Approaches
to
Planned Change

PUBLIC ADMINISTRATION AND PUBLIC POLICY

A Comprehensive Publication Program

Executive Editor

NICHOLAS HENRY

Center for Public Affairs
Arizona State University
Tempe, Arizona

Publications in Public Administration and Public Policy

Other volumes in preparation

Developmental Editors

Approaches to Planned Change

(in two parts)

Part 1

Orienting Perspectives and
Micro-Level Interventions

ROBERT T. GOLEMBIEWSKI

*The University of Georgia
Athens, Georgia*

MARCEL DEKKER, INC.   New York and Basel

Library of Congress Cataloging in Publication Data

Golembiewski, Robert T.
    Orienting perspectives and micro-level interventions.

    (His Approaches to planned change ; pt. 1)
    Includes bibliographical references and index.
    1. Organizational change. 2. Group relations
training. I. Title.
HD58.8.G64   pt. 1   658.4'06s   [658.4'06]   79-10310
ISBN 0-8247-6803-5

MARCEL DEKKER, INC.
270 Madison Avenue, New York, New York 10016

Current printing (last digit):
10 9 8 7 6 5 4 3 2 1

PRINTED IN THE UNITED STATES OF AMERICA

To that tiny stranger
   who first came and stayed to fill our home and hearts
   and minds
To that kaleidoscopic self
   which wondrously reveals an expanding crowd within:
   Dump and 'bott,' Bumbumniecki and Mad Gerbel,
   Mrs. Dettelson and Allison, Stephanie Dickinson,
   Rebecca Nurse, and the roaring mouse's Queen
To that mega-package of will and want
   that seeks to mark increasingly more of the world
   as her own
To that phenom and those phenomena of the past four years:
   Lordie, save us from four years more.
To that Tiger of the next years four.
In short, to Alice herself, who has evolved in as
   protean ways as this book, between then and now.

Preface

Approaches to Planned Change may be pardoned if it experiences a written work's equivalent of an identity crisis. Is it a second edition of *Renewing Organizations,* or no?

Let readers judge for themselves. Consider the two basic similarities between this work and its predecessor. Despite the 7 years that have passed since the publication of *Renewing Organizations,* the broad introductory framework of the original still seems serviceable and hence is substantially retained in the first three chapters below. These chapters provide an orienting structure for a literature that has sprawled and burgeoned wondrously over the last few years. Moreover, both writing programs propose that Organization Development clearly is here to stay. That conclusion was argued for in *Renewing Organizations,* and it seems certain now.

Now consider the points of difference between *Renewing Organizations* and this 1979 effort. Overall, to begin, perhaps 70 percent of the material below did not appear in any form in the earlier book. In addition to seeking to accommodate the great burst of research and experience that has accumulated since the appearance of the first edition, moreover, basic structural changes also characterize this effort. Not only have large portions of manuscript prominent in the first edition disappeared, but many of the retained portions have been variously shuffled about. This will emphasize relationships and insights that were not obvious earlier, as well as correct poor judgment and artless placement.

The most obvious difference from *Renewing Organizations* is that one book has now become two. The level of interaction constitutes the dominant criterion for the separation: Part 1 basically deals with micro-interventions, those aimed at individuals and small groups, while Part 2 focuses on macro-level interventions relevant to large organizations. Although dominant, the focus on levels of intervention is conveniently supplemented by other kinds of materials. In addition, that is, Part 1 begins with a number of introductory concerns and orienting perspectives, and Part 2 ends with a major block of materials relating to intervenors and the complex act of intervening.

Great pleasure fills me as I write this Preface, but I also recognize pain—
basically that pain involved in letting go. Each month brings fresh and exciting
experience and research that begs to be recognized and assimilated, and mulling
over the materials constantly suggests ways to highlight insights previously
slighted or unrecognized, constantly pinpoints places where the felicitous phrase
could better capture an idea and better attract the reader's eye and mind.
Hence, active waiting to let go has been a very rewarding posture on this project,
which is long past term. The fact is that I have put off completing this revision
several times—finding one excuse or another to set this work aside, to begin and
publish perhaps six other books while this revision waited. Waiting presents a
strong temptation even now, with two substantial piles of manuscript before me.

As in all human affairs, however, letting go can only be postponed so long.
For this revision—warts and blemishes and all—that time is now. The timing
could not be more appropriate, it just occurs to me. The two of us—wife and
husband, mother and father—have experienced a recent and major letting go
with two of our children who, born close together, boogied-off to college close
together. And our son will soon follow his sisters, his senior year in high school
now closing with a rush. The two-part volume thus constitutes just another
letting go, if long delayed, and a far less impactful one at that.

Robert T. Golembiewski

Contents

Chapter 5

DEALING WITH DYADS, WHEREVER

Applying Laboratory Values to Work, Home, and Social Settings   243

Section 3

SOME GROUP INTERVENTIONS

Chapter 6

BOUNDED AND EXTENDED INTERVENTIONS IN SMALL GROUPS

Some Developmental Trends and Two Case Studies   297

Contents of Part 2

Approaches
to
Planned Change

SOME INTELLECTUAL HANDLES AND FOCAL ISSUES
Preliminary Mapping of a Complex Territory

This is the second edition of this book and, in a real sense, titling the volume has posed trickier problems than assembling its bulky contents. The title of the first edition, *Renewing Organizations,* was selected only after long deliberation. Still, *Renewing Organizations* fell short of revealing the precise goals of this book. Some such title as "Toward Continuous Renewal for Organizations and Individuals" captures more of the book's actual flavor. Certainly, the thrust suggested by the key word "toward" is appropriate, but that alternative title implies more than can be delivered even today. We are but a little way down the road of understanding what continuous renewal implies, for individuals or for organizations. And, although we are beginning to see a little more daylight about how one goes about accomplishing "continuous renewal" for individuals and organizations, now is definitely not the time to rest on those tentative laurels.

Much has changed in the 6 years since the first edition went to press, but one constant remains. That is, so much experience and practice has accumulated since then that substantial portions of the first edition have a kind of antique quality about them. Hence, the second edition is completely overhauled, much of the older version having been dropped and much new bulk having been added. But the title has remained a problem, and this is the best that I can presently do: *Approaches to Planned Change,* with its two component parts being subtitled: Part 1, "Orienting Perspectives and Micro-Level Interventions," Part 2, "Macro-Level Interventions and Change-Agent Strategies."

Whatever their titles, the central thrust of these books is simple and (hopefully) substantial. The two-part volume deals with how individuals and organizations can go about making more effective choices, as well as coping better with change if that is what we choose or have thrust on us. The technology is new and only beginning to develop, and there is a very real doubt whether what we know is already far too little, far too late. But we still must try, even if only the attempt is possible, even if change is our contemporary Armageddon. Alvin Toffler put the necessity in perspective in his discussion of "future shock," the "shattering stress and disorientation that we induce in individuals by subjecting them to too much change in too short a time." He came away from his research "with two disturbing convictions":

> First, it became clear that future shock is no longer a distantly potential danger, but a real sickness from which increasingly large numbers already suffer. This psychobiological condition can be described in medical and psychiatric terms. It is the disease of change.
>
> Second, I gradually came to be appalled by how little is actually known about adaptivity, either by those who call for and create vast changes in our society, or by those who supposedly prepare us to cope with those changes. Earnest intellectuals talk bravely about "educating for change" or "preparing people for the future." But we know virtually nothing about how to do it.[1]

This second edition accepts the first of these two propositions and attempts to show how the state of the art extends beyond the limits sketched by Toffler in the second proposition. The flood of contemporary history, as Toffler documents it, certainly is attacking people and their institutions at their most vulnerable point. Beyond that, this volume attempts to provide some guidance for us in our institutions to generate constructive adaptation to historical challenges, a task which Toffler did not undertake.

A Model and Two Biases for Coping with Change/Choice
A Place to Start

Very early in the game is the appropriate time to begin sketching how this volume proposes to illustrate that, Toffler notwithstanding, quite a bit is known about how to "educate for change" and how to "prepare people for the future." Moreover, we are learning a lot more, fast. Thus, *Renewing Organizations* was published in late 1972, but it was soon behind the times in important particulars. Hopefully, this volume will experience a similar fate.

The approach here to revealing what we know about change is straightforward, if at times it may appear tedious. Basically, the underlying model is the straightforward one sketched in Figure 1. Our focus is on a technology for

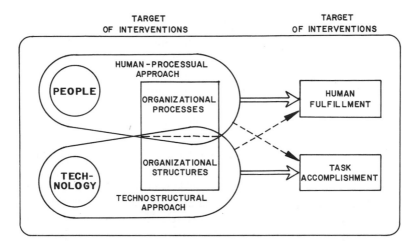

Figure 1   The basic model for coping with change/choice. [From Frank Friedlander and L. Dave Brown, "Organization Development," *Annual Review of Psychology*, Vol. 25 (1974), p. 315. Reproduced with permission, from the *Annual Review of Psychology*, Vol. 25. © 1974 by Annual Reviews, Inc.]

intervening in organizational processes and structures to heighten human fulfillment and task accomplishment. It is this simple, no matter what the complexity and detail that may at times be necessary below.

What follows will often be complex and detailed, not for their own sake but to make certain that critical points get the emphasis they deserve. Lest some important things be neglected, this volume has two major, self conscious biases. The first is to describe in detail the family of learning designs or interventions that are part of a burgeoning technology for successfully managing the processes of change. This can often be done with few words, although the reader may feel engulfed in a sea of terms like "third-party consultation" or "confrontation designs." The risk is worth running, for the reader needs to know what the interventions are and what they are intended to do. Hence, overkill is far preferable to allowing a subtle but significant design or feature to go unremarked.

The second bias of this volume is potentially even more troublesome but, alas, is also seen as very significant. This second edition seeks to illustrate and explain the dynamics induced by the several learning designs and interventions; it tries to test the consequences of specific learning designs; and it especially stresses that the values underlying any intervention are critical in giving constructive direction to the technology. These latter two aims may make this volume longish and even preachy; it will certainly require much space and time; and no doubt it will test every reader's forebearance at many points. But so be it.

Insisting on likely trouble in this case is not mere stubbornness. A little knowledge about a learning design may be insufficient, or even dangerous, in the absence of clarity about either values or underlying empirical processes. Moreover, we will either consciously guide our several technologies to where we want to go and how we expect to get there, or our technologies will run us, coercing us in directions we may not accept as our own, even in ways that we may abhor.

Hence, the goals of this volume may imply some extra effort, and even some redundancy, in both the writing and the reading of all that follows. The intent is to reduce the number of future surprises and perhaps to avoid real potential for pain later on.

Let these few words suffice here to provide some early direction, while realizing that it will be necessary to return again and again to the basic model and the two biases from which this volume starts. Hopefully, these several returnings will not be mere repetitions. Readers will make their own judgments about that matter, of course.

Three Perspectives on a Central Dilemma
Coping with the Constancy of Change/Choice

Three perspectives help develop much of the sense of the central dilemma that history is challenging us and our institutions at their most vulnerable point. *First,* the thrust of contemporary history can be characterized by a related set of words; change, revolution, turmoil, rootlessness, and so on. As one popular author expressed it: once reliable constants have now become galloping variables.[2] In effect, almost as much has happened in the past 50 years as happened in all earlier human history. Consider that there have been approximately 800 lifetimes of 62 years each in the past 50,000 years. Of these 800 lifetimes, some 650 were spent in caves.[3] Of these 800 human lifetimes, also, one or at most two have been spent with blood transfusions, air conditioning, first-generation mass transportation systems, television, medical services that can lay meaningful claim to improving the quality of human life, and formal education that extends beyond some small elite.

Second, and perhaps even more significant, the total effect is less and less a case of history just happening to us. More and more, we trigger deliberate change and conscious innovation—perhaps lust after it—even as we more clearly recognize the many unanticipated and sometimes overwhelming effects we thereby set in motion. We have met the enemy and they is us, as Pogo put it. And no truce seems likely.

The only real alternative is to get better and better at minimizing the negative effects of deliberate change and innovation. The problem remains whether we simply rush on to new and unsettling things, or whether we choose to say: Stop, enough is enough; we need a definite period to assimilate, to stabilize, to put down roots, perhaps to define progress as harking back to old values and institutions rather than progress as more and more. Indeed, to say "stop," and to say it meaningfully and effectively, will no doubt require very skilled and determined change or innovation.

Perhaps the greatest challenge involves mastering people effects. Clearly, there are people effects, massive ones. For example, rigorous research confirms what intuition suggested all along. The more change-episodes an individual experiences, the greater the likelihood that he will become ill, and have a more severe illness. An index of change has been developed, and it helps significantly in predicting the amount and severity of illnesses experienced by people in diverse populations.[4]

What is the overall flavor? Humans have become more travelers in time than to places and thereby have exponentially raised the costs of traveling. Travel to new places often results in "culture shock," as we find ourselves in new environments without the old cues that guided our lives. The new cues tend to be strange or incomprehensible, or even abhorrent. As Toffler notes, they account "for much of the bewilderment, frustration, and disorientation that can plague Americans in dealing with other cultures. The common consequences are breakdowns in communication, misreadings of reality, and inability to cope."[5]

These consequences of culture shock are mild compared to the costs of future shock, or rapid travel through time. A traveler in space usually can look forward to returning home, as one antidote to his culture shock. A traveler in time, even when he stays in the same place, finds his sense of a cultural home kaleidoscopically changing just as he gets familiar with it. Future shock is relief-less in this basic sense and is perhaps best reflected in the sense of things happening so evermore quickly that the brief encounter must do it all, even in romantic dalliance, especially for what Staffan Lindner calls the "harried leisure class." As he explains, "We had always expected one of the beneficent results of economic affluence to be a tranquil and harmonious manner of life. . . . What has happened is the exact opposite. The pace is quickening, and our lives in fact are becoming steadily more hectic."[6] Warren Bennis and Philip Slater capture the sense of it in an arresting book title, *The Temporary Society*.[7]

Third, humankind is, unfortunately, far less adept at dealing with galloping variables than with reliable constants. The results are most clear in the dry rot of our cities, but the effects are ubiquitous in all our institutions—political, social, and economic. These institutions are being sorely tested to provide the things that more and more people are seeking, indeed, demanding. Hence, our institutions now must not only catch up to these expanding demands, but they also can look forward to continuous renewal throughout the foreseeable future, to meet and hopefully to anticipate the demands to come. Moreover, institutions from one point of view reflect the spirit of humankind, and from another they mold our quality of life. Consequently, our ideas and attitudes must not only catch up with today's expanding demands, but also stand ready for continuous renewal in the tomorrows that can now be only dimly envisioned.

Boldly Facing the Major Issues of Choice
Renewal and Revolution as Alternative Strategies

There is no way of putting off either individual or organizational renewal, but a major choice must be made. Beyond a Pollyanna-like hope that matters will get better if they are left alone, two alternative approaches are available: rebellion against our institutions, with the goal of destroying them; or renewal of the institutions, with the goal of making them more effective. In short, it is a question of burning or learning, if we reject the alternative of lapsing into a growing irrelevance. Put otherwise, the central point is how we manage the choices available to us. Perhaps better said, the crux of it may be how we approach the choosing that will be done, either by conscious action or by bumbling default.

Renewal or Revolution?

Some would argue that only revolution offers any hope that our institutions will be renewed. True enough, in some cases. At the very least, however, massive efforts at renewal should precede that last resort, revolution. The thesis here proposes that this last resort in today's organizations is premature, for we have only recently begun attempts at major organizational renewal, at least with any real sophistication. The technology for renewal becomes increasingly available, and a profession for specialists in that technology is only now emerging.

Numerous additional reasons also support renewal. Consider only that revolutions seem generally better for smashing than creating, better for permitting a massive emotional orgasm than for constructive social action. One of the key reasons seems to be that revolution is oriented to the *ultimate end.* That is, any action that achieves the noble end may seem appropriate in revolution. This often enormously complicates putting the pieces back together again. In contrast, renewal should be more *means oriented.* In short, not just any action approaches the goals of a program of renewal. And there can be a world of difference in the two basic questions that rebellers and renewers tend to emphasize:

- "How do we destroy this need-depriving institution?" asks the revolutionary.
- "How can we improve on an imperfect but existing institution?" asks the renewer.

To revolt or renew poses serious dilemmas, then. I illustrate only. The problem for the revolutionary is that his zeal to change what exists can encourage neglect of the issues of what is to take its place, when, and how. The problem for the renewer is that her concern for having a working institution, even if imperfect, might make her overtimid where she should be bold. The cop-out temptation is clear: the certain, even if imperfect, institutions of today may become paralyzingly attractive when compared to the practical uncertainties of some hoped-for brighter new world.

This two-part volume attempts to slip between the horns of such dilemmas. For example, it urges changes in today's organizations, while seeking to do so within a more-or-less specific framework of values. At the same time, the volume urges caution in simply replacing what exists because it is imperfect, like all human works. In short, change should follow only clear need, and then only when the probability of success is high.

These are radical books, to put it directly, written from what is hopefully a disciplined perspective. In short, their approach accepts Harvey Cox's challenge. "If we choose to live responsibly in the world," he notes, "then we must face the issue of how we can harness organizational power for authentic human purposes."[8]

Overchoice or Underchoice?

This book and its companion also are dedicated to enlarging the *manageable and meaningful choices* open to individuals and organizations, via emphasis on a technology for renewal and change. Basically, that is, this two-part volume seeks to help us survive our modern freedom and to take advantage of the richness and diversity that is increasingly available and that, not incidentally, will be increasingly necessary in modern business and government organizations. The volume implies that, despite the patent problems it has brought and will bring, our continuing technological development has (in the words of Harvey Cox) "opened up new possibilities not present before." He concludes:

> In the world of work . . . secularization is not the Messiah. But neither is it the anti-Christ. It is a rather dangerous liberation; it raises the stakes, making it possible for man to increase the range of his freedom and responsibility and thus to deepen his maturation. At the same time it poses risks of a larger order than those it displaces. But the promise exceeds the peril, or at least makes it worth taking the risk.[9]

The concern about our surviving freedom distinguishes this work from the vast bulk of social commentary whose depressed theme is that we are increasingly coerced by repressive standardization and regimentation. In the orthodox commentary, the human was far freer in some past time. Then, in the words of the French mystic Jacques Ellul, "Choice was a real possibility for him."[10] The only issue in orthodox social commentary is how chronic the present condition is, and the usual agreement is that this condition is very chronic indeed.[11] The death throes may even now be upon us, some commentators tell us.

The contrasting view here urges that overchoice is more the modern problem than is underchoice. The kaleidoscopic profusion of today's life styles, and their substantial mutual tolerance, implies such an expanded range of choice, for example. Hence, the balanced view. This is no call to slack off on efforts at combating repression, standardization, or homogenization of human choice at every turn. But equipping individuals and organizations for expanded choice deserves at least equal attention. That attention here focuses on two basic questions. What attitudes and values permit individuals to constructively test the choices open to them, as opposed to those attitudes and values that wall them off from what they might become? And what skills does an individual need in order to exploit available choices, with some growing probability that change will have bearable costs?

Stressing overchoice does not mean, however, that all is clearly for the best in this best of all possible worlds. The present view is a more complex one. That is, this volume sees us today and tomorrow with a great and growing potential for choice, both as individuals and as organization members. For example, the choices open to the American poor or to blacks, however far short of parity they remain, have enormously enlarged in the past few decades. But enlarged choices are not necessarily manageable or meaningful. Thus, one can be coerced into change or face being discarded into some social refuse pile. Little choice exists in such "alternatives." "You can choose to be retrained, or to go hungry." Moreover, even if real choices are possible, the choices may be so numerous as to coerce the individual into an escape from freedom. No choice means no failure, from another point of view, while numerous choices imply correspondingly greater challenge and risk in the pursuit of heightened expectations. And there's the rub.

Hence the dedication of this volume to enlarging *manageable and meaningful choices* open to individuals and organizations, defined here in terms of an approach to change and renewal scaled to human dimensions. Simply, it aspires toward improving the odds that Everyman can adapt to his choice-filled world while minimizing the inherent shock.

This increased range of choices can be sketched here. Within an overall ethical or moral framework, the focus below on personal renewal will have several dominant emphases. The several thrusts toward increased choice for individuals include

From an Emphasis on		Toward an Emphasis on
Learning a skill	→	Learning to learn
Narrow needs satisfied by organizational membership	→	Broad range of needs satisfied by organizational membership
Being socialized in a narrow, stable, set of roles which may persist throughout life, such as being born into a caste system	→	Being socializable in a broad range of roles that can be variously activated as the individual grows and develops
Gaining satisfaction basically in more or less permanent identifications, attitudes, or skills	→	Gaining more satisfaction in identifications, attitudes, or skills that are quickly developed and which may be quickly extinguished

Several kinds of expanded choices to guide organization renewal also receive attention below, and they are at once clearer and more elusive. Their diversity can be suggested here, if at the expense of brevity and perhaps vagueness. The several thrusts toward expanded choices for organizational renewal include

From an Emphasis on		Toward an Emphasis on
Stability	→	Change or choice
Predictability and loyalty to an organization	→	Creativity and commitment to effective completion of task
Hierarchy and coercion by the few to control the many	→	Freedom that inheres in self-direction and self-control
Work relationships that are stable but difficult to develop and persist through obsolescence, or beyond	→	Work relations that are satisfying, yet can be established quickly and dissolved when no longer relevant

The Laboratory Approach and Organization Development (OD)
Elaborating Two Central Conceptual Frameworks

The discussion below describes ways to manage large and growing potentialities
for change and choice, within two related conceptual frameworks. The "laboratory approach" provides the all-encompassing framework, while Organization
Development (OD) is the more specific focus. The former begat the latter, as
it were, to facilitate coping with change and choice in organization contexts.
The four themes that follow will help sharpen the complementarities and distinctions between our two basic points of reference.

Laboratory Approach as Genus

The laboratory approach may be considered as *genus,* as one way of learning
which is at once convenient and potent. In brief, the laboratory approach has
a common base and aim. Thus, the approach constitutes an educational strategy
which rests primarily on the experiences of the learners themselves in various
social encounters. Also, commonly, the aim is to develop attitudes and competencies that aid learning about human relationships. In these basic commonalities, the laboratory approach involves "learning how to learn." "Essentially,
therefore," we are told, "laboratory training attempts to induce changes with
regard to the learning process itself and to communicate a particular method of
learning and inquiry."[12] The diverse forms and consequences of this "particular
method of learning and inquiry" constitute the targets of this volume.

The first three chapters in Part 1 consider this genus from two basic and
related points of view. They detail what may be called the *internal logic* or
broad theory of the laboratory approach, what it seeks to do via which specific
dynamics under which conditions. These chapters also will stress the *values* or
normative agreement on which the laboratory approach rests, the "why" of
what it seeks to accomplish. These early chapters thus seek not only to be clear
on what and when, to paraphrase *Jesus Christ, Superstar,* but are keenly concerned with why.

The laboratory approach also generates a number of species for learning or
change. These species include *strategies, designs,* and *interventions for change*
that are consistent with the laboratory approach. Explicating these species will
be the burden of the last three chapters in Part 1, as well as of the bulk of
Part 2. Each species will be treated in a similar way. It will be

- Defined and described
- Illustrated in applications relevant to individual or organization
  renewal, as appropriate
- Evaluated in terms of research relevant to its impact and consequences

These strategies, designs, and interventions deal with the *practicum* or the *techniques* of the laboratory approach and constitute the bulk of this two-part volume. As such, they complement the emphases in the first three chapters on the *internal logic* and the *values* or *normative agreement* underlying the laboratory approach.

Genus and species interactions thus constitute the vitals of this volume. Together, they—the laboratory approach and its derivative strategies for change, learning designs, and interventions—constitute the technology for renewal of concern.

Finally, two closing chapters of Part 2 will deal with the OD intervenor and the act of intervening. The focus there is on a major art form, the ways of applying specific OD interventions to achieve certain desired goals with as little fallout as possible, and especially with a minimum of unexpected fallout.

OD as Value-Loaded Species

The keenness below for "why" issues concerning the quality of organizational processes and products has a direct motivation. Paramountly, Organization Development is squarely in the business of dealing with both "desired" and "desirable" values, to use Solomon's revealing terminology.[13] Thus, an organization's executives typically seek such outcomes as high output, low turnover, and so on, and these desired values usually are significant goals of OD programs. At the same time, however, OD programs must deal with *desirable* values which should increasingly come to guide organization processes. These desirable values undergird the theoretical and personal framework within which the OD specialist works. At the broadest level, for example, it will be argued below that OD has an ontological relevance to human development. Values are not relevant only to OD. But OD is seen as facilitating movement toward important goals of human development which are in effect meta-values defining *the* desirable and progressively more human condition. OD also contributes to narrower organization goals that are managerially desired.

The commingling in OD of desired and desirable cannot be neglected, patently. This makes life complicated.[14] That is, values are relevant not only to how an organization goes about its business, but also to what an organization's business is. Ross powerfully illustrates the relevance to OD of broad values defining the desirable, the good life. If an organization is engaged in an immoral enterprise, Ross considers it a matter of moral irrelevance whether that organization is managed despotically or benignly. He notes convincingly that ". . . no aspect of organizational or procedural humaneness could justify the product of Auschwitz." The only moral OD approach to such organizations, Ross argues, will neutralize or destroy them. "The behavior of these organizations is such," he concludes, "that to make their products neutral or benign would entail making these organizations less effective, increasing waste, and encouraging discontent and disruption within them."[15] By "these organizations" Ross means not only those whose purpose was mass extermination, but also those which despoil the environment, exploit the consumer, aggregate tremendous social power, and so on.

This volume will certainly not settle the moral issues about which Ross writes, but neither will it permit readers to take the easy way out. Ross argues that many, or even most, OD practitioners do in fact take that easy way. He observes that "the OD professional is either unconcerned with, or supportive of (in value terms), what the client organization actually does. Evidently, process is seen as more important than purpose."[16] So it may be, although Ross's view is overstated from this writer's perspective. But as that view does apply, to that degree are OD professionals suffering (or perhaps, shortsightedly profiting) from a technical myopia.

The way out, if such exists, will be difficult indeed. For example, two careful observers conclude that we have of late passed over a major threshold, without recognizing it. An "organizational imperative" has become the "dominant moral force in our society," they argue, because modern organizations have been so successful. The needs of organization have come to overwhelm all other considerations, they note, "whether those of family, religion, art, science, law, or the individual." Individuals are rewarded for "value substitutions," and hence substitute they do, urged on by a now-pervasive belief as to their "moral malleability." Hence, for those observers it is both vital and apparently unlikely that we can turn telling attention to *the* central issue, now and for all time: "What is man that these things should or should not be done to him?"[17]

This two-part volume gives no support to a moral myopia, but neither does it provide magic spectacles that correct such shortsightedness. It tries to stake out an intermediate and viable position. This in-betweenness can be circumscribed in terms of three propositions. *First,* OD efforts must be judged in terms of two kinds of moral framework: the "internal" values related to organizational processes that inhere in the OD practitioner's theoretical framework, and "external" values that relate to organizational purposes. As OD becomes more potent, so does the interfacing of internal and external values become more critical. *Second,* the ethical burden of OD practitioners is particularly heavy because, for good or ill they have become identified as major modern carriers of humane values, because they are widely seen (in Ross's words) as seeking to move "corporate and other bureaucracies from punitive hierarchies toward nurturant commonwealths." *Third,* OD applications acquire awesome moral relevance because they typically relate to the quality of life in our major contemporary engines of power and purpose. OD applications consequently are suffused with issues of value.

The OD Cube: Diagnostic Focus, Locus, Designs

Let us take a third convenient way of illustrating the prime thrusts of this volume in dealing with OD, that sketched in Figure 2. To explain the sense of Figure 2,[18] OD programs *focus* on one or a variety of diagnosed problems. Moreover, each diagnosed problem has a *locus* at one or more levels of social organization, extending from the several roles that each individual plays to the complex social systems that encompass large numbers of actors. Finally, OD programs rely on a broad range of laboratory *learning designs or interventions*, intended to cope with various diagnosed problems, typically at several levels of social organization. Extensive discussion will develop the sense and meaning of the various labels in Figure 2, and especially of the several laboratory designs or interventions. Here note only that each topic in the volume can be located at one or more of the 858 coordinates of Figure 2. For example, Chapter 1 introduces process orientation, the core intervention of the laboratory approach. Process orientation is defined there as a shared commitment by interdependent persons to examine all aspects of their interdependence mutually, an examination with a technology guided by a common set of values. That introduction would have coordinates (0, 0, 16) on the three axes of Figure 2: diagnostic focus, locus, and designs. Later in Part 1, applications of this basic intervention will be illustrated at a variety of loci as they focus on a range of diagnosed problems.

OD as Group Oriented

This elaboration of our two central conceptual frameworks requires a fourth and final theme that comprehensively characterizes these volumes. OD basically reflects a variety of group-oriented strategies for conscious and deliberate change in social systems. In essence, changes in group-level phenomena such as social norms and values constitute the primary motivators of organizational change, via their influence on the behavior of individuals. This basic OD bias is hardly the only approach to change. Other approaches place their emphasis elsewhere. Alternatively,

- Technological or environmental conditions are seen as prime determiners of systemic change.
- Change is seen as largely unplanned and uncontrollable, whether it is serendipitous or calamitous.
- Change is seen as the basic product of an elite which seeks to generate unknowing and even unwilling change in large systems, as by guerrilla activities.

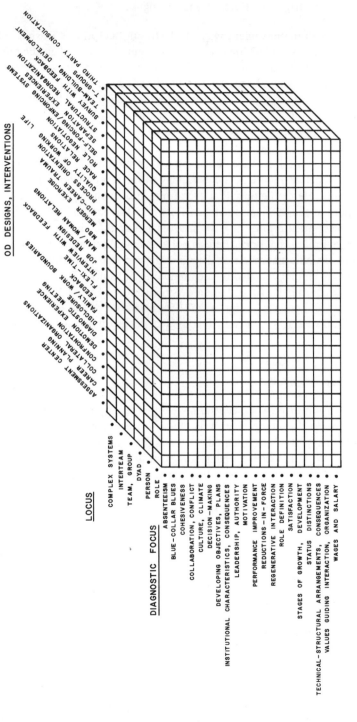

Figure 2 A schema for organization development.

- Change involves individuals subjected to "behavior modification" principles and techniques.[19]

The bias toward group-oriented strategies is dominant, then, but it is hardly an exclusive one. Simply, group-oriented strategies have a variety of general advantages for many OD purposes, a number of which are illustrated below. Other convenient sources also detail those advantages, especially with respect to individual-oriented strategies.[20]

OD as Technology or Transformation
What Is Involved?

This seems a convenient point at which to summarize some of what has been said thus far, as well as to seek to transcend what has gone before. That is, the view throughout is that Organization Development is a "technology" or, in a related but distinct sense, a "transformation." Using Vaill's suggestive formulation:

> A technology is a standardized method for converting energy in a purposeful way from one form, an "input," to another form, "output." The process of conversion is often called the "transformation." The operation by one or more men of the technology is the transformation.[21]

To say that OD is a technology or a transformation says it all, but at the risk of misleading. Let us minimize the risk by spelling out in some detail what is involved in this way of viewing OD.

Designs, Interventions

The standardized forms for converting energy in the OD mode are various designs or interventions for learning, such as those which are represented in the OD cube detailed a few pages earlier. Indeed, the unwary may only see designs or interventions.

There is a real danger here, which paradoxically burgeons in direct proportion to the sophistication and comprehensiveness of OD designs and interventions. Albert Speer should know; he was out-front on one of our first massive technological efforts as minister of armaments and war production in Nazi Germany. He sums up his experience as a fulfillment of a last duty to warn humankind: "The more technological the world becomes, the greater is the danger. . . . There is nothing to stop *unleased technology and science* from completing its work of destroying man."[22]

What are the major components of an "unleashed technology and science?" Speer believes he knows about two central pieces of the puzzle: one involves the large-scale emergence of the "technocrat," who knows everything about a limited something; and the other component features an authority figure willing and able to tie the narrow fixations of many technocrats to some broad and evil ends. In fact, the technocrat can be a very willing party in being a gun for hire for any cause, for the technocrat's desire to apply knowledge can be very strong, even compelling, and the high degree of compartmentation of technocratic specialties may dilute the sense of personal responsiblity. Hence, the anonymous technocrat may eagerly seek for personal affirmation of worth through use of one's technology, whatever the cause.[23]   Speer puts the pieces together for us in explaining his own tragic success:[24]

> Basically, I exploited the phenomenon of the technician's often blind devotion to his task. Because of *what seems* to be the moral neutrality of technology, these people were without any scruples about their activities. The more technical the world imposed on us by the war, the more dangerous was the indifference of the technician to the direct consequences of his anonymous activities.

OD technology will not finesse the dangers alluded to here. Determined efforts must be made to *leash* our technology and science, then, *suitably*. At a minimum, that requires being vigilant about excesses brought on by our own success, and that also requires being aware of obvious historical parallels.

Hence the appropriateness of Culbert's concern that the OD profession can lose momentum as an applied science unless the vision is far broader than designs or interventions, which are easy enough to describe and may be carried about comfortably but mindlessly in a kind of handy-dandy, all-purpose tool kit. Culbert cautions that, too often, we "rely on realism rather than philosophy. We practice intervention rather than diagnosis. We take pride in our principles rather than in our questions." Then he concludes: "too often we miss the connections between the situation in which our clients are struggling and the macro-problems faced by society."[25]

Guided by Culbert's concern, then, this two-part volume argues that the focus on designs or interventions has to be augmented by five other major perspectives. To the degree this augmenting does not occur successfully, so will Culbert's concerns become constraining realities.

Diagnosing Immediate Contexts

Fixation on designs or interventions can encourage neglect of *the* fundamental of OD applications: the diagnosis of the specific site of the application.[26] Patently, that is, the choice of any OD design presumes the prior diagnosis of an immediate situational context to assess the probability that the benefits of intervening in a specific way outweigh the costs of doing nothing or doing something else. It is painful, but necessary, to emphasize the point. For diagnosis often seems to be forgotten, and perhaps more so with the growth in the number of available designs or interventions that "have worked."

Beyond emphasizing the point, later discussion highlights diagnosis of the contexts in which specific designs have been applied. This requires space and much patience for both readers and author. But far better too much in this regard than too little.

Technique of the Intervenor

To some unknown degree, specific interventions work, or fail to work, because of the technique of the individual intervenor, the complex ways different intervenors practice the arts of their craft. There should be no surprise here. Both Artur Rubenstein and I might play the same piece, the same notes, on the same piano. Even poor musicologists can accurately judge that his and my techniques differ somewhat. So it is with intervenors.

The issues here are complex, but a word to the wise should suffice. Some of the designs below seem relatively foolproof; they seem to produce quite similar consequences whoever the intervenor and wherever the intervention. Other designs seem to reflect more intimately the character and quality of the intervenor. This distinction will be made below at several points, as a kind of warning to unwary enthusiasts.

Application/Discovery of Empirical Knowledge

Emphasis on OD designs or interventions is inadequate. Their application must at once rest on existing knowledge of empirical regularities, and ideally those applications also should trigger the discovery of new knowledge. Because of the still-early developmental stage of OD, one cannot in any extensive sense "learn the craft." Any delusions of this kind can be dangerous. Therein resides a significant problem with the increasingly common OD "cookbooks," which present numerous detailed designs but often provide little perspective on the specific diagnosed conditions that inspired them. Moreover, they generate little motivation for developing an increasingly complete network of theory that depicts the major covariants in nature.

Prescriptively, the OD intervenor should be in touch with existing empirical knowledge and also should be prepared to test, extend, and refine that knowledge. No comprehensive theory as yet describes in detail the processes by which various learning designs work or fail to work. So, the OD intervenor can expect to be surprised at times. Those surprises can provide significant learning opportunities. For when things do not work out as they should, they may signal that our existing knowledge base is somehow inadequate or even grossly unsuitable. And the prepared mind may be able to seize on such unexpected learning opportunities.

Some observers have taken a different route, by distinguishing OD from (let us say) "action-research."[27] The two are seen by some as involving the planned application of behavioral science knowledge via collaborative consultant-client relations. But OD and action-research are said to take different tracks, among which are the following.

Organization Development	Action-Research
Often uses "packaged" designs	Designs typically rest on detailed diagnoses of specific loci
May or may not include evaluation of results in specific terms	Usually involves evaluation of results in specific terms
Often does not result in new knowledge re behavioral science	Usually results in new knowledge re behavioral science

This volume rejects any such distinctions, which could be counterproductive if pushed very far. Rather, it defines OD as respecting dual commitments: to apply what is known, as well as to discover increasing chunks of that which now eludes our comprehension. This implies serious problems for both the readers and its author, for here we integrate two emphases typically at sixes and sevens. As Friedlander and Brown observe: "OD research has tensions built into it that are likely to lead either to 'action' (OD consulting) or to 'research' (development of organization theory), but not to both."[28] These tensions are acknowledged but not surrendered to. Hence, this revision seeks to emphasize both the "diagnosis of a specific situation," as well as the "study of general laws."

Higher-Order Perspectives

Again a simple point, but one often neglected in practice: designs or interventions should be selected to attain increasingly specific goals or values. Hence, Culbert sagely cites the OD specialist's need for "higher-order perspectives by which to orient ourselves."[29] Without being related to such guiding goals or values, OD designs approximate unguided missiles. Any one of them might do much good, or much harm, and any one of them might be too potent or too puny for the specific goals in question. One should not use a sledgehammer to drive carpet tacks, as it were, nor send a pussycat to slay dragons.

The opening three chapters of Part 1, especially, give multiple attention to higher-order perspectives for guiding the choice of specific OD interventions. The issues are subtle and devilishly interwoven, but they must be dealt with. Consider, for example, that OD seeks to increase both human fulfillment and task accomplishment. But what if these two broad values are somehow in opposition in a specific case? How much attention is to be given to each value, and in what priority? The issues are not trivial since, things being as they commonly are, task accomplishment is likely to get the benefit of even major doubts. Friedlander and Brown thus warn:[30]

> OD as a field runs the risk of encouraging and implementing subtle but persuasive forms of exploitation, curtailment of freedom, control of personality, violation of dignity, intrusion of privacy—all in the name of science and of economic and technological efficiency. Within the hierarchical fabric of everyday organizational power struggles, OD researcher/consultants typically represent the control needs of management. The needs of those lower in the organization for a higher quality of life, for an expanded range of occupational and life choices may seldom be known or acted upon by the consultant. The only choice for many such employees is to remain in or leave their organization.

Awareness of Macro-Context

Finally, specific OD interventions must be fine-tuned to suit specific broad contexts. The associated questions can be dramatic. For example, should an OD intervenor work to improve the efficiency of an organization like that running the horror camps in Nazi Germany? Would it not be preferable for an OD intervenor to choose designs in such a case that would shake and hopefully destroy such organizations?

Many other questions are less dramatic but of substantial and similar significance. Consider only two dilemmas. OD designs for improving communication in an organization surely should be sensitive to its past history of encouraging deviants to speak their mind, only then to release them or otherwise make life more difficult for them. Similarly, OD designs for bringing employees closer together certainly should take into account broad forces that otherwise separate one class of employees from another, as in apartheid policies. When do things get so bad that an intervention is contraindicated? That is a very difficult question, often beyond our capacity to answer without qualification. But sensitivity to the broader context clearly constitutes one requirement in such decision-making.

Not only punitive and autocratic macro-contexts need contraindicate an OD effort. Consider that class of cases in which subsystems desire OD interventions, even demand them, but where the parent macro-system is not supportive of even major signs of desirable change and, sooner rather than later, converts the gold of freer and more effective performance into bureaucratic dross. Thus, Dan Lortie of the University of Chicago describes the typical school system as a bowl of lukewarm Jello. An intervention in a subsystem in effect may successfully punch a fist into the bowl, splattering some Jello and temporarily displacing more of it, but without changing the Jello in any other way. Unless the intervenors are very skillful and resourceful, moreover, they will sooner or later withdraw that fist, and the Jello will assume its prior state.[31] Such experiences give pause to intervenors, even those eager to punch away!

Toward a Heightened Individual ⟷ Organization Exchange As Growing Need and Present Goal

Amid such complexity, several points seem to stand out starkly. *First,* the laboratory approach and its derivative learning designs constitute a significant modern phenomenon and perhaps, as some claim, even the most important learning technologies developed in the past three decades or so.[32] We shall see. In any case, two of the basic learning designs—"T-Groups" and "encounter groups"—have become notable parts of the contemporary culture, for good or ill.

 Second, whatever the diverse catalog of reasons underlying the prominence of the laboratory approach, one fact seems constant. More and more people seem to be demanding more and more from their relationships and institutions. Two contributing forces seem involved: many people are more explicitly needful than ever before, and many institutions and organizations are less and less successful in responding to those needs. Carl Rogers provides useful perspective on why so many people have been drawn to the laboratory approach. He asks:

> what is the psychological need that draws people. . . ? I believe it is a hunger for something the person does not find in his work environment, in his church, certainly not in his school or college, and sadly enough, not even in modern family life. It is a hunger for relationships which are close and real; in which feelings and emotions can be spontaneously expressed without first being carefully censored or bottled up; where deep experiences —disappointments and joys—can be shared; where new ways of behaving can be risked and tried out; where, in a word, he approaches the state where all is known and all accepted, and thus further growth becomes possible. This seems to be the overpowering hunger which he hopes to satisfy through his experiences in an encounter group.[33]

From this perspective, the laboratory approach reflects an effort to cope with freedom rather than to escape from sameness or isolation.

Third, coping with freedom is a critical theme in the material below. In important senses this work constitutes the necessary counterpart and logical consequence of the earlier interests reflected in my *Men, Management, and Morality*.[34] That earlier book emphasized that a real choice exists between two concepts for organizing—one that is in place virtually everywhere, and an alternative concept that is attractive in theory but has few real-life applications. This two-part volume emphasizes ways of approaching the latter organizing concept, to make the choice between the two concepts meaningful and manageable. Similarly, the earlier book stresses the relative usefulness of alternative models for organizing work under different conditions; this work sketches how an organization can change from one model to the other.

The theme of increased meaningful choice binds this volume to the earlier *Men, Management, and Morality*. It is appropriate, then, to introduce this volume with a paraphrase of Rousseau that highlighted one of the dominant themes of that earlier one:

> Men can be free within wide limits in organizations, but almost everywhere they are in unnecessary and ineffective bondage. This is a revolutionary tocsin, but it is more restrained than ringing pronouncements that men have only to break the chains of bondage. A great deal more, in point of fact, requires doing; and the doing requires a moral discipline and technical awareness beyond that of a simple call for unshackling man in organizations.
>
> This study details how men can be more free in organizations, but it has no vision of the end of the particularly human condition, the tension between the self and the social order. Freedom is not viewed as "free and easy," then. Rather, the emphasis is upon freedom as "free, responsible, and responsive."[35]

These words appear in the earlier book, but their usage here is different. The earlier book, at best, could describe alternative ways of organizing work *that have existed at various work sites*. This volume, at best, can suggest ways in which a specific structuring of work *can be realized at specific work sites*. The difference is enormous.

Rationale for a Second Edition
Is Another Time Around Really Necessary?

The considerations above may be quite convincing as to why a comprehensive overview of OD *was* necessary. But why go around another time? The question is especially apt, given the substantial number of comprehensive reviews of OD that were published in the few years following the appearance of the first edition.[36]

At the essential point, of course, the decision to go ahead on a second edition reflects an act of will rather than the weight of evidence for and against the effort. That act of will in this case rested on a complex rationale which encouraged a second go-round. Primarily, perhaps, the technology of OD had made such strides that it was increasingly important to establish the linkages of that burgeoning technology with central OD values and purposes, lest anyone forget or undervalue those linkages.[37] More specifically, the rationale supporting this second edition contains such elements as the following.

- Over 5 years of new literature have appeared between the two editions.
- The literature is burgeoning, in escalating quality as well as bulk, and the last comprehensive OD survey will be 3 to 4 years dated before the publication of this volume.
- Several critical breakthroughs have occurred in the literature, which do not get any or sufficient attention in available comprehensive surveys of OD.
- Earlier work fixated on interaction between members of small groups, while more recent designs pay significant attention to the structure of work in large organizations.
- A large number of new areas of application have developed.
- OD applications are becoming increasingly common in industrial and government settings, while earlier applications were limited to executive groups in high-technology organizations and soft goods.
- OD applications now touch all levels of work and organization, while the earlier focus was at "the top"; this enhances the social usefulness of OD and also implies the validity of its basic values and technology.
- The concept "OD" has been broadened in a number of ways that require careful attention, illustration, and analysis of the available literature.
- Many new OD designs have been developed recently in areas of great social concern,[38] for example, race, aging, male/female, and so on.

Another three developmental features of the literature also especially encourage a second edition. First, at four or five major places in this revision extended discussions detail why and how specific OD designs went wrong. Numerous readers commented about the absence of such material in the first edition, and in the OD literature generally.[39] Usually, critics note a painful disparity between OD preachment and practice: the usual counsel to others prescribes learning from their mistakes, but the common practice encourages neither publicly acknowledging failure nor assiduously seeking to profit from that experience. These observers correctly note that negative outcomes are particularly learningful for many people. Moreover, some argue that one learns little or nothing from success. Occasionally, some reader's suspicions were aroused by the emphasis on successful OD experiences. All three of these classes of readers should find the second edition provides substantially more opportunity for learning from failure as well as assurance that all does not always go well in OD, for reasons of which we are becoming increasingly aware.

Second, the OD literature is beginning to develop a pleasing specificity. Increasingly, that is, the literature refers to the degree of fit of a specific learning design to some (but not every) stage or phase in the development of an individual, a small group, or a large organization. Patently, to be able to note with increasing precision when a specific design is the design of choice, or when it is contraindicated, enhances the power of the technology. This growing tendency suggests the literature is really coming of age,[40] and reinforcing that desirable outcome provides much motivation for the present two-part revision. Several sections in the volume will highlight the fit between designs and approaches and host phases or stages. For example, following Harvey, one section below seeks to differentiate two distinct approaches to "process analysis," depending upon whether the host merely suffers from the classic "crisis of disagreement" or whether the appropriate diagnosis is the less often recognized "crisis of agreement."

Third, a real and growing need exists for treatments that at least aspire to comprehensiveness and that reflect the multiple and serious analytical and ethical issues facing Organization Development. I join Alderfer in his concern that "so few practitioners conceive of their work as creating, absorbing, and transmitting [the intellectual base of OD] to fellow professionals and clients."[41] Perhaps basically, that tendency helps reinforce the schizoid tension between theory and practice in OD. Fundamentally, this volume seeks to help bridge that unfortunate gap.

These introductory notes have a compelling quality to this author. Cumulatively, they encourage a second edition, even demand one. Hopefully, as the popular song says about love, this treatment will be better the second time around.

Notes

1. Alvin Toffler, *Future Shock* (New York: Random House, 1970), pp. 3, 4.
2. Warren G. Bennis, "Beyond Bureaucracy," *Trans-Action,* Vol. 2 (July-August 1965), p. 31.
3. Toffler, *Future Shock,* p. 15.
4. See, generally, the *Journal of Psychosomatic Research,* esp. Vol. 10 (1966), pp. 355-366, and Vol. 11 (1967), pp. 213-247.

5.   Toffler, *Future Shock*, pp. 12-13.

6.   Staffan B. Lindner, *The Harried Leisure Class* (New York: Columbia University Press, 1970), p. 1.

7.   Warren G. Bennis and Philip Slater, *The Temporary Society* (New York: Harper and Row, 1968).

8.   Harvey Cox, *The Secular City* (New York: Macmillan, 1965), p. 173. (Copyright Harvey Cox, 1965, 1966.)

9.   Ibid., p. 167.

10. Jacques Ellul, *The Technological Society* (New York: Vintage Books, 1967), pp. 77, 83, and 90.

11. Roderick Seidenberg, *Post-Historic Man* (Boston: Beacon Press, 1957).

12. Edgar H. Schein and Warren G. Bennis, *Personal and Organizational Change Through Group Methods* (New York: John Wiley and Sons, 1965), p. 4.

13. Lawrence N. Solomon, "Humanism and the Training of Applied Behavioral Scientists," *Journal of Applied Behavioral Science*, Vol. 12 (January 1976), esp. pp. 531-532.

14. W. Warner Burke, "Organization Development in Transition," *Journal of Applied Behavioral Science*, Vol. 12 (January 1976), pp. 24-29. Of course, some OD intervenors believe their work is value free, and this analysis disagrees with them. For an extensive effort to emphasize value issues, consult Donald D. Bowen, "Value Dilemmas in Organization Development," *Journal of Applied Behavioral Science*, Vol. 13 (October 1977), esp. pp. 545-590.

15. Robert Ross, "OD for Whom?" *Journal of Applied Behavioral Science*, Vol. 7 (September 1971), pp. 581-582.

16. Ibid., p. 581.

17. David K. Hart and William G. Scott, "The Organizational Imperative," *Administration and Society*, Vol. 7 (November 1975), esp. pp. 260, 272, and 285.

18. Based on the OD Cube developed by Richard A. Schmuck and Matthew B. Miles (eds.), *Organization Development in Schools* (Palo Alto, Calif.: National Press Books, 1971), p. 8.

19. E.g., Ed Pedalino and Victor U. Gamboa, "Behavior Modification and Absenteeism: Intervention in One Industrial Setting," *Journal of Applied Psychology*, Vol. 59, no. 6 (1974), pp. 694-698. Comprehensively, see Joel Fischer and Harvey L. Gochros, *Planned Behavior Change: Behavior Modification in Social Work* (New York: The Free Press, 1975).

20. Harvey A. Hornstein, Barbara Benedict Bunker, and Marion G. Hornstein, "Some Conceptual Issues in Individual and Group-Oriented Strategies of Intervention into Organization," *Journal of Applied Behavioral Science*, Vol. 7 (September 1971), pp. 557-568.

21. Peter B. Vaill, "Reflections on Technology," *Social Change,* Vol. 5, no. 4 (1975), p. 3.

22. Albert Speer, *Inside the Third Reich* (New York: Macmillan, 1970), p. 521. My emphasis.

23. David Schuman, *Bureaucracies, Organizations and Administration* (New York: Macmillan, 1976), pp. 13-37, presents a useful discussion of technology and technocrats.

24. Speer, *Inside the Third Reich,* p. 212.

25. Samuel A. Culbert, "Present Shock," *Journal of Applied Behavioral Science,* Vol. 10 (October 1974), p. 556.

26. See the useful emphasis in Richard Beckhard, "Strategies for Large System Change," *Sloan Management Review,* Vol. 16 (Winter 1975), pp. 43-56.

27. Mark A. Frohman, Marshall Sashkin, and Michael J. Kavanagh, "Action-Research as Applied to Organization Development," esp. p. 132, in S. Lee Spray (ed.), *Organization Effectiveness: Theory, Research, Utilization* (Kent, Ohio: Kent State University Press, 1976).

28. Frank Friedlander and L. Dave Brown, "Organization Development," *Annual Review of Psychology,* Vol. 25 (1974), p. 318.

29. Culbert, "Present Shock," p. 556.

30. Friedlander and Brown, *Organization Development,* p. 335.

31. Cited in Daniel Langmeyer, "Surviving An Intervention: The 'Jello' Principle," *Journal of Applied Behavioral Science,* Vol. 11 (October 1975), p. 456.

32. For a brief introduction, see Arthur Blumberg and Robert Golembiewski, *Learning and Change in Groups* (London: Penguin, 1976). Jane Howard, *Please Touch: A Guided Tour of the Human Potential Movement* (New York: McGraw-Hill, 1970), provides insightful personal reactions to some twenty learning experiences based on the laboratory approach.

33. Carl R. Rogers, *Carl Rogers on Encounter Groups* (New York: Harper and Row, 1970), pp. 10-11.

34. Robert T. Golembiewski, *Men, Management, and Morality* (New York: McGraw-Hill, 1965). For a kindred and broader work, see George E. Berkley, *The Administrative Revolution: Notes on the Passing of the Organization Man* (Englewood Cliffs, N.J.: Prentice-Hall, 1971).

35. Ibid., p. 7.

36. Jack K. Fordyce and Raymond Weil, *Managing with People* (Reading, Mass.: Addison-Wesley, 1971); W. Warner Burke and Harvey A. Hornstein (eds.), *The Social Technology of Organization Development* (Fairfax, Virg.: NTL Learning Resources Corp., Inc., 1972); Wendell L. French and Cecil H. Bell, Jr., *Organization Development* (Englewood Cliffs, N.J.: Prentice-Hall, Inc., 1973); Newton Margulies and John Wallace, *Organizational Change* (Glenview, Ill.: Scott, Foresman and Company, 1973);

Edgar F. Huse, *Organization Development and Change* (St. Paul, Minn.: West Publishing, 1975); Wendell F. French, Cecil H. Bell, Jr., and Robert A. Zawacki (eds.), *Organization Development: Theory, Practice, and Research* (Dallas, Texas: Business Publications, Inc., 1975); and Robert T. Golembiewski and William Eddy (eds.), *Organization Development in Public Administration* (New York: Marcel Dekker, 1978), in two parts.

37.   Fortunately, influential voices are emphasizing the relevance of OD values and purposes in taming the burgeoning technology. Illustratively, see Frank Friedlander, *Purpose and Values in OD* (Madison, Wisc.: Organization Society for Training and Development, 1976), esp. pp. 8-9.

38.   The point is made forcefully by Clayton P. Alderfer, "Organization Development," in Mark R. Rosenzweig and Lyman W. Porter (eds.), *Annual Review of Psychology*, Vol. 28 (1977), pp. 198-200.

39.   For the major effort in the literature to learn from error in OD applications, consult Philip H. Mirvis and David N. Berg (eds.), *Failures in Organization Development and Change* (New York: John Wiley and Sons, 1977).

40.   Only signal indicators of this tendency in the literature will be cited here. At the macro-level, fitting interventions to phases or stages get clear statement in Richard Beckhard and Reuben T. Harris, *Organizational Transitions: Managing Complex Change* (Reading, Mass.: Addison-Wesley, 1977). For micro-level counterpoint, see Harvey Levinson, "How Adult Growth Stages Affect Management Development," *Training HRD* (May 1977), pp. 42-47; and John Adams, John Hayes, and Barrie Hopson, *Transition: Understanding and Managing Personal Change* (Montclair, N.J.: Ellanheld, Osmun and Co., 1977).

41.   Mirvis and Berg, *Failures in OD and Change*, pp. 91-92.

Section 1

SOME ORIENTING PERSPECTIVES

Chapter 1

THE LABORATORY APPROACH TO LEARNING
Schema of a Method

This and the following two chapters provide a primer on the laboratory approach to learning, whose goal is to increase the effectiveness of individuals and to enhance the richness of their lives at work. This focal trio represents an important choice, conventionally made. Would that it were possible to say it all at once, but books must be written in series, not in parallel. In terms of the introduction, getting all the way around Organization Development requires three basic emphases:

- A human-processual approach, focusing on people and their relationships
- A technostructural approach, focusing on policies and procedures that specify task, job, and work relationships
- A large area of overlap, where organization processes and structures and human dynamics mutually influence one another

The subject matter of these first three chapters focuses on the human-processual approach, substantially although not completely. Basically, the development of OD as a technostructural approach and as overlap between organizational processes and structures is left to Part 2 of this revision. There, again, the focus will be substantial but not exclusive.

The focus of these three chapters is at once commonplace and complex. This first chapter develops the initial complexities in the commonplace events of establishing contacts between human beings, as we go about making a livelihood.

The complexity is both wonderful in its intricacies and awesome in relation to the infrequent sophistication with which Everyman copes with those intricacies. The second and third chapters provide specialized counterpoint. Chapter 2 concentrates on the values that should guide applications of the laboratory approach to individuals and organizations. The final chapter of this initial trio looks at Organization Development (OD) from various theoretical and practical perspectives.

Giving life to this intent is a difficult matter, but delay does not make it one whit easier. So we get on with it, now. The first of two major sections in this chapter briefly describes and illustrates the laboratory approach. The second section goes into greater detail about the laboratory approach, providing five perspectives on confronting as its basic goal.

Overall Features of the Laboratory Approach
Perspectives on Learning How to Learn

Preeminently, the laboratory approach is a distinctive way of learning. Hence our initial theme is "learning how to learn," which will involve four emphases:

- Four major characteristics of the laboratory approach
- An illustration of the laboratory approach in action
- Two basic processes of the laboratory approach
- The range of target phenomena of the laboratory approach

Four Central Characteristics

These characteristics suggest how the laboratory approach helps individuals "learn how to learn." *First,* the approach basically is an educational strategy for learning and inquiry. In this sense, the laboratory approach prescribes how a person goes about investigating and understanding complex social and psychological realities. In seeking to help people deal with complex human relationships and problems, the laboratory approach is both similar to many other types of education and distinct from them. Chris Argyris traces the major points of difference to assumptions about education:

> The traditional educational methods primarily emphasize substance, rationality, the inappropriateness of feelings, direction and control by the teacher, and so on. Laboratory education assumes that these emphases are not adequate by themselves. New ones need to be added such as the importance of maintaining the effectiveness of the learning group, the admission of all data that are relevant, including feelings, and the

enlargement of responsibility by giving students greater direction and control over their education.[1]

The emphases on feelings, group maintenance, and learner control, then, characterize the laboratory approach.

Second, the laboratory approach directs attention to a very special focus for learning and inquiry, the experiences of the learners themselves. Much traditional learning is centered "out there," as in subject matter like geometry. In contrast, the focus of the laboratory approach is "in here," on what goes on within and between the learners themselves. Learning via the laboratory approach is at once potentially threatening and rewarding. One can fail to understand geometry, and make it all right. Lack of self-understanding will probably have harsher consequences.

Third, the laboratory approach seeks to focus on the "in here" of interpersonal and intergroup relations in several very specific ways for quite discrete purposes. Attitudes, values, and skills are the key words to make the point with sufficient force. That is, the laboratory approach seeks to encourage certain attitudes about interpersonal and intergroup relations, and it also attempts to induce respect for certain values that should guide our relations with our fellows. Moreover, the laboratory approach provides experience with a range of behavioral skills consistent with these attitudes and values.

Fourth, the laboratory approach tends to emphasize learning in communities whose combined resources can encourage and enrich the learning of individual members. Such learning communities can facilitate inquiry in a variety of ways: developing an atmosphere congenial to search and experimentation; generating emotional support for the efforts of individuals; and providing enthusiasm when a learner succeeds or offering encouragement when he or she can only lay claim to struggle. In addition, a learning community permits vicarious learning. That is, individuals can identify aspects of themselves in others and profit from observing their learning attempts.

A Cameo in Action

These four features leave many gaps in understanding which only extended discussion can fill, so let us illustrate how the laboratory approach can generate powerful and involving learning experiences about interpersonal and intergroup relations. Consider one group that is learning how to learn via the laboratory approach, the members of a work team trying to improve their functioning on the job. The main speaker is Bob, an individual who was "drowning in responsibility" at work and who was so distant from his colleagues that they reported difficulty communicating with him. And Bob himself had begun to talk and act as if his productive life, and even enjoyable living, were over for him. His colleagues learned something about the man Bob, and he in turn learned something about them, when he talked about how "I saw myself inside . . . a loneliness." An observer provides this report of one episode in the learning of the work group:

> The room was still. "It's like being out on my boat, alone, surrounded by the sea. I go out at night when it is pitch black, with only the moon on the water to light the way. . . ."
>
> Some people in the group shuddered. It was a big risk in a small boat. . . .
>
> "Don't think I wasn't frightened when I first went out. It's dark and quiet, and the only sound is the water splashing against the side of the boat. A clear, cool spray hits my face. All around me darkness. Nothing. . . . At first the sea is rough, but then—far out—the sea is calm. I'm not frightened anymore. 25 miles—I'm following the stars. 35 miles—the moon glistens on the water. 45 miles—a fish jumps out of the sea—I'm startled! . . . It's quiet again. 55 miles—I can feel the excitement in me. I'm almost there—65 miles. I made it. I stand up in the boat and stare into the darkness, then up to the sky. Something surges over me. I throw my arms open wide and scream into the darkness. . . . I wait . . . listen. . . . Nobody hears me."
>
> People were crying for the lonely old man. There was the look of peace on Bob's face and slowly, somehow, the loneliness was leaving. He looked young, strong.
>
> Softly, I said, "Do you realize you've taken us with you? You've given us the privilege of being the first on your boat."
>
> People said, "Thank you, Bob." "You're a poet." "You've got great courage." "I could listen to you all night." "I've never known what a wonderful person you are."
>
> Jim asked, "How old are you, Bob?"
>
> "Forty-nine," Bob replied.
>
> Jim exclaimed, "Is that all! You've been acting like you're an old man—like your life's over, like your career with the company was finished. You've even looked old."
>
> Jack said, "You're a young, powerful person, Bob. Look at yourself."
>
> Bob's smile was young. He seemed to be overwhelmed with the adulation of the group—with the love that came by letting people in. . . .[2]

Feedback and Disclosure as the Central Processes

The two basic processes of feedback and disclosure help generate much of the powerful touching of persons just illustrated. Complex definitions are not necessary for present purposes. Feedback refers to information we give to others about themselves, and disclosure involves telling something about

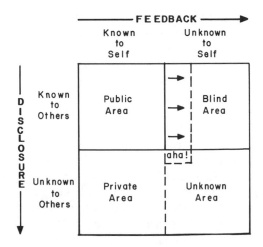

Figure 1 The Johari window. [Based on Joseph Luft, *Group Processes: An Introduction to Group Dynamics* (Palo Alto, Calif.: National Press Books, 2nd edition, 1970), pp. 11-15. For the most complete exposition of the Johari Awareness Model see Joseph Luft, *Of Human Interaction* (Palo Alto, Calif.: Mayfield Publishing, 1969).]

ourselves to others. Greater subtlety in these definitions will be introduced later.

The Johari window[3] in Figure 1 provides a covenient vehicle for demonstrating the centrality of the two processes. The window divides all interpersonal and intergroup reality into four cells. Elementally, the laboratory approach seeks to increase the size of the public area. Why? The rationale is direct: It permits individuals to isolate major areas of concern with dispatch and efficiency, which raises the probability of successful problem-solving. To the degree that the public area is cramped and narrow, individuals will be restricted in solving interpersonal and intergroup problems so that they remain solved.

Enlarging the public area requires careful attention. The applicable strategies include:

- Aha! phenomena, or flashes of insight
- Reducing the size of the blind area by giving feedback
- Reducing the size of the private area by self-disclosure

Aha! Phenomena, or Reducing the Unknown Area

The public area can be enlarged by flashes of insight that illuminate for both Self and Others material previously in the unkown area. These aha! phenomena often are the specific targets of psychoanalysis and the various psychotherapies, which seek the genetic roots of severe emotional disorders in experiences that an individual has suppressed into the unconscious mind. Somewhat similar learning opportunities can occur in the laboratory approach, when the individual assembles data of which he or she is aware at the conscious or preconscious levels and "puts it all together."

The case of a minister in a volunteer agency provides an example of an aha! experience. He and his colleagues met to do some work on their interpersonal relationships before beginning a new project and, almost from the start, the minister was locked in intense conflict with a new female staff member. All were surprised by the constant attacks of the minister, such behavior being decidedly out of character for him. But, the minister's colleagues encouraged him to work through his relationship with the woman and were ever alert to remind him "there you go again" when his attacks resumed. The minister himself was surprised, puzzled, and not a little ashamed of what he was doing. And he was unnerved because he realized the woman provided little provocation. Early one morning on arising, he had an aha! experience. The woman, he realized, reminded him of a parishioner from his early ministry. The other woman had created a major dilemma for the young minister: she demanded his wife and daughter in a lesbian relationship, and threatened suicide if the minister did not assent. He did not, and she did. The minister's anger and resentment toward this early parishioner apparently lurked within him, unresolved these many years, to be directed at the new staff member who, he reported, bore a striking resemblance to his young parishioner.

Reducing the Blind Area

Fortunately, increasing the public area does not require such massive insights. Consider reducing the size of the blind area, of eliminating a person's blind spots by telling them how we perceive their behavior. In the learning episode above, for example, Jim gave Bob some direct feedback. "You've been acting like you're an old man—like your life's over, like your career with the company was finished. You've even looked old." Feedback is the process by which Self learns how he or she appears to Others. And feedback is one thing we cannot do for ourselves, no matter what our skills and resources.

Reducing the Private Area

The public area also can be increased by decreasing the private area, as Figure 1 illustrates. Here, disclosure is the vehicle, as when Bob reveals much about himself to other members of his work team. He talks about his loneliness and his great need for human contact, in the context of his efforts to prove himself

Table 1 Some General Areas of Concern in the Laboratory Approach

Basic Goals for Outcomes	Kinds of Target Data	Kinds of Learning
Laboratory programs enhance authenticity in human relations by seeking to increase:	The focus is on public, here-and-now data, as they are experienced. These data include:	The laboratory approach generates three basic kinds of learning by participants, to varying degrees in individual cases:
Individual awareness about self and others	The specific structures developed, such as the leadership rank order	Learning that is largely cognitive and oriented toward techniques, as for effective committee functioning
Acceptance of others	The processes of group life, with special attention to getting a group started, keeping it going, and then experiencing its inevitable death	Learning that highlights deep emotional needs of which the participant was variously aware and that shows how such needs can be satisfied
Acceptance of self		
Laboratory programs seek to free individuals to be more effective while they are more themselves, both as persons and as members of organizations, by seeking to enhance the development of:	The specific emotional reactions of members to one another's behavior and to their experiences	Learning that demonstrates the significance of "unfinished business" and illustrates how and with what effects the press against the consciousness of such matters may be relieved
Sensitivity to self and others	The varying and diverse styles or modes of individual and group behavior, as in "fighting" or "fleeing" some issue that has overwhelmed group members	
Ability to diagnose complex social situations and to conceptualize experience in behavioral science terms		
Action skills, attitudes required to capitalize on increased sensitivity and enhanced diagnostic skills		

by going as far out to sea as his craft will permit. But, when he reaches his limit, he is starkly reminded of what it means to be so alone and so far from others, whether at sea or in everyday life.

This disclosure brought people into Bob's life, but not every disclosure is useful. Some kinds of disclosure can inhibit the development of relationships, for example. At a minimum, the timing and relevance of a disclosure can be critical. Too much disclosure too early can be as damaging as too little, too late. The concluding pages of this chapter provide additional insight about effective disclosure.

Some Preliminary Boundaries

Whether dealing with dramatic or everyday events, the laboratory approach extends the two basic processes of feedback and disclosure into broad areas of life. "I don't understand what you just said," for example, also is a piece of disclosure. At various times, that simple piece of disclosure can be highly relevant, even critical. Table 1 suggests this full range by providing three kinds of data. It elaborates on the overall goal of aiding the development of more humane relationships between more effective human beings. Moreover, Table 1 outlines some common target data for the laboratory approach. The list is not exhaustive, of course, but it should illustrate the phenomena that are of central concern in the approach. Finally, Table 1 indicates three kinds of learning which can be aided by the laboratory approach.

Table 1 rests on a basic tension between two needs, the need to know and the need for privacy. To be effective, we need to know about our blind spots, and we need to tell others how we perceive them. In short, we need to confront and to be confronted. Oppositely, we also need to preserve some sense of a private self, a domain that may be all the more precious because it constitutes the basic existential proof that we control some portion of our lives. Diversely, the tension ebbs and flows from situation to situation, but it is seldom absent from the human drama.

Greater Specificity About the Laboratory Approach
Perspectives on Confronting as the Basic Goal

The laboratory approach in its barest essential involves the delicate balancing of the need to know and the need for privacy, the ultimate human concern. That is, the option of neglecting the tension between the two basic needs is not really open. The only alternatives are to be more or less effective in balancing the two basic needs in opposition, more aware of why and how that balancing is sought.

The immediate focus is on five reinforcing themes which provide greater specificity about this delicate balancing. They involve:

- Introducing the "process orientation" as central to the laboratory approach
- Sketching how interpersonal competence rests on regenerative systems of human interaction
- Emphasizing the primacy of confrontation as the generic mode for inducing regenerative systems
- Establishing specifically how regenerative interaction systems require helpful feedback
- Developing the notion that relevant disclosure also underlies the development and maintenance of regenerative systems

Toward a "Process Orientation"

In its most elemental intent, the laboratory approach seeks to induce two conditions. The first is an awareness among people of their own processes of relating with one another. The second condition requires a commitment to analyze those processes, regularly. In effect, a process orientation reflects a shared norm which, in Herbert A. Shepard's words, involves "a joint commitment among interdependent persons to 'process analysis,' i.e., to shared examination of their relationship in all aspects relevant to their interdependence."[4] Shepard calls it "observant participation."

Broadly, the "process orientation" relates to a system's competence, whether that system is an individual, a small group, or a large organization. A large organization, for example, must be able to achieve its objectives, to maintain its internal environment while doing so, and also to adapt to its relevant external environment in order to exert necessary control over it. In the competent organization, Argyris proposes, its processes of carrying on these core activities tend to yield five outcomes.[5]

- The information needed to cope with the diverse factors relevant to the core activities will be both available and understandable to organization members who need that information.
- The information needed to cope is in such a form as to be usable.
- The system can afford the cost of gathering, understanding, and using the information.
- Problems are solved and relevant decisions are made and implemented in ways that neither create additional new and similarly grave problems nor induce the recurrence of the original problem.

- The four consequences above are accomplished while increasing—or at least while not decreasing—the capacity of system members to solve problems, make decisions, or take implementing actions.

Patently, testing whether a system's processes have such effects should have a very high priority. Fortunately, that testing need not always be a big deal, as can be established by further description of process analysis which involves describing its several major properties, and by sketching some guidelines that facilitate a process orientation.

Six Major Properties of a Process Orientation

Progress toward a better understanding of a process orientation can be made by introducing six major properties. *First,* process orientation is experiential. Its basic learning stimulus is not a case study or a theoretical presentation. The stimulus is, for example, that decision we have just made, and how we made it.

Second, the process orientation presumes a collaborative relationship in both diagnosis and prescription between participants in some social setting. In an organization, for example, these participants may include a consultant and the consultant's client. The consultant's purpose is not only to "get the patient well." The more significant purpose involves developing client interests and skills with diagnoses which will permit him to help judge his own interactional health, as well as that of his own organization. Even more, the purpose involves the client so intimately in joint problem-solving that his defensiveness is low and that, ideally, he internalizes any findings as his own. Perhaps paramountly, the goal of process orientation encourages the client to seek similar helping relationships with others.

Third, the process orientation is a continuous one. Short of collaborative death, there is no alternative to it. One can only do it better or worse, do it most often or hardly at all.

Fourth, the process orientation ideally operates simultaneously at individual, interpersonal, and intergroup levels. Moreover, several complex processes can simultaneously operate at each level. Schein describes in detail six such processes, which are listed here to suggest the reach of the process orientation. These human processes are:[6]

- *Communication,* as in who talks to whom
- *Member roles and functions in groups,* which can emphasize self-oriented behavior, performance of task or maintenance activities associated with preserving viable relations between members
- *Group problem-solving and decision-making*

- *Group norms and group growth*
- *Leadership and authority,* as in issues of who influences whom
- *Intergroup cooperation and competition*

The awareness and analysis of the complex interaction of such human processes at multiple levels constitute a demanding task, but nature comes that way.

Fifth, the process orientation can be enriched by contrasting "process" with "content" and with "structure." In a rough sense, process deals with how a decision is made and implemented. Content refers to the "what" of a decision—its quality, its logical or technical basis; and structure deals with issues such as who will formally implement the decision and what the procedures will be. The three levels variously interact. Consider structure and process. As Schein observed: ". . . the roles which people occupy partly determine how they will behave. It is important to have the right structure of roles for effective organizational performance." But structure does not predetermine process. Schein concludes: ". . . people's personalities, perceptions, and experiences also determine how they will behave in their roles and how they will relate to others."[7] The richness of human interaction lies in the subtle blending of these three levels of meaning.

Sixth, process orientation provides an additional path to increased organizational effectiveness, not an exclusive one. Schein captures the flavor of both features. He explains that:

> Obviously there is room in most organizations for improved production, financial, marketing, and other [functions]. I'm arguing, however, that the various functions which make up an organization are always mediated by the interactions of people, so that the organization can never escape its human processes. As long as organizations are networks of people, there will be processes occurring between them. Therefore, it is obvious that the better understood and better diagnosed these processes are, the greater will be the chances of finding solutions to technical problems which will be accepted and used by the members of the organization.[8]

In conclusion, these six properties suggest a working definition. The process orientation is one approach to augmenting personal and system effectiveness. It has an experiential thrust which encourages attention to a broad range of events at all levels in interpersonal and intergroup situations. The purpose of process orientation is to help individuals understand events around them, and to develop skills of diagnosis and prescription for effectively coping with their environment. The data are primarily those of everyday life—human actions and their impact on others in the full gamut of formal and informal relationships. A process orientation draws from life, in sum, and can contribute to it.

Guidelines and Some Interventions for a Process Orientation

The process orientation is no plea for general snooping or nosiness. Rather, a large family of techniques exists, with their use being guided by several "shoulds" or "oughts."

Chapter 2 provides detail about values that guide applications of the laboratory approach and its several technologies and techniques, but useful attention here can be directed to a set of operating guidelines that Jack Fordyce and Raymond Weil generalized from their own efforts in large-scale organizations. They highlight a number of guidelines applicable to the process orientation as conveived here.[9]

- We pay attention to individual as well as group needs.
- We pool the widest possible range of opinion.
- We systematically question established ways of doing things.
- We emphasize feedback and ongoing critique.
- We clarify interpersonal relationships by deliberately digging out garbage—that is to say, concealed feeling that blocks simple man-to-man understanding.
- We stress responsibility for sharing management of the enterprise.
- We encourage exploration of oneself and one's connection to others.

Later chapters will illustrate many of the methods for encouraging a process orientation. Exhibit 1 sketches briefly some of the more prominent interventions. Note that they are listed in order of their probable threat or confronting qualities. An important generalization should be kept in mind. "As a rule of thumb," Fordyce and Weil express the point, "the more confronting the method, the richer the response and the stronger the impulse to change. But groups [and individuals] vary considerably in their readiness to work with immediate methods."[10]

Two Emphases in Process Analysis

Fordyce and Weil help us see the many ways of skinning the cat of interaction via process analysis, and that all of them can be correct. This is true enough, but it is more immobilizing than helpful.

What is known, then, about specific kinds of process analysis and about how and when they work? As a convenient way of providing some early content for the concept, the immediate focus will be on two distinct emphases in "process analysis." This discussion will be multiply helpful: It will permit

Exhibit 1   Some Interventions for Stimulating Process Analysis in Organizations

---

Questionnaire and instruments soliciting written responses. Various questionnaires and instruments can be used to generate data about processes, typically with the assurance that only aggregate data will be reported to superiors. This increases openness by reducing risk. Some of these devices can be improvised on the spot, while others may have to be painfully developed for ad hoc use. Fortunately, a great many questionnaires and instruments have been developed and are "on the shelf," as it were.[11]

Interviews. These can provide great flexibility, especially for probing and exploratory purposes. Again, respondents typically are guaranteed anonymity.

Upward feedback devices. This set of designs uses groups of employees to generate information. The groups may be work teams, or they may be assembled de novo to get representation of specific interests or classes of workers. The group itself does the reporting, either in writing or via tape recording of a discussion. This method tends to raise the credibility of the product to the executive, coming as it does directly from the employees in whom the executive is interested. Obviously, however, the method makes greater demands on the time of the executive, especially in reading reports or in listening to tape recordings. Groups may be assured anonymity, or they might identify their products. One especially interesting version of this method is an edited tape recording of a real-time discussion, with the voices understandable but disguised.[12]

Questionnaire/instrument/interview followed by feedback to contributing parties. This is a classic method. In the typical case, a consultant interviews a manager and the manager's immediate subordinates, or the consultant might use a questionnaire or some instrument to gather the needed data. Then the summary findings and observations of the consultant are reported to all those interviewed in a total session. The method is intended to be quite confronting. Clearly, the method also can be a risky one for the consultant.

Pictorial representations. Sometimes pictures or collages can provide revealing information, perhaps due to the greater legitimation of fantasy or perhaps because of the regression encouraged by working with paste, scissors, and glue.

Representations in life. This method of gathering data can be impactful. Members of one work group, for example, seemed to be having real problems concerning influence, involving issues of competition. Most members acknowledged the problem but found it difficult to deal with in any but veiled and abstract terms. They agreed to a micro-design in which they were to occupy a vertical position in space corresponding to their influence in the group. Two stimuli were used. The first was an "is" stimuli: What level of influence does each individual exert? There was much mirthful relative arranging of selves in space after this first cue: some crouched, others stood tall, some lay on the floor, some stood on chairs, and so on. The ensuing discussion was animated, but not particularly revealing. "Are you really happy down there?" one member on a chair might ask a member on the floor. "Most times," might come the answer. "But you rubbed it in on that X contract."

Exhibit 1 (Continued)

The second stimulus was a "want": How much relative influence did individual members prefer? Again, vertical position in space was to indicate the degree of influence which each individual desired to exert. Considerable confusion followed, with one member seeking in some way to express his impressive desire for influence. Finally, he forcefully positioned one of his colleagues and proceeded to use her as an unwilling platform to reach a sturdy wagon-wheel lighting fixture. There he hung, head and shoulders above his colleagues in his need to exert influence. Literally, there was no way this man could satisfy his need for influence without stepping on someone, in this case an unwilling someone.

Slices of life. Modern recording equipment permits groups and individuals to confront self, as it were, by observing their own behavior. This might be done, for example by

- Listening to an audiotape of a conversation or problem-solving effort[13]
- Watching a videotape playback of a conversation or group interaction[14]

Videotape feedback seems to have a broad range of especially attractive features. For example, videotape can preserve the many nonverbal cues that can be critical in communication.[15] In addition, unlike interpersonal feedback, videotape allows the person direct access to his presentation of self, without the need to factor out of another person's reactions those induced by the presented self from those the observing person projects. Videotape feedback can also be processed without an outside consultant, thus avoiding such issues as confidentiality of data, the attempt to schedule a happening for the consultant's benefit, and the danger of the outside consultant being seen as judgmental, evaluative, or manipulative.

Direct confrontations: groups. The consultant can generate in vivo data by confrontations between groups having problems or merely intent on improving their relationships. The basic vehicle for generating data is a three-dimensional image, which each group develops in private. The three-dimensional image is a response to these three questions by (to make it simple) groups A and B:

- How do we see ourselves?
- How do we see the other group?
- How do we believe the other group sees us?

Description and analysis are at the group level only. Although the three-dimensional images are developed in private, the groups are told they will later be shared publicly.

Direct confrontations: meetings for two. These meetings are for any pairs, such as a manager and one of her subordinates, who wish to work toward some common goal more effecitvely. Usually a third party, a skilled resource person, sits in to help work on process. One effective way to conduct such a meeting for two is to have each party make three lists:[16]

Exhibit 1   (Continued)

- Positive feedback list: things the person values in the way the two people have worked together
- "Bug" list: things she has not liked or cannot tolerate in their relationships
- Empathy list: a prediction of what the other party has on his list

The lists then become the focus for analysis by the pair, aided by the third person. The procedure "is highly structured," Fordyce and Weil note, "but it is also foolproof."

---

making some useful if approximate distinctions about approaches to process analysis; it will highlight some central research issues; and it will emphasize certain useful lessons about process analysis. Throughout this section, the focus will be on a pioneering and insightful (but still limited) experiment by Raanan Lipshitz and John J. Sherwood.[17] They permit us a glimpse of the possible, of what can be done to bring greater clarity to what is a buzzing, blooming confusion of variables induced by people going about their work and their lives.

We begin with a basic distinction. Process consultation must be distinguished, at least in terms of degree, from expert consultation that is task-oriented. The latter might focus, for example, on the technology and procedures for pouring cement. In more or less sharp contrast, process consultation would focus on how a particular team of cement pourers went about their work, the emphasis being on their variable adjustments to one another and to the technological and procedural constraints and slack applicable to them or perceived by them.

This brief contrast does not establish a tidy unique sphere for process analysis. But it does circumscribe important features of the turf, and it does permit another step. Given this roughly defined territory, neglecting for the moment the several mixes appropriate in specific cases, at least two subspecies of process analysis can be distinguished:[18]

- Instrumental process analysis
- Interpersonal process analysis

Instrumental Process Analysis.   The several varieties of instrumental process analysis focus on work relationships. For example, one such approach emphasizes roles at work, how they complement or conflict, and how they can be tailored to permit greater effectiveness. Details about one such OD design, role negotiation, are provided in Chapter 5. Commonly, this subspecies emphasizes task and work, as in this three-phase design:

1. *Data-generating phase.* Work unit members exchange written messages concerning:

    a. Task behaviors by the recipient which sender sees as detrimental and would like to see stopped or reduced

    b. Task behaviors by the recipient which sender sees as helpful, and which sender would like to see started or intensified

    c. Task behaviors by the recipient which sender sees as adequate and which should be continued at about the present level

2. *Clarification phase,* in which any ambiguities, et cetera, in messages are raised and clarified

3. *Bargaining phase,* in which each pair of subjects seeks to write contracts about task behaviors, as in Y providing more of some behavior to X in return for some behaviors Y desires from X

Interpersonal Process Analysis.   This second subspecies puts the emphasis at a deeper, more human level. As Lipshitz and Sherwood explain,

> Interpersonal process analysis is concerned with feelings, attitudes, and perceptions which organization members have about one another. The purpose of the intervention is to improve the quality of human relations in all their manifestations: warmth, acceptance vs. rejection, trust and suspicion, etc.[19]

There are many ways of getting at this level of data. Several varieties of basic interpersonal process analysis are illustrated below in detail, as in Chapter 6 and Part 2, Chapter 4. One approach involves a set of six bipolar scales, for example, talkative-quiet, reasonable-greedy, and so on.[20] Group members rate themselves and all other members; they exchange ratings with others; and they discuss any regularities or inconsistencies between their self-ratings and the ratings received from others. The emphasis is thus on how the person is perceived by others, given a limited set of dimensions to save time and to focus analysis.

Some Central Research Questions and Answers.   Which kind of process analysis is best? Or better still, is some process analysis better than no process analysis? These simple questions have very complicated answers, of that we can already be certain, even though we are still very far away from providing any specific answers. In the spirit of illustrating how much we know about what we do not know, the focus below is on an intriguing experiment that manipulated these variables in small, temporary groups performing competitive experimental tasks.

- Process analysis versus no process analysis
- Instrumental versus interpersonal process analysis

- Presence versus absence of an outside consultant or resource person
- High versus low prestige of outside consultant

These conditions imply major questions, obviously. Does process analysis aid group attainment? If so, what kind of process analysis is better for which purposes? And should an outside consultant be involved? If so, does it make much of a difference whether participants see him as prestigeful or not?

The available answers are not up to the quality of the questions, however, in part due to the early stage of experimentation but more basically due to the complicated and often conflicting requirements of research necessary to provide those answers. Readers can consult the original source for provisional results.[21] Generally, however, the available results are mixed and sometimes conflicting. Consider this brief summary of the results on one key research question: Will task groups that use process analysis, with or without a consultant, improve their performance and cohesiveness more than groups which do not use process analysis? The results suggest the following:[22]

- No significant difference in productivity exists.
- A significant difference in cohesiveness exists.
- Overall differences seem to exist in the ways that two kinds of groups go about doing their work.

Useful Lessons from Unruly Data.   The research referred to is both fascinating and frustrating, and OD specialists will have to rely on the first feature to motivate the formidable work necessary to reduce the second. But three important lessons inhere in the seminal but still early work that has been done.

First, as the experimenters realize,[23] their results point up the crucial character of *prior diagnosis.* That is to say, their results cannot be interpreted definitely because they (and we) do not know whether specific experimental groups were in need of *any* intervention. Some groups may have been doing quite well, thank you, and might have perceived any process analysis as bothersome rather than helpful. Similarly, some groups might have been hung up on interpersonal issues, while others struggled with instrumental problems. Since the process analysis variants were assigned randomly, only dumb luck determined whether the needy or the satisfied were visited by the interventionist. Moreover, the needy did not necessarily require the specific variant the intervenor applied. That would make a difference, obviously.

Second, all experiments must distinguish short-range from long-run effects. That is, temporary groups might function well enough without process analysis, or any other intervention, for 30 minutes or an hour. It seems probable that groups with longer histories, and indeterminate futures, might prove very different targets for process analysis interventions.[24] They could be herniated by unresolved socioemotional garbage of the past; they could be buoyed through dismal adverstiy by past successes and established trust in one another; or such ongoing groups might fall somewhere in between on these and many other dimensions.

As the experimenters realize,[25] again, even if their results hold absolutely for temporary groups, they may be very wide of the mark for ongoing groups. So, conclusions should be drawn only tentatively from experiments such as the present one.

Third, the experiment sketched above implies a light at the end of the tunnel, even as it suggests that the tunnel is a very long one. This duality implies a realism that can be very valuable, especially in affairs of the human heart and will where the dominant tendency is to expect miracle cures and to believe they have been found. As the experimenters conclude:[26]

> The present study is not a crucial experiment. It does not prove, once and for all, that process analysis is beneficial, or that the value of a consultant is doubtful. It does not prove either that instrumental process analysis is the better approach, or that consultants should not worry about their prestige and reputation. What it does do is add in a relatively rigorous fashion to the painfully slow accumulation of knowledge that is available to those practitioners who are wondering about these questions.

Whence Come the Data re Process? And How?

"Instrumental" or "interpersonal" data about process can be generated in a variety of ways. And diagnosis and prescription based on such data also can be developed in numerous ways. The range of these variations in practice—and some sense of the trade-offs involved in choosing one variation over another— can be suggested by sketching two opposed modes that an OD intervenor could adopt with respect to a change-target, say, an executive team. The two modes are not polar opposites, but refer to different central tendencies by the intervenor.

A Hands-On Mode.   Many of the designs illustrated below involve the OD intervenor in a hands-on mode, given that members of the team are the source of all process data and also given that the common goal is to increase feedback and disclosure to facilitate group problem-solving. In the interview/feedback design, for example, the OD intervenor will play a major role in eliciting, interpreting, and then reporting data back to team members about their internal process. Designs such as survey/feedback have a similar hands-on quality, as in the technical complexities of developing and analyzing an opinion survey that may be responded to by hundreds or thousands of organization members.

The basic trade-off of the hands-on mode should be transparent. Intervenor expertise may come at the cost of lessened participant ownership of the data about process. Or, looked at from another perspective, organization members may use the external consultant as a safer vehicle than themselves for testing the readiness of their system for openness or change.

A Hands-Off Mode.   Many OD designs reflect a hands-off mode, in useful contrast. In such designs, the OD intervenor designs the broad outlines of a learning situation and perhaps gently enforces procedures that enhance a productive process orientation. But the intervenors typically play little or no role in the reporting or interpreting of data, unless things go very awkwardly. The several confrontation designs detailed below, especially in Chapter 6 and Chapter 1 of Part 2, have such a character. Or, group members might analyze their own performance captured on an audio or videotape.

The self-diagnosis design developed by Bartee and Cheyunsky illustrates the hands-off genre, and also provides a context for sketching the advantages of the mode.[27] Bartee's intervenor leads members of a group through a detailed procedure for a self-diagnosis of their own processes—a procedure not reproduced here to conserve space but conveniently available elsewhere[28] —which is repeated in each of five steps toward effective self-diagnosis. The steps include[29]

- Discussion and understanding of the general problem area
- Description of the present situation in the general problem area
- Exchange of information relevant to the present situation
- Development of a prioritized list of ideal desired situation
- Defining *the* problem as change in the present situation in order to approach the ideal situation.

Bartee sees a number of significant advantages in this hands-off mode. First, the intervenor controls that in which the intervenor is (or should be) most expert: the design of the learning situation, as well as the enforcement of the detailed procedure for self-diagnosis. Second, the client system becomes the authority for what information gets shared, when, and how. This realizes their special expertise, and acknowledges their special stake in the data. Third, clients consequently more likely will own the data generated, as well as accept the responsibility for what gets communicated. Fourth, since clients communicate in their own terms, this facilitates understanding and avoids intervenor jargon or theoretical interpretations that the data do not justify and/or that only encumber the process toward decision. Fifth, clients often learn much from observing self and others going through the procedures—information about style, strong points, inadequate information, and so on. Sixth, the self-diagnosis of process increases the probability that effective action will be taken.

General Rules?   There seem no profound rules for choice of modes. In general, the extremes of the hands-on mode can sacrifice important OD values, and fixation on extreme hands-off may create some unnecessary client frustration and in the rare case may even prevent an intervenor from highlighting that a group is missing something that is virtually certain to be hurtful later on. Moreover, the prevailing OD bias is toward far more hands-off than hands-on. But the really critical cases are those in which deviations are appropriate, and they would involve a level of detail far beyond that planned here.

Toward Competence Through Regenerative Systems

Despite such difficulties with establishing rigorous specifics, the evidence seems quite conclusive that process analysis in its manifold guises often "works": It can make interaction between people more fluid and satisfying, and it can make work groups more zestful and effective.

The implied question is simply disarming. Why does a process orientation work? No simple answer exists, that is clear, and only bits and pieces of an eventually satisfactory answer are presently known. But what is known is revealing, and also can be shared briefly. Broadly, the view here is that the process orientation "works" because it helps create "regenerative interaction systems" that link people, and because people at various levels of consciousness need and seek regenerative interaction systems.

Two Systems of Interaction

Hopefully, the skeletal explanation above is not simply a polysyllabic way of saying: No one knows why process analysis often seems to work. Putting some meat on the bare-bones explanation will test this hope. Consider a simple interaction model of four variables.[30] Figure 2 suggests the sense of two self-fulfilling

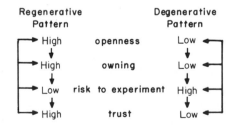

Figure 2   Two ideal systems of interaction.

systems of interaction, regenerative and degenerative. For simplicity, Figure 2 refers only to the interaction system that develops between any two people. Common sense understandings of risk and trust will suffice for now, but openness and owning must be distinguished. For example, Jim may tell me that some of my friends regard some of my behavior as reprehensible. If Jim is one of my friends, and if he feels that my behavior is reprehensible, then Jim was open about that attitude, but did not own it. He lets me judge which of my friends he is referring to.

In the degenerative pattern, one cannot win for losing. Consider the husband and wife whose relations are degenerative. During a long business trip away from home, the husband has second thoughts about the relationship. He decides to take a risk, to trust that his wife will understand if he openly talks about and sincerely owns his true feelings toward her. On the way home from the airport, the husband buys an extravagant bouquet of flowers to help begin a new era of good feelings. His wife has not gone through the same thoughts and feelings as her husband, however, and she perceives the flowers in the context of her low trust and high risk. "Well, what have you been up to now?" she reflexively and bitingly greets her husband. This increases the risk perceived by the husband and discourages the owning and openness he had planned on. "Why, you bitch," he blurts out. And so the best of intentions were interpreted so as to confirm a degenerative pattern. As was said, you cannot win for losing in degenerative systems.

A similar bouquet no doubt would have had more pleasant consequences, given a somewhat more healthy interaction system. In a real sense, regenerative systems increase the probability that two interacting persons cannot lose for winning. Less likelihood exists that misunderstandings and misperceptions will develop in regenerative systems, trivial events often being the materials out of which major impasses develop. Even if major issues develop between a pair of individuals interacting in a regenerative system, moreover, the prognosis is still good. At worst, trust permits confronting the issues, and the risk of doing so is low enough to discourage the continued festering of the issues in the closedness of silence.

The fact that the laboratory approach essentially attempts to provide experience and to develop skills for heightening regenerative systems, as well as for reversing degenerative ones, helps explain why the approach "works." That is, regenerative systems support individuals as they seek to establish and augment their interpersonal competence. This is no small matter. Directly, the drive to substantial and growing interpersonal competence is a major determinant of the emotional health of individuals. To hurry a patent conclusion, then, the laboratory approach is where it's at in significant senses in the matter of interpersonal and intergroup relationships.

Two aspects of this argument urging the centrality of the laboratory approach can usefully be dealt with in more detail. A minitheory of trust will suggest its complex role in regenerative systems, and it will also help establish the specific senses in which the quality of interpersonal and intergroup life can be affected in critical ways by high-trust versus low-trust conditions. Then, the relevance of regenerative systems to emotional health and interpersonal competence will be outlined.

A Mini-Theory of Trust and Its Consequences

The dynamics of regenerative systems get usefully elaborated by a focus on interpersonal trust, one of the four variables in the two basic models introduced above. The choice is not whimsical, for many reasons including two that get special emphasis here.[31] Thus, the centrality of trust in helping, or growthful, relations has long been emphasized. Moreover, recent empirical research helps establish some of the specific connections implied by the centrality of trust in various theoretical formulations relating to growth and development.[32]

The role of trust can be suggested briefly.[33] Overall, as Jack R. Gibb convincingly argues, low trust induces defensive behavior, which is perhaps the basic block to any learning. That is, learning or growth depends essentially on acceptance of self and others, and defensiveness inhibits that acceptance. A variety of studies can be marshalled in support of this efficacy of high trust, whether between therapist and client, members either of problem-solving groups or of sensitivity training groups, or parent and child.[34]

Recently, Dale Zand has successfully extended our appreciation of the centrality of trust to managerial effectiveness, in a very useful and revealing way. Zand's theoretical network is sketched in Figure 3 and is basically a four-element model that relies heavily on the contributions of Morton Deutsch[35] and Jack Gibb,[36] especially. Zand distinguishes the *intention* of a sender, as well as his *behavior*. The model admits the commonplace slippage between intent and action. The receiving actor, as it were, at once *expects* a certain level of trustworthiness from the sender and also *perceives* a specific level of trustworthiness in various behaviors. The possible richness encompassed by these components of the model should be obvious. For example, a low expectation about trustworthiness might lead to a congruent perception of the sender's behavior and intention, even though the sender and other observers might read high trustworthiness into both intention and behavior of the sender. In this regard, also, the model seems faithful to major features of social life.

Further Zand's model emphasizes the relevance of the character of the problem situation involving sender and receiver. Specifically, some issues involve a high degree of what Zand calls "objective uncertainty," and here the effects of high trust versus low trust are likely to be most pronounced.

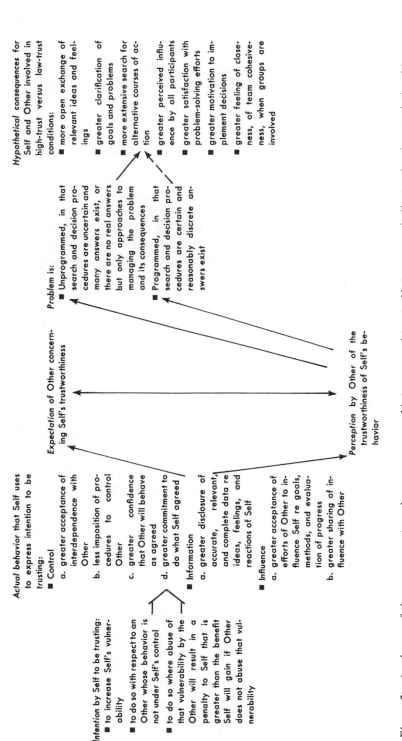

Figure 3 A schema of the components and consequences of interpersonal trust. Note: ——— indicates dominant relationship; — — indicates less-dominant relationship. [*Source*: Based upon Dale Zand, "Trust and Managerial Effectiveness," *Administrative Science Quarterly*, Vol. 17 (June 1972), pp. 230-233.]

Text within the figure:

Hypothetical consequences for Self and Other involved in high-trust versus low-trust conditions:
- more open exchange of relevant ideas and feelings
- greater clarification of goals and problems
- more extensive search for alternative courses of action
- greater perceived influence by all participants
- greater satisfaction with problem-solving efforts
- greater motivation to implement decisions
- greater feeling of closeness, of team cohesiveness, when groups are involved

Problem is:
- Unprogrammed, in that search and decision procedures are uncertain and many answers exist, or there are no real answers but only approaches to managing the problem and its consequences
- Programmed, in that search and decision procedures are certain and reasonably discrete answers exist

Expectation of Other concerning Self's trustworthiness

Perception by Other of the trustworthiness of Self's behavior

Actual behavior that Self uses to express intention to be trusting:
- Control
  a. greater acceptance of interdependence with Other
  b. less imposition of procedures to control Other
  c. greater confidence that Other will behave as agreed
  d. greater commitment to do what Self agreed
- Information
  a. greater disclosure of accurate, relevant, and complete data re ideas, feelings, and reactions of Self
- Influence
  a. greater acceptance of efforts of Other to influence Self re goals, methods, and evaluation of progress
  b. greater sharing of influence with Other

Intention by Self to be trusting:
- to increase Self's vulnerability
- to do so with respect to an Other whose behavior is not under Self's control
- to do so where abuse of that vulnerability by the Other will result in a penalty to Self that is greater than the benefit Self will gain if Other does not abuse that vulnerability

Zand notes that low trust adds a "social uncertainty" to whatever degree of objective uncertainty exists in a problem situation. Nature is not kind in this regard. Hence, applied behavioral science must labor to increase trust so as to facilitate effective responses to situations with a high objective uncertainty.

Figure 3 also sketches a number of major consequences that might be expected in high-trust conditions where the problem situation has a substantial objective uncertainty. Those consequences touch much that is central in social and organizational life.

Pretty clearly, Zand's model shares much conceptual ground with the regenerative/degenerative models above, as in its self-heightening features. For example, assume the interaction in Zand's model of a high-trust sender and a low-trust receiver. Because of his low expectations about the trustworthiness of the sender, the receiver is likely to read malice into the intentions of the sender. The sender not only tends to get the message; in addition, he might be concerned enough about misperceptions of his behavior and misjudgments of his intentions to punish the receiver. As sender becomes defensive or hostile, or noncommunicative, clearly he is also drawn into contributing to the intensity of the low-trust condition. This is the essence of spiral reinforcement. One can not win for losing, as was noted earlier.

Emotional Health and Interpersonal Competence

A second critical perspective on regenerative systems can be gained by tracing their interactions with emotional health, in broad terms, and with interpersonal competence, more specifically. The development by Argyris[37] of Robert White's[38] basic concept is relied on heavily in this section. The concept of interpersonal competence is a central one for the laboratory approach, related closely to its goal of heightening or inducing regenerative systems between individuals.

White defines interpersonal competence as the "capacity, fitness, or ability" of an individual to carry on those transactions that result in the individual maintaining, growing, and flourishing. White also argues persuasively that interpersonal competence tends to increase as[39]

- One's awareness of relevant factors increases
- The problems are solved in such a way that they remain solved
- The solutions involve a minimal deterioration of the problem-solving process

The centrality of regenerative interaction for interpersonal competence can be sketched briefly. A regenerative system will help insure that relevant factors are considered in problem-solving, especially via feedback or disclosure from other persons. Moreover, regenerative interaction between individuals will help assure that problems are solved in such ways that they remain solved, as by taking into account the preferences of relevant parties or by providing feedback early in the implementation of any solution should it prove to have unanticipated consequences. Finally, a regenerative system will raise the probability that individuals will believe that their inputs have been heard, which will help mightily to maintain the viability of a problem-solving process. Even an objectively correct solution, that is, may prove a failure if it is arrived at or implemented in ways that strain the processes or persons through which subsequent solutions will have to be made. In interpersonal relations, in sum, the specific way you skin a particular cat often counts less than how that way is chosen and implemented.

The relevance of regenerative systems to the development of interpersonal competence also can be suggested by highlighting the relationship between interpersonal competence and four conditions, following Argyris:

- Self-acceptance
- Confirmation
- Essentiality
- Psychological success

Self-acceptance refers to the confidence that an individual has in self, as well as to the degree that he or she regards self highly. Self-acceptance depends on knowledge about self, then, and the clarity of that knowledge will be influenced in significant senses by the quality of the interaction systems in which an individual operates.

The more regenerative the reaction systems within which an individual operates, on balance, the greater the individual's probable interpersonal competence. That is, a regenerative system implies that valid information will be available to parties in interaction, and each needs that information to know how the other sees him or her. More significantly, a regenerative system affects two crucial probabilities. It reduces the probability that feedback or disclosure will be perceived as hurtful or punitive. The high trust and low risk of experimentation in regenerative systems are the two factors which most directly raise these two crucial probabilities. Low trust and high risk can make any feedback or disclosure pointless and even punishing.

In conclusion, it is seldom easy to learn how others see us, to accept ourselves as others see us, or to change ourselves in ways that make our perception by others more acceptable to us. And degenerative systems complicate all three of these paramountly human concerns.

Confirmation of an individual occurs to the degree that others experience him as he sees himself. To the degree that an individual sees self as different from others experience her, her interpersonal competence is likely to be reduced. The rationale is both clear and compelling. Such an individual is not likely to be effective in gaining her objectives, or at least in gaining them for the reasons she expects. In a more fundamental sense, an individual who is more or less consistently disconfirmed may experience major problems associated with who she is or, to say much the same thing, with how she is perceived by others.

The quality of an individual's interaction system also affects confirmation in a more subtle and insidious way. In degenerative systems, an individual may experience a kind of bogus confirmation. This is perhaps even worse than getting confirmation from others concerning aspects of himself which an individual prefers to forget. Others may report they perceive the individual as a poet, for example, and he indeed sees himself as a souped-up if undiscovered Keats. In fact, these others really feel he is clumsy even in ordinary conversation, and a disaster with ballpoint in hand. But the others do not feel free to be open enough to own such a sentiment. And the individual may scribble on, uninformed by the kind of reactions he needs, or suspects, or may even want.

Essentiality refers to the condition under which an individual can express her central needs as well as to utilize her central abilities. The very term implies the sense of the concept. "What am I doing involved in this?" reflects one way we can express feelings of a low degree of essentiality.

Degenerative systems clearly would be unlikely to induce feelings of essentiality. Consider an individual who prefers to be a collaborative but who is locked into a narrowly competitive relationship. The result is low essentiality. There might be no way to avoid the interaction, and there would be no easy way to improve it. The high-risk level in a degenerative system, to illustrate, could inhibit raising the issue of the unsatisfactory pairing of the collaborative style preferred by the one person with the win or lose competitive style he actually experienced. This describes a vicious circularity, which is demeaning in an ultimately human sense.

Psychological success is a function of the degree to which an individual can define her own goals or meaningfully participate in their definition. Responding only to the goals set by others can generate feelings of failure, even when objective successes are achieved. Psychological success is also probable to the degree that goals are related to an individual's central needs, or abilities, or values. In addition, as the individual defines paths to attain her goals, the possibility of psychological success is heightened. Finally, attaining a realistic level of aspiration will induce psychological success. The point applies in two major senses. An aspiration level that is set too high can generate feelings of psychological failure no matter what the actual performance. That is, one can fail even as she does quite well. A level of aspiration that can be attained very comfortably also can generate feelings of failure, it being an "easy piece" and consequently too available to be motivating over the long run. In fact, the individual may despise herself for succeeding in such a facile way.

Regenerative systems are crucial for inducing the condition of psychological success, it should be clear. Such a system will facilitate an individual setting his own goals or participating in their definition, for example.

Toward Regenerative Systems Through Confrontation

These several perspectives on regenerative systems permit a major step toward providing greater specificity about the laboratory approach. Interpersonal competence is ineluctably linked via regenerative systems to confrontation, that is, to the very set of behaviors and attitudes that the laboratory approach basically seeks to increase. Confrontation is relatively rare, however, especially because it requires substantial interpersonal competence.

As a first step in building content into these two summary propositions, consider some "new business" between two individuals. Assume the new business relates to the unexpressed warmth that Joe feels for Jim. How is this new business to be handled? In order, these four modalities are characteristic means of responding to new business:

- Pairing
- Flight
- Fight
- Confrontation

The first two modalities are by far the most probable. Unfortunately, these modalities are the least likely to manage the new business. They raise questions about the individual's lack of courage and/or competence in facing the new business, which often begets new and more complicated unfinished business.

The generation of unfinished business, which remains as a press against the conscious mind or may even get deeply repressed, is not a trivial matter. Unfinished business constitutes a burden or excess baggage to which the individual can add and from which she can subtract, and which requires correspondingly variable energies to carry. Common usages suggest the point. "That's a load off my mind," we might say as we give a friend a piece of feedback that we consciously suppressed. The greater the energies devoted to unfinished business, crudely, the less energy an individual has to manage her socioemotional life. Hence, the less interpersonally competent she is likely to be. Unfinished business in the socioemotional realm can even become so great that it inhibits rational-technical performance.

Consider the four modalities individually. *Pairing* is perhaps the most common way of dealing with new business. Picture an impassioned sales director concluding an announcement of a new program with a request for questions or reactions. No response is forthcoming, and the sales director remains with his own fantasies. No sooner does the audience leave the meeting room, however, than reactions begin tumbling forth. Friends "pair," they get together to discuss informal reactions. "It'll never work," some say. "A great idea," is the sentiment others share. The sales director gets neither kind of input.

Pairing is at once understandable and perhaps even necessary, but it nevertheless avoids dealing with the new business generated by the request of the sales director. Pairing is especially understandable in degenerative systems, where the risk may be too great for public feedback or disclosure. And pairing may be necessary, as a way of comparing notes or perhaps even of preserving the handhold on sanity inherent in the fact that other people see things the same way. The issue avoided, of course, is why the questions and reactions that flowed so easily in the informal pairings were not shared with the sales director when he requested them. And this can cut many ways.

Flight is also a common response to new business. In this modality, the provoking stimulus is somehow avoided. In contrast, pairing deals with the stimulus, but not in the environment within which it was generated.

There are numerous ways to flee. One can observe the provoking stimulus, for example, and consciously choose to suppress it. Less directly, one can see what one wants to see instead of what exists.

Flight can have much to recommend it under various conditions, in the sense of strategically retreating to fight or confront another day. Strategic retreats can be both useful and necessary. Just as clearly, however, flight neglects the new business. The special danger of flight is that the accumulation of such unfinished business can begin to overburden interpersonal systems and perhaps lead to unforeseen blow-ups between people. Individuals will feel a reduced interpersonal competence as minor stimuli unexpectedly lead to massive responses. These are clear limitations on the usefulness of the flight response to new business.

Fight is an infrequent mode of dealing with new business. The low incidence of this mode is understandable, even though it may sometimes help clear the air between people. The mode implies win or lose competition, however, which often means that the approach creates as many problems as it solves. If nothing else, the resentment of the loser may be a factor to contend with sooner or later. Consequently, fight is usually a last-ditch strategy.

Confrontation, a fourth mode of dealing with new business, is at once quite rare and also the goal of the laboratory approach. The necessary and interacting amalgam is one of personal skills and appropriate environments. In terms of the vocabulary introduced thus far, confrontation requires interpersonal competence and regenerative interaction systems. Specifically, confrontation as used here implies four interacting skills and attitudes in people.

First, the confronting person must "know where she is." That is, she must know what she is thinking or feeling, she must know how she is reacting. In the common vernacular, a confronting person must "be in touch with herself." This assumes certain skills, as well as attitudes that call for the application of such skills as a part of daily life. For most people, at least much of the time, this first requirement for confronting is well within their normal reach.

Second, confrontation requires that a person know why he is where he is. If he feels angry, for example, he needs to know what induced or triggered his anger. More dynamically, the individual needs confidence and experience that he can trace his reactions or thoughts back to some precipitating stimuli, at least in substantial part. If he feels warm and accepting, the same requirement holds. In short, self-insight and analysis are required. Without such insight and analysis, catharsis may result, but controntation remains improbable.

Third, the confronting person must be able to express where she is, as well as why she is there. In part, personal courage is required. In part, also, this presumes regenerative systems. There will be precious little confrontation, in sum, if we have to wait on courageous heroics. Environments must permit, encourage, and even reward confronting behavior. Otherwise it will remain in critically short supply.

Fourth, the person intent on confronting must master a difficult balance. He must be able to achieve the three conditions described immediately above, while permitting and even encouraging others to do the same. The point applies particularly to those in positions of power or authority. They may be able to achieve the first three conditions with ease, while complicating or prohibiting a similar achievement by others.

That the thrust of the laboratory approach is toward confrontation through interpersonal competence gives it "a very real toughness," in Sheldon Davis's words, which is too little noted. "In dealing with one another, we will be open, direct, explicit," Davis notes as he develops his view. "Our feelings will be available to another, and we will try to problem-solve rather than be defensive. These values have within them a very tough way of living—not a soft way." Davis sees too little of this view in the behavioral sciences, which often seem to him to value the building of happy teams of employees who "feel good about things." He prefers concentration on building such relationships between individuals and groups that they "can function well and can zero in quickly on their problems and deal with them rationally, in the very real sense of the word." Davis concludes:

> There is no real growth—there is no real development—in the organization or in the individuals within it if they do not confront and deal directly with their problems. They can get together and share feelings, but if that is

all they do, it is merely a catharsis. While this is useful, it has relatively minimal usefulness compared with what can happen if they start to relate differently within the organizational setting around task issues.[40]

Toward Regenerative Systems Through Helpful Feedback

This chapter ends as it began, again emphasizing the central roles of feedback and disclosure, but this time in a more specific way which gives special relevance to creating and maintaining regenerative systems of interaction. The overall point here applies pretty much across the board, whether feedback and disclosure are induced in a T-group or in some other learning vehicle of the laboratory approach. Whatever happens in the laboratory approach, at whichever level of organization, has its immediate origins in feedback and disclosure supplied by individuals in interaction. Hence, the critical nature of the two processes and the profound importance of the values or operating guidelines that underlie them.

Some Generic Issues

Feedback and disclosure may be distinguished crudely. The former refers to information, both verbal and nonverbal, we give others about how we see them or react to them, and disclosure involves revealing something about oneself to another. Not that the two come distinct in nature. Typically, indeed, every piece of feedback tells or implies to the Other something about the sending Self, and hence is commingled with self-disclosure. Similarly, disclosure often implies feedback from the Self to the Other, if only: "I believe you can be trusted with this information." Moreover, the two processes also are subtly linked in another way: One typically triggers the other.

   Feedback may be viewed as information concerning the efficacy of some data processor's adaptations to an environment. And the stakes are high, even incredibly high. As one source expresses the criticality of feedback to both sender and receiver: "Feedback, then, is a way of giving help; it is a corrective mechanism for the individual who wants to learn how well his behavior matches his intentions; and it is a means for establishing one's identity—for answering Who am I."[41] Feedback, in sum, is central to the quality of life and living in providing persons with information about the adequacy of their behavior. The more timely and accurate the feedback, the better the performance.[42] The rationale is uncomplicated. Individuals desire to be competent, to make happen successfully what they want to have happen. Thus, individuals are motivated to adjust when they learn that their behaviors are perceived as differing from their core concepts, or are ineffective or maladaptive.[43] In fact, it is not too much to say that all of us deeply need such information to remain sane and human.

Human beings and large organizations, then, are alike in that they are no better in adapting than their feedback is timely and validly reflects what exists.

Human beings and organizations will be *no better* in adapting than their feedback is timely and valid; however, they can be *worse*. That is, people in organizations must be appropriately programmed to deal with as well as to provide feedback. The ideal is not providing just any feedback that is to be processed in just any way. How the feedback is given and how it is responded to are of great significance. Hence, the following gives attention to some properties of helpful feedback, and to some guidelines for giving and processing helpful feedback.

Some Specific Properties of Helpful Feedback

Detailing the properties of helpful feedback is like eating an artichoke, a peeling off of layers of meaning. Even the six such levels distinguished here are more suggestive than definitive. A large research literature exists,[44] and many designs for variously inducing feedback are available.[45] We here stress the dominant central emphases in that research and practice, as they appear to the author.

Enhances Mutual Interpersonal Competence. At the most general level, feedback that will help both Self and Other in enhancing their mutual interpersonal competence has the following major properties.[46]

- The information exchanged is minimally distorted, which requires that both Self and Other have a relatively high degree of self-awareness and self-acceptance.

- The information is relatively consistent and noncontradictory; consequently, it does not pose ambiguities or double-binds.

- The information is directly verifiable by Self and Other, which is to say that it should be neither interpretative nor based on inferred categories.

- The information is descriptive and minimally evaluative as to "good" versus "bad," and so on.

- The information contributes to effective problem-solving, "effective" taken to mean that the solution does not generate other problems of equal or greater magnitude and that the solution enhances or at least maintains the viability of the problem-solving processes.

Facilitates Autonomy. Perhaps the major property of helpful feedback is that it facilitates autonomy, increases the chances of learning accompanied by feelings of psychological success. As the autonomy of the learner is facilitated, goes the extended rationale, so grows the feeling of being in control of the learning and confidence about transferring it to other situations. This thrust toward personal autonomy via community is patent in Leland Bradford's view of the centrality of feedback. "Each individual needs to get accurate information about the difference between what he is trying to do and how well he is doing it," he observed. "He needs to be able to use this information to correct or change his actions. Then, *basically, he is steering himself.*"[47]

Chris Argyris is also insistent on the point, and he relentlessly follows that insistence to its logical consequences. He thus urges that all laboratory learning designs offer participants frequent opportunities to[48]

- Define their own learning goals
- Develop their own approaches to meeting the goals
- Relate both goals and approaches to central needs of participants
- Choose a challenging level of aspiration that extends their present abilities but does not overwhelm them

The underlying notion is one of the growth-oriented person seeking self-enhancement and aid in more effective coping. That model person is not survival oriented or deficiency oriented, in Argyris's vocabulary.

Seeks a Special Level.   Relatedly, helpful feedback focuses on preconscious or conscious processes, as is implicit in the emphasis above on information that can be verified directly by Self and Other. Feedback oriented toward eliciting the so-called unconscious processes is not a deliberate goal of the laboratory approach. Indeed, unconscious processes often are approached via a second kind of information, information relying on inferred categories that can be validated only in terms of some theoretical or conceptual framework.[49]   Compare two ideal responses to a long, evocatively rich description that invokes images of floating on dark and stormy waters, of a feeling of drowning with only impassive rocks looking on, and so on. Probing this imagery for unconscious materials would take one route. Thus, the speaker might be asked to close her eyes, to again imagine her feeling of drowning, while taking special note of those "rocks." What feelings in her do they evoke? Does she sense anything familiar in them? The trend of the questions should be clear enough. They seek to explore the ontological roots of one interpretation of the images as reflecting a separation from fellow humans and, perhaps, as implying some precipitating rejection by a critical person earlier in life. In sharp contrast, an appropriate here-and-now response might be: "You confuse me when you use all that complex imagery. I have to struggle for meanings. It would help me if you would take one theme at a time, and relate it to how you're feeling and reacting now. Maybe I could help more then."

Insight is possible via the use of both kinds of information, but the appropriate learning situations are quite dissimilar. For example, Leonard Horwitz notes that: "Therapeutic and training groups emphasize two different methods of insight giving: the training group depends more upon personal feedback from one's peers, while the therapy group depends largely on the therapist's interpretation of transference to him."[50] That is, at the level of basic T-group design, reliance on directly verifiable information "encourages peer observation in the form of mutual evaluations in which each member has the opportunity of hearing a consensus opinion about his role in the group."[51] In contrast, reliance on information inferred from a conceptual scheme implies a unique role for the person most in touch with the conceptual scheme, that is, the therapist.

Feedback has a number of advantages in those insight-producing situations which are brief and whose goal is to make persons more aware of how they come across to others. For example, feedback utilizes the great social pressure implicit in its approach to insight. Group scapegoating must be guarded against. But a dominant or unanimous opinion coming from members of a group can make the individual uniquely aware of aspects of himself which he has heard about from others, but which he has been relatively free to discount as more-or-less random and perhaps even hostile, if consistent, observations. Finally, and crucially, emphasis on information that is directly verifiable intends to avoid the profound regression that the therapist seeks to induce in order to surface unconscious conflicts that impair functioning.[52]

Relies on a Contingent Process. The fourth property of helpful feedback involves a delicately contingent process. As C. Gratton Kemp observes: "verbal feedback should await the development of mutual trust and a pattern of interchange and support from person to person. Some verbal feedback is laden with anxiety, and the skill needed to evaluate constructively is slow to develop."[53] In terms of degenerative systems, then, the foundations of helpful feedback are sufficient increases in interpersonal trust and sufficient reductions in risk. If achieved, these predisposing states will support increased openness and owning, and they will induce a readiness on the part of the sender and the receiver of the feedback. Figure 4 sketches the sense of the two conditions.

The mini-models in Figure 4 do not imply that no feedback will occur in the cycle of mistrust.[54] Some harmful feedback can occur, but the far more probable condition is one of withholding or masking at least verbal feedback. Nature is kind in this regard, however. To the degree that a cycle of mistrust exists, so also is any expressed verbal or nonverbal feedback likely to be devalued, misinterpreted, or rejected as the effort of a stranger or enemy to hurt.

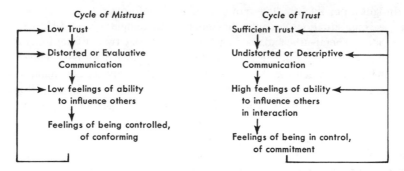

Figure 4 Two cycles for characterizing interpersonal relationships. [*Source*: R. T. Golembiewski, *Renewing Organizations: The Laboratory Approach to Planned Change* (Itasca, Ill.: F. E. Peacock, 1972).]

Does Not Destroy Defenses. Derivatively, helpful feedback does not seek to assail and destroy a person's defenses. The intent of the laboratory approach is to induce an analytical view of one's defenses, of how they help and hinder learning, of how they are variously functional or dysfunctional for the individual's goals. Change in the defenses may be appropriate, or it may not be. But it is cavalier to contemplate assailing and destroying a person's defenses. That is, an individual's defenses exist for at least two significant reasons: these conceptual systems have proved at least modestly useful in the past, and they imply major values that help guide an individual's life.[55]

Rather than assailing or destroying defenses, in fact, the laboratory approach creates a climate of trust that legitimates safely looking at one's defenses, in part through the eyes of others. Jack R. Gibb details the point in broad sweep when he rejects a "climate which induces defensiveness" for a "climate of supportive communications." He explains that the person who perceives or anticipates threat must devote an appreciable part of his energy to defending himself, which reduces the energy available for learning or change. The defensive person, Gibb notes, is too busy to be of much help to himself or others:

> he thinks about how he appears to others, how he may be seen more favorably, how he may win, dominate, impress, or escape punishment, and/or how he may avoid or mitigate a perceived or anticipated attack. . . . The more "supportive" or defense reductive the climate the less the receiver reads into the communication distorted loadings which arise from projections of his own anxieties, motives, and concerns. As defenses are reduced, the receivers become better able to concentrate on the structure, the content, and the cognitive meaning of the message.[56]

Gibb emphasizes a people process rather than a language process, and he stresses that fundamental improvements in communication consequently require improvements in interpersonal relationships. Improving communications thus often means behaving in ways that reduce threat. How is this challenge of reducing defensiveness to be met? Based on his study of recordings of numerous discussions, Gibb isolated two contrasting climates and six categories of behavior characteristic of each of them. The contrasting nature of these two climates can be suggested economically, although reference to the original piece is necessary to provide details.

Defensive Climates Tend to Be Induced by	Supportive Climates Tend to Be Induced by
1. Evaluation	1. Description
2. Control	2. Problem orientation
3. Strategy	3. Spontaneity
4. Neutrality	4. Empathy
5. Superiority	5. Equality
6. Certainty	6. Provisionalism

The laboratory approach, in its essentials, rests on learning designs that help demonstrate the significance of climate to communication, as well as the difficulty of inducing the appropriate climate. The task is formidable. To illustrate the point, consider the subtlety of shifting behaviors from evaluation to description. "Anyone who has attempted to train professionals to use information-seeking speech with neutral affect," Gibb explains, "appreciates how difficult it is to say even the simple 'who did that?' without being seen as accusing."

The common thrust of these considerations should be patent. Helpful feedback requires more respecting of defenses than it does assailing or destroying them, thereby creating conditions favorable to an increase in accurate listening.[57] An assault on a person's defenses might be "Stop that behavior, stupid." The laboratory approach advises: "When you behave that way, I have these reactions." The style does make a difference.

Is Most Effective in Group Situations. Feedback is usually most impactful and helpful in a group situation. Patently, consistent feedback coming from many or all members of a group makes powerful stuff. The group context also provides individuals with substantial security against getting bushwhacked by an unscrupulous individual or two. In addition, the group situation provides a wide range of resources. Thus, some members may not like X in member A, but others may provide support for A or even report they find charming in A what others find repelling. These diverse resources can provide shelter from even intense feedback, while the individual determines a long-run course of action.

Frederick Stoller describes both the short-run probabilities and the ideal in this regard:

> Most people either succumb completely to pressure or unequivocally oppose it and it is only when they have had the opportunity to experience it clearly and see it through that they seem to have the option to deal with pressure in a more differentiated fashion—to pick and choose what they want to resist and what they want to accept; the free individual has the option to stand up against or go along with.[58]

And it is free individuals that the laboratory approach seeks to nourish: free in the essential sense of being in command of more of the information that permits them greater control over their interpersonal and intergroup relations.

Six Specific Guidelines for Helpful Feedback

The properties above demonstrate that the laboratory approach does not legitimate just any kind of feedback, but we must get much more specific about the kind of feedback considered ideal. The focus in this section is on six guidelines for helpful feedback, and the basic design is straightforward. The guidelines for feedback will be listed below, and their application to a sample piece of feedback will be illustrated.

Readers might help make this section more experientially meaningful to themselves by writing a piece of feedback they would like to send to someone. Write in it prose, as you envision yourself saying it to the intended target. You can later measure your piece of feedback against the guidelines, after they have been described and illustrated.

Exhibit 2 details value-loaded guidelines for helpful feedback, for a starter. These guidelines will be briefly described and illustrated.

Emphasis on the Here-and-Now.   First, helpful feedback is based on a scratch it when it itches principle. As much as possible, feedback should refer to ongoing situations, to the here-and-now. The rationale is both practical and profound. As the here-and-now is emphasized, practically, so is it easier to deal with more-or-less immediately verifiable data, unclouded by recollections that have grown dim. More profoundly, as the here-and-now is emphasized, it becomes easier to avoid several kinds of inappropriate behaviors. Less likely, for example, is the amateur psychiatry that seeks ontological there-and-then roots for behavior.

Emphasis on the Individual Act.   The second guideline for helpful feedback prescribes that it should emphasize individual acts, attitudes, or values, as opposed to the total person. The purpose is dual: to zero-in on the specific phenomenon of concern, and to do so without unnecessarily raising the target's defenses or

Exhibit 2   Three Guidelines for Helpful Feedback

Guidelines for Helpful Feedback	Sample Feedback
Emphasis on the here-and-now versus the there-and-then	"George, you are a stereophonic SOB. And I know why. Your father rejected you as a child."
Emphasis on the individual behavior, attitude, or value, versus the total person	
Emphasis on feedback that is non-evaluative in at least three senses:	
It is nonjudgmental	
It is noninterpretive	
It reports the specific impact on the Self of Other's behavior, attitude, or value	

without denigrating the target as a person. The difference in wording of feedback can be profound. Compare "I hate you" with "You hurt me when you didn't recognize me at the party," when the common stimulus is a perceived social snub. The underlying rationale for this guideline is elemental. A denigration of the total person is most likely to induce a flight response, or perhaps even fight. Neither of these probable responses fosters what helpful feedback requires: hearing the full import of the message by the target, and keeping defenses low enough, or porous enough, so that both target and sender can expend maximum energy in problem-solving, as opposed to facade maintenance.

Emphasis on Nonevaluative Feedback.   The third guideline is far more complex and subtle. Helpful feedback should be nonevaluative and descriptive, in at least three more-or-less distinct senses. In the most elemental sense, feedback should be nonjudgmental. That is, it should be characterized by an absence of evaluations like "good" or "bad," especially as these evaluations refer to a total person.

Relatedly, effective feedback should be noninterpretive. Consider the husband who complains that the potatoes at dinner were hard. "Poor dear," his wife may respond by leaping to an interpretation, "had a hard day at the office, I see." Such interpretations may imply serious problems. They often are a way of not hearing what the sender intends, or of devaluing it. In addition, the interpretation often will be inaccurate. The husband above might retort: "I had a wonderful day at work, as a matter of fact. I repeat: the potatoes were hard." The subsequent dialogue might go several ways, none of them very promising.

Finally, interpretations of many sorts deal with data that are not immediately observable, or that may even be validatable only against some theoretical schema. Back to the wife again, to illustrate. She might reply soothingly, recalling (she believes) some potent stuff from Home Ec 217, "Your Happy Home." "I know how difficult it is for you to be open with me, dear, given how you were dominated by that other woman in your life, your mother. Now just tell me all about how rough your day was. You can trust me, I'm not out to tie you to my apronstrings." And all that from some underdone potatoes.

Finally, feedback should be nonevaluative in the sense that it reports the feelings in Self induced by the Other's act, attitude, or value. As the sender of the feedback is in touch with her reactions—as she is aware and accepting of herself—so are such reports descriptive rather than evaluative.

The rationale for this guideline has several components, foremost among which is an equivalent of the rule of best evidence. That is, the Self represents the world's expert about such relations, literally. Moreover, such reactions are vital to any Other intent on testing or improving his interpersonal competence. In short, others basically need to know whether their actions have the intended effects. Of great importance, also, this guideline reinforces an emphasis on the here-and-now, which is central in the laboratory approach.

The sample piece of feedback in Exhibit 2 helps illustrate these first three guidelines, if in a negative way. The reader can assume the basic responsibility for the effort. Note here only the skeleton of such an evaluation:

- The emphasis is basically on the there-and-then, for example, in the alleged childhood of George.
- The emphasis is on George as a total person, who is an SOB from whatever angle one views him.
- The sample feedback:

    Judges George as a total person (stereophonic SOB)

    Interprets why George is the way he is (childhood experiences)

    Fails to report the specific impact on the sender of George's unspecified acts, attitudes, or values, although the general tone clearly reflects George's negative impact on the sender

Guidelines 4, 5, and 6 for helpful feedback can be described and illustrated as complements to the first three, as shown in Exhibit 3.

Emphasis on Facilitating Change.   The fourth guideline acknowledges that effective feedback typically refers to some kind of action or choice: doing something different; or doing more of something; or just continuing to do something. As such, helpful feedback should have three attributes, following the basic Lewinian model of change. At the very least, a piece of feedback

Exhibit 3   Three Additional Guidelines for Helpful Feedback

Guidelines for Helpful Feedback	Sample Feedback
Emphasis on facilitating change in three ways:	"George, you are a stereophonic SOB. And I know why. Your father rejected you as a child."
By helping to "unfreeze" the old behavior, attitude, or value	
By suggesting replacements that may be tried	
By reinforcing any new behavior, attitude, or value	
Emphasis on "trust in leveling," on psychological safety of target of feedback	
Emphasis on creating and maintaining an "organic community"	

should encourage the target to look at some part of self or behavior. Two elements are involved: a specificity by the sender about what the sender is directing attention toward; and a receptivity by the target, which is often a function of the degree to which he perceives the immediate climate as helpful and supportive. The desired condition is described as "unfreezing," where the target feels secure enough to view some part of himself and to evaluate its contribution to his interpersonal competence. The antigoal is typified by the tightly wound Don Knotts character. "Are you ner—," begins a question. "No!" the character replies before the question is finished. And we laugh, with some compassion, knowing how hard it will be for that character to learn from his experience when he so quickly rejects even what is so obvious at all.

Moreover, feedback that facilitates change will imply or suggest replacement behaviors, attitudes, or values. Consider the anticase. "You say I distrust you," says one person. "I'd like to change that. Perhaps you could help by telling what there is about me that evokes such a strong reaction." The unhelpful response is: "I don't know. There's just something about you that rubs me the wrong way." Unless this unpromising dialogue goes much further, no change is a very solid bet, except a change for the worse.

Finally, on the issue of choice and change, helpful feedback will provide reinforcement for any new behaviors, attitudes, or values with which the target of feedback might experiment. At a minimum, this implies a willingness of others to respond openly concerning reactions to the new or intensified acts. Further, reinforcement implies openness to point up any backsliding, as well as social support for the effort and for any progress.

Emphasis on Psychological Safety.   Helpful feedback will emphasize the
psychological safety of the target of the feedback, a kind of contract about
"trust in leveling" that binds both sender and target. For the sender, this fifth
guideline implies feedback that is requested rather than forced and that meets
the needs of the target as well as the sender. For the target, the guideline implies
that she is in control of the feedback process and can indicate both when she
wants more feedback and when she has had enough.

Emphasis on Creating a Community.   Helpful feedback is more likely in the
context of a community of learners or a society dedicated to mutual help. The
T-group is the prime example of such a learning-helping community. In its
broad philosophical perspective, the goal is to create in a T-group a true moral
and ethical order, a basic agreement concerning fundamentals that alone can
permit individuals to differ and to be different without opting for isolation or
scapegoating.

T-groups are not always and everywhere appropriate or convenient, of
course, and alternative designs might be more appropriate. Whatever the design,
the use of group settings can be of great value. If nothing else, they can provide
consensual validation. Moreover, group settings can contribute to the feelings of
safety of the target of the feedback. Both features are implicit in such questions
as: "That's how I see Fred. I wonder if others have a different perception of
him?"

The sample feedback in Exhibit 3 permits convenient illustration of these
final three guidelines. Again, the reader can do much of the work. In outline,
however, it may be helpful to note that in the sample piece of feedback:

- The emphasis does not facilitate change because:
  The target is not clear about what old behaviors, attitudes, or values
  might be changed.
  The replacement behaviors are not clear, short of a return to the womb
  to start over again.
  There is consequently no clear, promised reinforcement of any changes;
  in fact, quite the contrary seems implied.
- The emphasis is clearly not on the psychological safety of the target,
  even though presumably some needs of the sender are being met.
- The emphasis is on a one-to-one relationship, and the "community" in
  that dyadic relationship seems oriented only indirectly toward helping
  and learning.

Toward Regenerative Systems Through Relevant Disclosure

This chapter also ends as it began in another sense, with some greater specificity
about disclosure designed to build on the foundations of earlier discussion. The

discussion cannot be as detailed as that on feedback, and the issues here are more subtle in many senses. But the issues are all the more unavoidable for that.

Some Generic Issues

Disclosure has not received the attention lavished on feedback,[59] and the neglect seems momentous. H. M. Lynd seems to measure his statement of this profundity: "a person who cannot love cannot reveal himself,"[60] and vice versa. Similarly, Egan observes that groups rest on the agreement of participants "to make some efforts to reveal the person within to other members." He explains that this assumes that "responsible self-disclosure is a kind of royal road to community. This sharing of the human condition—in its sublimity, banality, and deformity—pulls people together."[61]

The specific focus here on disclosure has more modest purposes, three of which deserve highlighting. *First,* disclosure is seen as a common quid pro quo for feedback, and hence it is of great importance. The model piece of disclosure in the laboratory approach, that is, often contains a clear or implied request for feedback. For example, this statement at once discloses and seeks feedback: "I'm very concerned with how you see me."

Second, more broadly, there seem to be major reasons why a person should disclose, perhaps even needs to disclose in some ultimate sense. Samuel A. Culbert notes of non-self-disclosure that "one general consequence does stand out." That consequence is "the added difficulty a non-self-disclosing person faces in obtaining information about the reality or objective aspects of relationships in which he participates."[62] That constitutes a major consequence, indeed, one associated with such effects as the probable onset and severity of mental illness.

Third, "congruent" or "authentic" relationships represent a two-way street—"an accurate matching of experiencing, . . . awareness, and communication" between two or more people.[63] Oppositely, some interpretations of "being congruent" or "being authentic" imply "letting it all hang out," whether in feedback or disclosure. This implies one-way authenticity or congruence, and perhaps even a narcissistic dead-end that makes impossible what it seeks to enhance.

Overall, strong reasons urge rejecting the conclusion that, because more disclosure can be a good thing, unlimited disclosure consequently ranks as the very best thing. To be sure, particularly as a countervalue to overcontrolled behavior imposed by restrictive societies or organizations, disclosure within broad limits can be a tonic. There "the problem for many people is not going 'too far' with congruency but dealing with over-controlled behavior."[64] But the limits are easily passed.[65] Hence, Argyris[66] urges thinking of authenticity as an interpersonal phenomenon rather than a personal state or characteristic.

He conceives of human relationships as "the source of psychological life and human growth," especially in that such relationships can involve increasing awareness and acceptance of self and others. Authentic relationships are, in fact, those in which an individual enhances her awareness and acceptance of self and others, while she does so in ways that permit others to do the same. Consequently, for Argyris, one can no more be authentic independently of others than one can cooperate with self. A person's authenticity, then, will be a mutual function of the capacity to create authentic relations with others, as well as their capacities to create authentic relationships with that person. It is easy but ultimately futile to serve aces in tennis if there is no player on the other side of the net. This is not how the game is played.[67]

Some General Guidelines for Relevant Disclosure

What kinds of disclosure seem better adapted to inducing increased awareness and acceptance by both Self and Other? Our knowledge remains scanty, so brevity is appropriate here. Six features of disclosure will be emphasized.

First, disclosure will be helpful as it is perceived as appropriate to the situation in which the disclosure is made. Extreme examples are easy enough to handle, such as the high probability of the inappropriateness of the child in a theater who loudly discloses during a tender scene his intentions to use the restroom facilities. Existing research implies that broader situational appropriateness is likely to be very complicated, including the self-esteem of the discloser as well as the status and style of the target of the disclosure.[68]

Second, the motivation seen as prompting a disclosure will be significant in determining its impact on the relationships existing between sender and receiver. Culbert stresses the perception by others of the congruence between what the discloser states or implies are his motives, and what motives the receiver attributes to him. He concludes: "To the extent that the communicator is seen as congruent, the receiver is likely to accept his participation at face value and to be open to the possibility of viewing his communications favorably."[69] In contrast, communications that are viewed as incongruent will tend to evoke guarded or defensive reactions, at least until the receiver can decide on a strategy to protect his interests.

Third, timing will be critical in the impact of a piece of self-disclosure. "*Now* you tell us" suggests a disclosure that could have been made earlier.

Fourth, self-disclosure apparently has different effects, depending upon whether its orientation is toward the past, present, or future. Disclosures from the past can be significant, but they also can develop into complicated histories that critically depend on the perceptual filters of the person supplying the narrative. The appropriateness of past-tense disclosures to ongoing situations also may be unclear. Hence, Egan notes that past-tense disclosures often are "history," or pseudo-self-disclosure. He notes of "history" that:

It is actuarial and analytic, and usually has a strong "there and then" flavor. It clicks off the facts of experience and even interpretations of this experience but leaves the person of the revealer relatively untouched; he is accounted for and analyzed, but unrevealed. The person relates many facts about himself, but the person within still remains unknown. History is often a long account. It is long and often steady because it fears interruption. Interruption might mean involvement, and a person engages in history to avoid, rather than invite, involvement.[70]

Disclosure about the future also can be meaningful, but resolution may flag and recollection may dim when the chips are down.

For such reasons, and especially to avoid the pitfalls of a there-and-then orientation, Culbert gives central status to present-tense disclosure. He explains that such disclosures typically have the highest interpersonal relevance, generate the greatest amount of feedback, and make for the greatest receptivity to the feedback of others. The conclusion is direct. "Hence, present-tense disclosures, all other things being equal," Cublert notes, "are believed to possess the highest potential for increased self-awareness and personal growth."[71]

Fifth, growth in awareness and acceptance of self and others seems to be a curvilinear function of self-disclosure. Some research[72] supports common sense[73] in this regard. Too much self-disclosure can be as destructive to interpersonal relationships as too little. The former overwhelms the other person, while the latter starves the relationship.

Effective self-disclosure, then, may be characterized as being uninhibitedly appropriate, and to the correct degree. In most cases, this poses no great problem, even given the lack of specific content of the terms "appropriate" and "correct." By and large, too little self-disclosure characterizes most interpersonal relationships. So, "more" is a generally applicable prescription for self-disclosure. Questions of how much remain beyond general prescription. As Culbert notes,

> The problem of too much disclosure is less clear-cut. What constitutes *too much*, under *what* circumstances, and by *whom* is a thoroughly complex issue. Appropriateness, motivation, timing and tense all enter in. Moreover, what constitutes the *optimal* amount of self-disclosure is a no less complicated issue.[74]

Sixth, self-disclosure can be useless or perhaps even dangerous under certain conditions. Uselessness is Egan's basic concern, by far. He sees it as a probable outcome to the degree that self-disclosure is[75]

- Exhibitionistic rather than oriented toward establishing or deepening a relationship
- Not responded to with support and acceptance by the receivers

- History, in the sense defined above
- First promised by someone who then reneges on the promise
- Incomplete in a situation where completeness is required

More broadly, self-disclosure may even be threatening sui generis, and perhaps acutely so for some people. Egan observes: "Self-disclosure both crystallizes and, in a sense, reifies aspects of the self that a person would rather live with silently—however painful the living—than face."[76]

Some General Features of Irresponsible Disclosure

At the possible expense of some repetition, general features of irresponsible disclosure can be sketched. That is, although most systems have disclosure deficiencies, the prognosis here is not the more disclosure, the better. The quality of feedback can be significant, as can be illustrated by five kinds of irresponsible disclosure borrowed from Steele.[77] First, disclosure can be irresponsible if it is offered with the expectation that no reactions or repercussions will occur. Such an expectation signals that the sender has low commitment to the disclosure process, and will bail out very early in the game; better no such disclosure. Second, anonymous disclosure can be irresponsible. It suggests the sender would like the best of all worlds: to send the signal, but with little investment. That implies a weak learning link. Third, some disclosers do so in ways that entail risks only for others. Such disclosure has many names, none of them especially attractive. And the sender may be naive or even vicious. Fourth, some disclosures deal with information that was shared with the understanding that confidentiality would be maintained. Such disclosure need not improve an interaction system. Obviously, it might have precisely the opposite effect. Fifth, disclosure should not be a one-way street. Steele labels people who disclose by overwhelming others as "blasters." They disregard the characteristics of receivers: their feelings as well as their abilities to hear and respond to the disclosure.[78] Blasters will tend to generate irresponsible disclosure.

Process as Complementary, Not All-Consuming
Four Emphases Concerning a Neglected Point

A point made above in passing requires reinforcement here, even at the risk of possible overkill. The emphasis on "process" can be very powerful in diagnosing and prescribing for organizational choice or change, so much so that its only complementary character gets too little attention. Four emphases here provide necessary correction of this common underattention. In turn, these themes will be stressed.

- Process analysis can be approached in many ways at many levels of organization, and quite different approaches/skills will be appropriate (for example) for small target organizations and large ones.

- Process interventions seek to encourage unity and cooperation although they often get derided because they "create trouble where none existed," and moving from the latter to the former often will require a range of techniques, theory, and knowledge.

- Appropriate interventions often must give close consideration to "content" issues as well as to "process."

- Process interventions typically get triggered by experience, but they should be embedded in theoretical networks of growing comprehensiveness and specificity that will help associate experience with specific networks of covariants—information critical for anticipating strings of consequences, for isolating strategic targets for choice or change, and so on.

Interventions in Large as Well as Small Systems

Most experience with process analysis derives from small collections of people, and the T-group or sensitivity training group constitutes perhaps the most useful and convenient locus for beginning to work on appropriate skills and perspectives.[79] Not surprisingly, then, this two-book set gives fulsome attention to process analysis in micro-systems. Chapter 6 of this first part, for example, provides the major reflection of this emphasis. It details two cases of interventions in small groups that focus on process issues. Without doubt, the most favored design family of OD is called "interview/feedback" and relies substantially on the observational, data-eliciting, and interpreting capabilities, as well as on the presentation skills, of an intervenor. Interview/feedback, in turn, can contribute to that burgeoning set of learning designs usually called "team-building" or "team development," which will be highlighted not only in Chapter 6 but also at several other points in this two-part volume.

When the target system comprises much or all of a large organization, a process orientation is no less valuable, but different data-gathering methods and interpretive skills become useful, if not necessary. That is to say, the focus remains on basic feedback and disclosure processes, but a large population with numerous subunits may encourage or even require reliance on survey/feedback designs that test opinions and attitudes across sometimes huge ranges, that utilize advanced electronic data-processing methods, and that permit sophisticated

statistical treatment of multiple comparisons of the data.[80] Chapter 3 of Part 1
provides an introduction to survey/feedback designs; Chapters 6 and 7 of
Part 2 draw attention to one specific way of using survey data to determine the
effects of an OD intervention, and also provide overall perspective on survey/
feedback processes and institutions, respectively.

Interventions Encourage Unity as Well as Make Trouble

Perspectives commonly differ about process interventions, in extreme ways.
Thus, OD aficionados strongly emphasize the good works of a process orientation: They stress the good feelings that often develop between parties to insightful process analysis, and they often suggest that newly released energies can
become available for task performance. Oppositely, critics bemoan the fact
that such interventions simply "make trouble" where none had existed before,
at least on the surface, and critics likely will emphasize the large gobs of time
and effort consumed by the "non-work" of process analysis.

On whose side does truth lay? Well, some rests firmly on both sides. The
pages above develop the positive case for process analysis. If the truth be told,
however, process analysis can be time consuming. Moreover, especially in the
early bloom of experience with the orientation, neophytes may "process everything to death"; and any reasonable effort *will* release material that had been
suppressed, or forgotten, or even was seen earlier as of little or no concern—
material that may come tumbling forth even from relationships that had seemed
quite placid. This can be variously seen as troublesome, or even as scary.

Hence, the position here: Process analysis can be time consuming, and it
may "make trouble," usually for good reason but sometimes for absolutely no
reason at all, except perhaps to try out the commitment of self and other parties
to the process orientation. Nevertheless, the present view urges that the time—
even that spent chasing down blind alleys—can be most rewarding, on balance,
and especially in the long run.

To be more specific, the present position follows that of the laboratory
approach,[81] such bodies of thought as the "gestalt orientation,"[82] and more
general behavioral science approaches.[83] Consider their common approach to
conflict. Unlike the common wisdom that urges letting sleeping dogs lie, these
approaches take a pro-active stance which rests on five major propositions that
combine beliefs as well as predictions about probable outcomes. *First,* conflict
or contention is not only ubiquitous but it can be vital to the effective functioning of individuals and groups. Depending on how it is managed or resolved,
conflict can be either divine nectar, pure poison, or somewhere in between. At
least, conflict usually implies one most attractive feature: a level of arousal, a
high-energy system. Suppression of conflict typically leads to various degrees
of withdrawal or checking out—low levels of arousal or low-energy systems.

That is, suppression of conflict may preoccupy so much energy that little exists for other uses. In short, you can't make somethin' from nothin'.

Second, relatedly, we are usually not very good at suppressing conflict or contention, especially in the long run, even when substantial energy is resolutely applied. Typically, suppressed conflict acts like the proverbial "snake in the grass." The unresolved tension associated with the conflict tends to get turned against someone or something at some time or other. Like the chastised employee who goes home and kicks the dog, not untypically, the target often will be the wrong someone or something, and the timing may be so inappropriate as to leave both kicker and kickee chagrined, puzzled, or even guilty about why what happened did happen. As such matters thus get more complicated, still greater energies have to be mobilized against surprise manifestations of the conflict. And this leaves still less energy available for other purposes. The cycle clearly has been set to repeat on itself, to intensify.

Third, not only do conflicts defy easy repression, by persons as well as by their institutions, successful repression often will prove to be "love's labour lost." That is, conflict or contention may signal an opportunity as much as (or more than) a problem—an opportunity to seek a new way, develop a more satisfying relationship, build a better mousetrap, or whatever. Successful repression thus may simply forfeit an opportunity.

Fourth, people typically and often unnecessarily create their own prisons with respect to suppressing conflict. The fear of dealing with conflict is often both very real *and* also spurious in that the "imagined catastrophic predictions of the outcome" of confronting the conflict are usually far too somber.[84] Given very real exceptions, suppressing or avoiding conflict usually will be more costly "than the possible temporary discomfort and turbulence involved in confronting the conflict."[85]

Fifth, despite these benign probabilities, this approach does not recommend precipitating parties in conflict into seeking a resolution of their differences. Oppositely, this two-book revision abounds with contrary prescriptions: concern about voluntarism and owning; emphasis on psychological safety; the development of tolerable levels of risk and trust; and so on through a very long catalog. Various designs below seek to help parties become more aware of the issues separating them; to test one another's readiness to do more than complain, repress, or avoid; and to set their own pace in moving toward dealing with the issues in contention. For example, Chapter 5 in Part 1 details such a careful design for couples experiencing problems associated with business travel and summarizes its consequences.

Interventions Deal with Content as Well as Process

The power of process interventions sometimes obscures the patent fact that *something is being talked about,* and especially in organizations that something may have a technical, rational, or semantic content which can only be neglected at one's peril. This notion is hardly novel. Indeed, facilitating such content/ process linkages often motivates that teaming of inside/outside intervenors.

Although this third notion hardly qualifies as novel, it can stand much repetition lest it be forgotten. Consider Crosby's advice to look for "commonalities" in the content of conflict situations that provide mutual ways out. Crosby illustrates:[86] ". . . in a school conflict, one citizen insisted that youth could not be trusted to decide on the expenditure of $3,000. In the heat of the argument, he mentioned $500 would be different. His opponent said that they could be trusted but we should help them. The seeds for compromise are in the '$500' and the 'need for help' statements. That's where I started." Or consider a personal example. A Tennessee mountain man—serving as my guide on a rough boar-hunting trip—was complaining about his wife's rigid control over the processes of their married life. As the story haltingly came out over several campfires, my unlettered guide told me his behavior was controlled in an elemental way: His wife dominated him with the "fact" that she would bear him no male children unless he behaved as she prescribed. She was a tough mate, but the situation was equalized somewhat by a new "fact," which I supplied: the male controls the child's sex, although not by an act of the will. Now that was a piece of content that had a profound effect on the processes of one dyad.

The leverage in such content-oriented attention has been described at length by Jeffrey W. Eiseman, first in a conceptual overview of integrative framework construction (IFC),[87] and then in a paper replete with examples and illustrations of how the approach can and does work.[88] Briefly, Eiseman describes IFC by noting that it seeks to help[89]

> parties trapped in deteriorating patterns of interaction change to self-enhancing patterns. One step in that process, Integrative Framework Construction (IFC), consists of constructing an integrative conceptual framework which builds upon each party's "theories-in-use," demonstrates that everyone's desires are compatible, and provides a way of thinking about the conflict which all parties can support.

IFC cannot be accorded brief justice, but a substantial sense of Eiseman's intent can be communicated with economy. Consider this initially polarized and stymied pair of wants/needs:[90]

Individual I: "I ought to be granted autonomy."
Individual II: "You ought to be collaborative."

Eiseman notes that a major content issue is at the heart of an interpersonal process characterized by more heat than light. Thus, Individual I may be equating autonomy with a desired resoluteness and may see it as a defense against becoming deferential or obsequious, and Individual I also may see collaboration as flaccid self-sacrifice. Eiseman focuses on the content of such assumptions by Individual I and also on associated ones by Individual II which both contribute to conflict. Solid theoretical and research reasons can help show the inadequacy of these content positions, Eiseman basically argues, and a more appropriate conceptualization provides a common ground on which Individuals I and II can build less contentious relationships. Eiseman provides overall perspective on a useful content-oriented intervention:[91]

> since we are autonomous to the extent that our behavior is influenced by our long-term goals and central values, and since we are collaborative to the extent that our orientation is mutualistic . . . , it is possible to be both autonomous and collaborative. In a work setting characterized by both autonomy and collaboration, deference is minimal, each person is vested with extensive discretionary authority, and everyone treats long-term goals and central values seriously, including one's own.

This hurries Eiseman's fuller and more satisfying analysis of the example, of course. But what is the upshot? Acceptance of such a reconceptualization can help reduce or dissolve the contention between Individuals I and II. Each can have what each prefers.

This example helps make an important point. A process orientation in this case might have directed early and continuing attention to the feelings and reactions crackling between Individuals I and II. And, that approach might have worked, or it could have been variously counterproductive. For example, in settings where the disclosure of feelings is taboo or substantially proscribed, an emotional emphasis might have generated concern, fear, even guilt, and these easily could have confounded the learning process or even overloaded it. This two-part volume contains several other applicable designs, such as the discussion in Chapter 5 (Part 1) of role negotiation, which might be useful in contexts like the one alluded to above which define feelings as largely or wholly out of bounds.

Interventions Involve Theory as Well as Experience

The several emphases above often point in one direction: toward the primacy of diagnosis. Not only must the intervenor be insightful about the choice among numerous process-oriented designs, in small units as well as large ones, to make more progress and less trouble. That intervenor also may have to choose between process and content-based interventions, as well as complex combinations of them. And, all this implies the criticality of serviceable theories, models, or perspectives on reality.

In summary, this analysis takes this posture about the role of theory. Yes, there is wisdom in the insistence on experience and how we all can mold it, within wide limits. And substantial justice inheres in the contemporary vulgarism that theories or models can be so much intellectualized hogwash. Moreover, feelings can be central for many purposes, and their impact can be dissipated or even deflected by too much "head-talk."

But even the best things can be extended too far and, consequently, the following argument seeks to provide theoretical perspectives at many points. The purposes? Such theory fragments commonly seek to summarize experience so that we are not compelled to relive every moment and count each situation as absolutely unique; to provide insights for diagnosis; and to suggest covariants that might be usefully manipulated to change a system's state or processes. Alike in these basic senses, the theory fragments detailed below will differ in their comprehensiveness, specificity, and the confidence appropriate to each of them. And their foci clearly differ. How and why some OD interventions seem to work, for example, get attention in both books. Illustratively, Chapter 4 in this part sketches several stages of adult development, as a necessary prelude to fine-tuning specific OD designs or families of them to the particular developmental stages of a target population. Moreover, Chapter 2 in Part 2 is perhaps the most insistent about its theoretical framework—in this case, with a focus on the structuring of organization relationships and designing of jobs. And a fuller catalog of related theoretical initiatives would soon grow to an unwieldy length for present purposes.

The emphasis on theories or models is definitely provisional, however. In most cases, the theoretical discussion serves to remind the reader about what it would be very useful to know but which, except in bits and pieces, still lies well beyond our present grasp.

Notes

1. Chris Argyris, "On the Future of Laboratory Education," *Journal of Applied Behavioral Science*, Vol. 3 (April 1967), p. 153.

2. Reproduced by special permission from Arthur H. Kuriloff and Stuart Atkins, "T-Group for a Work Team," *Journal of Applied Behavioral Science*, Vol. 2, no. 1, (January 1966), pp. 84-85. Copyrighted by NTL Institute, 1966.

3. Joseph Luft, *Group Processes* (Palo Alto, Calif.: National Press Books, 1963), pp. 10-15.

4. Herbert A. Shepard, "Explorations in Observant Participation," in Leland Bradford, Jack R. Gibb, and Kenneth D. Benne (eds.), *T-Group Theory and Laboratory Method* (New York: John Wiley and Sons, 1964), p. 379.

5. Chris Argyris, *Intervention Theory and Method* (Reading, Mass.: Addison-Wesley, 1970), esp. pp. 36-37.

6. Edgar H. Schein, *Process Consultation* (Reading, Mass.: Addison-Wesley, 1969), pp. 15-75.

7. Ibid., p. 11. Reprinted by special permission from Schein, *Process Consultation: Its Role in Organization Development* (Reading, Mass.: Addison-Wesley, 1969).

8. Reprinted by special permission from Schein, *Process Consultation: Its Role in Organization Development* (Reading, Mass.: Addison-Wesley, 1969), p. 9.

9. Reprinted by special permission from Jack K. Fordyce and Raymond Weil, *Managing with People* (Reading, Mass.: Addison-Wesley, 1971), p. 77.

10. Ibid., p. 137.

11. Frank A. Heller, "Group Feedback Analysis: A Method of Field Research," *Psychological Bulletin,* Vol. 72 (August 1969), pp. 108-117.

12. Alton Bartlett, "Changing Behavior as a Means of Increased Efficiency," *Journal of Applied Behavioral Science,* Vol. 3 (July 1967), pp. 381-403.

13. Thomas J. Bouchard, "Personality, Problem-Solving Procedure, and Performance in Small Groups," *Journal of Applied Psychology Monograph,* Vol. 53 (1969), pp. 1-29.

14. R. Jack Weber, "Repetitive Self-Observation and Changes in Interaction Behavior in Small Task Groups," mimeographed (Hanover, N.H.: Dartmouth College, 1972); and Gordon A. Walter, "Effects of Video Tape Feedback and Modeling on the Behaviors of Task Group Members," mimeographed (Vancouver, B.C.: University of Vancouver, 1974).

15. Ray L. Birdwhistell, *Kinetics and Context* (Philadelphia: University of Pennsylvania Press, 1970).

16. Fordyce and Weil, *Managing with People,* p. 114.

17. Raanan Lipshitz and John J. Sherwood, "The Effectiveness of Third Party Process Consultation as a Function of the Consultant's Prestige and Style of Intervention," Institute for Research in the Behavioral, Economic, and Management Sciences, Paper no. 559 (June 1976), Krannert Graduate School of Management, Purdue University, Lafayette, Indiana.

18. The distinction derives from Roger Harrison, "Choosing the Depth of an Organizational Intervention," *Journal of Applied Behavioral Science,* Vol. 6 (April 1970), pp. 181-202.

19. Lipshitz and Sherwood, "The Effectiveness of Third Party Process Consultation," p. 7.

20. Ibid., p. 13.

21. Ibid., esp. pp. 18-26.

22. Ibid., pp. 21-23.

23. Ibid., pp. 38-39.

24. Chester C. Cotton, "When Is Reality Not Enough?: The Realism Paradox in the Simulation of Hierarchical Organization," *The Teaching of Organizational Behavior*, Vol. 1 (December 1975), esp. pp. 26-27.

25. Lipshitz and Sherwood, "The Effectiveness of Third Party Process Consultation," pp. 35-37.

26. Ibid., p. 39.

27. Edwin M. Bartee and Fred Cheyunsky, "A Method for Process-Oriented Organizational Diagnosis," *Journal of Applied Behavioral Science*, Vol. 13 (January 1977), pp. 53-68.

28. Ibid., pp. 60-71.

29. Ibid., pp. 59-60.

30. The model is a synthetic one, but is supported by a variety of research. See, for example, the relationship of risk and trust sketched in John Lillibridge and Sven Lundstedt, "Some Initial Evidence for an Interpersonal Risk Theory," *Journal of Psychology*, Vol. 63 (1967), pp. 119-128.

31. Overall, see Robert T. Golembiewski and Mark McConkie, "The Centrality of Interpersonal Trust in Group Processes," in Cary Cooper (ed.), *Theories of Group Processes* (New York: Wiley, 1975), pp. 131-185.

32. See especially Carl R. Rogers, "The Interpersonal Relationship: The Core of Guidance," *Harvard Educational Review*, Vol. 32 (Fall 1962), pp. 416-429; Frank Friedlander, "The Primacy of Trust as a Facilitator of Further Group Accomplishment," *Journal of Applied Behavioral Science*, Vol. 6 (October 1970), pp. 387-400; and Dale Zand, "Trust and Managerial Effectiveness," *Administrative Science Quarterly*, Vol. 17 (June 1972), pp. 229-239.

33. Jack R. Gibb, "Climate for Trust Formation," in Bradford, Gibb, and Benne, *T-Group Theory and Laboratory Method*, pp. 279-309; and Carl R. Rogers, *On Becoming a Person* (Boston: Houghton Mifflin Co., 1961), esp. pp. 39-58.

34. Melvin J. Seeman, "Counselor Judgments of Therapeutic Process and Outcome," in Carl R. Rogers and R. F. Dymond (eds.), *Psychotherapy and Personality Change* (Chicago: University of Chicago Press, 1954), pp. 99-108; Friedlander, "The Primacy of Trust"; and Alfred Lee Baldwin, Joan Kalhorn, and Fay H. Breese, "Patterns of Parent Behavior," *Psychological Monograph*, Vol. 58, no. 268 (1945), pp. 1-75.

35. Morton Deutsch, "Cooperation and Trust: Some Theoretical Notes," in Marshall R. Jones (ed.), *Nebraska Symposium on Motivation* (Lincoln: University of Nebraska Press, 1962), pp. 275-319.

36. Gibb, "Climate for Trust Formation."

37. Chris Argyris, *Intervention Theory and Method* (Reading, Mass.: Addison-Wesley, 1970), pp. 16-20, 38-39.

38. Robert W. White (ed.), *The Study of Lives* (New York: Atherton Press, 1963), pp. 72-93.

39. Chris Argyris, "Explorations in Interpersonal Competence," *Journal of Applied Behavioral Science,* Vol. 1 (January 1965), p. 59.

40. Sheldon A. Davis, "Organic Problem-Solving Method of Organizational Change," *Journal of Applied Behavioral Science,* Vol. 3 (March 1967), pp. 4-5. For substantial detail on confrontation, see Gerard Egan, "Confrontation," *Group and Organization Studies,* Vol. 1 (June 1976), pp. 223-243.

41. NTL Institute for Applied Behavioral Science, "Feedback and the Helping Relationship," in Robert T. Golembiewski and Arthur Blumberg (eds.), *Sensitivity Training and the Laboratory Approach* (Itasca, Ill.: F.E. Peacock Publishers, 1971), p. 73.

42. James N. Mosel, "How to Feed Back Performance Results to Trainees," *Training Directors Journal,* Vol. 12 (February 1958), pp. 37-47; and R. Jack Weber, "Effects of Videotape Feedback on Task Group Behavior," *Proceedings, Annual Convention, American Psychological Association, 1971,* Vol. 6, pp. 499-500.

43. Kenneth J. Gergen, "Self Theory and the Process of Self-Observation," *Journal of Nervous and Mental Disease,* Vol. 148 (November 4, 1969), pp. 224-237.

44. Bradford, Gibb, and Benne, *T-Group Theory and Laboratory Method,* esp. pp. 130-131, 156-159, and 429-433; and Walter Mead, "Feedback," in Robert T. Golembiewski and Arthur Blumberg (eds.), *Sensitivity Training and the Laboratory Approach* (Itasca, Ill.: F.E. Peacock, 1977), pp. 66-69.

45. For example, Gail E. Myers, Michele T. Myers, Alvin Goldberg, and Charles E. Welch, "Effect of Feedback on Interpersonal Sensitivity in Laboratory Training Groups," *Journal of Applied Behavioral Science,* Vol. 5 (April 1969), pp. 175-185.

46. Chris Argyris, "Conditions for Competence Acquisition and Therapy," *Journal of Applied Behavioral Science,* Vol. 4 (March 1968), pp. 147-177, provides a valuable conceptual analysis of healthy feedback. For more specific guidelines re useful feedback, see Mead, "Feedback: A 'How to' Primer for T-Group Participants."

47. Leland P. Bradford, "A Fundamental of Education," *Adult Education,* Vol. 6 (April 1952), p. 85. My emphasis.

48. Argyris, "Conditions for Competence Acquisition and Therapy," pp. 153-154.

49. Alvan R. Feinstein, *Clinical Judgment* (Baltimore, Md.: Williams and Wilkins, 1967).

50. Leonard Horwitz, "Transference in Training Groups and Therapy Groups," in Golembiewski and Blumberg, *Sensitivity Training and the Laboratory Approach* (1971), p. 188. Originally published in *The International Journal of Group Psychotherapy*, Vol. 14 (1964), pp. 202-213.

51. Ibid., p. 189.

52. Ibid., p. 190.

53. C. Gratton Kemp, *Perspectives on the Group Process* (Boston: Houghton Mifflin Co., 1970), p. 184.

54. Gordon L. Lippitt, *Organizational Renewal* (New York: Appleton-Century-Crofts, 1969), p. 90.

55. Roger Harrison, "Defenses and the Need to Know," in Golembiewski and Blumberg, *Sensitivity Training and the Laboratory Approach* (1971), pp. 80-83.

56. Jack R. Gibb, "Defensive Communication," *Journal of Communication*, Vol. 11 (September 1961), p. 144.

57. Argyris, "Conditions for Competence Acquisition and Therapy," p. 157.

58. Frederick H. Stoller, "A Stage for Trust," in Arthur Burton (ed.), *Encounter* (San Francisco: Jossey-Bass, Inc., Publishers, 1969), p. 90.

59. Gordon J. Chelune, "Self-Disclosure: An Elaboration of Its Basic Dimensions," *Psychological Reports*, Vol. 36 (February 1975), pp. 79-85.

60. H. M. Lynd, *On Shame and the Search for Identity* (New York: Science Editions, 1958), p. 241.

61. Gerald Egan, *Encounter: Group Processes for Interpersonal Growth* (Belmont, Calif.: Wadsworth Publishing Co., 1970), p. 193. Broadly, see Sidney M. Jourard, *Self-Disclosure* (New York: Wiley Interscience, 1971).

62. Samuel A. Culbert, "The Interpersonal Process of Self-Disclosure: It Takes Two to See One," in Golembiewski and Blumberg, *Sensitivity Training and the Laboratory Approach* (1973), p. 75; and David Nason, "Disclosure in Learning Groups," in Golembiewski and Blumberg, *Sensitivity Training and the Laboratory Approach* (1977), pp. 70-78.

63. Carl Rogers, *On Becoming a Person* (Boston: Houghton Mifflin Co., 1961), p. 308.

64. William G. Dyer, "Congruence and Control," *Journal of Applied Behavioral Science*, Vol. 5 (April 1969), pp. 161-173.

65. Ibid., pp. 164-165.

66. Chris Argyris, *Interpersonal Competence and Organizational Effectiveness* (Homewood, Ill.: Dorsey Press, 1962), p. 21.

67. For evidence that disclosure is fundamentally a process of social exchange—as opposed, for example, to modeling—see John D. Davis and

Adrian E. G. Skinner, "Reciprocity of Self-Disclosure in Interviews," *Journal of Personality and Social Psychology,* Vol. 29 (June 1974), pp. 779-784.

68. Craig W. Ellison and Ira J. Friestone, "Development of Interpersonal Trust as a Function of Self-esteem, Target Status and Target Style," *Journal of Personality and Social Psychology,* Vol. 29 (May 1974), pp. 655-663.

69. Ibid., p. 77. That is, the suspicion of gamesmanship is likely to induce gamesmanship in return.

70. Gerard Egan, *Encounter: Group Processes for Interpersonal Growth* (Monterey, Calif.: Wadsworth Publishing Company, 1970), pp. 234-235.

71. Culbert, "The Interpersonal Process of Self-Disclosure," p. 78.

72. Ibid., p. 75.

73. S. M. Jourard, *The Transparent Self* (Princeton, N.J.: D. Van Nostrand Co., 1964).

74. Culbert, "The Interpersonal Process of Self-Disclosure," p. 79.

75. Egan, *Encounter,* pp. 241-243.

76. Ibid., p. 207.

77. Fritz Steele, *The Open Organization* (Reading, Mass.: Addison-Wesley, 1975), pp. 43-48.

78. Ibid., p. 47.

79. Arthur Blumberg and Robert T. Golembiewski, *Learning and Change in Groups* (London: Penguin, 1976), esp. pp. 24-104.

80. To sample the relevant and growing literature, see David Nadler, *Feedback and Organization Development* (Reading, Mass.: Addison-Wesley, 1977); and Robert T. Golembiewski and Richard J. Hilles, *Toward the Responsive Organization* (Salt Lake City, Utah: Brighton Publishing Co., 1979).

81. For overall perspective, see Kenneth D. Benne, Leland P. Bradford, Jack R. Gibb, and Ronald O. Lippitt (eds.), *The Laboratory Method of Changing and Learning* (Palo Alto, Calif.: Science and Behavior Books, Inc., 1975).

82. Stanley M. Herman and Michael Korenich, *Authentic Management: A Gestalt Orientation to Organizations and Their Development* (Reading, Mass.: Addison-Wesley, 1977), esp. pp. 115-121.

83. Allan Filley, *Interpersonal Conflict Resolution* (Glenview, Ill.: Scott, Foresman, 1975).

84. Herman and Korenich, *Authentic Management,* p. 116.

85. Ibid.

86. Robert P. Crosby, "Managing Conflict in Large Group Meetings," *Social Change,* Vol. 8, no. 2 (1978), p. 9.

87. Jeffrey W. Eiseman, "A Third-Party Consultation Model for Resolving Recurring Conflicts Collaboratively," *Journal of Applied Behavioral Science*, Vol. 13 (July 1977), pp. 303-314.

88. Jeffrey W. Eiseman, "Reconciling 'Incompatible' Positions," *Journal of Applied Behavioral Science*, Vol. 14 (April 1978), pp. 133-150.

89. Ibid., p. 133.

90. Ibid., p. 139.

91. Ibid., p. 140.

Chapter 2

THE LABORATORY APPROACH TO CHOICE AND CHANGE
Values that Guide Applications for Individuals and Organizations

As with any technology for learning, the laboratory approach faces some critical and complex issues. Are the effects attributable to the technology worth achieving? If so, with what confidence can specific effects be expected? What safeguards exist or can be developed to raise that confidence? And what of the potential side effects of the technology? Or is the cost/benefit ratio for the laboratory approach favorable enough to encourage running the risks over the longer run?

Basically, answers to all these questions rest on choices between values, given a knowledge of a technology's empirical effects. What is desired and desirable? The simple questions pose the central concerns for applications of the laboratory approach to individuals in organizations, and mammoth concerns they are. Without fairly specific choices between values, we cannot decide between technologies for learning or change, nor can we determine whether any technology is worth the effort. To put the point in somewhat different terms, this chapter is key to all three of the basic orientations to OD described in the introductory section of this volume. Those basic orientations to OD emphasize:

- People, in a human-processual approach that deals with the dynamics of their relationships
- Technology, in a technostructural approach involving policies and procedures that define work relationships
- An area of major overlap between behavioral processes and formal structures or technologies

Value judgments underlie questions about which of these approaches to take when, and how. Simply, that crucial but often neglected point expresses the basic thrust of this chapter.

None of the required choices between values is easy to make, but two degrees of difficulty can be distinguished: tough and awesome. More seriously, the first two sections of this chapter deal with some general and easier issues of common goals for individuals and organizations. Substantial agreement exists about many of these broad "shoulds" or "oughts," in fact. The last two sections of this chapter hunt more elusive game. They become more specific, and the issues they raise become less tractable. These sections focus on the value sensitivity required in the laboratory approach because of its "reach" and because of its "grasp."

Briefly, to deal with "reach," the laboratory approach deals at multiple levels with persons as affective and valuing beings, using learing designs that tap a broad range of affective and valuational states, from superficial to profound, and everything in between. Hence, acute value sensitivity is a crucial part of the game.

Briefly, also, to deal with "grasp," applications of the laboratory approach in organizations significantly complicate the required value sensitivity. For the focus is not only on valuing individuals, but also on individuals in contexts where personal well-being is not the only (or sometimes, even a major) consideration. Sometimes, no doubt, personal well-being is not even *a* consideration. Organizations, that is, constitute variously benign contexts for the work of the laboratory approach, and pure intentions are rarely sufficient in themselves. This compounds the required value sensitivity, raising it to some exponential power— a $(\text{value sensitivity})^2$ or $(\text{value sensitivity})^3$. To do OD, or not to do OD? This can be a profoundly significant moral choice for institutions as well as for their members. Hence, a later section of this chapter raises several central normative or ethical concerns, even though it cannot promise to provide any ready solutions. And for contrast, the concluding section will compare the treatment of values in OD and Behavior Modification, which are the dominant contemporary approaches to change.

Some Common Goals for Individuals
Toward Authentic, Helping, Related Persons

Basically, this section accepts one piece of the complex action. It focuses on factors that guide the application of the laboratory approach, on constraints expressed in terms of explicit values as well as those that are implicit in the properties of the learning technology. Therefore, this section has a strongly prescriptive orientation. It cannot be otherwise. As far as possible, the aim is to present the essence of the laboratory approach, basing the presentation on the consensus of afficionados. At other points, this section becomes an intensely personal product.

Meta-Values Toward Open Interpersonal Systems

Every technology dealing with humans rests on some set of meta-values, or basic goals. They may be explicit, or they may be what Alvin Gouldner called a "metaphysical pathos" of implicit understandings, hopes, and aspirations. In effect, these meta-values constrain applications of the technology. Sometimes in unambiguous terms, and sometimes via what one can call "spirit," these meta-values help determine what should be done and what should be avoided, how it should be done, and when it should be done.[1]

The laboratory approach always has given up-front attention to its meta-values, which diversely contribute to a sense of open interpersonal systems. Or, perhaps the concept of mutually helpful and vulnerable systems more fully suggests the total spirit of the laboratory approach. The following discussion of five meta-values will help the readers make their own choices. Column A of Exhibit 1 summarizes these meta-values.

Acceptance of Inquiry

A significant constraint for applications of the laboratory approach rests on a deep acceptance of inquiry as the norm in relationships with others. "It is what we don't know that can destroy our relationship" could well serve as a motto. The more common and opposed meta-value is reflected in such maxims as "familiarity breeds contempt." The difference between these two guiding values is profound. The true acceptance of inquiry involves a mutual accessibility of persons to one another, as well as a potential vulnerability to each other and a real commitment to the possibility of being influenced by the other. The opposed meta-value legitimates a more distant relationship and, if only in a superficial sense, a safer relationship.

The acceptance of inquiry—indeed, the rejoicing in it—has two basic logical consequences. Thus, the laboratory approach is preoccupied with testing reactions or perceptions or interpretations. The tentativeness recognizes only two absolutes: the certainty of the complexity of the observed phenomena, and the inevitability that reactions to the phenomena will be diverse. The laboratory approach has a significant place for "subjective truth," then. Considerable attention is devoted to how various people differently perceive the same stimuli and to how the same stimulus generates diverse responses. Since as many truths as observers often characterize such situations, a hypothetical spirit is very useful for eliciting this diversity of human responses. In addition, experimentalism logically mates with the acceptance of inquiry, especially in the sense that a perceived need may motivate an innovation. Inquiry would be a contraceptive experience were it not linked closely with experimentation.

Expanded Consciousness and Recognition of Choice

A second meta-value, an expanded consciousness and recognition of choice, inheres in the acceptance of inquiry. The linkages are direct: an expanded consciousness or awareness generates wider choices; choice permits experimentation that could lead to change; and freely made choice also helps assure that the individual will own the change rather than (at best) accept its imposition. These linkages constitute a circular process that seeks to enhance the potential for learning, as well as the owning of and commitment to its consequences.

That is, choice is central in the laboratory approach. As Warren Bennis expressed his emphasis on expanding choice and creating options:

> I care much less about a participant's learning that he talked too much and will, in the future, talk less, than I do about his recognizing that choice exists and that there are certain clear consequences of under- or over-participation. I care much less about producing a "cohesive" group than I do about members' understanding the "costs" and gains of cohesiveness, when it's appropriate and worth the cost and when it may not be. I care far less about developing shared leadership in the T-Group than I do about the participants' recognizing that a choice exists among a wide array of leadership patterns. In short, I care far more about developing *choice and recognition of choice points than I do about change.* Change, I think, is the participants' privilege, but choice is something trainers must emphasize.[2]

The total sense of it is that persons are free and responsible to the degree that they make informed choices.

Collaborative Concept of Authority

Consistent with an expanding sense of choice, the laboratory approach also reflects a collaborative concept of authority. In laboratory learning situations, the role of the participant is by design a far more influential one than in traditional learning situations. In some variations of the laboratory approach, indeed, this ability to influence extends to all details but the scheduling of the time and place of the initial meeting. Beyond that, the participants share responsibility with any professional staff concerning all future planning, even living accommodations for the rest of the experience, if indeed it is not canceled at the outset by mutual consent.[3]

A complex rationale supports this collaborative concept of authority. Basically, the political and social heritage of Western civilization rests on a substantial and growing sense of popular influence over the environment. "No taxation without representation" and "power to the people" are merely two forms of the same heritage. More narrowly, the collaborative concept of authority is rooted in a desire to improve the quality and efficiency of the learning process. Specifically, learning can be considered a form of the broader process of influencing behavior, and the various forms can have profoundly different consequences. To illustrate, Herbert Kelman has distinguished three forms of influence:[4]

- Compliance, in which case the influence is accepted to receive some reward or avoid some punishment controlled by the influencing agent
- Identification, in which case the influence is accepted so as to maintain or develop a satisfying relationship with the influencing agent
- Internalization, in which case the influence is accepted because it is congruent with the learner's own value system

These three modes can interact in complex ways. For example, influence or learning based on compliance that is accepted can become a part of an individual's own value system, in which case future acceptance of similar influence attempts can be based on internalization.

The laboratory approach attempts to induce identification and especially internalization as the basic processes in its influence or learning attempts. Clearly, these two forms of influence imply collaborative authority. The emphasis in the laboratory approach rests on very deep value preferences about the quality or style of learning processes. In terms of our operating vocabulary, learning based on identification→internalization will increase the probability that learners will retain the learning and apply it outside the specific learning situation.

The basic qualities of the required concept of authority include a pervasive sense of cooperation and collaboration, as well as a commitment to resolve conflicts openly in a problem-solving sense. The collaborative concept of authority, in words reminiscent of Mary Parker Follett, allows the problem situation to determine which skills and resources are appropriate and consequently, who should influence decisions. An opposed style might rely on command/obedience, with problems being solved by authority figures presumed to have the skills appropriate to the generality of problem situations.

Mutual Helping Relationships in Social Settings

Reinforcing this concept of shared authority, the laboratory approach emphasizes the development of mutual helping relationships in social or community settings. Here, helping is seen as perhaps *the* distinctive human attribute that requires cultivation and development, and the social setting assumes the role of an optimal (perhaps even natural) locus for mutual helping. This world view assumes a diversity of notions, among them the classical concept of man as a social animal. In addition, the emphasis upon community reflects a reasonable belief that social units have an extraordinary and perhaps unique capacity to induce massive forces to reinforce learning or change.

The helping relationships stressed by the laboratory approach are not always optimally achieved, of course, but the necessary ingredients seem obvious enough. For example, learning designs based on the approach tend to generate substantial (even unparalleled) exchanges of warmth, or support, between members. Such exchanges can help cement a community of learners. All but universally, psychosocial growth is seen as depending upon some degree of warmth or nurturance. The effects of lack of maternal nurturance can be profound,[5] and, more or less, the need persists even through old age.[6] Similarly, the laboratory approach rests on acceptance of the Other as is, on what has come to be called "unconditional positive regard."[7] Acceptance does not imply approval, but rather a valuing of the Other, in the senses of a respect and a concern. Relatedly, designs based on the laboratory approach attempt to stress the psychological safety of participants, an important and difficult matter.[8]

Authenticity in Interpersonal Relationships

This fifth, and final, meta-value of the laboratory approach is the equivalent of the hackneyed "tell it like it is." It emphasizes the expression of feelings as well as the analysis of the behaviors inducing them, in sharp contrast to traditional technologies for learning.

The rationale for the meta-value of authenticity rests on its patent centrality in communication, as well as on its broader significance. Thus, minimally distorted communication facilitates both individual and group development. That is, failure to be authentic in the senses of "leveling" and "expressing feelings" to elicit similar behaviors from others can accumulate so much unfinished business as to overburden interaction.

Authenticity seems critical in broader senses as well. For example, contemporary constructs of mental health tend to emphasize outcomes in which the individual as he or she knows self is much the same person known to others.[9] This congruence of the person and the person perceived by others has generated some empirical research that implies the value of the concept.[10] Clearly, this congruence rests squarely on the ability of both Self and Other to be authentic.

Values Guiding the Development of Specific Competencies

"Operating values" comprise a second major set of constraints on applications of the laboratory approach. The term "operating" may be awkward, but it nonetheless directs attention to value-loaded guidelines consistent with the meta-values. The operating values also can help guide the development of specific competencies, such as attitudes or behavioral skills. This focus on values guiding the development of specific competencies has a most serious purpose. It seeks to emphasize that the laboratory approach does not support the concept that "anything goes regardless of consequences." Two critics of the "let it all hang out in any way" approach complain that

> instead of creating interpersonal awareness it may foster personal narcissism. If an individual says anything he wishes, then he may come to assume that just because he feels like expressing himself is justification enough to do so. This may preclude effective communication, for he then ignores whether the other person is receptive to his message, and he ignores the effect of his message on the other person. Communication may not be seen as an interpersonal event but merely as the opportunity to express oneself. The principle of "optimal communication" is ignored for the principle of "total communication."[11]

Column B in Exhitit 1 lists one such set of operating values that guide applications of the laboratory approach, the guidelines for feedback discussed in Chapter 1. The guidelines propose normative constraints that applications of the laboratory approach should respect and serve to distinguish "optimal communication" from simpler but simplistic "total communication."

Immediate Goals and Transferable Learning

Column C of Exhibit 1 can be used to permit similarly convenient treatment of some immediate goals of the laboratory approach, awareness about which can be transferred from a learning situation to a real-time context. For example, increased insight and self-knowledge gained in a T-group should be transferable to a work situation, in whole or part.

Illustrations of the Mix of Values in Action

The contribution here[12] to reinforcing the sense of the value-loaded quality of the laboratory approach builds on the content of Exhibit 1, which lists meta-

Exhibit 1   Three Sets of Normative, or Value, Constraints on Applications of the Laboratory Approach

(A) *Meta-Values of Laboratory Approach*	(B) *Operating Values of Laboratory Approach*	(C) *Immediate Goals of Laboratory Approach*
1. An attitude of inquiry reflecting (among others): a. a hypothetical spirit b. experimentalism	1. Emphasis on here-and-now occurrences	1. Increased insight, self-knowledge
2. Expanded consciousness and recognition of choice	2. Emphasis on the individual act rather than on the total person acting	2. Sharpened diagnostic skills at (ideally) all levels, i.e., the levels of the: a. individual b. group c. organization d. society
3. A collaborative concept of authority having as two core elements: a. spirit of collaboration b. open resolution of conflict via a problem-solving orientation	3. Emphasis on feedback that is nonevaluative in that it reports the impact on the self of other's behavior, rather than feedback that is judgmental or interpretive	3. Awareness of, and skill practice in, creating conditions of effective functioning at (ideally) all levels
4. An emphasis on mutual "helping relationships" as the best way to express man's interdependency with man, or man's basic social nature and connectedness	4. Emphasis on "unfreezing" behaviors the trainee feels are undesirable, on practice of replacement behaviors, and on "refreezing" new behaviors	4. Testing self-concepts and skills in interpersonal situations
5. An emphasis on "authenticity" in interpersonal relations, a high value on expressing feelings and their effects	5. Emphasis on "trust in leveling," on psychological safety of the trainee 6. Emphasis on creating and maintaining an "organic community"	5. Increased capacity to be open, to accept feelings of self and others, and to risk interpersonally in rewarding ways

Source: Adapted from Edgar H. Schein and Warren G. Bennis, *Personal and Organizational Change through Group Methods* (New York: John Wiley and Sons, 1965), pp. 30-35; and Leland P. Bradford, Jack R. Gibb, and Kenneth D. Benne, *T-Group Theory and Laboratory Method* (New York: John Wiley and Sons, 1964), pp. 10, 12.

values, operating values, and immediate goals of the laboratory approach. Disagreements among practitioners may exist about details in the exhibit, but not about its essence.

No easy way comes to mind for illustrating the complexity of Exhibit 1, but some of its uses can be established. Consider a competitive exercise in a learning design based on the laboratory approach which uses groups. Sue, who has suffered with the muddling through characteristic of early meetings, seizes the opportunity provided by the time pressure of the exercise to whip her group into shape. She is well pleased with her efforts initially, but in the end her group loses badly. Moreover, Sue learns soon thereafter that the commitment she thought she had been instrumental in developing existed largely in her own mind. This news comes from the postexercise analysis of questionnaire data gathered at various stages of the game about the involvement of group members, members' confidence in their team strategy, and so on. These data showed that most members of Sue's group privately reported low involvement and lack of confidence in their team, and hence in Sue.

Exhibit 1 provides a way of analyzing Sue's experiences. Her reactions will be compared to the exhibit via a shorthand, such as reference to (A-1) to indicate that the postexercise analysis encouraged Sue to take a critical and experimental approach toward her own behavior, as designated by item 1 in column A.

Let us assume that (like most of us) Sue did not enjoy losing the competitive exercise, particularly in the presence of prestigious peers. But Sue is disturbed that her group "held out on her" and "let her down" by failing to communicate their feelings and expectations. Her sense of her own experienced and anticipated competence has been disconfirmed. If the level of trust is high enough (B-5), and if group members generally accept the meta-values of laboratory work (A-1 through A-5), Sue can begin learning from this disturbing challenge to her skill and to herself (C-4). This learning will occur if both Sue and her colleagues (in post-mortem discussions) can act authentically and share their feelings and reactions (A-5).

Sue can take diverse tacks to learning, to increasing her awareness. What did she do that encouraged other group members to lead her down the primrose path (C-1)? What cues did she miss that she might be sensitive to in similar situations (C-2 and C-3)? These are among the questions dealing with the here-and-now (B-1) that Sue can raise.

Only other group members can provide answers to such questions in their own reactions and feelings about the here-and-now, however, and Sue soon learns she will receive roughly in proportion to her giving of self. She has somewhat opened (C-5) her Private Area by disclosing that she is troubled about her role in the exercise. That revelation may earn her some constructive feedback (B-3) that shares with her the impact her behavior had on others (A-4). Her initial openness also may save Sue from the lack of feedback that essentially rejects her as well as her specific actions (B-2) during the competitive exercise. Indeed, perhaps paradoxically, Sue can only gain acceptance as a person as her actions are considered significant enough to react to, whether positively or critically, and as the atmosphere permits her to be herself with minimal feelings of risk and defensiveness (B-5 and B-6).

But Sue must go further still if she wants to learn more. For example, she must be able to accept the integrity of the feelings of her colleagues (C-5), rather than deny them or search for underlying motives. This is a mutual enterprise, clearly. And, the mutual giving and accepting of reactions, in turn, will contribute to the cohesiveness of the group (B-6). For it signals to other group members that they need not withhold their reactions (B-5) for fear that they will be disparaged or discounted. The results are generally happy, for the hiding of reactions not only creates unfinished business but also deprives everyone of data and thus inhibits everyone's learning. Moreover, as the sense of community in her training group grows, so will Sue feel more free to risk further exploration (A-1 and C-5) of the dynamics of the competitive exercise. And, when Sue acknowledges that even the "strong person" can be free only as she acknowledges her interdependence with those about her (A-4 and B-6), as well as her independence of them, then a really firm foundation will have been established for learning.

Learning can take a variety of directions, once this foundation for true exchange has been established. Two basic directions can be distinguished. From that foundation, group members can collaboratively (A-3) help Sue survey the range of alternatives open to her (A-2), help her to work toward modifying awkward behaviors (B-4), and reinforce her efforts to experiment with other behaviors (A-1 and B-4). Also from that foundation, Sue may decide that change is not appropriate, given her backhome setting. The climate at her work may violate such values as those in Exhibit 1, for example, or the individual may not feel able to integrate the new behaviors into her repertoire. In that case, Sue may have gained insight about the consequences she might expect from how she must behave. In addition, Sue has made a conscious choice among alternatives, and that act in itself may make it easier for her to understand and accept that part of herself.

These notes are sketchy and may seem lifelessly stilted, but they illustrate the dynamic linkages that underlie Exhibit 1. Meta-values, operating values, and immediate goals will simultaneously if variously serve to constrain the laboratory approach and thereby they will shape its products. But two major questions remain.

Why Expose Self to Laboratory Learning?

Bernard Lubin and William Eddy provide a useful response to this central question. In their view, the laboratory approach meets a variety of needs that encourage exposure to it:[13]

- Participants have been conditioned to inhibit the expression of the emotional aspects of their communications, which reduces interpersonal effectiveness.

  The laboratory approach legitimizes feelings and facilitates experiencing, expressing, and examining the emotional aspects of communication.

- Participants, however well they may function interpersonally, have developed resistances against attending to certain classes of cues about the effects of their behavior on others. This inhibits their potential for learning newer, more functional behaviors.

  The laboratory approach provides an opportunity for each participant to receive information about how his behavior is seen, as well as to learn about his impact on others.

- Even though participants might have opportunities in everyday life to receive information about their interpersonal performance, it is difficult to practice new behaviors because of the real or imagined risk.

  The laboratory approach encourages and provides opportunities for the practice and analysis of new behavior.

- Although participants function more or less effectively in leadership and membership roles in a variety of groups back home, such factors as the need to meet a schedule make it likely that individuals will have neither the opportunity to examine decision-making, communication, or problem-solving processes, nor the leisure to analyze their roles in these back-home processes.

  The laboratory approach to learning provides opportunities to learn about the many forces at work in groups, as well as to study one's own performance in relation to these forces.

- Participants may have considerable cognitive knowledge about the "principles" of leadership, communication, group dynamics, etc. However, they may not be able to translate this knowledge into action, for a variety of reasons.

  The experience-based laboratory approach may help them to act on their knowledge.

Is Such Learning for Everyone?

Even granting the motivation for exposure to the laboratory approach inherent in such factors, a second question remains. Should individuals avoid learning designs based on the laboratory approach?

This question is difficult to answer, because learning experiences can differ so profoundly in impact. Thus, T-groups seem to have the highest rates of negative experiences, but even here the record is far from clear.[14] Team-building experiences, while often very intense, seem far less worrisome with regard to psychiatric casualties, but here the firm evidence is practically nonexistent.

Perhaps the most helpful response to the question of whether such learning is for everyone, to take another tack, rests on a description of the kinds of individuals who seem to learn via the labortory approach. In sum, they are relatively healthy individuals who are capable of interacting with others and who

have an interest in improving their degree of effective coping. Chris Argyris
emphasizes three prime atributes of relatively healthy individuals. Such
individuals have[15]

- A relatively strong ego that is not overwhelmed by conflicts and
  doubts, but can entertain them
- Defenses that are "low" enough, or "porous" enough, to allow the
  individual to hear what others say about him, with accuracy and minimal threat and without the major mediation of a therapist or educator
- An ability to communicate throughts and feelings with minimal
  distortion

Some Guiding Implications for Learning Designs

The various value-loaded considerations implicit in Exhibit 1 come to a special
point when applied to the design of specific learning experiences. Argyris has
done us the service of developing the senses in which such values specifically
guide or constrain specific application of the laboratory approach. He develops
four implications for learning designs, which are presented in the form of direct
quotations in Exhibit 2.

Argyris's implications for learning design stand on their own, and the
temptation to redo his competent work will be resisted. The implications will
become part of the frame of reference that will help us understand and evaluate
various applications of the laboratory approach.

Some Common Goals in Organizations
Toward the Nonbureaucratic Enterprise

When applications of the laboratory approach occur in large organizations,
additional normative constraints become relevant. These goals or values refer to
a basic observation: We all need constraints on our behavior to live more
securely, and yet we chafe under those constraints. Bertram Forer elegantly
makes the point:[16]

> The fact of his structuring indicates that [man] has relinquished some
> freedom to experience, wish, and act in order to maintain continuity,
> recognizability, stability, and predictability and in order to insure
> continuing relationships with important persons. Self-maintenance and
> relationship maintenance are both essential to life but are often at odds. He
> has become a person whose sense of self, whatever it has happened to be, is
> his most important possession and often his most threatened one. A major
> issue in his life, then, has to be how to maintain the sense of self through
> the sequential events of his life, both directing the course of life and dealing

Exhibit 2   Some Implications Guiding the Design of Laboratory Experiences on the Laboratory Approach

Implication I

1. All participants who attend laboratory programs of any type will have a certain degree of self-awareness, self-acceptance, and interpersonal competence.
2. These qualities will greatly influence and be influenced by the laboratory program.
3. The faculty should strive to plan activities that will tend to maintain (or increase) the present degree of self-awareness, self-acceptance, and interpersonal competence.
4. The faculty may strive to plan activities that will tend to increase the present degree of self-awareness, self-acceptance, and interpersonal competence.
5. Since man is incomplete without others, the faculty should not plan any educational activities that erode or deteriorate man's basic need for human connectedness or his responsibility toward others (in order that they and he can help themselves become more self-responsible).

Implication II:

1. The faculty should strive not to plan any activities that encourage unnecessary dependence, psychological failure, withdrawal, conformity, and mistrust.
2. The faculty should strive to plan activities that will increase the participants' knowledge of and skill in developing more effective groups, intergroups, and organizations.
3. Since the laboratory program is a system, the faculty should strive not to create one that is close to the traditional organizations, with their closedness, group inefficiencies, and intergroup rivalries.

Implication III:

No matter what the central learning target is (individual, group, organization), the learning processes used should not damage the targets that have been made peripheral. Learning, for example, that has the group as its primary target should be planned so that those types of educational activities be used that minimize damage to aspects of the individual and vice versa.

Implication IV:

Learning activities, no matter what their target, that create conditions for psychological success, confirmation, and essentiality are to be maximized. Learning activities that create conditions for psychological failure, disconfirmation, and nonessentiality are to be minimized.

Source: Chris Argyris, "On the Future of Laboratory Education," *Journal of Applied Behavioral Science*, Vol. 3, no. 2 (April 1967), pp. 155-159. Reproduced by special permission. © Copyrighted by NTL Institute, 1967.

with uncontrollable assaults and repercussions, and at the same time retain other persons.

Some Dysfunctions of "Pyramidal Values"

Let us direct attention to the difficulties for interpersonal and intergroup relations that exist in organizations whose structure is based on the "bureaucratic model." Basically, the bureaucratic model often acts as a dysfunctionally restrictive "They" which constrains the "I" in ways that increasingly frustrate organizational as well as personal needs/demands. Specifically, Figure 1 sketches some "pyramidal values" characteristic of today's organizations which encourage a variety of consequences that constrain spontaneity, adaptability, and effectiveness, as Figure 1 suggests.

Pyramidal Values Common in Organizations

■ The significant human relationships at work are those directly related to getting the job done; they have a task or technical preoccupation.

■ Effectiveness in human relationships increases directly as behavior is rational and logical, as communications are unambiguous. Conversely, effectiveness decreases as behavior becomes more emotional and nonrational.

■ Human relationships are most efficiently motivated by consciously and clearly defined directives, authority, and controls. Rewards and penalties are used to reinforce rational behavior and achievement of objectives.

Some Typical Consequences of Pyramidal Values

■ Individuals get and give less direct information about their interpersonal impact on each other. Such information may be suppressed at various levels of consciousness, where it cannot be dealt with. Or the information may be communicated in veiled ways, in which case:
 a. it will be disguised or raised in the context of rational, technical, or intellectual issues
 b. it will be difficult to deal with

■ Increases occur in the denial of feelings or reactions, in closedness to new ideas, and in demands for stability.

■ Interpersonal competence will decrease as individuals:
 a. are less likely to be open about and own their reactions, ideas, and feelings
 b. experience reduced trust in one another
 c. react to increased risk by reducing their willingness to experiment or change
 d. are less effective in solving problems

■ As interpersonal competence declines, increases are probable in pressures toward conformity and toward dependence on authority figures, both of which circularly lead individuals to get and give less information about their interpersonal impact on each other; etc.; etc.

Figure 1 "Pyramidal values" and some of their typical consequences in organization. [*Source:* Chris Argyris, "T-Groups for Organizational Effectiveness," *Harvard Business Review* (March–April 1964), Copyright © 1964 by the President and Fellows of Harvard College, all rights reserved.]

The pyramidal values have a broad potential for mischief as prevailing guides for behavior. "What causes dynamic, flexible, and enthusiastically committed executive teams," Argyris asks rhetorically, "to become sluggish and inflexible as time goes by?" He sees a major cause in the build-up, beyond some easily surpassed limit, of consequences like those in Figure 1.[17]

Subsequent chapters will raise detail aplenty, but, broadly, two reasonable responses exist to the challenge implied by the pyramidal values. The first seeks to ameliorate the difficulties in interaction resulting from the bureaucratic model and its organization values. The second strategy seeks new models for organizing work, to preclude the very emergence of the difficulties that are attributed to the bureaucratic model. Patently, these two goals seek the development of nonbureaucratic organizations, or even antibureaucratic organization. The two strategies can be complementary, but their advocates have on occasion taken out after one another, and differences have been polarized into unalterable opposites.

Toward Developing New Skills and Attitudes

Argyris well represents those who propose to undercut the pyramidal values by seeking to develop new attitudes and skills in members. Basically, he prescribes a two-pronged approach to avoiding the consequences of the pyramidal values, which can generate substantial barriers to collective effort. Thus, Argyris argues that a modified set of organization values should guide collective effort. These values provide that:[18]

- The important human relationships do involve those related to achieving organizational objectives, but these important relationships also include those necessary to sustain or develop the organization's socioemotional system as well as those related to adapting to the external environment.

- Human relationships increase in effectiveness as both technical and interpersonal data become conscious, discussable, and increasingly controllable.

- Directives, authority, and controls can influence human relationships, but the most effective influences will occur through authentic relations between individuals, internal commitment, and feelings of psychological success.

The induction of this modified set of values is seen as a problem in reeducation, purely and simply, for which required reeducation the laboratory approach is a prime learning vehicle. Argyris outlines the reeducation program in terms of this three-phase sequence: unfreezing and analysis of old behaviors, attitudes, and values; choice and practice of replacements, if appropriate; and refreezing of the new behaviors, attitudes, or values, should they lead to the desired consequences.[19]

The sense of the Argyrian approach is, simply, that bureaucratic organizations rest on troublesome values and norms, and new member skills/attitudes must be developed to avoid falling back into old ruts. He sees mere change in structure as a snare and a delusion. People must be changed first — or rather, more strictly, the inadequacies of their "theories-in-use" must be highlighted so individuals can make a clear choice to change those theories if they generate awkward consequences — and all this must occur before alternatives to the pyramidal values can have any chance at all. Conveniently, the required new values and norms may be thought of as trending toward the evolution of an "open organization." This is not to say that differences in authority and status will disappear. Rather, these differences will be conditioned in diverse ways by a set of values such as the one below. As a first approximation, approaches to these guiding organization values are consistent with the laboratory approach:[20]

- Full and free communication
- Greater reliance on open confrontation in managing conflict, where participants psychologically own at least the causes of the conflict and its consequences, as well as (hopefully) agree on approaches to managing the conflict, as contrasted with a reliance on coercion or compromise
- Influence based on competence rather than on personal whim or formal power
- Expression of emotional as well as task-oriented behavior
- Acceptance of conflict between the individual and the organization, to be coped with willingly, openly, and rationally

Toward Basic Structural Change

Other observers build on Argyris's beachhead, but they focus on structural change. They also propose to avoid the consequences of the pyramidal values, but by changing the basic concepts for organizing in which these values inhere. Bureaucracy is also the demon these observers seek to exorcise. Some bravely proclaim that its end has come,[21] more or less, while others see it as increasingly inappropriate under a wide variety of conditions to which today's organizations are routinely exposed. But, all agree that the kind of consequences sketched by Argyris can in significant measure be laid on the doorstep of the bureaucratic model. Out it must go, consequently, root and branch.

Basically, the bureaucratic model is seen as a social invention whose time has come and, to greater or lesser degree, has gone. The bureaucratic model rests on propositions such as these five:

- A well-defined chain of command that vertically channels formal interaction

- A system of procedures and rules for dealing with all contingencies at work that reinforces the reporting insularity of each bureau

- A division of labor based upon specialization by major function or process that vertically fragments a flow of work

- Promotion and selection based on technical competence, which is defined consistently with the first three items

- Impersonality in relations between organization members and between them and their clients

These propositions imply a guiding metaphor and an overall bias. The guiding metaphor of the bureaucratic model is a precision clock. Once appropriately designed and machined, it would go on ticking away with awesome regularity. Moreover, the overall bias is strongly elitist and authoritarian. "Only those higher in the hierarchy are to be trusted with judgment or discretion," Alvin Toffler concludes. "Officials at the top make the decisions; men at the bottom carry them out. One group represents the brains of the organization; the other, the hand."[22]

The strength of these propositions under one set of conditions has become their weakness under another set. Toffler put the point simply. The "typical bureaucratic arrangement is ideally suited to solving routine problems at a moderate pace," he noted. "But when things speed up, or the problems cease to be routine, chaos often breaks loose."[23] Things indeed have "speeded up," to make a complex story simple if not necessarily sweet. Figure 2 suggests some of the diverse senses in which the conclusion holds. Basically, instead of a precision watch, the guiding metaphor for many of today's organizations is a kaleidoscope. Contemporary organizations increasingly have to respond to emphases like those in the right column, while the bureaucratic model is designed for more stable and simple conditions implied by the emphases in the left column. Variability and change become the watchwords, and "project teams" or "task forces" come and go in bewildering profusion. The bureaucratic model awkwardly fits both the pace and the structure that are increasingly characteristic of organizational life. Rather than building permanent organizations, one observer notes acutely, we need to create "self-destroying organizations . . . lots of autonomous, semi-attached units which can be spun

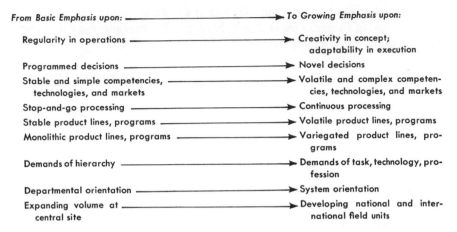

From Basic Emphasis upon: ─────────────────────► To Growing Emphasis upon:

Regularity in operations ─────────────► Creativity in concept;
                                          adaptability in execution

Programmed decisions ──────────────► Novel decisions

Stable and simple competencies, ──────────► Volatile and complex competen-
   technologies, and markets   cies, technologies, and markets

Stop-and-go processing ─────────────► Continuous processing

Stable product lines, programs ──────────► Volatile product lines, programs

Monolithic product lines, programs ────────► Variegated product lines, pro-
                                              grams

Demands of hierarchy ──────────────► Demands of task, technology, pro-
                                         fession

Departmental orientation ─────────────► System orientation

Expanding volume at ──────────────► Developing national and inter-
   central site   national field units

Figure 2   Two sets of emphases to which organizations can respond. [*Source:* Robert T. Golembiewski, "Organization Patterns of the Future," *Personnel Administration*, Vol. 32 (November 1969), p. 11.]

off, destroyed, sold bye-bye, when the need for them has disappeared."[24] Toffler notes that we need an "adhocracy" model to replace bureaucracy, consistent with the growing emphasis on temporary organizations versus permanent ones.

The specific form of the organizing concepts suitable for this adhocracy is still evolving, but a preview is possible here. To use common catchwords, the new concepts will be "organic" rather than "mechanical," and they will emphasize "collaboration-consensus" more than "coercion-compromise." In somewhat more detail, even a few contrasts establish the social and emotional gulfs between traditional organizing concepts and those needed to respond to increasingly common contemporary demands. The contrasts are basically borrowed from Herbert Shepard's seminal contribution, but the translation in Figure 3 is free and may not be entirely faithful to the original.

Toward the Healthier Organization

These perspectives on persons and organizations clearly rest on a rough distinction between the healthy and the less healthy, and that distinction implies a complex of normative and empirical considerations. It is possible to be a little more specific about this central thrust toward healthier organisms, whether they be individuals or organizations.

Directly, the attention to interpersonal and intergroup processes here rests on a simple model that has three components:

$$\text{human inputs} \Rightarrow \text{Interpersonal and Intergroup Processes} \Rightarrow \text{outcomes}$$

Human processes intervene in critical ways between inputs and outcomes, and any improvement in these processes will result in the liberation of energy. That energy can be converted to various uses, such as the facilitation of change. The failure to implement a decision that was made only by disrupting interpersonal or intergroup processes illustrates the resistance that can be attributed to inadequate process.

Within this broad input/output model, the quality of interpersonal and intergroup processes is seen as having critical linkages with individual and organizational effectiveness. For example, adequate organizational processes will facilitate individual growth, and growing individuals can improve the quality of organizational processes. Moreover, ineffective organizational processes are associated with chronic symptoms. Fordyce and Weil, for example, stress three such symptoms. Dependency and/or rebelliousness by subordinates can develop

Emphases in Systems of Coercion-Compromise	Emphases in Systems of Collaboration-Consensus
■ Superordinate power used to control behavior, reinforced by suitable rewards and punishments	■ Control achieved through agreement on goals, reinforced by a feedback system that provides continuous feedback about results
■ Emphasis by leadership on authoritarian control of the compliant and weak, obeisance to more powerful, and compromise when contenders are equal in power	■ Emphasis by leadership on direct confrontation of differences and working through of any conflicts
■ Disguise or suppression of real feelings or reactions, especially when they refer to powerful figures	■ Public sharing of real feelings, reactions
■ Obedience to the attempts of superiors to influence	■ Openness to the attempts of others to exert influence, whatever their status
■ Authority/obedience used to cement organization relationships	■ Mutual confidence and trust used to cement organization relationships
■ Structure is power-based or hierarchy-oriented	■ Structure task-based or solution-oriented
■ Individual responsibility	■ Shared responsibility
■ One-to-one relationships between superior and subordinates	■ Multiple-group memberships with peers, superiors, and subordinates
■ Structure which is based on bureaucratic model and is intendedly stable over time	■ Structure which emerges out of problems faced as well as out of developing consensus among members is intendedly temporary or at least changeable

Figure 3   Two contrasting managerial systems. [*Source:* Based on Herbert Shepard, "Changing Interpersonal and Intergroup Relationships in Organizations," in James G. March (ed.), *Hand of Organizations* (Chicago: Rand McNally, 1965), pp. 1128-1131.]

in response to "chiefs [who] play at being powerful fathers [and] Indians [who] obey submissively or revolt or run away." Defensiveness and narrowness of perspective are two other chronic symptoms of inadequate processes.[25]

The notion of health or illness is patently very close to the surface of such conceptions involving the quality of interpersonal and intergroup processes. Such notions are largely metaphorical at present, but attempts are being made to specify appropriate content. The content-filled metaphor then can be subjected to empirical test, and thus to rejection or to amendment. A useful approach is that of Fordyce and Weil, who propose a number of indicators of organizational health/illness. To illustrate, they define "unhealthy" and "healthy" in terms of a large number of descriptive statements. These statements are illustrated in Figure 4.

Despite a variety of problems, such an approach has its virtues. Consider the problems of measuring the degree to which various organizations possess the several characteristics. Nonetheless, the approach does provide useful first

Unhealthy Organizations	*Healthy Organizations*
■ There is little personal investment in organizational objectives except at top levels.	■ Objectives are widely shared by the members and there is a strong and consistent flow of energy toward those objectives.
■ People in the organization see things going wrong and do nothing about it. Nobody volunteers. Mistakes and problems are habitually hidden or shelved. People talk about office troubles at home or in the halls, not with those involved.	■ People feel free to signal their awareness of difficulties because they expect the problems to be dealt with and they are optimistic that they can be solved.
■ Extraneous factors complicate problem-solving. Status and boxes on the organization chart are more important than solving the problem. There is an excessive concern with management as a customer, instead of the real customer. People treat each other in a formal and polite manner that masks issues—especially with the boss. Nonconforming is frowned upon.	■ Problem-solving is highly pragmatic. In attacking problems, people work informally and are not preoccupied with status, territory, or second-guessing "what higher management will think." The boss is frequently challenged. A great deal of nonconforming behavior is tolerated.
■ People at the top try to control as many decisions as possible. They become bottlenecks and make decisions with inadequate information and advice. People complain about managers' irrational decisions.	■ The points of decision-making are determined by such factors as ability, sense of responsibility, availability of information, work load, timing, and requirements for professional and management development. Organizational level as such is not considered a factor.
■ When there is a crisis, people withdraw or start blaming one another.	■ When there is a crisis, the people quickly band together in work until the crisis departs.
■ Conflict is mostly covert and managed by office politics and other games, or there are interminable and irreconcilable arguments.	■ Conflicts are considered important to decision-making and personal growth. They are dealt with effectively, in the open. People say what they want and expect others to do the same
■ Minimizing risk has a very high value.	■ Risk is accepted as a condition of growth and change.

Figure 4   Some indicators of organizational health. [*Source:* Selected from Jack K. Fordyce and Raymond Weil, *Managing with People* (Reading, Mass.: Addison-Wesley, 1971), pp. 11-13. Reprinted with permission.]

approximations of the typical outcomes toward which the process orientation trends. And, the approach does at least imply the possibility of empirical testing and verification, on the basis of which some more measurable typologies might be built. In fact, some research in this direction will be reviewed in later chapters, using another set of measures on the adequacy of an organization's processes.

Organization health also can be estimated in terms of a variety of other criteria. John Gardner provides an intriguing illustration in his focus on "organizational dry rot."[26] A checklist of diagnostic questions permits some judgment of the degree to which any organization has the disease. The following selected questions suggest the fuller range of the questions that Gardner would ask of any organization, questions that all bear on the effectiveness of coping with change. Gardner asks:

- Does the organization have an effective program for the recruitment and development of talented manpower?
- Has the organization an environment that encourages individuality and releases individual motivations?
- Is there an adequate system of two-way communication in the organization?
- Does the organization have a fluid and adaptable internal structure?
- Are there ample opportunities and situations where the organization provides a process of self-criticism?
- Does the organization have the ability to cope with vested interests?
- Has the organization developed effective face-to-face groups for accomplishment of work goals?
- Does a climate of trust exist between individuals and groups in the organization?

As Gardner suggests, moreover, it is not only that the answers to such questions are significant. More paramount are the processes of raising such questions— frequently and willingly—as an organization's members review their purposes, policies, and procedures.

Value Sensitivity in Dealing with Human Affect
The Normative Reach of the Laboratory Technology

The preceding two sections deliberately oversimplify, and it is time to begin providing necessary complexities in this section and the next. Here the emphasis is on the person. Later, the emphasis will be on the organization.

Let us put the essential matter up front. The laboratory approach has been involved until now with values because it emphasizes learning via an affective point of entry. Hence, the prime need for value sensitivity in the laboratory approach, for it typically begins by dealing with persons as affective, with what they value and how they value it. And, the approach basically maintains that human beings should both represent themselves and be dealt with in their valuing fullness.

Broadly, the individual is seen as a valuing and feeling entity. That is, behavior is significantly influenced by the values a person places on experience, as well as by the feelings associated with those valuations. The individual may be more or less aware of these affective and value bases for his or her behavior, more or less conscious about their impact on others with whom he or she interacts. But that affective impact is nevertheless often substantial, perhaps always so. This will especially be the case in degenerative relationships. Hence, the basic learning progression for the laboratory approach is

$$\text{Affective} \quad \rightarrow \quad \text{Behavioral} \quad \rightarrow \quad \text{Cognitive}$$

This basic progression does not imply that cognition or behavior are without influence on valuation or feeling. The progression does reflect the basic assumption that the affective emphasis is strategically impactful, at least in many cases.

Behavior and cognitive learning or change need not always begin with an affective entree, of course. Subsequent chapters will illustrate other ways in which laboratory values can be approached.

In the interest of starting where much of the action is, however, the basic learning progression above, the linkage of affect→behavior→cognition, will be made more explicit. The laboratory approach helps and encourages individuals to determine what they need and want affectively to meet their own needs and motives. In turn, this sensitization should induce the search for appropriate behavioral skills, as well as thought about the kinds of life situations which both require and foster such skills. In organizations, for example, cognitive concerns often center around the design of structures, procedures, or policies that can reinforce the behaviors that are considered desirable by the organization's members.

Eight Affectively Relevant Levels

The broad and deep involvement with values of the laboratory technology may be indicated more directly. The outline below sketches eight affectively relevant levels of a total life span,[27] all of which are preferences which can activate behavior seeking their attainment, and all of which are tapped by the laboratory approach.

1. *Basic needs or drives* are generically inferred from states of well-being or threat experienced by the individual. That is, the need for food is defined as basic because of the consequences for the organism's integrity and survival when that need is unsatisfied, or poorly satisfied.

Two sets of these needs may be distinguished. First, there are the well-known physical states based on biochemical processes, imbalances in which induce behavior. The visceral states—hunger, thirst, and so on—are the clearest illustrations.

Second, evidence also strongly suggests the existence of an ontological set of social and psychological needs. In the theoretic work of Maslow[28] and Argyris,[29] for example, the individual is seen as trending from the satisfaction of lower-level needs toward the satisfaction of higher-level needs. Failure to do so will result in frustration, fixated behavior, and so on. Basically, the laboratory approach essentially constitutes a set of values that increases the probability that an individual can increasingly become aware of and satisfy these basic social and psychological needs.

2. *Basic affective states* are associated with various degrees of well-being/threat, such as fear, satiation, anxiety, anger, comfort, and so on. Evidence suggests that these subjective states can be influenced by learning, as when an organism develops defenses that permit managing the impact of an affective state, or that even mask an affective state. The evidence also suggests that these affective states are somehow primal. In sum, they are not merely learned responses, although the individual typically learns acceptable ways to express them and even to experience them.[30]

3. *Motives* are conceived of as powerful if usually derivative activators of behavior. They refer to the specific modalities in which the individual seeks satisfaction of basic needs or drives. Scott[31] distinguishes two basic motives: psychological and social. Psychological motives activate specific patterns of quest for maintenance of mental integrity and balance. Social motives induce behaviors that seek to develop stable patterns of association with others. Thus, an individual's basic social motivation[32] might be toward patterns of association that stress affiliation, achievement, or power, or various combinations thereof.

Such social motives are seen as learned.[33] This learning can occur in the process of meeting the basic needs or drives, as well as in the process of seeking to avoid undesirable affective stages (for example, anxiety) and/or to approach desirable affective states.

4. *Values* are in effect higher-order attitudes, valuational "shoulds."[34] In Scott's[35] words, a "value, or moral ideal is . . . an individual's concept of an ideal relationship (or state of affairs), which he uses to assess the 'goodness' or 'badness,' the 'rightness' or 'wrongness' of actual relationships that he observes or contemplates." For example, a person may have compassion or pity toward the disadvantaged. His or her behavior will depend, in part, on values concerning how one should respond to those for whom one has compassion.

5. *Beliefs* refer to purported existential states, some of which can be proved or disproved in a direct sense, and others of which are at least temporarily beyond proximate proof or disproof. Some negative beliefs about various categoric groups, for example, can be tested rather directly. Belief that the sun rotated around the earth was first challenged on deductive grounds, however, and only recently by direct observation. Belief in an ultimate moral order escapes such proof or disproof, finally, at least within a human context.

Beliefs can activate behavior, it is important to note, whatever their potential for being proved or disproved. Indeed, some have argued that beliefs will be motivators in direct proportion to the degree that any belief, or logical deductions from it, is not testable or provable. In any case, the term belief suggests an intensity which distinguishes it from attitudes and opinions, which intensity also can significantly influence behavior.

6. *Attitude,* or an inferred base of behavior, in Allport's classic definition[36] is a "mental and neural state of readiness organized through experience, exerting a directive or dynamic influence upon the individual's response to all objects and situations with which it is related."

Attitudes can have cognitive aspects, then, and they can trigger behavior. The thought component is most prominent in the organization of experience underlying attitudes. Thought may also intervene in decisions to behave consistently with the attitude.

Attitudes also are affective vectors, as it were. As Kiesler notes:[37] "The principal aspect of an attitude is the degree to which it is positive or negative toward something."

7. *Opinions* are usefully distinguished from attitudes, as by the Hartleys.[38] Many situations are problematical in that they "involve new and strange objects or new combinations or arrangements of familiar objects. . . . In this process of assessing the situation, participants draw on past experience, bring to bear attitudes that seem to be relevant; but they cannot rely, except tentatively, upon these attitudes to carry them through the situation. With a greater or lesser degree of rationality, a definition of the situation, a conception of the kind of action appropriate to it, will be worked out; it is just such a definition that seems to be referred to, on both the practical and the scholarly level, as opinion."

8. *Set, or frame of reference,* refers to the general structure that an individual tends to impose on experience.

By extension, then, a person's behavior can be influenced in two major ways via an affective approach. For example, a changed attitude or value can motivate behavioral change, or consideration of such change. Moreover, if no value or attitudinal change occurs or is even considered, major learning is still possible. Thus, individuals can become more aware of their affective lives, of interactions between what they desire and how they behave, and so on. Major potential for behavioral choice and change inheres in such enhanced awareness.

Laboratory Approach and Affective Impacts

Three points highlight significant interactions of the laboratory technology and the eight affectively relevant levels in the outline above. *First*, various learning designs based on the laboratory approach can tap the full affective range. For example, a T-group design could help a person realize that one of his sets or stereotypes is wildly inapplicable. Or such an experience might sensitize an individual to the strength of her affiliative motives, of which she had become increasingly unaware over time. Or an individual might learn something about the subtle range of defenses he has developed to avoid being in touch with his own feelings or affective states, as well as those of others.

Second, the affective range above contains at least two different classes of change targets. Sets or attitudes, for example, have a substantial potential for change. Change in sets or attitudes may be simple, and may also be desirable in that it enhances the individual and her associations. In contrast, the laboratory technology is oriented toward pointing up the character and impact of basic affective states or motives, rather than toward changing them. These "higher" affective levels are "givens," in critical senses. That is, they are not only more difficult (or perhaps, impossible) to change, as a practical matter. Moreover, change at such levels implies serious ethical issues about tampering with the essential person, playing god, and so on.

Third, to risk a simplification, designs based on the laboratory approach challenge participants to two kinds of effort in relation to the full affective range sketched above. The effort involves

- Comparing the values of the laboratory approach with one's normal complement of "lower" effective levels: values, beliefs, attitudes, opinions, and sets, in the language of the outline

- Testing whether the values of the laboratory approach enhance meeting one's "higher" affective levels—basic needs, basic desired affective states, and social needs—as he or she hopefully comes to recognize the latter more clearly as a result of a learning design based on the laboratory approach.

Based on such a dual test, the prudent individual makes his or her choices. It is just that deliciously simple, and just that maddeningly complex.

Value Sensitivity in Dealing with OD
The Normative Grasp of the Laboratory Technology

The need for value sensitivity in organizational applications of the laboratory approach is even more paramount than when only individuals are considered, as above. Two perspectives provide related proof of the point. *First,* organizational development (OD), the organizational expression of the laboratory approach, rests on values that are at once complementary and contradictory. *Second,* organizations are neither benign nor neutral contexts, raising significant value issues of what is done within them, to whom, and how, with what probable consequences. That is, asking for openness in some organizations may be as ill-advised as shouting "Fire!" in a crowded theater.

Consequently, the reach of the laboratory approach in organizations can easily exceed its normative grasp. Specifically, there are numerous choices in conflict relevant in any OD intervention, conflicts which are not resolvable in terms of the broad set of values introduced earlier in this chapter. Hence, the need for caution, it being so easy to go too far. But the costs of being timid are often too great to pay. Hence, the need for informed risk-taking.

OD Rests on Complementary/Contradictory Values

Relying on the work of Hainer,[39] Friedlander usefully demonstrates that OD reflects significant aspects of three broad values or philosophic predispositions.[40] They are

- Rationalism, which emphasizes logic, consistency, and determinism in describing the world
- Pragmatism, which emphasizes usefulness and effectiveness, what "works"
- Existentialism, which puts the primacy on personal and immediate experience, on the subjective sense of phenomena and reactions to them

Note that Exhibit 3 provides substantial detail about these three systems of predispositions or beliefs, described in terms of nine basic categories of differences. The reader is referred to Friedlander's demonstration of how these three broad belief systems underlay the development of OD, which he puckishly presents as a delightful soap opera concerning the lives and loves of Rati, Prag, and Exi.

In addition to not gilding Friedlander's fanciful lily, this brief treatment is motivated by the fact that it suffices here to illustrate the senses in which

Exhibit 3 Some Differences Between Three Sets of Values Relevant to OD

	Rationalism	Pragmatism	Existentialism
Purpose	To discover truth	To improve practice	To experience, choose, commit
Basic activity	Think (knowledge building)	Do (acting)	Exist (being)
Learning paradigm	Conceptualize → define → manipulate ideas	Practice → experiment → valid feedback → improvement	Experience → choose → commit
Terms are	Precisely defined	Tentatively defined	Need not be defined
Meaning emerges from	Definition (concepts)	Practice (results)	Experience (perception)
Ingredients for learning	Concepts, assumptions, logic	Practice, experiment, feedback	Awareness and confrontation of one's existence
Locus of knowledge	The conceptual model	The organizational practice	The individual experience
Reality is	Objectivity and truth	Workability and practice (validity)	Subjective perception
Causes of good communication	Semantic precision	Consensual listening and understanding	Shared feeling and resonance

Source: Frank Friedlander, "OD Reaches Adolescence: An Exploration of its Underlying Values," The Journal of Applied Behaviroal Science, Vol. 12, no. 1 (1976), p. 14. Copyright by NTL Institute, 1976. Reproduced by special permission.

these three systems imply both potentialities and dilemmas for OD. "All three values are essential ingredients of OD," Friedlander observes, "yet each lends to OD a different and sometimes contradictory identity."[41] More fully, he illustrates the sometimes divergent forces deriving from the three systems in this revealing way:[42]

> Rationalism pushes contemporary OD toward becoming more scientific, more theoretical and conceptual, more logical, more mathematical; toward abstract models; toward building theories; toward understanding the determinants of our organizational, social, and personal worlds. Pragmatism pushes OD in the direction of becoming more useful—how does OD increase effectiveness, performance, productivity; how can OD determine expected or alternative organizational processes and structures; and how can it feed back information into the organization to reduce the gap between the way it is now and the way it would be better? Existentialism within OD pushes the organization to become more humanistic, more aware, more emerging, more person-person oriented.

Friedlander summarizes the useful contributions of each of these three orientations to thought in a revealing way: "The rationalist learns by thinking," he observed, "the pragmatist by doing; and the existentialist by becoming aware."

Both the implied potentialities and dilemmas should be clear enough. For example, rationalism can lead to the development of models or theories that will permit the achievement of the goals of pragmatism: greater usefulness and effectiveness of interventions. This is true in the long run. But, we live in the short run, for many purposes. And, this elemental fact can generate irresolvable dilemmas, or at least painful choices between imponderables. In the short run, that is, the pragmatist will urge seeking something that works, anything. The rationalist will insist, however, that such adventuresomeness will only delay the long-term development of that model of the world which alone will permit effective applications in the real world. Meanwhile, the existentialist is more concerned with immediate responses to what's going on inside self.

Diversely, these three basic belief systems underlie the analysis that follows, and severely complicate it. When push comes to shove, that is, what does OD prescribe: a greater openness to personal experience; a greater awareness of theories of relationships in the world; or a down-to-earth getting on with it, whatever and however? To choose "all of the above" is both correct and insensitive to the common, insistent need to emphasize one or the other. Basically, this volume tries to choose "all of the above," and pays the costs of length, complexity, and integrations that do not quite come off.

But so be it: There is no easy way out. The goal here will be to exploit the potentialities of the richness represented by the three belief systems; the ambition will be to raise consciousness about as many resulting dilemmas as possible; and the hope will be that some little may be done to blunt the impact of the horns of some of those harsh dilemmas.

Organizations Are Neither Benign nor Neutral Contexts

That the normative reach of OD may severely test its grasp also inheres in two facts: organizations are neither as benign as most training or educational sites, nor are they neutral as to preferred outcomes. These two facts heighten the ethical or value consequences of OD interventions, purely and simply. Two perspectives serve to expand on those dual enormities.

First, many observers insist rights that organizations not be considered mere technical structures—organizations get infused with value as to what is to be done, by whom, and (especially) how things get done.[43] Consider this list of operating values that I deduced from observing the top-level marketing group of one corporation, and reported back to its members for purposes of analysis and action-planning. The operating values, along with brief illustrations, include:

• "We are a family." Illustratively, frequent and overt sharing of portions of meals occurred among organization members. "Have some of my salad; I'd just love a tad of your lobster bisque."

• "Kill a big rat; have high aspirations and goals." Allusions to big deals and plans were numerous. Big risks also were encouraged, typically along with the complaint that not enough risk-taking occurred.

• "Work hard and play hard." By the fact of having been retained, organization members had demonstrated their ability to work hard, and thus were granted the right to "play hard," privately as well as during R&R periods on company meetings and business. The boundaries seem broad, but limits clearly existed. Thus, one member played high-stakes poker all night and until 5 or 6 AM the next morning, and then slept through a significant meeting. "Don't do that again," his boss noted when the individual finally appeared during mid-afternoon. "That" referred only to sleeping through a meeting. "Playing hard" was still OK, failure to "work hard" brought quick censure.

• "We tolerate a very broad range of behaviors." For example, one executive noted his desire to assume control over the product line presently run by a fellow executive, publicly and insistently in the presence of that executive and numerous peers, superiors, and subordinates.

• "Everyone is, or should be, a big girl or boy." Requests for help were seldom if ever made, and unsolicited help, even when helpers wanted very much to intervene, was considered inappropriate because that "might signal loss of confidence in the other person." Organization members reported they often "worked very hard" not to intervene, the usual verbalization being that "ours is a tough industry and everybody has got to make it on their own."

• "We have a high degree of confidence in our formal and informal methods of social control." For example, numerous organization members played high-stakes poker after off-site business meetings, with pots sometimes running into the thousands of dollars. The players included organizational peers as well as superiors and subordinates.

Hopefully, the gentle reader will avoid the temptation of evaluating this set of values, or of forgetting the general point. Thus, it is easy to point to inconsistencies, or at least sources of tension, between the several values in the set above. And, to be sure, the values above clearly are both unusual and uncommon. For example, most organizations would discourage high-stakes games among members, especially among bosses and subordinates, for what should be obvious reasons that all boil down to a concern that social controls could not encompass the dynamics that might be set loose. But this set of values plays the same role in this organization as more garden variety values play in other organizations. They prescribe certain behaviors and proscribe others, and hence define the quality of the prevailing systems of social control.

The general point here should be obvious, whatever the prevailing set of values. The application of any technique in such valuational contexts raises substantial ethical problems. Specifically, the values intended to be served by the technique may be perverted by the ambience or culture of the host organization. Thus, Albert Speer innovated variants of participative management practices to avoid the excessive bureaucratization elsewhere flourishing in Hitler's Germany. In many respects well ahead of his managerial time, Speer emphasized:[44]

- Collegial decision-making
- Problem-solving rather than legalistic definition and protection of jurisdictions
- Temporary systems versus permanent ones
- Decentralization of trust, responsibility, and initiative

These are major elements in many contemporary, even humanistic, views of management. And they are usually offered as serving lofty ethical goals: freedom, self-determination, self-policing, and so on. In Nazi Germany, however, Speer "utilized these theories and practices to promote the goals of one of the most inhumane societies in the history of mankind. . . ."[45] The differences are momentous.

Other observers will argue that what happened in Speer's case is no fluke, indeed, that it was to be expected. They see two chances that an "organizational imperative" will not dominate human values: slim and none. This "imperative" requires five specific "cultural value commitments" if it is to survive. These can be outlined in terms of five sets of paired values, which indicate the kind of movement beyond traditional values that the "imperative" requires:[46]

- From individuality to obedience
- From the indispensability of the unique individual to dispensability
- From community to specialization

- From spontaneity to self-conscious planning
- From voluntarism to an organizational paternalism

Some observers are worried that, from the very start, OD aficionados basically accept these (or similar) imperatives, and that the needs of individuals will be sacrificed to organization demands most of the time, as these are interpreted by organizational and quasitherapeutic elites.[47] "In resolving the alleged conflict between the individual and the organization," Strauss concludes, "stress is placed on changing people. The [humanistic ideal] is to be imposed benignly from the top."[48]

These brief comments imply a serious issue of choice whether to do OD. That is, however noble the professed goals underlying OD interventions, some danger—or perhaps an absolute inevitability—exists that those values will be perverted by the inexorable demands of the organizational system. OD interventions may be tolerated only when they basically serve to stabilize the system, as in "cooling out" those members who develop antagonistic feelings toward some system.[49] Human needs will be responded to, in this view of the world, only (or mostly) when they happen to coincide with the organizational imperative.

Second, knotty ethical issues inhere in restraints on individual freedom that can develop in organizations experiencing OD programs. Given the rewards or penalties that organizations can dispense, and given how these can energize the baser as well as the loftier motives in man, the stakes can be high and the danger remains real.

How to provide reasonable guarantees for individual freedom in organizations? Following Walton and Warwick,[50] "freedom" in such cases can be taken to include at least:

- Informed consent of participants
- Participation that is basically voluntary, and certainly is not based on coercion
- Rejecting manipulation as a strategy, manipulation meaning "deliberate attempts to change personal qualities or the structure of the physical or social environment without the knowledge of the individuals concerned"
- Developing some reasonable guarantees against misuse of information generated in the course of the intervention

Organizational sites often make it difficult to act in ways that respect these guidelines for individual freedom. The dangers of trespass exist even for those of great goodwill.[51] For example, organizations are usually hierarchical in form and substance. Hence, it may be difficult for a subordinate to beg off participating in an organizational application of the laboratory approach, which he knows his superior favors, even when his superior says it "will not be held against him." The degree of coercion perceived in such cases will vary, of course. In other cases, an employee can be so uptight that she cannot even verbalize her concern. Or the subordinate might feign enthusiasm when he feels terror. In such cases, the supervisor can easily delude herself into believing that enthusiasm reflects the voluntary participation that she honestly desires.

Such possibilities urge cautious testing, and imply difficult issues for judgment, in any organizational application of the laboratory approach. When does "some perceived coercion" become "too much"? What is a "reasonable guarantee" that information will not be misused, when the ambitious or unscrupulous are known to exist? And so on, and so on. This two-part revision seeks to be sensitive to such questions and tries to illustrate some experience in coping with them.

OD and Behavior Modification
Brief Comparisons of Differential Emphases on Values

This introduction to issues concerning the desired and desirable in OD will profit from a comparison with today's second most prominent newer approach to learning. This second approach is variously referred to as behavior modification (BM), Skinnerian psychology, or operant behaviorism, and its most popular and villified expression is B. F. Skinner's *Beyond Freedom and Dignity*.[52] The OD/BM debate can be introduced conveniently in these terms:[53]

> The very title of B. F. Skinner's book implies the nature of the issues that exist between proponents of environmental restructuring [and OD advocates] as a way to a better life. [OD intervenors] tend to put definite priority on the freedom and dignity of the individual so that he can make informed choices; Skinner says that this priority is misguided. . . . [He argues] that behaviour is primarily a function of positive and negative reinforcements from the environment and that the real problem confronting mankind is to understand better how behaviour is shaped [so that] we will be able to restructure the environment.

Values in Behavior Modification

The sprawling area of Behavior Modification is not one about which simple conclusions may be drawn,[54] despite a host of efforts to do precisely that— efforts taking too little care with, and reflecting too little respect for, the arguments of people like Skinner. But five major points seem clear enough. First, in a broad sense, we are all behavior modifiers. We positively reinforce the behavior we like in others, and we will often repeat the behaviors reinforced by others. Without question, then, observers like Skinner have got their finger on a real pulse point of the human condition. Their core insight has great meaning and application, no doubt about that.

Second, how to apply that core insight? Here the issues are painfully unresolved, from the OD point of view. Indeed, BM settles *the* important issues, from the perspective of an OD intervenor and all humanists, only by definition. *The* issues relate to questions of value or preference. These questions take such a form, to simplify:

- What should we do?
- What means are desirable for achieving such ends?

These two prototypic questions can take many forms. Illustratively, a humanist would raise such questions about Behavior Modification applications:

- What behaviors should be shaped or reinforced?
- What constraints should restrain the shaper or reinforcer of behavior in his or her choice of reinforcing stimuli?
- What safeguards should be provided for persons exposed to the BM technology?

In brief, the task for Behavior Modification indicated a decade ago by Perry London still requires doing. London accepted the BM core insight about reinforcement and perhaps contingencies, and urged getting on to *the* issues. He notes: "What remains is to determine the characteristics of this technology, the rules for implementing control, and the purposes which it should serve."[55]

The BM literature is impossibly subtle, or cavalier, or simply neglects such issues of relevance to many. For example, Skinner writes that we really know what we want—peace versus war, lawfulness versus crime, nourishing food versus famine, and so on—and that we only lack the wit to get on with it.[56] Or he tells us reinforcers are defined only by the fact that they affect behavior, and, by implication, it seems that any reinforcer is thereby equivalent to any other. The issues he avoids or finesses appear momentous. Can individuals be shaped or reinforced toward war and crime, as well as peace and lawfulness? Apparently so. Should they be so shaped and reinforced? Such questions do not get the attention they deserve in the BM literature. The neglect of values is even raised to a methodological principle with regard to reinforcement. Locke's formidable BM critique puts the point well, although his emphasis may be more on empirical issues than on values. Locke observes:[57]

> Because the concept of reinforcement is defined solely by its consequences, if an alleged reinforcer does not reinforce, it is not a reinforcer. If it does,

it is. Since the concept of reinforcement itself has no content (no defining characteristics independent of its effects on behavior), how are behavior modifiers to know what to use as reinforcers?

Clearly, short of random search, this puts the BM intervenor directly in the complex business of conceptualizing, valuing, and choosing. But, this is awkward, because Skinner himself has proposed that "the environment" induces all behavior (and thinking, valuing, feeling?).[58] Indeed, Locke sees that point as a basic BM premise. He notes:[59] "Determinism: With respect to their choices, beliefs and actions, individuals are ruled by forces beyond their control (... these forces are environmental). Individuals are totally devoid of volition."

Even with such analysis by infinite regression, observers like Skinner cannot successfully avoid issues of choice and, consequently, questions of values. When push comes to shove, Skinner generally but narrowly redefines values. As Carpenter notes:[60]

> Fundamentally, Skinner's psychology is a psychology of values. Positive values are assigned to those events that are rewarding, while negative values emerge from experiences that bring aversive stimulation. The human is a value-making creature in the sense that his own behavior produces results that are sorted into positive and negative effects.

And whence derives this ultimate value-making capacity? Most of those in Behavior Modification seem to resist getting inside the skin of people, but Carpenter reasonably guesses that Skinner would argue that people are value-making because of "natural selection," in the sense that those people tend to survive to reproduce their own kind who respond appropriately to the significant consequences of their own behavior.[61]

Third, there is enough ambiguity in (let us say, Skinner) that some observers see an essential commonality between OD and BM, as does Gamboa.[62] For this writer, the word of Skinner on such a matter prevails, and he acknowledges no such commonality;[63] quite the contrary, in fact.

What encourages some observers to see such a commonality between OD and Behavior Modification? Basically, such observers associate a common sense of personal growth and survival with both approaches to learning. Thus, Carpenter explains that Skinner's thought implies that individuals have the ability to relate their behavior to experienced consequences in regular ways. And what does that implication imply, in turn? Carpenter notes:[64]

> In addition, there is some genetic or built-in tendency to sort consequences into "good" and "bad" classes that are generally associated with survival. An organism avoids noxious conditions because it is genetically wired to sustain its physical safety. Good consequences are those that meet the needs of survival and growth. Skinner avoids using the concept of "need" as I have just used it, because he thinks that is not necessary.

OD practitioners typically take very different positions on the matters related to needs and/or values. All but uniformly, that is, they see "need" as a vital construct, in numerous possible forms, and evaluate behaviors as more or less useful for filling the requirements of healthy growth and development associated with such needs. This prescriptive mode clearly differs from BM. Many other OD practitioners also would define appropriate behavior in terms of "shoulds" or "oughts" independently of the individual, such as those deriving from cultural prescriptions, ethical statements, or even some transcendental moral order.[65] This posture departs substantially from that implied in BM systems of thought.

Fourth, observers like Gamboa and Carpenter may be correct, but the comments above reflect the opposite view here, that profound conceptual distance exists between BM and OD on the issues of needs and values. Exhibit 4 seeks to summarize a number of significant differences in the two treatments of values or preferences. Briefly, most OD practitioners do stress individual growth and survival, as in Maslow's hierarchy of needs, the Argyrian dimensions for self-actualization, Herzberg's distinction between motivators and satisfiers, and similar constructs.[66] In contrast to Skinner, however, these constructs are content filled and variegated, and their truth value exists at least in part independently of a specific individual's response to them. That is, individuals can be "sick" or "misguided" and may eagerly adopt counterproductive behaviors. This approach poses problems, but those problems seem less formidable than the infinite regression or perhaps vagueness that BM brings to bear on the matter.

Relatedly, many OD practitioners stress the specific moral or ethical thrusts of their evolving body of theory and practice,[67] with zesty disputation as well as reasoned calm. Indeed, a central survey article opines that value and ethical issues rest at the very heart of the near-future progress of organization development.[68] This stands in marked contrast to the spareness in this regard of systems like Skinner's, whose values seem two in number, "good" or "bad," that is, reinforcers or nonreinforcers for a specific target behavior for an individual at a specific time and place, which is not to neglect the large number of stimuli that are "neutral" in regard to shaping or reinforcing the target behavior. Relatedly, the BM literature does not seem much concerned with values related to their interventions. Illustratively, one careful student devotes 15 of some 400 pages to such issues, and almost all that bulk is devoted to legal constraints on BM interventions, as contrasted with the basic values or goals of their interventions.[69]

Fifth, then, this analysis recognizes the BM core insight but rejects the trappings in which it commonly gets dressed. This approach shares much basic conceptual territory with Nay,[70] who rejects the choice between the "extrinsically-controlled man" of BM along with extreme formulations of "self-directed man." Reinforcement certainly plays a major role in our behavior, he notes.

Exhibit 4 Comparisons of Two Approaches to Learning

	Behavior Modification	Typical OD Design
Direction of interventions	Basically unilateral, a doing unto others	Intendedly multilateral and reciprocal, a doing unto each other
Model of person	Except for the differential capacity of individuals to be reinforced by some stimuli and not others, BM determinedly avoids "going beneath the skin" and hence defines or limits the range of interventions only to those that can be made with effect	Rests on some sense of human "needs" and/or values that define or limit the range of interventions that can and/or should be made
Emphasis on	Participant change, with no concern for choice and even some ambiguity about whether "choice" exists	Participant choice, with concern about the dimensions of choice as well as about how to enhance its reality and probability
Safeguards for "subjects"	Some reference to benign intent of reinforcer, but the basic safeguard is that behavior can be shaped or reinforced only by stimuli that are somehow appropriate for specific individuals	Major concerns about safeguards, with substantial although hardly complete agreement about sufficient safeguards—e.g., informed consent, deliberate choice to participate, several points at which individuals might reassess participation, and so on
Change-agent role	Determine goals toward which shaping or reinforcement will be directed, with little or no role for participants	Legitimates and specifies certain processes, norms, and designs for moving toward goals which participants have major roles in defining and elaborating

But so does consciousness and choice. Nay's balanced view, in brief, proposes that:[71]

> The individual is . . . capable of being aware of those events that come to define and control his behavior, and capable of making deliberate choices to alter them. The relative importance of the extrinsic environment or

intrinsic phenomena in controlling behavior might vary across persons as well as across specific behaviors. . . . The extent to which extrinsic events come to control a behavior perhaps depends on the degree to which the individual is aware of their controlling properties, can make a conscious choice, and has developed a sufficient behavioral repertoire to alter them.

This much having been said, some caveats are in order. Thus, OD practitioners do not have some complete and comprehensive ethical or value framework; they can publicly fuss about differences in normative emphases, as well as about neglect by their brethren of ethical or value issues;[72] and concern by OD practitioners about "mere technology" not rooted in values is common.[73] But, *the* crucial point inheres not in its finished quality but in the fact that ethical or value specificity is more or less front-and-center in OD thought. Normative concern is alive and vital there. Moreover, significant conceptual and empirical issues do bedevil the available versions of needs that OD practitioners typically attribute to individuals,[74] needs that are kinds of human gyroscopes that steer healthy persons toward what they need to function in satisfying and growthful ways. Again, the OD view does clearly emphasize a content-filled view, in contrast to BM spareness, whatever the present inadequacies of specific developmental versions of needs or goals.

Value-Relevant Comparisons of Two Approaches to Learning

Caveats aside, however, Exhibit 4 does focus on two approaches to learning that differ significantly in their treatment of issues of values, ethics, or preferences. Consider only the first point in the exhibit. Thus, OD is seen as determinedly multilateral and reciprocal in concept, which does not maintain that no narrowly manipulative applications exist. The various designs described below diversely reflect the energy put into broad psychological ownership of OD designs and the learning to which they lead—by administrative superiors as well as subordinates, for example. BM has a distinctly different character in this regard. Revealingly, BM applications known to this author typically have the character of some few doing unto others. This neglect may avoid some difficult questions, and it is certainly understandable, given that early BM applications clustered in "total institutional" settings for the mentally ill, the retarded, the profoundly disturbed, and so on. However understandable, the practical and intellectual consequences of neglect can be profound. Imagine a teacher of BM seeking to shape docile behaviors among his active students. Assume also that the students are armed with BM technology, but they are using it to seek to shape freedom-granting behaviors by the teacher. The BM technology provides no clear directions concerning such cross-purpose situations. Numerous OD designs in this volume and its companion dote on just such situations as the raw material for confronting and for learning.

A Crucial Sense in Which OD Is Value Loaded
Cross-Cultural Applications of OD Interventions

In general, perhaps *the* crucial proof that OD is value loaded inheres in this common observation: a host organization must be "culturally prepared" for an OD application. That observation implies a profound truth. Values must be taken very seriously in OD applications—from two directions, as it were. The values characterizing OD interventions and potential host organizations, as well as the fit between the two, must be taken into conscious account. Neither major alternative seems attractive: to count on being lucky; and to settle for a low batting average.

"Cross-Cultural" in a Generic Sense

More specifically, to what can "cross-cultural" refer? Of course, the term can have numerous levels of meaning. Four come to mind immediately:

- Many observers have noted that each organization or group tends to "become infused with value,"[75] and hence, even apparently identical organizations may have significantly different cultures or "climates" to which the same OD intervention might apply well or not at all.[76]

- Commonly, the "public sector" is seen as constituting a significantly different and more difficult target for OD designs than do "business" hosts.[77]

- Seasoned observers caution that OD applications in a "military culture" will differ profoundly from counterparts in "civilian" hosts,[78] with especially marked normative biases in the military reinforcing the primacy of status and the integrity of the "chain-of-command."

- Voices are beginning to be heard urging a careful distinction of "American OD" from "non-American OD," the general idea being that the same OD intervention will variously suit different societies, cultures, or economic systems.

These examples inexorably force a direct conclusion. An OD intervenor must be conscious of values related to both interventions and hosts. The point holds for an intervenor with "American-only" experience who has been retained by a Socialist-bloc country; and it holds, if perhaps more subtly, for the intervenor planning on making the same intervention in two subunits at proximate loci in the same parent organization. Hence, the absolute primacy of careful, prior diagnosis of potential hosts for OD applications. Chapter 2 in Part 2 will especially draw attention to useful conceptual foci for diagnosing relevant normative, value, and cultural differences in hosts.

"Cross-Cultural" in a Macro-Sense

Let us restrict attention here to the broadest sense of cross-cultural OD applications. The focal questions take this prototypical form: Will an OD intervention play in Azerbaijan as well as in Dubuque, Iowa?

Three points seem crystal clear about this macro-usage of the cross-cultural. First, relatively little research exists that deals with the issue in any specific and detailed ways,[79] and that research reflects no consistent pattern. Thus, one specific team-building design used many times in this country[80] seems to have quite similar effects on three continents.[81] And, T-group designs also seem to have broadly similar consequences.[82] But, evidence reflecting the criticality of value and cultural differences can be found easily. Research on diplomatic personnel supports the definite preference of the British for high social distance, while Arabs prefer to move in close.[83] It takes little imagination to envision the tragicomic encounters that might derive from these two tendencies.

Second, whatever else, available research suggests that cross-cultural OD applications must be considered in terms of internal and external consequences. Team-building is pretty much team-building, for example, in my experience— whether the locus is at Long Lines of AT&T or in a refinery in a socialist country—when "internal" criteria are relied upon. At the same time, however, "external" criteria can exert a profound influence at various stages in an OD application resting on team-building experiences. Thus, any interteam designs of even modest size may involve a local representative of the Communist Party, the appropriate labor union(s), and officials of relevant governments. At the very least, this complicates the dynamics of extending team-building designs. Multiple and incompletely congruent systems also appear in many other contexts, of course, and they commonly dilute the impact of OD designs.[84]

We have no large literature dealing with this internal and external issue related to organizations in cross-cultural settings, macro-variety. "Transfer of learning" or "re-entry" from a "learning culture" to a "back-home culture" have long been with us, of course, but this relates to a different point than the one here. Nonetheless, there is every reason to expect such effects, now quite well documented in attempts to use the laboratory approach to bridge cultures as (for example) in the conflict between Protestants and Catholics in Ireland. In small training groups, real progress typically can be made. So, "internal" criteria—greater understanding of others, warmth and empathy toward them, and so on—will signal the kind of learning characteristic of the laboratory approach.[85] However, such progress can be negated—may even be dangerous—

when the trainees reenter the broader social context which remains unchanged and hostile to the training goals.[86]

Third, hope concerning cross-cultural OD applications nonetheless waxes strong, which implies some combination of growing need and useful experience. As one sign of the times, for example, the first conference on international OD applications will be held in 1979. Western European countries saw early OD applications, but the approach has now spread to Japan, Latin American countries, Africa, and also is showing some more recent vitality in countries such as Poland.

Factors Encouraging Cross-Cultural Applications

The factors encouraging cross-cultural applications can be illustrated briefly, since they seem well in-hand. Only four factors get some attention here. First, many countries yearn for "progress," and hence are attracted to practices in countries like the United States which are seen as having strong records in that particular. Cross-cultural consultants often will hear references to the desires of other nationals to pick and choose from among "American model business practices," where OD now has a substantial and even spectacular place.

Second, common professional attitudes and strivings among the world's managers also encourage OD applications in cross-cultural contexts. The point holds in at least two senses. Thus, large numbers of the world's managers have received "Western" training, either by travel or by attending their own national schools of management and administration that were variously influenced by Western experts and standards. Many Western universities, for example, were both aggressive exporters (by serving on development missions throughout the world) and also importers (by accepting foreign nationals as students). In a far more subtle sense, moreover, managerial professionalization has induced strong and common forces: needs as well as strivings.[87] For example, "high technologies" imply a swing from the authority of position to the authority of knowledge, even in otherwise totalitarian or authoritarian systems. That swing is not inevitable,[88] but it does tend to occur with profound consequences for management.[89] And there seems no doubt that this profound movement has contributed much momentum to OD.

Third, the requirements of technology often will reinforce such professional needs and strivings for autonomy, or at least influence. The argument does not need fulsome repeating. In general, technological demands raise the bargaining power of required professionals and managers. The point was first made forcefully in the West by James Burnham's *The Managerial Revolution,* and got socialist counterpoint two decades later in sources such as Milovan Djilas's *The New Class.* Enough said.

Fourth, many countries seek to build an industrial and commercial base while "consumerism" grows apace. This requires running faster to stand still, in some cases, and raises the attractiveness of approaches like OD that give real promise of facilitating what needs to be done.

Factors Inhibiting Cross-Cultural Applications

These encouraging factors are powerful, patently, but they face major inhibitors. Often, these inhibitors reflect serious value clashes between the OD technology and potential loci for application. These inhibitors may also work on OD intervenors, who must make judgments about risk/benefit ratios, where the downside potential may be very high. Such decisions always must be made, of course, as one experienced intervenor sardonically reflects in this title of a conference paper: "Tell Me Exactly What You Think, Even If It Costs You Your Job."[90] In "closed systems," not uncommon across the world, that paper's title might reflect far greater negative consequences.

Four classes of such cross-cultural inhibitors may be illustrated. First, many cultures have strong autocratic or authoritarian biases that can run seriously counter to OD values and practices. Briefly, such cultures may reflect this catalog of features:

- Social mobility may be limited, as in a traditional caste system or in a persisting class structure.

- Relationships between people in organizations might be characterized by high degrees of formality, even stiffness, great "social distances," and so on.

- Many members of the culture may be fatalistic, believing that their fates are substantially or completely determined, which demotivates choice or change.

- Many members may be comfortable in a dependent role in a paternalistic relationship, on definite balance.

- Concern about task performance may be very low, with emphasis far less on task than on loyalty to family, persons, or political identifications.

Second, and obviously, language itself may cause serious problems, in combination with value differences. I recall expressing my admiration for an overseas colleague in a crisis situation: "Atta baby," I said. My colleague was not fluent in idiomatic American, and much later expressed his furious resentment that I had been so familiar with him as to refer to him as infantile. That one got untangled, after a while.

Third, various political and institutional features may inhibit some OD interventions, or at least encourage reflective pause by the OD intervenor. There may be some important lines that should not be crossed, as that between what may be called "politics" and "administration." Moreover, since those lines sometimes have moved substantially, in the past, even apparently firm precedents may not be reliable. I recall one conversation with a senior official in a socialist country. I marvelled at the very aggressive consumer-oriented emphasis then current in his country, which peaked for me in some roughing-up on national TV of major government officials, by both a panel of commentators and telephone callers complaining about the inadequacy of certain government services. "Wonderful," he said. "Their administration was not adequate, and they needed to know what the people were feeling," my informant told me. "And it was the callers' socialist responsibility to speak out," my source added. "But what about a caller who criticized higher-level officials like my informant?" I asked. "What should he do?" The response was chilling:

> We expect no such calls. But were such a call made, the caller would need do nothing but give his name and address, and wait.
>
> We would take care of the rest.
>
> That kind of caller would not be contributing to enhanced managerial performance, you see. He would be meddling in politics.

Fourth, many cross-cultural OD applications may be inappropriate for the special phase of development common in organizations in the host culture. Aspects of this difficult issue, on a smaller scale, get some attention in Chapter 2 of Part 2.

Hedging Bets Concerning Value Conflict

The intended message here is not: Checkmate. The OD intervenor has some room to maneuver in cases of a clash of values. For example, an intervenor can variously protect the anonymity of his sources. One especially potent approach relies on a tape recorder that masks voices but not their message. Or interview and feedback designs might be used for a similar purpose, as will be illustrated at several points in this two-part volume. Relatedly, OD interventions that focus on structures and policies may raise less obvious questions than do interaction-centered designs. Basically, this first part deals with interaction-centered interventions. Part 2 shifts attention to structures and policies.

Whether bets are hedged or not, however, one point should be clear enough. OD is a value-loaded technology, and that fact can be neglected only at the intervenor's and especially the client's expense.

Notes

1. Warren G. Bennis, "Goals and Meta-Goals of Laboratory Training," *NTL Human Relations Training News*, Vol. 6, no. 3 (1962), p. 4.

2. Bennis, "Goals and Meta-Goals," p. 4.

3. Gurth Higgin, "The Scandinavians Rehearse the Liberation," *Journal of Applied Behavioral Science,* Vol. 8 (November 1972), pp. 643-663.

4. Herbert C. Kelman, "Processes of Opinion Change," *Public Opinion Quarterly,* Vol. 25 (Spring 1961), pp. 57-78.

5. R. I. Watson, *Psychology of the Child* (New York: John Wiley & Sons, 1959).

6. Gerard Egan, *Encounter: Group Processes for Interpersonal Growth* (Belmont, Calif.: Wadsworth, 1970), p. 260.

7. Carl R. Rogers (ed.), *The Therapeutic Relationship and Its Impact* (Madison, Wisc.: University of Wisconsin Press, 1967).

8. John P. Campbell and Marvin D. Dunnette, "Effectiveness of T-Group Experiences in Managerial Training and Development," *Psychological Bulletin,* Vol. 70 (August 1968), pp. 73-104.

9. Marie Jahoda, *Current Concepts of Positive Mental Health* (New York: Basic Books, 1958).

10. G. T. Barrett-Lennard, "Dimensions of Therapist Responses as Causal Factors in Therapeutic Change," *Psychological Monographs,* Vol. 76, no. 43 (1962).

11. Louis A. Gottschalk and E. Mansell Pattison, "Psychiatric Perspectives on T-Groups and the Laboratory Movement," *The American Journal of Psychiatry,* Vol. 126 (December 1969), p. 835.

12. This section is based on Robert T. Golembiewski, "The Laboratory Approach to Organization Development," *Public Administration Review,* Vol. 27 (September 1967), pp. 215-217.

13. Bernard Lubin and William B. Eddy, "The Laboratory Training Model: Rationale, Method and Some Thoughts for the Future," *International Journal of Group Psychotherapy,* Vol. 20 (July 1970), pp. 315-316.

14. Cary L. Cooper, "How Psychologically Dangerous Are T-Groups and Encounter Groups?," *Human Relations,* Vol. 28, no. 3 (1975), pp. 249-260.

15. Chris Argyris, "T-Groups for Organizational Effectiveness," *Harvard Business Review,* Vol. 42 (March 1964), p. 67.

16. Bertram R. Forer, "Therapeutic Relationships in Groups," in Arthur Burton (ed.), *Encounter* (San Francisco: Jossey-Bass, 1969), p. 28.

17. Argyris, "T-Groups for Organizational Effectiveness," p. 61.

18. Ibid., pp. 61-63.

19. Ibid., pp. 63-73. Argyris' ideas have a long and distinguished development. For extensions of his thought, see his *On Organizations of the Future* (Beverly Hills, Calif.: Sage Publications, 1973); and Argyris and Donald A. Schön, *Theory in Practice* (San Francisco: Jossey-Bass, 1974).

20. Philip E. Slater and Warren G. Bennis, "Democracy Is Inevitable," *Harvard Business Review,* Vol. 42 (March 1964), pp. 51-59.

21. Warren Bennis, "Organizations of the Future," *Personnel Administration,* Vol. 30 (September 1967).

22. Alvin Toffler, *Future Shock* (New York: Random House, 1970), p. 125.

23. Ibid.

24. Donald A. Schön, quoted in *Commission on the Year 2000,* Vol. I (Cambridge, Mass.: American Academy of Arts and Sciences, 1965), p. 106.

25. Jack K. Fordyce and Raymond Weil, *Managing with People* (Reading, Mass.: Addison-Wesley, 1971), p. 8.

26. John W. Gardner, "How to Prevent Organizational Dry Rot," *Harper's Magazine,* October 1965, p. 21.

27. The approach is suggested by David G. Bowers, *Perspectives in Organizational Development* (CRUSK—Institute of Social Research, University of Michigan, Ann Arbor, n.d.), pp. 21-22.

28. "Self-actualization" is the summum bonum of needs in such concepts, and it has often been rooted in a framework of a "hierarchy of needs." For a conceptual wellspring, see Abraham H. Maslow, *Motivation and Personality* (New York: Harper and Row, 1954). In his latest (and posthumous) work, Maslow calls for a "humanistic biology" to deal with the ontological goals or needs for individuals he posits to exist. Just as deprivation of the need for food can cause disease, Maslow argues, so also does the deprivation of "the basic-need satisfactions of safety and protection, belongingness, love, respect, self-esteem, identity and self actualization. . . ." He sees such needs as related to the "fundamental structure of the human organism itself," in the same ways and via the same logic that established the more strictly biologic needs. He explains: "the classical way of establishing a body need, as for vitamins . . . has been first a confrontation with a disease of unknown cause, and then a search for this cause. That is to say, something is considered to be a need if its deprivation produces disease." His list of social-psychological needs was inferred in a similar manner, if in a preliminary way, as explanations for "spiritual or philosophical or existential ailments" that are seen as deriving from deprivations of basic social-psychological needs, or what Maslow calls "instinctoids." *The Farther Reaches of Human Nature* (New York: Viking, 1971), pp. 22-23.

29. Chris Argyris, *Personality and Organization* (New York: Harper and Row, 1957), esp. pp. 49-53, provides a specific model of the dimensions of self-actualization. Note: Attempts to develop and rigorously test such "needs models" have run into major unresolved difficulties. For example, consult Gerald R. Salancik and Jeffrey Pfeffer, "An Examination of Need-Satisfaction Models of Job Attitudes," *Administrative Science Quarterly,* Vol. 22 (September 1977), pp. 427-456; and Clayton P. Alderfer, "A Critique of

Salancik and Pfeffer's Examination of Need-Satisfaction Theories," *Administrative Science Quarterly,* Vol. 22 (December 1977), pp. 658-669.

30. Ezra Stotland, *The Psychology of Hope* (San Francisco: Jossey-Bass, 1969), p. 31.

31. William G. Scott, *Human Relations in Management* (Homewood, Ill.: Richard D. Irwin, 1962), pp. 80-82.

32. David C. McClelland, John W. Atkinson, Russell A. Clark, and Edgar L. Lowell, *The Achievement Motive* (New York: Appleton-Century-Crofts, 1953).

33. A similar notion has been the key one in a number of theoretical systems, as in Harry Stack Sullivan, *Conceptions of Modern Psychiatry* (New York: W. W. Norton & Co., 1953), pp. 19-23.

34. Milton Rokeach, *Beliefs, Attitudes, and Values* (San Francisco: Jossey-Bass, 1968).

35. William A. Scott, *Values and Organizations* (Chicago, Ill.: Rand McNally, 1965), p. 3.

36. Gordon W. Allport, "Attitudes," in C. Murchison (ed.), *A Handbook of Social Psychology* (Worcester, Mass.: Clark University Press, 1935), p. 798. See also Charles A. Kiesler, *The Psychology of Commitment* (New York: Academic, 1971), p. 4.

37. Kiesler, *The Psychology of Commitment,* p. 4.

38. Eugene L. Hartley and Ruth E. Hartley, *Fundamentals of Social Psychology* (New York: Alfred A. Knopf, 1952), p. 657.

39. R. M. Hainer, "Rationalism, Pragmatism, and Existentialism: Perceived but Undiscovered Multicultural Problems," in Evelyn Glatt and Maynard W. Shelly (eds.), *The Research Society* (New York: Gordon and Breach, 1968), pp. 7-50. The analysis can be further elaborated, as by including such other isms as materialism, defined as related to personal income and organizational productivity. Allyn A. Morrow and Frederick C. Thayer, "Materialism and Humanism: Organization Theory's Odd Couple," *Administration and Society,* Vol. 10 (May 1978), esp. p. 86, focus on the long history of attempts to reconcile two contradictory premises, and they recommend giving up in that regard by abandoning materialism, as by separating work from income.

40. Frank Friedlander, "OD Reaches Adolescence," *Journal of Applied Behavioral Science,* Vol. 12 (January 1976), pp. 7-21.

41. Ibid., p. 7.

42. Ibid., pp. 17-18.

43. Ethan A. Singer and Leland M. Wooton, "The Triumph and Failure of Albert Speer's Administrative Genius," *Journal of Applied Behavioral Science,* Vol. 12 (January 1976), pp. 79-103.

44. Ibid., pp. 82-85.

45. Ibid., p. 79.

46. David K. Hart and William G. Scott, "The Organizational Imperative," *Administration and Society,* Vol. 7 (November 1975), esp. pp. 269-282.

47. Patrick E. Conner, "Assumptions and Values in OD: Some Critical Observations." Paper presented at the Annual Meeting, Academy of Management, August 1975.

48. George Strauss, "Organizational Development: Credits and Debits," *Organizational Dynamics,* Vol. 1 (Winter 1973), p. 15.

49. Richard E. Walton and Donald P. Warwick, "The Ethics of Organization Development," *Journal of Applied Behavioral Science,* Vol. 9 (November 1973), p. 686-688.

50. Ibid., pp. 689-693.

51. Gordon A. Walter, "Organizational Development and Individual Rights." Faculty of Commerce and Business Administration, University of British Columbia, Working Paper No. 286 (November 1974).

52. B. F. Skinner, *Beyond Freedom and Dignity* (New York: Alfred A. Knopf, 1973).

53. Arthur Blumberg and Robert T. Golembiewski, *Learning and Change in Groups* (London: Penguin, 1976), pp. 135-136.

54. For a careful treatment of the capstone work of the leading figure in the tradition, see Finley Carpenter, *The Skinner Primer* (New York: The Free Press, 1974). From a management and organization perspective, Craig Eric Schneier provides a comprehensive analysis in "Behavior Modification in Management: A Review and a Critique," *Academy of Management Journal,* Vol. 17 (September 1974), pp. 528-548.

55. Perry London, *Behavior Control* (New York: Harper and Row, 1969).

56. Ibid., pp. 40-41.

57. Edwin A. Locke, "The Myths of Behavior Mode in Organizaitons," *Academy of Management Review,* Vol. 2 (October 1977), p. 544.

58. B. F. Skinner, "The Steep and Thorny Way to a Science of Behavior," *American Psychologist,* Vol. 30 (1975), pp. 42-49.

59. Locke, "The Myths of Behavior," p. 543.

60. Carpenter, *The Skinner Primer,* pp. 12-13.

61. Ibid., p. 13.

62. Victor V. Gamboa, *Beyond Skinner With Dignity: An Investigation of the Application of Behavior Modification in Industrial Settings.* Unpublished doctoral dissertation, University of Michigan, Ann Arbor, 1974.

63. "Conversation with B. F. Skinner," *Organizational Dynamics,* Vol. 1 (1973), p. 40.

64. Carpenter, *The Skinner Primer,* p. 15.

65. Robert T. Golembiewski, *Men, Management, and Morality* (New York: McGraw-Hill, 1965).

66. For a brief review of such "growth psychologies," consult Robert T. Golembiewski, "Structuring the Public Organization," in H. George Frederickson and Robert Agronoff (eds.), *Public Administration for the Professionals* (Itasca, Ill.: F.E. Peacock, 1979).

67. Illustratively, see Donald D. Bowen, "Value Dilemmas in Organization Development," *Journal of Applied Behavioral Science*, Vol. 13 (October 1977), pp. 543-557.

68. Frank Friedlander and L. D. Brown, "Organization Development," in M. R. Rosenzweig and L. W. Porter (eds.), *Annual Review of Psychology*, Vol. 25 (Palo Alto, Calif.: Annual Reviews, 1974).

69. W. Robert Nay, *Behavioral Intervention* (New York: Gardner Press, 1976), pp. 319-334.

70. Ibid., pp. 3-13, presents a useful contrast of three approaches to treatment or learning.

71. Ibid., p. 9.

72. For example, see Richard E. Walton and Donald P. Warwick, "The Ethics of Organization Development," *Journal of Applied Behavioral Science*, Vol. 9 (November 1973), pp. 681-699.

73. Ethan A. Singer and Leland M. Wooton, "The Triumph and Failure of Albert Speer's Administrative Genius," *Journal of Applied Behavioral Science*, Vol. 12 (January 1976), pp. 79-103.

74. See Salancik and Pfeffer, "An Examination of Need–Satisfaction Models."

75. For example, see Robert T. Golembiewski, Frank Gibson, and Gerald Miller (eds.), *Managerial Behavior and Organization Demands* (Itasca, Ill.: F.E. Peacock, 1978), esp. pp. 350-360.

76. The point is elaborated in Fritz Steele and Stephen Jenks, *The Feel of the Work Place* (Reading, Mass.: Addison-Wesley, 1977).

77. Consult, for example, Leonard Goodstein, *Consulting with Human Service Systems* (Reading, Mass.: Addison-Wesley, 1978).

78. Fred Schaum makes such an argument in detail in Chapter 7 of Robert T. Golembiewski and Richard J. Hilles, *Toward the Responsive Organization* (Salt Lake City, Utah: Brighton, 1978).

79. For a major exception, see David Berlew and William E. LeClere, "Social Intervention in Curacao," *Journal of Applied Behavioral Science*, Vol. 10 (January 1974), pp. 29-52.

80. The prototype design was reported in Robert T. Golembiewski and Alan Kiepper, "MARTA: Toward an Effective, Open Giant," *Public Administration Review*, Vol. 36 (January 1976), pp. 46-60.

81. R. Wayne Boss, David J. Gouws, and Takeshi Nagai, "The Cross-Cultural Effects of An OD Intervention: A Conflict-Confrontation Design," *Southern Review of Public Administration,* Vol. 1 (March 1978), pp. 486-502.

82. Cary L. Cooper, Ned Levine, and Koichiro Kobayashu, "Developing One's Potential: From West to East," *Group and Organization Studies,* Vol. 1 (March 1976), pp. 43-55.

83. Micro-sociology has isolated many such interesting and useful proclivities. For broad perspective, see Robert Sommer, *Personal Space: The Behavioral Basis of Design* (Englewood Cliffs, N.J.: Prentice-Hall, 1969).

84. Marvin Weisbord, for example, explains the great difficulties in successful OD interventions in hospitals in similar terms of several partially congruent systems. See his "Why Organizational Development Hasn't Worked (So Far) In Medical Centers," *Health Care Management Review,* Vol. 1 (Spring 1976), pp. 17-28.

85. Robert T. Golembiewski and Arthur Blumberg (eds.), *Sensitivity Training and the Laboratory Approach* (Itasca, Ill.: F.E. Peacock, 1977), esp. pp. 1-120.

86. Leonard W. Doob and William J. Foltz, "Voices from a Belfast Workshop," *Social Change,* Vol. 5, no. 3 (1975), pp. 1-3 and 6-7.

87. Mason Haire, Edward Ghiselli, and Lyman W. Porter, *Managerial Thinking* (New York: John Wiley and Sons, 1966), esp. Chapters 4 and 5.

88. An extreme case-in-opposition is the havoc wrought to Soviet agriculture when professionals (in this case, biologists, agronomists, and so on) were forced to subject knowledge to hierarchy and to ideology, under the threat of death in many cases. For chilling details, see David Joravsky, *The Lysenko Affair* (Cambridge, Mass.: Harvard University Press, 1970).

89. See Robert T. Golembiewski, Frank Gibson, and Geoffrey Y. Cornog (eds.), *Public Administration* (Chicago, Ill.: Rand McNally College Publishing, 1976), esp. pp. 135-159, 227-249, and 482-504.

90. Sherman Kingsbury, "Tell Me Exactly What You Think, Even If It Costs You Your Job." Paper presented at Annual Meeting, Academy of Management, San Francisco, Calif., August 1978.

Chapter 3

THE LABORATORY APPROACH
TO ORGANIZATION DEVELOPMENT
Perspectives on Practice and Theory

This chapter has a dual and hopefully integrated character. It seeks to elaborate on both the practice and the theory of Organization Development (OD). This involves sketching the burgeoning practical experience in one of the booming areas of the behavioral sciences during the last decade or so. Moreover, this chapter emphasizes the still-massive gaps in that knowledge, especially in our theoretical comprehension of what goes on in OD efforts.

The emphasis on OD *as practice* will concentrate on illustrating the range of OD designs, as well as on sketching some of their essential features. The primary focus in this chapter will be on the "laboratory stem" or the "interaction-centered" features of OD, although that focus will not be a monomania. Full-scale OD programs typically also will involve variable emphasis on policies and procedures, as well as structures for jobs and organizations. Part 2 of this revision will emphasize these latter features. Very often, interaction-centered designs will pave the way for an emphasis on policies, procedures, and structures. The common element tying together these two classes of designs is provided by the values discussed in Chapter 2. A tolerable simplification of those OD values is that they urge shifting the balance in all relationships—from dyadic ones to membership in huge collective enterprises—from repression toward freedom, as far as that is possible.

The focal emphasis on OD *as theory* is easy to state, but it is impossible at present to deal with satisfactorily. The focal question may be put in a few words: Why does the technology called the laboratory approach to OD seem to work? It will take many, many words to establish that we have no really complete answer to this focal question.[1] Although there is no satisfactory way to deal with this key question, some beginnings to an answer are hazarded here, and their thrust is simple. The laboratory approach to OD seems to work because it provides for both individuals and organizations what they seem to need, and need very badly. This humble point will be developed in some detail, with the initial focus on individuals and then later on organizations.

Perspectives on OD as Practice
Descriptions and Designs

OD has evolved as a response to what needs doing for individuals in organizations. While we wait for the development of valid and reliable indicators of various degrees of "health" or "illness," an unenlightened organizational world whirls on, and OD specialists can either leap aboard to try to help, or they can pout. Short of the millennium, that is, numerous designs need to be developed that seek to approach the goals of the laboratory approach to OD, both particularistic and comprehensive designs. This section proposes to

- Detail some initial content for the OD concept
- Sketch some overall features of OD as an educational process
- Highlight five special characteristics of OD
- Circumscribe the scope of OD in numerous particulars
- Provide a substantial sense of the range of OD designs

OD at Four Levels of Meaning

Four levels of meaning—philosophic, operating, strategic, and tactical—give some initial working content to the term Organization Development. Philosophically, OD is nothing less than "a reorientation of man's thinking and behavior toward his organizations," in the words of Lyman K. Randall, and "views man and change optimistically." He adds that OD ideology also stresses that

> people have the capability and motivation to grow through learning how to improve their own work climate, work process, and their resulting products. It accepts as inevitable the conflicts among the needs of individuals, work groups, and the organization but advocates openly confronting those conflicts using problem-solving strategies.[2]

In an operating sense, OD programs have several major distinguishing features. They are (1) *planned* programs, that (2) involve some meaningful *system* of work, (3) that are managed by the *top responsible officials* who are both aware of and committed to the program and its objectives, (4) which are conceived as *long-term efforts,* (5) whose thrust is to improve *organizational effectiveness* by (6) *interventions* that focus on interpersonal and group process via (7) the applications of behavioral science knowledge basically through *experiential learning* which (8) is *action-oriented* rather than concerned only with increases in knowledge, skills, or understanding.[3]

What about the major directions in which these operating features are applied? Alexander Winn explains that OD "implies a normative, re-education strategy intended to affect systems of beliefs, values and attitudes" that will permit more timely and effective responses to technological or broader social changes. In turn, these normative and behavioral changes may also trigger, facilitate, and reinforce compatible restructuring of formal work and reporting relationships.[4]

Tactically, OD programs can be used to induce a broad family of organizational changes. Only a huge list could exhaustively catalog those uses. OD programs can analyze and help change or review:[5]

- Managerial strategies
- Organization climates that are inconsistent with individual needs or changing environmental demands
- Organization structures and related job roles
- An organization's culture or associated norms
- Ineffective patterns of intergroup collaboration
- Communication systems that block or distort the flow of information
- Inadequate planning processes
- The motivation of a workforce
- Policies and procedures that were adaptations to an environment which is changing
- Patterns of relationships between individuals and groups, as in mergers or unmergers

In sum, it is necessary to take a systems view in an OD effort, to consider the probable effects of a change in one part on other parts. The organization is seen as a network of overlapping individual and group systems, with the OD goal being a more effective integration and meshing of all systems.

OD as an Educational Process

To make a critical point again, OD also can be described as an educational process which constitutes a new way of looking at the human side of life in organizations. In Beckhard's terms, this involves enhancing the attitudes and skills of organization members that relate to "self-awareness, communication skills, ability to manage conflict, and tolerance for ambiguity—all essential requirements for the organization leader in today's and tomorrow's world."[6] Resting on such common social and psychological foundations, OD programs can flower diversely, as the bulk of this volume will testify.

Sherwood provides useful detail about OD as an educational process. According to Sherwood,[7] OD seeks to develop "self-renewing, self-correcting systems of people who learn to organize themselves in a variety of ways according to the nature of their tasks, and who continue to cope with changing demands the environment makes on the organization." The underlying educational process is one which identifies applicable human resources in the organization, expands them, and allocates them to improve the problem-solving capabilities of the organization. Somewhat more specifically, again relying in part on Sherwood, the laboratory approach to OD can be described as (1) a long-range effort to consciously introduce planned change into an organization in ways that involve its members, both in diagnosis of problems and prescriptions of change, (2) an effort which involves an entire organization, or some relatively coherent and meaningful subsystem of an organization (3) working toward the goal of greater organizational effectiveness by enlarging the array of reasonable organizational choices and by increasing the probability of self-renewal and constructive adaptation, by (4) intervening in the ongoing activities of an organization in ways that facilitate learning by broad segments of its members and that also facilitate the making of choices from among alternative ways to proceed (5) with the common resultant need to change behaviors or values or attitudes, which must be distinguished from "changing personality," which has the flavor of changing men into angels, and (6) with the common need to deal with "system problems" and "structure problems," as well as with "people problems."

Five Specific Characteristics of OD

Several characteristics implicit in these global descriptions of OD as an educational process deserve spotlighting. *First,* the basic OD learning strategy is experiential. As in the T-group, the locus is "in here" rather than "out there."

Second, the laboratory approach to OD emphasizes the "how" as contrasted with the "what." It fixates on action—on the specific action, on processes or methods for achieving, testing, and (if necessary) changing interpersonal and intergroup relationships required for effective performance. Many policies, procedures, or structures will be compatible with this specific "how."

This broad statement requires tethering in two senses. Paramountly, the laboratory approach to OD does not serve as a gun for hire for any purpose. In sharp contrast, applications of the laboratory approach need to be constrained by broad ranges of values that define the essentials of the philosophy and internal logic of this specific technology for change. Relatedly, the laboratory approach to OD is not essentially a technology for "management by consensus," as some critics take pains to contend. The technology primarily stresses the quality of interpersonal and intergroup relationships, as well as the adequacy of communication networks to isolate and resolve current problems. The technology is compatible with many organization structures and mechanisms for decision-making.

A broad consensus does motivate the laboratory approach to OD, but one more elemental than some decision-making mechanism or structure. That primal consensus, in the words of Kenneth D. Benne, urges that individuals in organizations go beyond "the conventional and parochial certainties of unquestioned group identifications and loyalties." He concludes that:

> In affirming the inescapability of grappling with the demands of groups and organizations, contemporary men must at the same time learn how to alter, how to build and rebuild group and organizational patterns, even as they participate in them, with an eye to the values of personal freedom and spontaneity. Such learning is facilitated by the kind of clear-eyed and socially supported look into the abyss which T-Group experience provides.[8]

In its dominant focus on action—on methods *for achieving, testing,* and *changing* interpersonal relationships for effective performance—OD constitutes a truly revolutionary departure from much organizational analysis, which tends to be *concept oriented.* In the laboratory approach—and especially in interaction-centered designs—one may almost say there is no such thing as a bad concept for change. Only more or less adequate behavioral commitment to a concept determines success or failure, to exaggerate the point somewhat.

Third, the laboratory approach to OD fixates on increasing valid information, generating additional and reasonable choices, and developing active resources in the host organization. In principle, these may seem reasonable fixations, and benign ones in the bargain. In practice, however, increasing information and choices usually requires raising issues that some power-wielders may prefer to leave undisturbed. That is, the laboratory approach to OD can raise issues that strike to the heart of the organizational ties that bind. These are not tasks for the fainthearted: increasing information, raising alternatives, and developing resources.

Fourth, the development of a collaborative relationship preoccupies the laboratory approach to OD. Basically, changes or choices must be made and the underlying information gathered in ways that enhance the commitment of organization members to the decision.

On this point, OD applications walk a tightrope. The subtleties can be illustrated. Essentially, OD works with existing organizational centers of power. But, OD programs will at least increasingly challenge these centers of power to become more open to a wide variety of influence attempts.[9] The situation has inherent in it a broad range of possible perversions. This range includes OD practitioners serving as lackeys of the power-wielders or acting as quiet subverters of all authority. The *via media* is a hard road.

Fifth, OD programs have a relational thrust. Overall, they seek to relate individual needs and organization goals, to increase their congruence for mutual benefit. The tendency to attempt to make a whole from some set of parts, to relate several sets of needs or demands, is also common in OD efforts.

The Scope of OD

Beyond such general features, substantial agreement exists about the boundary conditions that circumscribe a successful application. Three such boundaries help stake out the territory of OD: (1) the typical set of objectives underlying OD programs; (2) some assumptions implied by these typical objectives; and (3) some broad agreements about the linkages of individual learning with organization change, as well as about the inadequacies of the available research as it relates to these agreements.

These three kinds of boundaries conveniently imply why the technology tends to work; and they also suggest the broad range of payoffs for individuals and their organizations when the technology does work. Hence, the three sections below do multiple duty.

Major Objectives of Typical OD Programs

Within the context of releasing the human potential within an organization, specific OD efforts will emphasize major objectives such as these:[10]

- To create an open, problem-solving climate throughout the organization so that problems can be confronted, rather than fought about or fled from
- To build trust among individuals and groups throughout the organization, whether the linkages are vertical ones between superiors and subordinates, horizontal ones between peers, or diagonal ones between individuals of different ranks in different units of organization
- To supplement the authority associated with role or status with the authority of knowledge and competence
- To locate decision-making and problem-solving responsibilities as close to the information sources as possible
- To make competition where it exists contribute more to the meeting of work goals, as where organization units compete in producing a good or service more efficiently and effectively, as opposed to win/lose competition

- To maximize collaboration between individuals and units whose work is interdependent

- To develop a reward system which recognizes both the achievement of the organization's mission (profits or service) and human development (growth of people)

- To increase the sense of ownership of organization objectives throughout the work force

- To help managers to manage according to relevant objectives rather than according to "past practices," or according to objectives which do not make sense for one's area of responsibility

- To increase self-control and self-direction for people within the organization

- To create conditions where conflict is brought out and managed

- To increase awareness of group "process" and its consequences for performance—that is, to help persons become aware of what is happening between and to group members while the group is working on the task—for example, communication, influence, feelings, leadership styles and struggles, relationships between groups, how conflict is managed, and so on

These common OD objectives come to a sharp focus in which, basically, the organization is seen as a system in need of continuing innovation, where the goal is nothing less than the creation of a more humane and effective organization.

Some Assumptions of Typical OD Efforts

As with all systems of social theory and practice, the conceptual foundations of OD also include a variety of more-or-less explicit assumptions about how the world is or ought to be. This is neither good nor bad; it is simply inevitable. The prudent person can only be as clear as possible about these assumptions. In that spirit, Exhibit 1 is a continuation of the persistent effort in these early pages to make the OD foundation as explicit as possible. Some of the assumptions have various degrees of empirical support, while others are more in the nature of value preferences.

Diverse OD Designs for Common Goals

No wonder, then, that a broad range of learning designs has been developed to do the multitudinous things that OD intervenors aspire to accomplish. This section introduces several OD designs for working toward the common goals of a more effective and satisfying worksite.

Exhibit 1   Some Assumptions Underlying Typical OD Objectives

- Work which is organized to meet people's needs as well as to achieve organizational requirements tends to produce the highest productivity and quality of production.
- Most members of organizations are not motivated primarily by an avoidance of work for which tight controls and threats of punishment are necessary—but, rather, most individuals seek challenging work and desire responsibility for accomplishing organizational objectives to which they are committed.
- The basic building blocks of organizations are groups of people; therefore, the basic units of change are also groups, not simply individuals.
- The culture of most organizations tends to suppress the open expression of feelings which people have about each other and about where they and their organization are heading. The suppression of feelings can adversely affect problem-solving, personal growth, and satisfaction with one's work.
- Groups which learn to work in a constructively open way by providing feedback for members become more able to profit from their own experience and become more able to fully utilize their resources on the task. Furthermore, the growth of individual members is facilitated by relationships which are open, supportive, and trusting.
- "People support what they help create." Where change is introduced, it will be most effectively implemented if the groups and individuals involved have a sense of ownership in the process. Commitment is most assuredly attained where there is active participation in the planning and conduct of the change.
- The basic value underlying all OD theory and practice is that of *choice*. Through the collection and feedback of relevant data—made available by trust, openness, and risk—more choice becomes available to the organization and to the individual, and hence better decisions can be made.

Source: From John J. Sherwood, *An Introduction to Organization Development,* Experimental Publication System. Washington, D.C.: American Psychological Association, no. 11 (April 1971), Ms. no. 396-1. Copyright 1971 by the American Psychological Association. Reprinted by permission. Also reprinted in J. W. Pfeiffer and J. E. Jones (eds.), *1972 Annual Handbook for Group Facilitators* (Iowa City, Iowa: University Associates, 1972).

The Range of OD Designs

Our focus is on a continuum. It extends from special and limited-purpose OD designs, and extends through comprehensive efforts to change large sociotechnical systems. Designs at each end of this continuum will get some attention, in turn. All these designs seek in common to improve an organization's health, and they rest on the participants' willingness to seek to work more collaboratively. Building from that essential agreement, OD designs proceed by simultaneously:[11]

- *Working with* the people who are affected by particular proposed changes in the organization.
- *Linking* to all those who can influence the outcome.
- Forming a tentative *general goal* which, by joint process, will convert to a specific group goal.

- Working on *changing the quality of relationships* from one in which the individual is conditioned to isolation, destructive competition, and interpersonal conflict ("I'm up—you're down") to one of collaboration and healthy competition ("we"). To bring about such a change, the manager must encourage direct and open communication and set an example.
- Building active *feedback* loops from all knowledgeable sources so that organization members can perceive the shape of events as realistically as possible and can monitor their organization's progress.

And now on to examples of both limited-purpose and comprehensive OD designs.

Some Limited-Purpose OD Designs.   Exhibit 2 sketches a number of special and limited-purpose designs. Generally, the designs are run in the presence of skilled resource persons, who often are called change agents or interventionists.

The designs do not constitute peas in a pod. They differ widely in crucial particulars—the breadth of their purposes, the complexity of the phenomena likely to be encountered, the probable level of threat experienced by participants, and the skills required for successful coping by participants. Some are best applied only after participants have some prior experience with the values, skills, and behaviors consistent with the laboratory approach.

More or less, the first four designs in Exhibit 2 deal with the diagnosis of existing and limited situations. These designs are:

- Manager in a consulting pair
- Manager's diagnostic meeting
- Team diagnostic meeting
- Goal-setting and planning groups

Skilled resource persons in such designs normally can provide gentle if necessary guidance consistent with the goals of the laboratory approach. This generalization holds even for rather large populations who are naive about OD goals, values, and attitudes.

For the last three designs in Exhibit 2, particularly, the emphasis is more decisively on changing some existing and complex situation, as well as on diagnosing it. There is a quantum difference between the four designs named above and the following three:

- Third-party interventions
- Internal team-building
- Interface team-building

Exhibit 2   Some OD Designs

- *Manager in a Consulting Pair.* The parties are a manager and a resource person from outside the manager's immediate organization, with the manager and consultant developing a close and continuing relationship for the purpose of early sharing of problems and possible solutions.
- *Manager's Diagnostic Meeting.* The learning group is the manager, an outside resource person, and some one or few resources with organizationwide responsibility, such as personnel managers.

  The focus is on diagnosis of the manager's workteam, to consider the need for change or improvement under conditions of low threat to the manager.
- *Team Diagnostic Meeting.* The learning group is an organizational family, a manager, and his immediate work group.

  The diagnosis may center on specific tasks or problems, or it may have a summary quality, as by considering issues:
  - a. What we do best
  - b. What we do worst
- *Goal-Setting and Planning Groups.* These may either be individual pairs of superiors-subordinates, or they may be individual family teams throughout the organization.

  The focus is on systematic review of performance that leads to the setting of targets or goals, that are the products of mutual commitments. Progress toward the goals or plans will be mutually reviewed.
- *Interface Groups.* The learning groups may be composed of different functional specialties, such as sales and engineering, labor and management, the managements of two organizations working through a merger, or organizational insiders and an outside group such as customers or clients.

  As many as 100 or more persons may participate, usually meeting for a day or less, and the emphasis is on groups rather than individuals. These three factors limit the intensity of the design.

  As Sherwood explains, such groups are "a problem-solving mechanism when problems are known to exist. An action-research format is used. The entire management group of an organization is brought together, problems and attitudes are collected and shared, priorities are established, commitments to action are made through setting targets and assigning task forces."[d]

  Three types of interface groups are common:
  - a. *Mirror Groups.* This design allows some inside group to get feedback from one or more key clientele groups to whom it relates. e.g. customers, suppliers, or inside users of the target group's services.

    This is a one-way confrontation. The target group sees itself mirrored, as if were, by the clientele group. The target group does not mirror back.

    The design can end with proposals to improve conditions, which usually are generated by mixed teams each having members from the target group and from the clientele groups. The mixed teams report back their suggestions to the total group.
  - b. *Goal-Setting Interface Groups.* Representatives from several related groups of organization units meet to set goals for action or change, usually on quite specific issues.

    The basic work is typically done in mixed subgroups of five or six members representing each group or unit so as to facilitate cross-fertilization in the collection of information and the setting of goals.

    The subgroups report back to the total population of participants, and some known procedure is used to integrate the results. For example, a manager might take the results as inputs to guide his decision-making. Or a steering committee composed of one representative from each subgroup might prepare a composite report for all participants, or for some manager or group of managers.
  - c. *Confrontation Groups.* Here two or more groups are brought together, such as black employees and white employees, to begin building a relationship or to repair a defective one. The groups share perceptions of how they see themselves and others, with the intent of surfacing issues, letting the groups know how they are perceived, and permitting groups to compare their own group concepts with perceptions of others.

    The intent of such a design is to "clear the air," to provide a realistic and open base on which to build relationships. Such a meeting typically concludes with an action phase: What can be done to do what needs to be done?
- *Third-Party Interventions.* These OD interventions use a skilled third person to help in the diagnosis and resolution of difficult human problems between two individuals or two groups.

Exhibit 2   (Continued)

The purpose is to provide an outside perspective that may be unavailable to the parties in difficulty, and to use the third person as a trusted agent to begin rebuilding relationships between the parties.

■ *Internal Team-Building.* The learning group consists typically of a manager and one or more levels of his immediate subordinates, up to a limit of 15 or so participants.

The focus is on work problems, and especially on their early identification and solution. The broad emphasis is on interpersonal, procedural, and organization blockages to effective functioning. The design is distinguished by depth of analysis, scrutiny of interpersonal relations, and focus on individuals.

Interpersonal relations in team-building can be variously improved, as by working on: (1) increased openness and owning of ideas and feelings; (2) heightened mutual trust, acceptance, and understanding of team members; or (3) changing patterns of communication.

Procedural and organizational blockages can receive major attention, as by adapting differentiated procedures for different tasks or by analyzing patterns of delegation to isolate and possibly eliminate their awkward consequences.

■ *Interface Team-Building.* Involves two or more groups, separate organization units, simultaneously dealing with the same kinds of issues that are encountered in internal team-building.

This design is extremely complicated and demanding, since it also deals with complex intergroup phenomena such as intergroup competition or the presence of two or more coequal authority figures.

---

[a]John J. Sherwood, *An Introduction to Organization Development,* Experimental Publication System. Washington, D.C.: American Psychological Association no. 11 (April 1971), Ms. no. 396-1.
Source: R. T. Golembiewski, *Renewing Organizations: The Laboratory Approach to Planned Change* (Itasca, Ill.: F. E. Peacock, 1972).

Substantial proportions of the learning populations, at least, will have appropriate values, attitudes, and behavioral skills prior to experiencing the last three kinds of designs. The first two chapters of Part 1 define these appropriate values, attitudes, and behavioral skills. In their absence, the three designs immediately above are unlikely to be effective.

The three kinds of interface groups may be considered intermediate in complexity and in skills and attitudes required of participants. They can be ranked in terms of increasing threat and potential complexity, as below. The three kinds of interface groups pose somewhat more formidable challenges than the first three OD designs, more or less in this order:

- Mirror groups
- Goal-setting interface groups
- Confrontation groups

These different designs imply differing needs for prior experience by participants. Certainly no later than immediately before or after the time an organization progresses to OD designs using interface groups, a dose of T-group experience is recommended to provide some in-depth experience with the laboratory approach. "Sensitivity training may be viewed as basic training" for the latter three OD designs, at least, to quote Jack Fordyce and Raymond Weil, who make a similar distinction between OD designs.[12]

A Comprehensive OD Design.   Without doubt the most comprehensive OD design is based on Robert Blake's Managerial Grid®* whose inner logic can be sketched here.[13]   Basically, Blake's educational program rests on an elaboration of the Grid described below, around which are built six overlapping phases of an OD program.   The first two phases deal with managerial development, more specifically, and the latter four phases with organization development proper.

Phase I: Grid Seminars.   The introduction to the Grid design for OD is a week-long seminar, spent either in stranger or cousin groups of small size. Cousin groups are members of the same total organization who generally have not worked with one another before and who will not do so immediately after the training. The heart of the experience includes a variety of team tasks, in which individual and group problem-solving styles are interpreted in terms of the "Grid." In one exercise, for example, each participant gets feedback from members of his team concerning their impressions of his managerial style. Using a 9 X 9 grid, whose axes are "concern for people" and "concern for production," a participant may be described as a

- 1,1 Manager, who has minimum concern for both people and production
- 1,9 Manager, who gives thoughtful attention to the needs of people and helps induce a comfortable, friendly, but slow-paced tempo at work
- 5,5 Manager, who trades off satisfactory morale for satisfactory output
- 9,1 Manager, who seeks high levels of efficiency in operations by arranging work so that human elements interfere in minimum degree
- 9,9 Manager, who seeks significant accomplishment at work through committed people, whose interdependence rests on relationships of trust and respect

Phase I constitutes a pump primer and is not expected to produce immediate effects in organizations; it basically seeks to expose participants to a certain kind of face-to-face feedback experience.

Phase II: Team Development.   This is the initial on-the-job extension of Phase I, in which each manager and his or her subordinates make use of grid experience and vocabulary to explore managerial styles and operating practices. The thrust is to use 9,9 concepts at work and to develop a 9,9 style.

*The word "Grid" is a registered service mark of Scientific Methods, Inc.

Phase III: Intergroup Development.   The focus here is on extending 9,9 concepts and style beyond individual work groups. The goal is to move groups from win or lose competition to joint problem-solving, and complex subdesigns are tailored to individual situations in specific organizations.

Phase IV: Organizational Goal-Setting.   The orientation here is to move toward areas that require commitment at many organization levels, as in cost control or labor-management relations. In contrast to earlier phases which use learning vehicles representing one or a few hierarchic levels, devices like the "diagonal slice" are used to develop special task forces composed of individuals representing several functions and several levels of organization.

Phase V: Goal Attainment.   Given the problem areas isolated by the special task forces, other teams are set up throughout the organization to sharpen statements of problems, clarify goals, and assign responsibilities for necessary action.[14]

Phase VI: Stabilization.   This phase serves to reinforce changes made in earlier phases, as well as to evaluate and build on that experience to inhibit regression.

Survey/Feedback in OD Designs

Whether the OD design is limited purpose or comprehensive, survey/feedback features are likely to be prominent in them, more or less in direct proportion to the size and geographical dispersion of the host organization. Basically, survey/feedback

- Utilizes the power of survey research techniques to gather data about the host organization
- Uses such information as feedback to the host organization
  To test the adequacy of the organization's information processing
  Perhaps to motivate change, as by posing dilemmas or problems and inducing motivation to resolve them
  To provide a benchmark pretest against which to measure the effectiveness of any subsequent efforts at change

Survey/feedback approaches come in a kaleidoscopic array of variants,[15] but they basically seek to induce processes of disclosure and feedback for purposes very much like those sketched above for individuals. Survey/feedback technology is merely an adaptation to the large size of many organizations, as well as to the common dispersal of their subunits over wide geographic areas.[16] The goal of the technology is much the same as the goal of a person who approaches a friend, and notes: "It is important for me to know how you perceived me in that incident. Please level with me, whether the information is good or bad."

Survey/feedback variants are illustrated at a number of points below. Sometimes the "survey" is based on depth-interviews by a consultant, who reports his findings to some managerial group or work unit. Chapter 6 (Part 1) contains several examples of such interview/feedback designs. Sometimes the "survey" involves large numbers of responses to a laboriously constructed and tested questionnaire. The underlying technologies and skills differ substantially, but their goal is the same: to stimulate disclosure and feedback conveniently.

Survey/feedback designs have long been central in what has come to be known as OD,[17] and every evidence implies a sharply growing reliance on that class of designs.[18] While not yet *the* design of choice, survey/feedback has contributed substantially to the growing effort to develop large organizational systems that are more efficient and effective, more productive and more humane. Early OD tended to emphasize individual team-building, often at the top level of organization, with interview/feedback being the common design, following the precedent of the earliest team-building efforts.[19]

Guidelines for Survey/Feedback Designs.   Over the years, several more or less firm guidelines have come to be accepted as especially useful for generating the kind of systemic change envisioned by survey/feedback. These guidelines include such common features,[20] despite numerous variations.

- *Preliminary planning involves members of the organizational elite, typically utilizing an independent, external consultant.* The purposes are multiple, but basically seek to increase the survey instrument's credibility and to enhance the probability that the elite will later use the resulting data for action-planning. Such involvement is especially critical when the survey instrument implies a model of organization excellence,[21] as several possible instruments do.[22] If top management does not accept this implied model, of course, much mischief may derive from action plans based on the data.

- *The survey instrument is administered to all members of the target system.* Sampling often would be technically adequate, but the total population is usually surveyed for motivational and symbolic reasons.

- *Typically, the external consultant processes the survey data, arrays the results, suggests approaches to diagnosis, and often provides help in analyzing the data.*

- *Data feedback from the consultant begins at the top of the target system, either to the top manager or executive team.*

- *If the initial feedback is to the top manager only, a meeting with subordinates is held soon thereafter to* discuss and interpret the data, make diagnoses of problem-areas, develop plans for action based on these diagnoses, and prepare to introduce data at the next hierarchical level.

- *Commonly, especially in large systems, "waterfalls" or "cascades" of data feedback*—an "interlocking chain of conferences"—*are then provided for successive lower organization levels.*[23] An external consultant may be available or the managers may handle such iterations by themselves.

Why and How Survey/Feedback Designs Seem to Work.   Primarily, survey/feedback designs have proliferated for two reasons. They permit the convenience of survey methods, which are all but necessary in large target systems. Moreover, such designs seem to have attractive motivational consequences. This is a powerful combination.

The motivational potentialities of such designs seem quite obvious. On the basis of experience with an early survey/feedback effort, for example, Baumgartel concluded:[24]

> an intensive, group discussion procedure for utilizing the results of an employee questionnaire survey can be an effective tool for introducing positive change. . . . It may be that the effectiveness of this method, in comparison to traditional training courses, is that it deals with the system of human relationships as a whole (superior and subordinate can change together) and it deals with each manager, supervisor, and employee in the context of his or her own job, problems, and work relationships.

Massive subsequent experience with survey/feedback designs adds much reinforcing detail to Baumgartel's conclusion, but does not shake it in the least. Conveniently, Figure 1 abstracts this experience as to the motivational sources engaged by such designs. The figure should be self-explanatory. Basically, it provides that three components of survey/feedback designs—the data generated, the intensified interaction due to rounds of meetings, and the orientation toward "process" as well as "task"[25]—can contribute to more effective personal and organizational performance. The model patently has self-heightening features, as in the probabilities that effective performance will encourage additional flow of data as well as be induced by it.

Some Significant Qualifiers.   These general descriptions require tethering in several senses, lest enthusiasm overreach the available research and experience. Four qualifiers have a special salience.

First, although no definitive theory describes what happens, when, in survey/feedback designs, substantial confidence seems appropriate. A growing body of empirical research establishes the general efficacy of the design,[26] but hardly without deviant cases[27] or without partial confirmations that suggest the need to investigate intervening variables that may affect outcomes.[28]

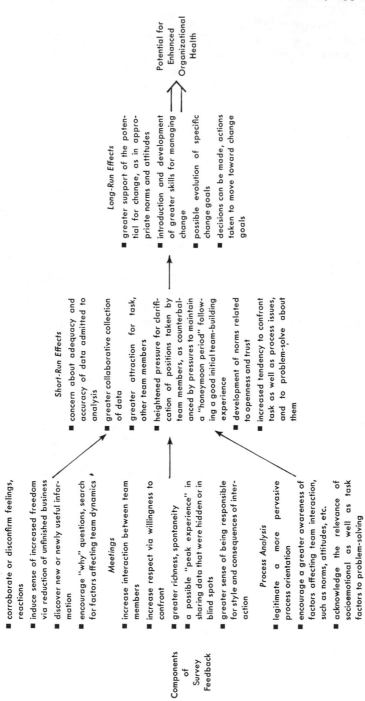

Figure 1 Idealized schema of survey/feedback design components and consequences. [Following Charles T. McElvaney and Matthew B. Miles, "Using Survey Feedback and Consultation," pp. 116-117, adapted from Richard A. Schmuck and Matthew B. Miles (eds.). *Organization Development in Schools* (LaJolla, Calif.: University Associates, 1976). Used with permission.]

Second, accumulating evidence implies that at least some aspects of survey/ feedback designs have a rather broad-band applicability in diverse cultures. The reader is directed to some recent research, both in industrially-developed[29] as well as in developing areas.[30]

Third, we still lack any clear appreciation of the cross-cultural effects of survey/feedback designs. But anecdotal evidence implies that some contextual factors contraindicate some OD designs.[31] Possibly, also, survey/feedback designs might be especially potent in some cultures, as where face-to-face confrontation is culturally proscribed.[32] For now, Gostkowski's advice seems most reasonable. The usefulness of survey research cannot be considered universal; it can be expected to vary with such conditions:[33]

- The general legitimacy of making contacts outside of primary groups or immediate reference groups
- The degree of direct expression by individuals of their own concerns, which is a function of institutions, mores, political freedom, and so on
- The degree to which respondents are acculturated to surveys and accept them as a "data-gathering device"

Such conditions, obviously, vary in major ways from one survey site to another, from one political jurisdiction to another, and from one organization to another.

Fourth, it appears that various differences between organizations in the "same" culture also may be important determinants of which OD techniques apply with what consequences under specific circumstances. The contingency theorists beginning with Lawrence and Lorsch[34] imply this caution, for example. Research is scarce, however, and promises only that increments in knowledge will be difficult to achieve.[35] Some empirical work does trace similar effects of the same OD design in two different kinds of target systems, for example, with the degree of effect varying in regular ways.[36] Associated issues are considered in some detail, especially in Chapters 8 and 9 of Part 2.

Flow Chart of a Typical OD Program

Whether OD programs are limited in purpose or comprehensive, to conclude this section on the range of learning designs, they tend to share a common developmental form, as in the flow chart in Figure 2. The flow chart is stylized, but it does depict the major generic activities in an OD program as well as the sequence of these activities.

The flow chart in Figure 2 of a typical OD program should be self-explanatory, in the main, but one feature deserves highlighting. That is, succeeding waves of an OD program typically deepen the intensity of the design elements. Thus, the interview-cum-feedback of the first wave is a less intense design than the team-building or sensitivity training that often come in the second wave.

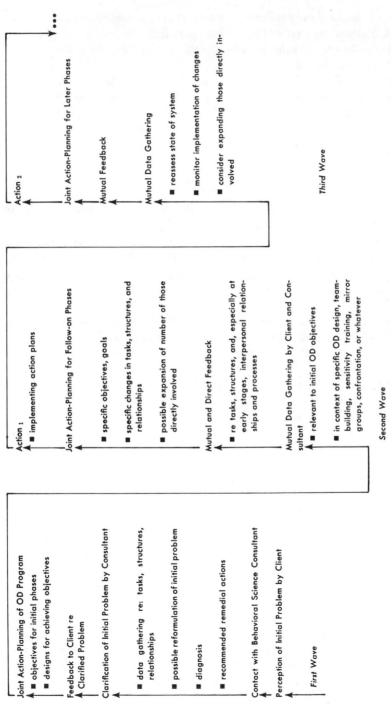

Figure 2 A flow chart of a typical OD program. (*Source:* Patterned after the Model of Wendel French, "Organization Development: Objectives, Assumptions and Strategies," copyright 1968 by the Regents of the University of California. Reprinted from *California Management Review,* Vol. 12, no. 2, pp. 23 to 34 by permission of the Regents.)

Moreover, succeeding waves of an OD program typically expand the number of organization members who are directly involved. These are not linear tendencies, however. As the circle of those involved expands to very large numbers, OD designs typically become less intense.

Perspectives on OD as Theory, I
Why the Technology Seems to Work for Individuals

There are numerous possible ways of viewing the laboratory approach as it applies to individual learning.[37] The vantage point here views the laboratory approach in the context of a model of developmental plateaus, each of which provides a socioemotional base for possible cycling to a new and higher level of understanding and awareness of self. Success is not certain, of course, and even hurtful regression is possible.[38]

An Existential Learning Theory

C. M. Hampden-Turner has developed one such cyclic model of special value.[39] He proposes an "existential learning theory" in the form of a "cycle of accumulating human experience" sketched in Figure 3. Three aspects of an individual's past developmental cycles generate a "base," or jumping-off point:

- The quality of his cognition, or that universe which includes the breadth of an individual's understanding, his sensitivity to the needs of others, or his ability to develop effective strategies for satisfying needs
- The clarity of her identity, or the quality of the ways in which an individual sees herself: for example, her awareness of self in relation to others, her consciousness of her behavior in various roles, and her growing differentiation from other people as a responsible individual actor
- The extent of his self-esteem, or the degree to which an individual values himself and others, the degree to which he can accept himself and others as needing to grow and to help others do so

These three factors in combination, Hampden-Turner notes, determine a person's level of overall interpersonal competence. See stage 4 in Figure 3, which proposes that the individual orders these three factors into a resultant state labeled "experienced and anticipated competence" (EAC). EAC provides a plateau from which an individual can attain greater development or learning. Conceivably, also, these three factors combine to form a plateau from which regression can occur.

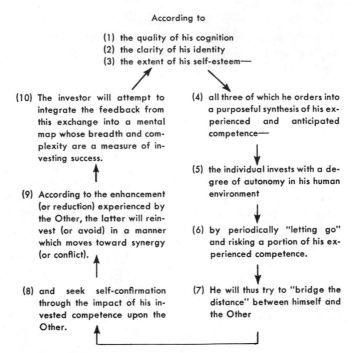

According to

(1) the quality of his cognition
(2) the clarity of his identity
(3) the extent of his self-esteem—

(10) The investor will attempt to integrate the feedback from this exchange into a mental map whose breadth and complexity are a measure of investing success.

(4) all three of which he orders into a purposeful synthesis of his experienced and anticipated competence—

(5) the individual invests with a degree of autonomy in his human environment

(9) According to the enhancement (or reduction) experienced by the Other, the latter will reinvest (or avoid) in a manner which moves toward synergy (or conflict).

(6) by periodically "letting go" and risking a portion of his experienced competence.

(8) and seek self-confirmation through the impact of his invested competence upon the Other.

(7) He will thus try to "bridge the distance" between himself and the Other

Figure 3   A cyclical model of individual development or learning. [*Source:* C. M. Hampden-Turner, "An Existential 'Learning Theory' and the Integration of T-Group Research," *Journal of Applied Behavioral Science,* Vol. 2 (October 1966), p. 368.]

The laboratory approach seeks to improve the probability of a new and higher level of insight and understanding. Hampden-Turner takes pains to establish, specifically, that the laboratory approach intends to improve the three components of overall competence he outlines: quality of cognition, clarity of identity, and extent of self-esteem. Early research implies that the approach can lay substantial claim to succeeding in this intention. For example, the laboratory approach emphasizes the development of increasing self-awareness in individuals, as well as an appreciation of the impact of their behavior on others.[40] A growing research literature suggests that this is achieved more often than not.[41] Subsequent chapters will deal with this literature in detail.

Given a certain level of "experienced and anticipated competence," as in Hampden-Turner's model, a cycling experience may begin. As stages 5 and 6 in Figure 3 represent, the individual willingly offers some part of her self-related "base" to others for acceptance or rejection. As her interaction systems are regenerative, to that degree will the individual be willing to expose herself to test her self-concepts at any particular plateau of understanding.

Stages 5 and 6 are critical in human growth or development; perhaps they are even the ultimate human act. Consider four points which establish the relation of the present model with the previous discussion of regenerative systems. *First,* the individual must act with a substantial degree of autonomy if he is to really *own* the results of the testing of self. As the individual is forced into such an investment, so will he be likely to resist any possible learning. Indeed, he may even feel psychological failure as he succeeds in learning. *Second,* the individual must strive to be *open* in dealing with others about self. That is, her base of experienced and anticipated competence will be meaningfully tested only to the degree that openness characterizes her interaction with others. By not informing others, in sum, she may only be handicapping herself. *Third,* the individual also must *risk* by "letting go." Hampden-Turner expresses the point with a penetrating directness: "I discover that I am valuable and meaningful to the Other only through risking that I am worthless and meaningless."[42] *Fourth,* such letting-go will be a function of the *trust* that the individual experiences in the situation he invests in. The sense of the critical nature of stages 5 and 6, and hence of regenerative systems, is captured in this summary statement by Jack and Lorraine Gibb:

> The central dynamic of the growth process is a movement from fear to trust. Latent fear predisposes individuals to build social structures around role relations, develop strategies for mask maintenance, attempt to manage motivations by various forms of persuasion, and maintain tight control systems. The individual camouflages his fears to himself by building role barricades; he camouflages his humanness with an idealized presenting self; he reacts to imposed motivations by attempting to impose motivations on others; and he protects himself from intimacy by defending or rebelling. With experience in high trust environments, however, he tends to be more personal; he replaces facades with intimacy and directness; he becomes more search-oriented and self-determining; and he develops the capacity for making interdependent relationships with relevant and significant others.[43]

In the very act of letting go, the individual exposes herself to feedback which could imply rejection or modification of her base of experienced and anticipated competence. The process is delicate because of the inevitable differentiation of Self and Other, as stages 7 and 8 in Figure 3 attempt to suggest. To use the feedback of the Other, the individual must somehow "bridge the distance" between Self and Other. Dynamic counterforces are involved. Thus, the individual strives to preserve his differentiated Self, to maintain a gap between Self and Other. Paradoxically, the differentiation of Self requires the confirmation that only Other can supply. Hence, the need to bridge the Self/Other gap, as well as the need to maintain it. Martin Buber expressed the point powerfully: he cites "the wish of every man to be confirmed as to what he is, even as what he can become, by men; and the innate capacity in man to confirm his fellow men in this way."[44] However, to find yourself really means risking the loss of some part of yourself to others. In Kenneth Benne's words, the process "involves some of the deepest dilemmas of personal and social life, the dilemma of self and society . . . of conservation and of apartness partially overcome in an association which, while firm and security-giving, yet enhances and affirms rather than eclipses and derogates individual variation and difference."[45]

These dynamics have other paradoxical qualities. When we expect others to be just like ourselves before we can learn from them, for example, we will learn little. This will preserve our sense of experienced and anticipated competence, but only in a bogus way. Moreover, we need Other to be differentiated from us if Other is to provide us this essential human service. But the Self cannot be surrendered to the Other. The common idiom suggests how valueless such surrender is to development or learning. "If that's the way you say I am," goes the idiom, "then that's how I am." This is at least a statement of dependence, which limits the degree to which an individual can accept any learning as her own. Consequently, what we commonly call conformity cannot play a major role in bridging the Self/Other gap.

The subtleties of the latter point have escaped some critical observers,[46] and perhaps even many devotees of sensitivity training. For example, some observers see in sensitivity training a vehicle for the development of consensus and for the subjugation of the individual to it. Commitment to any interpersonal relationship does imply a loss of individual freedom, but the quid pro quo is personal development. There are pitfalls aplenty in bringing off this paradoxical exchange, to be sure. But just as surely, there is no alternative to taking the risk, short of arrested development. Ashley Montagu sensitively captures the point in his discussion of an individual's identification with a group:

> In this process the consciousness of self may actually increase, the sense of personal identity may become even more vivid, and one's ties to one's society more firmly established than ever. Individuation, as the development of personal identity, is neither the contrary nor the contradictory of social identification, it *is* social identification.[47]

To return to Figure 3, the developmental payoff for individuals occurs at stages 9 and 10. Both Self and Other can grow individually while they facilitate each other's growth. Basically, the differentiated Self and Other provide insights or aspects that can be integrated into Other and Self, respectively. Tolerance of the initial differentiation, that is to say, facilitates further differentiation while it intensifies the sense of shared contributions to development or learning. Such dual effects magnify the results of the separate investments of Self and Other, and encourage additional investments.

The cycle of learning then can feed on itself, finally, on the products of stages 9 and 10. A complementary enhancement of Self and Other, that is, will contribute to raising the plateau of "experienced and anticipated competence" symbolized by stages 1, 2, and 3 in Figure 3.

The outcomes are not necessarily happy ones, although they dominantly tend to be. The process of individual development or learning also can come un-glued at stages 9 and 10 in Figure 3. The result could be a reduced sense of over-all competence, perhaps even a seriously impaired sense.

The Implied Exchange

Looked at from a simple exchange point of view, the laboratory approach helps individuals do what they cannot really avoid: to find more of themselves at the risk of losing themselves. To the degree that the laboratory approach increases the probability that this risky but necessary process be managed somewhat more successfully, so does it help provide what the individual badly needs.

Perspectives on OD as Theory, II
Why the Technology Seems to Work in Large Organizations

Suggesting why OD seems to work in large organizations will require a long line of argument, with many of the punch-lines coming toward the very end of this long section. Specifically, the analysis builds through these stages:

- Developing the distinction between "family" and "stranger" experiences and their role in OD
- Suggesting how a mutual meeting of individual and organization needs basically explains the acute relevance of OD applications to management and to employees
- Evaluating the adequacy of available theories of learning or change

This analysis will often be unsatisfying, for there is much we have yet to learn about why the OD technology seems to work in large organizations.

Worksite as End Point or Starting Point?

Demonstrating that much is yet to be learned poses no problem. Consider the basic question: Where to start OD? We have no good answer to this question, in part because of lack of knowledge but also because of the multidirectional potency of the technology. Two basic macro-designs could guide any specific OD effort. Circumstances will encourage the choice of one or the other alternative, although no clear guidelines exist for making the choice. But, the laboratory technology seems robust, whatever the preferred approach. That is, along with illustrating the difficulties raised by the choice between the macro-designs, the two alternatives provide different perspectives on why the technology seems to work.

Stranger Experiences → Family Experiences

The orthodox entree into the laboratory approach to OD began with stranger experiences in a basic T-group, neglecting for present purposes today's reality that some variant of "team development" or "team-building" is the most likely design for openers. There organization members get safe experiences with values, attitudes, and behaviors consistent with the laboratory approach, safe in the sense that participants can savor the experience without concern about preserving appearances with organizational peers or superiors.

The orthodox entree then builds toward family designs that involve individuals who are associated at work. At some point, enough persons trained at off-site locations will be seeded into the organization so that they can begin to spearhead changes at work. The system will "go critical," in effect, when some unspecified proportion of an organization's membership has a positive experience with laboratory values. The proportion need not be very large, if it includes enough organizational influentials.

Several details sufficiently describe this orthodox macro-design. To begin, organization members work on personal learning, which they may later transfer individually and gingerly to work. They probably will make more aggressive attempts at transfer in family or marriage relations, and success there may increase the motivation to make applications at work. In such diverse ways, an increasing number of an organization's members may have a "positive experience" with laboratory values, which means that those values are dually seen as contributing to personal growth and as applicable at work, realistically as well as ideally. At some point, "enough" members have a positive experience and begin to emphasize transfer learning in the host organization, deliberately, as well as begin to work on environmental learning.

The rationale for the orthodox progression is transparent. Organization members can gain experience with the laboratory approach under anonymous conditions which encourage experimentation and risk-taking, while they reduce the costs of "failing" or "losing face" in front of workmates with whom continuing relations are necessary. Overall, the high degree of voluntarism possible via the initial reliance on stranger experiences no doubt helps individuals extract benefit from the experience. As voluntarism decreases, the tendencies to fight the experience, or to deny it, will grow. Conveniently, the rationale presumes that the personal learning from the stranger experience will variously penetrate

into work. For example, a basic T-group experience can be of varied usefulness
in inducing personal learning that can generate organization change. Consider
only that:

- The basic T-group can provide an arena to develop and to test new skills
  and insights applicable to interpersonal situations that may be modified
  for use at work.

- The experience in the basic T-group can reveal the nature and importance of differences between "public" and "private" attitudes. A
  positive experience in the stranger experience can encourage an organization member to confront similar differences at work in such ways as
  to own them, analyze them, and perhaps reduce them to enhance
  performance in the organization.

- The stranger experience can point up the limitations of existing organization norms.

- The experience in the basic T-group at least can illustrate in life that
  some alternatives to common organizational norms are available.

- The basic T-group can help generate new norms for work and help en-
  force them as well, as by inducing a desire in individuals to try to
  achieve at their work some of the gratification of needs they experienced in a basic T-group.

Family Experiences → Possible Stranger Experiences

Particularly of late, some proponents have stood the usual sequencing of the
laboratory approach to OD on its head, as it were. They prescribe that learning
experiences for the immediate work group should initiate an OD program. These
initial experiences may be T-groups or any number of variously circumscribed
spin-offs which will be described and discussed below. If individual organization
members prefer, after the initial experience with their work team, they may subsequently arrange for a stranger experience to deepen insights that they begin to
develop in their family experience.

The late Alexander Winn was an early proponent of this alternative macro-
design for OD. Based on his experience of a decade at Alcan: Canada, he
concludes that ". . . programmes of team development contribute substantially
to individual growth but . . . the reverse is not necessarily true."[48] Hence Alcan:
Canada moved from a massive reliance on stranger T-group experiences through
stranger experiences with Alcan's diverse workforce who did not work together
and probably never would. The firm finally came to rely more and more on
sensitivity training experiences for work teams as the basic opener for OD effects.
Winn explains that the family experience differs from a stranger T-group in
important ways:

Quite frequently, it becomes a variation of a work conference in which, in addition to the manifest, overt topic or agenda, the covert, the hidden, the process and the here-and-now are explored. The explorations of the family T-Group are obviously not limited to the data the group generates in its confrontation at the meeting. Their past experiences, the "carry-overs," the "hang-ups," their anxiety and frustration, their feelings of hostility as well as of warmth, become the here-and-now data as well. The real authority figure, not a surrogate, is present along with one's work partners from one's own as well as other functionally related departments. By making explicit the many blocks to inter-personal, intra-group, and inter-group communication, and by seeking to break through these, it becomes the most powerful way to affect the social system.[49]

The rationale for this second macro-design is less straightforward than for the stranger → family progression. *First,* beginning with stranger experiences resulted in personal learning, but transfers into the workplace were unsatisfyingly slow at Alcan: Canada, according to Winn:

As should have been expected, the stranger and semi-stranger T-Group experience affected the individual where he was most involved in a deep personal sense and where his ambivalent feelings had the strongest resonance— in his home. It is thus in the nuclear family, i.e., in a culturally prescribed environment of lesser mobility and greater trust that the individual has found a more receptive ground for experimentation with his own behavior than in an affectively neutral industrial organization.[50]

Directly, the question of transfer was not solved by the stranger → family progression.

Second, in part, this lack of transfer reflects the elemental fact that Alcan: Canada trainees had great problems seeing how they could translate into work the often profound learning gained in stranger T-groups. The stranger T-group can be so emotionally charged, or can deal with such novel topics, that the organization member is at once caught up in the dynamics and very unclear about how it all applies back at work. He speculates that the fantasied costs of transfer may seem too high, especially in the case of organization members who participated in an all-male stranger T-group where the expression of feelings was accompanied by displays of crying, hugging, or whatever. Organization transfer might appear remote, at best. At worst, as Winn concludes, homosexual anxieties may inhibit organization members "from being close to another man, whether it be his superior, peer or subordinate. He may select the fight-flight modality which will support, by distance or contradiction respectively, his individuality in the back-home environment."[51]

When the work team together experiences a sensitivity training experience, patently, transfer comes directly. The situation implies a discipline, or holding-back, that is at once bane and boon. Family T-groups may have "shallower experiences," and defenses may be higher. On the other hand, the experience has a "what you see is what you get" quality which, at its best, implies a realistic tethering of expectations about change and learning. As Winn suggests:

> The organizational family T-Group experience does not have to reshape the individual's underlying personality characteristics, but it does alter his expectations of himself and others about what is legitimate behaviour. The group reaches the point in its team development when the members begin to behave in a more open and authentic way, and when they can resolve conflicts more effectively. The organizational T-Group establishes a frame of reference for working through and managing conflicts. Resolution is not a Utopian answer but a workable solution to immediate issues. In a way, conflicts are accepted as a price we all have to pay for living in a complex industrial society. As new issues arise, they are again confronted openly. Effective and continuous conflict resolution is but the basis of an effective decision-making process so central to our organizational lives.[52]

Third, even if the organization member clearly sees the applicability at work of her learning in a stranger T-group, she often is not able to act on her insight. This reflects a practical and theoretical issue. Practically, the learner later faces the problem of somehow getting her work colleagues to the learning plateau she reached. Theoretically, Alcan: Canada's experience reflects the critical gap between insight and action. This will especially be the case where the learner moves from the supportive and warm environment of the stranger T-group to the more affectively neutral if not hostile environment of the worksite.

A Critical Open Question

To the betting person, the considerations above suggest that you make your choice and pay the price. For example, Winn sees only enough evidence to make a negative conclusion. He concludes:

> There is not enough evidence that the "seeding" and saturation with stranger or semi-stranger T-Groups is a prerequisite for an effective organizational family lab. There were as many instances when past T-Group experience triggered off the individual's defenses against an organizational family lab as there were examples when such prior exposure to stranger T-Groups was pertinent and helpful.[53]

The character of the evidence necessary to permit finer decisions about beginning with stranger or family experiences can be sketched in terms of the unique approach of Reed M. Powell and John Stinson.[54] They compare the differential impact of standardized T-Group experiences in family and stranger settings on the performance of simulated business firms.[55] Each firm had five members. The 15 firms first had 6 to 8 hours of experience with the simulation.

Table 1   Selected Impacts of Laboratory Training on Operations of Simulated
Firms

	Mean Scores on Selected Dependent Variables		
	Five Family-Trained Firms	Five Stranger-Trained Firms	Five Control Firms
1. Average accumulated profit	$186,600[a]	$445,380	$440,080[a]
2. Average increase in stock price	$.12[a]	$5.75[b]	$10.25[a]
3. Average change in cohesiveness	+.349[a,b]	−1.39[b]	−1.484[a]
4. Average change in leader-initiating structure behavior	−5.304[a]	−3.826[c]	+3.17[a,c]
5. Average change in task-oriented behavior by leader	−3.41	−3.096	−.91

[a]Difference between family-trained and control firms was statistically significant by Mann-Whitney U test.
[b]Difference between family-trained and stranger-trained firms was statistically significant.
[c]Difference between stranger-trained and control firms was statistically significant.
Source: Reed M. Powell and John F. Stinson, "The Worth of Laboratory Training,"
Business Horizons, Vol. 14 (August 1971), p. 92.

After matching the firms for performance in these initial trials, three clusters of
firms are distinguished:

- Five family-trained firms whose members had a T-group experience
  together
- Five stranger-trained firms whose members each had a separate T-group
  experience
- Five control firms whose members had no training

Subsequently, each firm spent 12 to 16 additional hours in further trials on the
simulation. The basic experimental data involve comparisons of the initial 6 to
8 hours of simulation time with the final 12 to 16 hours.

The findings of the Powell-Stinson experiment suggest the complex issues
involved in the question: Should the initial experience be in a stranger or in a
family experience?

- Although the T-group experience was a brief one and was oriented
toward task rather than relationships,[56] the experience tended to be impactful.
The decrease in leader-oriented behavior[57] in rows 4 and 5 in Table 1 supports

this conclusion, when either family-trained or stranger-trained firms are compared to control firms.

• Family-trained firms seemed more able to transfer the effects of their training into their simulated worksite. Rows 4 and 5 in Table 1 suggest the point. Relatedly, row 3 shows that the cohesiveness of family-trained firms increased, while stranger-trained and control firms experienced sharp decreases. This is expected. Given that cohesiveness is a measure of the resultant attraction of a group for its members,[58] the data imply that the family T-group experience helped induce more satisfying and enjoyable interpersonal relationships that persisted throughout the simulations.

• The family-trained firms did not work together as productively on the technical task as the other two kinds of firms (see rows 1 and 2 in Table 1). Powell and Stinson see clear cause and effect. They note: "... it seems reasonable to assume that the participants had a limited amount of time to devote to the simulation; as more time was devoted to improving interpersonal relationships, less was available for productive activities."[59] These findings imply issues which Powell and Stinson cannot resolve, which is not to demean this seminal research but only to describe its limits. The unresolved issues include:

• The simulations were brief, so the effects sketched might not have been maintained over a longer period. Major questions remain moot in the absence of such longitudinal data. For example, would the decreases of cohesiveness in stranger-trained and control firms over the longer run have caused a deterioration in task performance?

• Above interpretation of the data assumes that as cohesiveness increases, productivity decreases.[60] Other research strongly suggests, in contrast, that the actual relationship can be more complicated. Low cohesiveness implies low productivity on tasks that require collaborative effort, in this alternative view. Up to a substantial point, increases in cohesiveness are associated with increases in productivity. At very high levels of cohesiveness, however, either very high productivity or very low productivity may be expected. High cohesiveness implies substantial group control over member behavior. And both very high and very low productivity require that behaviors of all group members be narrowly distributed, which is to say highly controlled.[61] We do not know whether the Powell/ Stinson data contain any high cohesiveness/low productivity cases, which would profoundly affect average data.

• Moreover, the reward schedule for participants is not clear. Specifically, participants were told that their academic grades would be affected by their performance on the simulations. Apparently, this potential reward was not great enough to engage the high cohesiveness of the family-trained firms. Or, alternatively, their socioemotional needs were stronger than their aspirations for grades, or that portion of them which would be affected by their simulation performance.

    •   The training in this case may have encouraged an extreme emphasis on a homogenized social inclusion, as contrasted with membership that acknowledges differential abilities and interests.[62] The "honeymoon period" which characterizes the early stages of many T-groups is based on homogenized social inclusion, and available data do not reject the possibility that the Powell-Stinson groups were caught at such an early stage of development. As Powell and Stinson explain their T-group design:

> Throughout . . . there was a considerable emphasis on developing consensus in decision making. Compromise and one-man decisions were discouraged. Rather, T-Group participants were encouraged to ensure that all points of view were heard and thoroughly discussed, that all members contributed to the decisions as much as possible, and that the groups arrived at a consensus on their decisions.

> It is probable that this concentration on participation and consensus encouraged [the appointed] formal leaders to reduce the strength of their leadership.[63]

Yes, indeed.

    The laboratory approach is oriented toward truth as well as love, however, despite the likely early fixation on warmth, inclusion, and so on. If the truth is that various differentiations among a group's membership are appropriate because of their varying knowledge and skills, the laboratory approach should facilitate that differentiation and help cope openly with its inevitable fallout. Such differentiation can be risky for a group's members, but necessary to progress beyond early stages of development.

Toward Mutality as the Basic Goal

Whereever entry is first made, the laboratory approach contributes to a heightening mutuality of organization demands and satisfaction of member needs. These few comments imply, in summary, the basic reasons why the OD technology works in organizations. That is, the mutual payoffs of the technology for individuals and large organizations constitute the basic motivator for adopting the OD technology.

    The basic argument here is direct. Especially in the last decade, organizations have demanded increasingly more of their employees. Increasing skills, longer periods of socialization and training, and, especially, greater tolerance for change, instability, and tension: these characterize the broadening spiral of today's organization demands. Relatedly, this seems one of those times when the gap between organization demands and satisfaction of member needs is considered critically large by enough people to make a significant difference. Cries by the young that they "want more than a job" may be viewed sardonically by those for whom "just any job" in 1935 or in 1975 would have answered their most urgent prayer. Clearly, however, the stakes required to induce playing various organization roles have been sharply raised in the period of a few decades. The view here, perhaps primitive, urges that these stakes have increased just as have the demands that organization life makes on more and more people.

From the point of view of an exchange model, two possibilities exist. Thus, new incentives can be developed to insure that organization demands will continue to be met, even as they spiral outward at unprecedented rates. Alternatively, individual expectations can be lowered. This General Bullmoose strategy is at best a temporary expedient. At worst, the strategy conjures up images of depressions, of Great Leaps Forward that go backward in major respects.

From a major perspective, then, this volume seeks to contribute to the satisfaction of individual needs necessary to assure that organization demands will be met. Overall, the laboratory approach aims to identify major human needs, and to suggest how they may be met in organizations. The specific immediate contributions here to that overall aim are: (1) to sketch one way of viewing the linkages of individual needs and organization demands and (2) to use the notion of regenerative communication systems to suggest the ways in which the laboratory approach can contribute to mutuality in organizations.

Linking Individual and Organization Needs/Demands

The essence of OD programs is to link individual needs with organization demands, as Figure 4 suggests. "Needs" are to be understood broadly as prerequisites for effective functioning, or at least aids to such effective functioning. The assumed contribution to effective functioning of each of the items mentioned, in turn, rests on empirical findings[64] as well as on (hopefully reasonable) hypotheses when research is inconclusive or is lacking.[65]

The schema in Figure 4 is simple. It begins with a basic premise, that mutuality in meeting individual and organization needs will be associated with high output and member satisfaction. This basic premise is supported in two ways. Some individual and organization needs are outlined, for the purpose of showing how they imply competence in interpersonal and intergroup relations, and the figure also lists some learning designs whose consequences—such as increased openness and individual commitment—can clearly be related to the satisfaction of individual and organization needs. The intent is to depict a self-heightening system.

Mutuality via Regenerative Systems

The thrust toward mutuality in OD can be established in a somewhat more specific way, as in Figure 5, which sketches how degenerative interaction systems can create serious problems in organizations. The usefulness of

Basic Premise: To the degree that individuals can meet their own needs while meeting organizational needs, two simultaneous conditions become increasingly probable:

■ satisfaction of organization members will heighten
■ output will increase, both in terms of quality and quantity

Individual

Organization

An individual's basic needs center around *self-realization* and *self-actualization*. The former involves a person seeking himself as he is in interaction with others, with the goal of increasing the congruence between his intentions and his impact on others. Self-actualization refers to the processes of growth by which an individual realizes his potential.

An efficient organization will develop an appropriately shifting balance between *institutionalization* and *risk-taking*. The former refers to *infusing with value* the activities of the organization, so as to elicit member support, identification, and collaboration. Risk-taking is necessary in *innovating* more effective ways to deal with existing activities and in *adapting* to environmental changes in society, markets, technologies, and so on.

An individual whose basic needs are being met experiences corresponding *psychological growth,* the prime conditions for which, and consequences of which, are:
■ a growing awareness of the needs and motivations of self and others
■ a lessening of the degree to which his relationships and actions are distorted, especially via more actively inducing feedback from others and by more effectively interpreting it
■ an increasing ability to modify behavior in response to feedback about its impact on others, to respond appropriately rather than stereotypically
■ a growing tendency to seek or develop conditions that promote psychological growth for self and others
■ an expanding capacity to determine goals and internal motivations for self

An organization's successful balancing of institutionalization and risk-taking will depend upon:
■ the increasingly complete use of *people as well as nonhuman resources*
■ the development and maintenance of *a viable balance between central control and local initiative*
■ fluid lines of *communication*—vertically, horizontally, and diagonally
■ *decision-making processes* that solve problems that stay solved without creating other problems
■ *infusing the organization with values* that support its existence as a stable institution and that also motivate its developmental change as an adaptive structure

An individual who experiences psychological growth will be correspondingly motivated to search for *work, challenge, and responsibility.*

An organization with such a working balance of institutionalization and risk-taking will develop appropriate norms that support efforts of organization members to search for *work, challenge, and responsibility.*

Satisfaction of both individual and organization needs will be facilitated by, if such satisfaction

An individual's growth and self-realization are facilitated by interpersonal and intergroup relations that are *honest, caring, and non-manipulative.* Individuals can gain convenient experiences with these personal needs and with ways of satisfying them in such learning designs derived from the laboratory approach as sensitivity training. This is a managed process of gaining experience with attitudes and skills for inducing greater openness about positive and negative feelings, attitudes, or beliefs. Such openness leads to greater trust and reduced risk in communicating and is intended to suggest possible transfers into other environments.

does not in fact crucially depend upon, *skill and competence in interpersonal and intergroup situations.*

Organizational family teams can be exposed to such learning designs derived from the laboratory approach as sensitivity training, with the intention of increasing *confidence, trust, and responsibility* that can be applied directly to solving organizational issues. Skill and competence in interpersonal and in intergroup situations can be increased in sensitivity training groups composed of strangers, that is, but the real test is the application of such learning in life-relevant situations. Such application will require that substantial numbers of organization members learn appropriate interpersonal skills, as well as that they internalize a set of values which support and reinforce such learning.

Persons in groups which develop greater openness tend to *identify strongly* with other members and with the goals of the group.

Groups characterized by strong identification with members and goals become *increasingly capable of dealing with issues facing their members,* and hence increasingly capable of *influencing their environment in desired ways.*

Groups whose members identify strongly and who can influence their environment are likely to be effective reinforcers of decisions about change. Such groups also can provide emotional support necessary to sustain required changes in the values, attitudes, or behaviors of their members.

Figure 4 A simplified model of findings-hypotheses underlying an organization development program based on the laboratory approach. [*Source:* Adapted from Robert T. Golembiewski and Stokes B. Carrigan, "Planned Change in Organization Style Based on Laboratory Approach," *Administrative Science Quarterly,* Vol. 15 (March 1970), p. 81.]

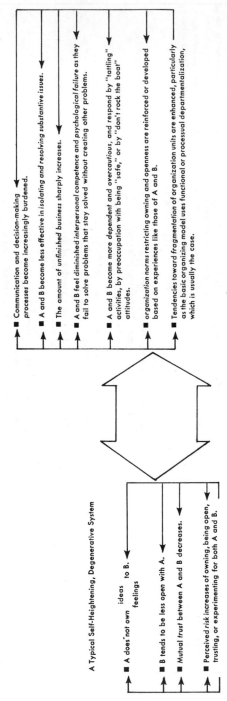

Figure 5 A degenerative system and some of its typical outcomes in organizations. [*Source:* R. T. Golembiewski, *Renewing Organizations: The Laboratory Approach to Planned Change* (Itasca, Ill.: F. E. Peacock, 1972).]

Some Typical Organizational Outcomes of Degenerative Systems

- Communication and decision-making processes become increasingly burdened.
- A and B become less effective in isolating and resolving substantive issues.
- The amount of *unfinished business* sharply increases.
- A and B feel diminished *interpersonal competence and psychological failure* as they fail to solve problems that stay solved without creating other problems.
- A and B become more dependent and overcautious, and respond by "tattling" activities, by preoccupation with being "safe," or by "don't rock the boat" attitudes.
- *organization norms* restricting owning and openness are reinforced or developed based on experiences like those of A and B.
- Tendencies toward *fragmentation of organization units* are enhanced, particularly as the basic organizing model uses functional or processual departmentalization, which is usually the case.

A Typical Self-Heightening, Degenerative System

- A does not own ideas to B. feelings
- B tends to be less open with A.
- *Mutual trust* between A and B decreases.
- Perceived *risk* increases of owning, being open, trusting, or experimenting for both A and B.

regenerative systems for individuals was (hopefully) established earlier. Here, the discussion supports the mutual value of regenerative systems to organizations as well as to individuals.

Figure 5 is an ideal construct, relating how two self-heightening sets of relations can explain the genesis of what are offered as common problems in organizations. Note, for example, the circular reinforcement of effects suggested by the figure. To illustrate, increases in unfinished business between individuals and organization units can lead to the development of organization norms that restrict the interaction which alone can support the communication and decision-making processes necessary to reduce unfinished business. Moreover, Figure 5 also implies another wheels-within-wheels feature. That is, the model allows that organization norms restricting interaction can reinforce degenerative systems which exist between individuals, or can induce degenerative systems even in cases where individuals have the best of collaborative intentions. This captures the essential meaning of the abortive romance between a Hatfield and a McCoy, or a Montague and a Capulet.

Tersely, OD has as one of its major purposes the development and maintenance of regenerative systems between individuals and groups. The intended outcome reduces consequences like those sketched in Figure 4, which contribute to the organizational fragmentation that is so much with us. In this sense, OD attempts to develop greater centripetal forces in the face of growing centrifugal forces. These centrifugal forces can be conceived of as the major resultant of the delayed double spiral referred to above: expanding organization demands and lagging satisfaction of individual needs in organizations. Primarily, this impairs the exchange relationship between organizations and many of their members.

Let us become somewhat more specific, in terms of both intent and difficulty. The essential burden of this two-part volume will be to detail how and why individual and organization needs can be met—a mutuality that may be approached via three basic orientations: changes in interaction; changes in the technical organization of work and in supporting procedures, policies, and structures; and changes in the complex interaction between human and technical processes. Sometimes, it will be convenient to begin with one of these approaches or another. Typically, a complex effort will require effort at all three levels, in orderly sequence or in bewildering simultaneity. Commonly, however, the initial OD focus will be on interaction-centered designs, which focus on enhancing the validity and reliability of information in human/technical systems. Illustratively, a typical OD application might begin—following Exhibit 3—to work on defective feedback systems consistent with generally accepted principles for improvement or enhancement. Exhibit 3, in effect, extends to the organizational level the earlier emphasis on feedback between individuals. Improvements in the quantity and quality of feedback, in turn, might well facilitate rational or technical problem-solving.

Exhibit 3   Problems with Feedback Systems and Principles for Their Improvement

Problems with Feedback Systems	Principles for Improving Feedback Systems
1. Absence of valid and reliable data, usually about organization processes but also about performance.	1. Generate reliable and valid data about organization processes and performance.
2. Emphasis on inappropriate or misleading measures of processes or performance.	2. Rely heavily on users of data to design systems of data flow.
3. Inefficient and restricted distribution of data, often at high levels of organization.	3. Broad distribution of data to all levels of organization.
4. Inadequate or ineffective uses of data by managers.	4. Train managers in effective use of data.
5. Resistance to changes necessary to improve the flow of data and to permit effective action, often supported by norms proscribing "squealing," "informing," and so on.	5. Careful design of the process for acting on data, including the development of appropriate norms for sharing data and for problem-solving.

Source: Based on David A. Nadler, Philip Mirvis, and Cortlandt Cammann, "The Ongoing Feedback System," *Organizational Dynamics*, Vol. 4 (Spring 1976), p. 65.

Clearly, many organizations stand in need of such improvement or enhance-ment of their feedback systems. Witness especially how some systems turn on their "disloyal" members who surface data about problems with the performance or processes of their organizations, usually after arduous and nerve-wracking struggles to generate some response via normal channels, only to come to be vili-fied by the systems they sought to aid.[66] A. Ernest Fitzgerald, who while working for the Air Force blew the whistle on enormous C-5A cost-overruns, provides one of the more recent examples of how organizations tend to be more hierarchy-serving than problem-solving. Let us put aside the practical issue of how much of this "loyalty" we can afford in our organized society. The patent price of such loyalty? Organizations demanding it coerce us and repress that which is the best in humankind.

This much having been said, the practical and theoretical difficulties imped-ing improvement in feedback systems can be enormous. Consider here only a technical issue: What specific kind of feedback is most effective? Here we must be more tentative for, clearly, we cannot simply argue that the answer is: More. That may be an appropriate short-run answer, of course. Much greater detail will be required in the long-run and, so far, progress has been uneven. As the review in Chapter 1 reflects, quite a bit is known about effective guidelines for feedback. But consider such major open issues as the relative effectiveness of three kinds of feedback: that which reports perceptions of reality as well as expectations (ideal and actual feedback); that which reports perceptions (actual-only); and that which reports expectations (ideal-only). One comparative study revealed these surprising findings:[67]

- Ideal-only was most effective in producing intended behavioral change.
- Actual-only was the least effective.

Clearly, those findings relate to very important practical problems, not only in behavioral change but also in such activities as budgeting.[68] Clearly, also, rela-tively firm answers to such implied critical questions about feedback still remain to be developed.

Some Available Theories of Learning or Change

One cannot yet really detail why and how the OD technology works, however, despite the useful descriptions above. Basically, we lack a comprehensive theory of learning or change, which would be most useful to have, for more-or-less obvious reasons.

Progress toward the development of a learning theory or model has been sufficient only to pose a dilemma. On the one hand, much support exists for a global model that explains the intended effects of the laboratory approach. But, the model is so general that important issues are left unresolved, or are still the subjects of basic disagreement. On the other hand, quite specific models of change also exist, but these generate conflicting research findings.

Hence, the unsatisfactory choice, which this section's subheadings below highlight: one can choose an accepted but general model; or one can choose among several specific models of learning or change that have variable degrees of empirical support. The discussion below provides detail about these choices.

An Accepted but General Model of Change

The classic Lewinian model of change has received wide acceptance as reflecting the global processes of the laboratory approach. Lewin proposed three stages of attitudinal change: (1) unfreezing, (2) changing, and (3) refreezing. With some elaboration, that three-phase model has proved serviceable in describing the broad processes of learning or change in the laboratory approach, both in small learning collectivities like the T-group as well as in large organizations.

Lewin's Model in Small Groups. Lewin's three-stage model applied to small learning groups usefully highlights central processes of choice and change. They may be sketched briefly.[69]

Stage 1. Unfreezing
1. Some stimulus points up an unexpected feature of an individual's coping mechanisms, his defenses, self-concepts, or whatever. The unstructured nature of a T-group, for example, provides an unsettling experience which brings into question an individual's capabilities to adapt and hence helps motivate looking at self with the minimal defensiveness and distortion. Generally, disconfirmation or lack of confirmation about some aspect of the self is the trigger, and especially so if (for example) the disconfirmation is consensually validated by several observers. ("You say you are not anxious, but we all see you as terrified and seeking support from the authority figure.")
2. The stimulus induces a potentially motivating concern, perhaps anxiety, guilt, shame, or anger. At least initially, such feelings may induce defensiveness, or avoidance of the meaning of the stimulus-situation as applied to the self. Such reactions or feelings also may prove motivators right from the start, however, for they can trigger a concern to change or to understand in people whose defenses are appropriately low. In either case, agreement exists about the conditions required to activate such potentially motivating concerns.
3. The concerns—perhaps anxiety, guilt, shame, or anger—become motivators as the person experiences a sense of psychological safety for self and others, and as barriers to experimentation and change are removed. This suggests the development of a regenerative system, where trust is high enough and risk low

enough to induce openness and owning. Low openness and owning may be considered the primary barriers to change. ("The guy you describe isn't me; I'd tell you people if he were. Honest.")

Stage 2. Changing

4.   The individual openly scans her interpersonal environment for new information about herself. As a person feels psychologically safe, she is open to the inputs of others. These inputs clarify, modify, or perhaps even change the focus of the original stimulus. ("Now I see. You said I wasn't cooperating at first. Now I hear you saying that you felt I rejected you.") As Edgar Schein and Warren Bennis explain, the "changee . . . may begin to view himself from the perspective of an array of others. As his perspective, his frame of reference, shifts, he develops new beliefs about himself which, in turn, lead to new feelings and behavioral responses."[70]

5.   If some change seems appropriate to him after scanning, the individual seeks to identify some model to guide his change. In a T-group, the trainer very often provides such an early model. As the individual experiences the other group members as differentiated, he can isolate a broad range of specific attributes as models. An individual can then decide whether to try to integrate these attributes into his existing behaviors and attitudes.

6.   The individual practices replacement behaviors or attitudes implied by, or deduced from, the model. Here, a supportive T-group can be very useful. Its members can confirm or disconfirm progress, provide emotional support for experimentation, and encourage continued effort. True mutual learning may take place. ("I beamed when you said you were angry, just when I perceived you to be angry. We're on the same wave-length at last. You used to deny you were angry when I was certain I perceived the signs. That induced my distrust of you, and my mistrust in my own radar. I couldn't help you much, then, even really talk with you.")

Stage 3. Refreezing

7.   The replacement responses must be integrated with the rest of the learner's personality, defenses, and attitudes.

8.   They must be integrated as well into her significant ongoing relationships outside of the immediate learning situation. The issue is particularly relevant when the learning occurs in a T-group and the individual wishes to transfer the replacement responses into her real-world relationships. The "transfer issue" will receive major attention below.

As useful as this three-stage model is, however, it has serious inadequacies. For example, the three-stage model is moot on many significant questions which often begin with: "How much . . . ?" Specifically, if some unfreezing is useful, some point surely exists beyond which additional unfreezing does not facilitate

learning, or may even be detrimental to learning. Similarly, given that some feedback is a good thing, in what strengths should it be given?

Lewin's Model in Large Organizations.   Gene W. Dalton studied a number of
successful OD interventions, and found that they also could be interpreted in
terms of Lewin's basic developmental stages. Schematically:[71]

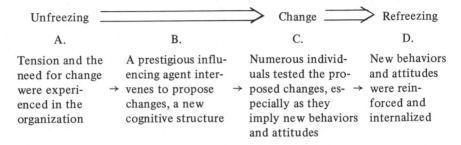

| Unfreezing | $\Longrightarrow$ | Change $\Longrightarrow$ | Refreezing |

A.	B.	C.	D.
Tension and the need for change were experienced in the organization	→ A prestigious influencing agent intervenes to propose changes, a new cognitive structure	→ Numerous individuals tested the proposed changes, especially as they imply new behaviors and attitudes	→ New behaviors and attitudes were reinforced and internalized

Dalton also isolated four subprocesses, each of which is characterized in successful OD efforts by movement from one condition in the left column below to its
paired condition in the right column. Specifically:

Generalized goals	→	Specific objectives
Old social ties	→	New relationships which support the intended changes in behavior and attitudes
Self-doubt and a diminished sense of self-esteem	→	A heightened sense of self-esteem
External pressure for change	→	An internalized motive for change

Dalton's combination of three sequences and four subprocesses generates a
model of the influencing process in organizations, as in Figure 6 which accords
quite well with several descriptions of successful programs of change in organizations. Specifically, the model begins with tension as an antecedent condition.
This chafes existing interpersonal and intergroup relationships and also lowers
the self-esteem of organization members. The collective friction and individual
concern about lowered self-esteem generates some leverage for change, and can
provide a prestigious influencing agent with an opportunity to intervene. The
task is substantial. As Dalton notes: ". . . unless there is to be protracted
resistance, someone must gain the acceptance and possible support of individuals
not seeking change and even those who feel threatened by it."[71]
    Internal agents who seize such opportunities tend to act in ways that seem
at apparent odds, the available descriptive literature suggests. They provide an
impetus to change, often in the form of a statement of generalized objectives that
have the effect of shaking or replacing prior social ties. These objectives

Tension Experienced within the System	Intervention of a Prestigious Influencing Agent	Individuals Attempt to Implement the Proposed Changes	New Behavior and Attitudes Reinforced by Achievement, Social Ties and Internalized Values—Accompanied by Decreasing Dependence on Influencing Agent
Tension →	General Objectives established, new cognitive structure offered →	Growing specificity of objectives—establishment of subgoals →	Achievement and resetting of specific objectives →
	Prior social ties interrupted or attenuated →	Formation of new alliances and relationships centering around new activities →	New social ties reinforce altered behavior and attitudes →
Lowered Sense of Self-Esteem →	Esteem-building begun on basis of agent's attention and assurance →	Esteem-building based on task accomplishment →	Heightened sense of self-esteem →
	External motive for change provided by influencing agent →	Improvisation and testing by experience of new cognitive structure induced by generalized objectives of influencing agent →	Internalized motive for change, resulting from: Verification through experience of the new cognitive structure Application of new cognitive structure and improvisation with it A psychological owning of the new cognitive structure by organization members who make it their own →

Figure 6   A model of the successful change process in organizations. [*Source:* Adapted from Gene W. Dalton, "Influence and Organizational Change," p. 81, in Anant R. Negandhi and Joseph P. Schwitter (eds.), *Organizational Behavior Models* (Kent, Ohio: Comparative Administration Research Institute, 1970).]

constitute a "new cognitive structure," in effect, a new way of conceiving what
is to be done and how it is to be done. Moreover, the influencing agent is perceived as acting in ways that enhance rather than deprecate the self-esteem of the
individuals who are affected. Essentially, the message is: "I know things have
not gone well, but I believe you can do better."

These ways of behaving that characterize successful internal managers of
change can be illustrated briefly. Consider this description of a new plant manager's first meeting with all his supervisors. The manager, an observer tells us,
described "a few basic goals" that he expected to reach, despite the fact that he
had heard of Plant Y's bad reputation and had been warned that many of its
personnel were not competent at their jobs. However, the manager expressed
optimism, even if of the wait-and-see variety: "I am willing to prove that this is
not so, and until shown otherwise, I personally have confidence in the group."[72]

This brief illustration supports rich speculation. The manager's expressed
confidence might heighten self-esteem. The generalized objectives propounded
by the influencing agent also might contribute to self-esteem, in the sense that
they leave ample room for the contributions and influence of other organization
members. This is particularly the case since successful change agents typically
begin to actively listen to their subordinates and to react to them, which is some
of the stuff of inducing heightened self-esteem via moving toward regenerative
interaction sequences.[73] In any case, Dalton concludes that:

> Interestingly, a movement toward greater self-esteem seems to be a facilitat-
> ing factor not only in the establishment of new patterns of thought and
> action, but also in the unfreezing of old patterns. The abandonment of
> previous patterns of behavior and thought is easier when an individual is
> moving toward an increased sense of his own worth. The movement along
> this continuum is away from a sense of self-doubt toward a feeling of posi-
> tive worth—from a feeling of partial inadequacy toward a confirmed sense of
> personal capacity. The increased sense of one's own potential is evident
> throughout this continuum, not merely at the end. This may seem a para-
> dox, but the contradiction is more apparent than real.[74]

Beyond this point, Figure 6 should be self-explanatory, and that is at once
its value and its limitation. Dalton's schema seems to adequately describe the
major features of successful programs of change, but it awaits the modifications
and elaborations that will come with empirical testing.

Specific but Conflicting Models of Change

As noted, both varieties of Lewin's basic model provide general guidance, but fall
short of giving specific answers to such questions as: How much feedback is too
much?

The rest of the literature does no better at providing what is needed, as can
be illustrated by sketching three more specific models of the change process.

Unfortunately, those three models recommend conflicting courses of action, and available research does not yet have sufficient power to determine which recommendation is more appropriate under what circumstances.

The three focal models have a basic common feature. They postulate that a motive force for change inheres in "discrepant situations," in cases of a difference between some stimulus and a person's "internal anchors" of attitudes or perceptions. The obvious question is confronted in three different ways by three different models of change.[75] That question is: What degree of discrepancy is optimum for inducing learning or change?

Model I. Big Bang Hypothesis.   Roughly, this model provides that the greater the discrepancy between a stimulus and an individual's internal anchors, the greater the probable change in her attitudes and opinions so as to reduce that discrepancy. The tension induced by discrepancy acts as a motivator. Many studies[76] report such an effect, which has been incorporated in theoretical syntheses like Leon Festinger's theory of cognitive dissonance. As he notes: ". . . the discrepant reality which impinges on a person will exert pressures in the direction of bringing the appropriate cognitive elements into correspondence with that reality. . . . The strength of the pressures to reduce the dissonance is a function of the magnitude of dissonance."[77]

Model II. Either/Or Hypothesis.   Model II introduces a major intervening variable in the discrepancy/change sequence—the degree of "ego involvement." Roughly, high ego involvement means that the person experiencing a discrepancy feels strongly about the stimulus issue, that the issue is a central one. Depending upon the degree of ego involvement, a great discrepancy will trigger either greater change or lesser change than a small discrepancy.

That is, Model II includes two general cases. When ego involvement is high, Model II predicts a contrast effect when discrepancy is great, and an assimilation effect when the discrepancy is smaller. That is, a great objective discrepancy is likely to be perceived as even more discrepant than it is, given a high ego involvement. A contrast effect will inhibit change in the direction of the stimulus. This prediction contradicts Model I, as Figure 7 shows. When ego involvement is low, however, as in the second general case as shown in Figure 7, Model II predicts the same effect as Model I. That is, when a person experiencing a discrepancy does not feel strongly about a stimulus issue, Model II predicts an assimilation effect, whether the discrepancy is greater or lesser. In either case, the course of least resistance for the person experiencing the discrepancy is to move attitudinally toward the discrepant stimulus or to perceive it as less discrepant than it is. Observed change will be greater toward the more discrepant stimulus, but change toward the less discrepant stimulus also will occur. General Case 2 in Figure 7 depicts these relations.

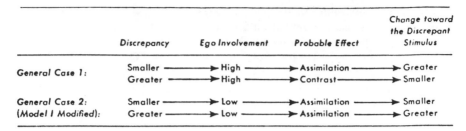

Figure 7   Two general cases in change Model II. [*Source:* R. T. Golembiewski, *Renewing Organizations: The Laboratory Approach to Planned Change* (Itasca, Ill.: F. E. Peacock, 1972).]

In addition, the second general case of Model II is limited by some students to narrow ranges of discrepancy. Increases in discrepancy will yield linear attitudinal change only up to a point, they argue. Beyond that point, the rate of change decelerates and then turns negative. As James O. Whittaker explained:

> the relationship was curvilinear. Small discrepancies yielded small change, moderate discrepancies yielded the maximum change, and the degree of change tended to diminish as the discrepancies became even larger.
>
> We suspect that on issues that are low in involvement, the discrepancies would need to be much greater than those we employed before decreasing change would result.[78]

Model III.   Balance Hypothesis.   Model III emphasizes the balanced state rather than the degree or direction of change. Thus, Fritz Heider writes of the interaction of "sentiments" and "units" in terms in which the concept of balanced state

> designates a situation in which the perceived units and the experienced sentiments co-exist without stress; there is thus no pressure toward change, either in the cognitive organization or in the sentiment. . . . That sentiment, unit formation, and balanced state have something to do with each other can be stated as a general hypothesis, namely: the relationship between sentiments and unit formation tends toward a balanced state.[79]

Model III also is distinguished in two other major senses. Thus, Model III—unlike Model I—admits both assimilation and contrast effects. Unlike Model II, moreover, the intervening variable is not the ego involvement of the subject confronted by the discrepancy. Rather, the intervening variable is the character of the object of the discrepancy. As Fritz Heider explains: "It has been assumed, and with good support from experimental findings, that 'Assimilation appears when the differences between the substructures [of a unit] are small; contrast appears when the differences are large.' "[80]

An example may clarify the significant differences between the three models. Assume A does not like B, whom A later discovers is the anonymous author of a sensitive and moving poem of which A has said: "Only a beautiful spirit could have written it." How does A handle the discrepancy?

- Model I. A would come to like B more in direct proportion to the degree of the discrepancy between A's original sentiments about B and about the poem.

- Model II. It would depend on A's degree of ego involvement with B:

  If A is ego-involved with B, the larger the discrepancy between A's original sentiments about B and about the poem, the less likely A is to favorably change his sentiments toward B (general Case 1 in Figure 7).

  If A is not particularly ego-involved with B, the larger the discrepancy between A's original sentiments about B and about the poem (at least up to some undetermined point), the more likely is A to favorably change his sentiments toward B (general Case 2 in Figure 7).

- Model III. A new balance would develop between A's sentiments toward B and his original definition of B as a unit. The initial unbalanced combination of positive sentiments about the poem and negative evaluation of the author as a unit could be resolved in several ways:

  By A seeing the person-author B, as a total positive unit; consequently, A comes to like B more

  By A deciding he really does not like the poem, thereby creating a balance with B seen as a totally negative unit; consequently, B is disliked at least as much as originally

  By A doubting or denying B's authorship of the poem; in which case B is disliked as much or more than originally; and so on

The choice between these alternative resolutions presumably will depend on the magnitude of the differences between B's "substructures," that is, B as person and B as author. The greater the difference, the more likely are alternative resolutions like the latter two directly above.

The three models above derive from simple experiments in which discrepancy is induced by design. But they also seem relevant to the laboratory approach, many of whose central dynamics involve the highlighting of discrepancies. These discrepancies include, for example, differences between how a person sees herself and how others perceive her to be.

Which Model Best Accounts for Change?   Research does not yet permit us to choose definitely between the three models, but some insight is possible. Statistical details and methodological issues are omitted here, but they are available for the interested student.[81] The data for the test come from a mass team-building experience at one site for 33 sales regions of a national marketing organization, including all first-line managers and all salesmen reporting to them. The experience was considered a successful one—by the consultants, by several levels of management, as well as by most participants who made their reactions variously known.

Do the data reveal an optimum discrepancy for learning? That is, a discrepancy can exist between how a person behaves/believes and some challenging stimulus. Motivating energy is often attributed to such discrepancies, with resulting pressure to change attitudes or behaviors to reduce any discrepancy. In the present case, organization members initially described actual climate as falling short of their attitudes as to what it should ideally be. Their ideal climate was consistent with the values underlying the lab approach to OD. Presumably, the OD experience showed individuals that it was possible to change in ways that individuals preferred.

The research question: Was there a relationship between individual actual/ideal discrepancies and how much change individuals reported as a result of the OD experience? The simple models in Figure 8 help test the question. The models are analogues of Models I and II above, in effect. Heider's "balance model" defied analysis, although it has a variety of attractive features. This is inelegant, but unavoidable at this early stage of research. The alternative models are here called:

- *Accelerating* because it proposes that the greater the discrepancy before an OD intervention, the greater an individual's change motivated by a desire to reduce dissonance.

- *Decelerating*, because it implies that change in OD programs occurs more by assimilation than by contrast. Hence low discrepancies are associated with larger changes.

- *Reversible*, which is perhaps the dominant model underlying OD theory. Bennis[82] and Harrison[83] reflect such a model, for example. This variant, in effect, combines an accelerating effect for low-to-intermediate discrepancies, with decelerating change for intermediate-to-high discrepancies.

The particular interest here is in "optimum prior discrepancy," the discrepancy between what an individual would like his organization's climate or style to be, and how he perceives that climate before an OD experience. "Discrepancy" here has both attitudinal and behavioral components, in sum. In effect, the OD intervention in this case provided most participants with an experience that legitimated their preference as to organization climate, while it also encouraged behaviors appropriate for more closely approaching that preferred climate.

The specific measure of prior discrepancy uses respondent self-reports on the Likert Profile of Organizational Characteristics, Form E.[84] The Profile consists of twenty-four items which seek to measure aspects of an organization's

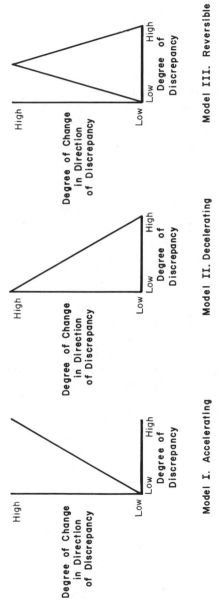

Figure 8   Three alternative models of the relationship between discrepancy and degree of change toward that discrepancy.

comprehensive climate or style, perceived both as: *Now,* where the respondent sees his organization on each item, and *Ideal,* where the respondent would like his organization to be. Differences between Ideal and Now ratings before the OD intervention provide the operational measure of prior discrepancy in this research. Ideal scores measure personal preferences about organization climate, in sum, and Now scores measure actual organization conditions as perceived by the respondents.

The twenty-four Likert items are not reproduced here to conserve space, but they can be clustered in four qualitatively different "systems of management," that is, distinct managerial climates or styles. The systems are:

1. Exploitative-authoritative
2. Benevolent-authoritative
3. Consultative
4. Participative group

Systems 1 and 4 are taken to be the antigoal and goal, respectively, of OD applications.

Overall, the OD design in this case intended to move the climate or style of thirty-three regional sales units in the direction of Likert's System 4, the Participative Group system. In effect, the design had three purposes. Thus, it legitimated looking at possible discrepancies between individual preference and organization style. Moreover, the design intended to make participants aware of actual discrepancies, where necessary. Finally, the design emphasized an approach to reducing any discrepancies by providing an impactful learning experience with appropriate values, attitudes, and behavioral skills.

The design's efficacy was tested by a simple research design, $O_1 X O_2$ in form, where O = Observation and X = OD Intervention. A pretest with the Likert Profile preceded the OD intervention by a month, and the posttest was administered approximately three months after the X. The four-month interval between the two administrations was a guesstimate about the length of time required for any attitudinal/behavioral changes to develop in the regional units, whose members came together only episodically. Both administrations were by mail, sent from the firm but returned to the senior author's university address. For convenience, data from the first administration are identified as Now 1 and Ideal 1, and the second administration data are Now 2 and Ideal 2. Of the original total of 430 sales persons, 406 responded to the first Likert administration, and 341 to the second one some 4 months later. The sample here is the 329 sales personnel who responded both times, or some 76 percent of the original N.

Which model accounts for change? Table 2 provides some preliminary data about individual respondents and their self-reports. The underlying data array— which reflects a huge matrix of 329 respondents $\times$ 4 Likert systems $\times$ 24 Likert

Table 2   Some Summary Data from Member Self-Reports About Climate of
Regional Units as Measured by Likert Profile[a]

	Initial Likert System of Management by Individual Respondent			
	System 1	System 2	System 3	System 4
1. Average number of respondents rating their region on Now 1 as	12	63	164	90
2. Mean Now 1 scores[b]	3.1	8.1	12.8	17.2
3. Mean Ideal 1 scores[c]	16.5	16.5	17.4	17.6
4. Mean discrepancy scores, or Ideal 1 Now 1[d]	13.4	8.4	4.6	0.4
5. Mean Now 2 scores[e]	9.8	11.6	13.6	15.0
6. Mean Now 2-Now 1 scores[f]	6.8	3.7	0.8	-2.2

[a]*Note:* Overall F-scores for rows 2-6 were statistically significant in all cases. As is conventional when overall F-values are significant, each paired comparison in rows 2-6 was tested for statistical significance using Duncan's multiple-range test. The test permits comparisons of each of the six possible pairs of the four Likert Systems on each of the twenty-four items, or 144 comparisons in all for each row.
[b]All 144 possible pairs of differences far surpass the 0.01 level.
[c]Of the 144 possible pairs of differences, seventy do not attain the 0.05 level. Of the seventy-two comparisons involving only Systems 2, 3, and 4, fifty-one do reach the 0.05 level.
[d]All 144 possible pairs of differences far surpass the 0.01 level.
[e]Of the 144 possible pairs of differences, 127 surpass the 0.05 level.
[f]Of the 144 possible pairs of differences, 132 surpass the 0.05 level.

items—supports four generalizations. *First,* most respondents rate their region's climate as System 1, 2, or 3, initially.

Second, Ideal 1 scores for all respondents indicate a strong preference for System 4, which is to say that respondents attitudinally prefer an organization climate consistent with the thrust of the laboratory approach to OD

Third, respondents who initially rate their regions in System 1 have the highest prior discrepancy scores by far, while System 4 respondents approximate a mean discrepancy of zero. Row 4 in Table 2 suggests this regularity. Tests of the differences between the means of the discrepancy scores, classified in terms of the four Likert systems, achieve huge F-levels.

Fourth, Table 2 suggests, and a complicated analysis not reported here strongly reinforces, that the Accelerating model of discrepancy/change best fits the data. Consider only the general support in Table 2 via a comparison of rows 4 and 6. As the mean discrepancy score decreases, in sum, so do respondents report less change in pre- versus postintervention Likert self-reports. For the lowest prior discrepancy scores, in fact, the mean change has a negative value. More specifically, relying on a table not reproduced here, the Accelerating model of discrepancy/change best accounts for changes on twenty-two of the twenty-four Likert variables. Two cases—Items 1 and 21—are deviant. The Reversible model fits them best. Note also that all twenty-two cases fitting the Accelerating model reflect statistically significant between- versus within-variance for the four Likert systems. The two cases of the Reversible model also attain statistical significance.

Some Tentative but Profound Implications.   This test generates a number of implications which, if necessarily tentative, touch profound concerns in OD programs. Most dramatically, *first,* the data imply the value of an appropriate theory of learning or change.

   Second, the data urge major attention to the tailoring of OD designs to the characteristics of change-targets. Indeed, the data imply that the discrepancies between perceived and ideal organization climate are massive covariants of change. By implication, a learning design appropriate for one degree of discrepancy might be seriously inappropriate for another degree.

   The dynamics underlying this potentially crucial interaction are not clear. Possibly, the design worsened the objective situation in which low-discrepancy respondents found themselves after the OD design. Alternatively, the postdesign regression reported by low-discrepancy respondents may be due simply to the fact that the public team-building design impressed on them the unrealism of their initial assessments of their unit's climate or atmosphere. This is a benign effect, as effects go, and probably beneficial. But it does suggest that a different design was appropriate for those whose prior discrepancies are low. For example, it appears that "social desirability"[85] might be related to the reporting of low-priority discrepancies, with some persons having a strong tendency to see and report what is socially acceptable or desirable, as contrasted with what exists.[86] If such a hypothesis is tenable, a two-stage OD design is indicated.

   Whatever the case, the next step seems obvious. Research using different OD designs for individuals and groups at different take-off points is indicated. For example, low-discrepancy respondents might profit from a more impactful design than the present one. Or, perhaps it is better to leave well enough alone, as long as respondent reports that relationships in his or her organization are more or less what he or she prefers them to be.

   Third, the results suggest that discrepancy is directly associated with change or learning. This finding has great potential importance, both in theory and for practice. However, how far the manifest regularity in the present data may be extended is not clear. Thus, a more impactful design—such as a week-long family T-group—might generate a different pattern of change or learning. Credibly, for example, a high-impact design might threaten high-discrepancy respondents so as to inhibit or preclude attitudinal or behavioral change. Fortunately, this kind of issue not only needs attention but is researchable.

Perspectives on OD as Practice/Theory
Fine-Tuning Overbounded and Underbounded Systems

The complex discussion above suggests that we will be a long time at our work, and also that the details of future working resolutions can only now be guessed at. But one point seems crystal-clear. The basic need involves integrating numerous aspects of what we typically call "practice" and "theory," without being at all specific about what that means but nonetheless certain about the diverse pushes and pulls that are conjured up by those designations.

The point has been repeated by all and sundry, so we need tarry here long enough only to sketch one general but useful way of looking at that practice/theory interaction. Alderfer develops one such perspective,[87] which can be briefly introduced here, that amounts to seeing OD as a technology for fine-tuning systems of human behavior. Alderfer sees some systems as "over-bounded"—too constricted by policies, procedures, and structures, and perhaps as existing in environments so enriched that survival is easy, coping mechanisms atrophy, and systems piddle along. Other systems are "under-bounded"—at internal sixes-and-sevens, even though their environments may be such as to demand direct and forceful action. Exhibit 4 details some of the salient characteristics of all systems, and sketches the two opposed ways in which they can get out-of-line. Chapters 2 and 8 in Part 2 provide detailed counterpoint of the present approach toward emphasizing that host organizations can differ in profound and regular ways.

We need not burden this discussion with the many practice/theory interactions implied by Exhibit 4. *The* theoretical issue clearly concerns choosing OD interventions appropriate to the "boundedness" of the host, interventions that also reflect the values we seek to realize at work. The associated practical need involves the development of ways and means to initiate behavior and norms consistent with this theoretical system. But, eschew examples and focus on the patent conclusion. The practical significance of theoretical understanding to modulate pendular swings of systems to one boundary state or the other cannot be overstated. One can call the goal "conservative" or "reactionary," from one perspective; or one can look at the goal as a kind of golden mean between extremes. But when the name-calling is done, some such modulation of extremes will go far toward determining both the efficiency and the effectiveness that we will be able to achieve in our cooperative activities. And that success or failure, in turn, will essentially define the quality of our lives.

Exhibit 4   Characteristics of Overbounded and Underbounded Systems

System Characteristics	Boundary State	
	Overbounded	Underbounded
Authority relations	Well-defined hierarchy and decision-making	Unclear authority sources, overlapping authority
Role definition	Overly specified and constraining roles; strict "job definition"	Uncertainty about limits or priorities of roles
Management of human energy	Difficult to release energy; dammed-up and blocked resources	Difficult to harness energy; physical and emotional dispersion
Communication	Easy to convene groups; problems with distortion and invalid information	Difficult to promote communication; absence of communication
Affect	Egocentric; ethnocentric; suppression of (strong) emotions	Negative internal and external emotions
Economic conditions	Stable and wealthy economic conditions	Uncertainty about sources of funding; "tight" money
Time frame	Relative long-term security; loss of responsiveness to change	Survival-oriented, crisis-oriented mentality

Source: From Clayton P. Alderfer, "Organization Development: The Profession and the Practitioner," p. 104, in Philip H. Mirvis and David N. Berg (eds.), *Failures in Organization Development and Change: Cases and Essay for Learning* (John Wiley & Sons, New York, 1977).

Notes

1. The conclusion is a common one, as in W. Warner Burke, "Organization Development in Transition," *Journal of Applied Behavioral Science,* Vol. 12 (January 1976), pp. 33-360.

2. Lyman K. Randall, quoted in Warren H. Schmidt (ed.), *Organizational Frontiers and Human Values* (Belmont, Calif.: Wadsworth, 1970), p. 22.

3. Richard Beckhard, *Organization Development: Strategies and Models* (Reading, Mass.: Addison-Wesley, 1969), p. 9.

4. Alexander Winn, "The Laboratory Approach to Organization Development: A Tentative Model of Planned Change," *Journal of Management Studies,* Vol. 6 (May 1969), p. 161.

5. Beckhard, *Organization Development,* pp. 16-19.

6. Ibid., p. 40.

7. John J. Sherwood, *An Introduction to Organization Development,* Experimental Publications System. Washington, D.C.: American Psychological Association, no. 11 (April 1971), Ms. no. 396-1. Also reprinted in J. W. Pfeiffer and J. E. Jones (eds.), *1972 Annual Handbook for Group Facilitators* (Iowa City, Iowa: University Associates, 1972).

8. Kenneth D. Benne, "From Polarization to Paradox," in Leland P. Bradford, Jack R. Gibb, and Kenneth D. Benne (eds.), *T-Group Theory and Laboratory Method* (New York: John Wiley and Sons, 1964), p. 243.

9. Samuel A. Culbert and Jerome Reisel, "Organization Development: An Applied Philosophy for Managers of Public Enterprise," *Public Administration Review,* Vol. 31 (March 1971), p. 162.

10. These objectives derive from a variety of sources, primarily from Sherwood, *Introduction to OD,* and NTL Institute for Applied Behavioral Science, "What is OD?" *News and Reports,* Vol. 2 (June 1968), p. 1.

11. Jack K. Fordyce and Raymond Weil, *Managing with People* (Reading, Mass.: Addison-Wesley, 1971), p. 18.

12. Ibid., pp. 89-90.

13. For greater detail, see Robert R. Blake and Jane S. Mouton, *The Managerial Grid* (Houston, Tex.: Gulf Publishing, 1964). See also their *The New Managerial Grid* (Houston, Tex.: Gulf Publishing, 1978).

14. Robert R. Blake, Jane S. Mouton, Louis B. Barnes, and Larry E. Greiner, "Breakthrough in Organization Development," *Harvard Business Review,* Vol. 42 (November-December 1964), p. 135.

15. Bernard M. Bass, "A Systems Survey Research Feedback for Management and Organizational Development," *Journal of Applied Behavioral Science,* Vol. 12 (June 1976), pp. 215-229.

16. For an ambitious example, see Paula Franklin and Richard Franklin, *Tomorrow's Track: Experiments with Learning to Change* (Columbia, Md.: New Community Press, 1976).

17. Wendell L. French and Cecil H. Bell, Jr., *Organization Development* (Englewood Cliffs, N.J.: Prentice-Hall, 1973), esp. pp. 25-29.

18. Mark A. Frohman, Marshall Sashkin, and Michael J. Kavanagh, "Action-Research as Applied to Organization Development," esp. pp. 142-152, in S. Lee Spray (ed.), *Organizational Effectiveness: Theory, Research, Utilization* (Kent, Ohio: Kent State Press, 1976); and Edgar F. Huse, *Organization Development and Change* (St. Paul, Minn.: West Publishing, 1975), esp. pp. 163-174.

19. Chris Argyris, *Interpersonal Competence and Organizational Effectiveness* (Homewood, Ill.: Dorsey, 1962).

20. Floyd C. Mann, "Studying and Creating Change," in Warren Bennis, Kenneth Benne, and Robert Chin (eds.), *The Planning of Change* (New York: Holt, Rinehart, Winston, 1961), pp. 605-613. For overall perspective, consult: David A. Nadler, *Feedback and Organization Development* (Reading, Mass.: Addison-Wesley, 1977); David G. Bowers and Jerome L. Franklin, *Data-Based Organizational Change* (La Jolla, Calif.: University Associates, 1977); and Robert T. Golembiewski and Richard J. Hilles, *Toward the Responsive Organization* (Salt Lake City, Utah: Brighton, 1979).

21. David Bowers and Jerome Franklin, "Survey-Guided Development Using Human Resources Measurement in Organizational Change," *Journal of Contemporary Business,* Vol. 1 (Summer 1972), pp. 43-55.

22. Rensis Likert, *The Human Organization* (New York: McGraw-Hill, 1967).

23. Mann, "Studying and Creating Change," p. 609.

24. Howard Baumgartel, "Using Employee Questionnaire Results for Improving Organizations: The Survey 'Feedback' Experiment," *Kansas Business Review,* Vol. 12 (December 1959), p. 6.

25. Arthur Blumberg and Robert T. Golembiewski, *Learning and Change in Groups* (London: Penguin, 1976), pp. 57-74.

26. Frohman, Sashkin, and Kavanagh, "Action Research," pp. 142-152; and David A. Nadler, "Use of Feedback for Organizational Change: Promises and Pitfalls," *Group and Organization Studies,* Vol. 1 (June 1976), pp. 177-186.

27. Charles T. McElvaney and Matthew B. Miles, "Using Survey Feedback and Consultation," in Richard A. Schmuck and Matthew B. Miles (eds.), *Organization Development in Schools* (Palo Alto, Calif.: National Press Books, 1971), pp. 129-130, detail the results of one administration of the design which was disappointing to them.

28. Particularly significant here is a recent attempt to test the adequacy of a survey/feedback design, compared to a control condition. The results suggest higher satisfaction of needs in the former condition, but with no significant differences in performance. Herbert H. Hand, Bernard D. Estafen, and Henry P. Sims, Jr., "How Effective Is Data Survey and Feedback as a Technique in Organization Development?" *Journal of Applied Behavioral Science,* Vol. 11 (September 1975), esp. pp. 342-343.

29. Cary L. Cooper, Ned Levine, and Koichiro Kobayashi, "Developing One's Potential," *Group and Organization Studies,* Vol. 1 (March 1976), pp. 43-55.

30. Wayne Boss, David J. Gouws, and Takeshi Nagia, "The Cross-Cultural Effects of Organizational Development Interventions: A Conflict/Confrontation Design," *Southern Review of Public Administration,* Vol. 2 (March 1978), pp. 486-502.

31. Alexander Winn, "Social Change in Industry," *Journal of Applied Behavioral Science,* Vol. 2 (April 1966), pp. 170-184.

32. Charles J. Cox and Cary L. Cooper, "Developing OD Skills in Japan and the UK: An Experiential Approach," *Journal of European Training,* Vol. 5, no. 1 (1976), pp. 4-11.

33. Zygmunt Gostkowski, "Toward Empirical Humanization of Mass Surveys," *Quality and Quantity,* Vol. 8 (March 1974), p. 12.

34. Paul R. Lawrence and Jay W. Lorsch, *Organization and Environment* (Boston: Harvard University Graduate School of Business, 1967).

35. E.g., James C. Taylor, *Technology and Planned Organizational Change* (Ann Arbor, Mich.: Institute for Social Research, 1971); and Jay W. Lorsch and Stephen A. Allen III, *Managing Diversity and Interdependence* (Boston: Harvard University Graduate School, 1973).

36. Robert T. Golembiewski and Stokes B. Carrigan, "Planned Change Through Laboratory Methods: Toward Building Organizations to Order," *Training and Development Journal,* Vol. 27 (March 1973), pp. 18-27.

37. For overall perspective, consult Malcolm Knowles, *The Adult Learner: A Neglected Species* (Houston, Texas: Gulf Publishing, 1973). For extensive summaries of a variety of models of learning, see Ernest R. Hilgard, *Theories of Learning* (New York: Appleton-Century-Crofts, 1966). More conveniently, see Freemont A. Shull, Jr., Andrew L. Delbecq, and L. L. Cummings, *Organization Decision-Making* (New York: McGraw-Hill, 1970), esp. pp. 78-81.

38. Leland P. Bradford, "Membership and the Learning Process," in Leland P. Bradford, Jack R. Gibb, and Kenneth D. Benne (eds.), *T-Group Theory and Laboratory Method* (New York: John Wiley and Sons, 1964), pp. 190-215.

39. C. M. Hampden-Turner, "An Existential 'Learning Theory' and the Integration of T-Group Research," *Journal of Applied Behavioral Science,* Vol. 2 (October 1966), pp. 367-386.

40. Bradford, Gibb, and Benne, *T-Group Theory and Laboratory Method,* p. 279.

41. Douglas R. Bunker, "Individual Applications of Laboratory Training," *Journal of Applied Behavioral Science,* Vol. 1 (April 1965), pp. 131-147.

42. Hampden-Turner, "An Existential 'Learning Theory,' " p. 376.

43. Jack R. Gibb and Lorraine M. Gibb, "Role Freedom in a TORI Group," in Arthur Burton (ed.), *Encounter* (San Francisco: Jossey-Bass, 1969), p. 43.

44. Martin Buber, "Distance and Relation," *Psychiatry,* Vol. 20 (May 1957), p. 101.

45. Kenneth D. Benne, "From Polarization to Paradox," in Bradford, Gibbs, and Benne, *T-Group Theory and Laboratory Method,* pp. 235-236.

46. William Gomberg, "Job Satisfaction: Sorting Out the Nonsense," *AFL-CIO American Federationist* (June 1973).

47.   Ashley Montague, *On Being Human* (New York: Abelard-Schuman, 1950), p. 76.

48.   Winn, "The Laboratory Approach to Organization Development," p. 163.

49.   Ibid., p. 160.

50.   Ibid., p. 158.

51.   Ibid., p. 159.

52.   Ibid., pp. 159-160.

53.   Ibid.

54.   Reed M. Powell and John F. Stinson, "The Worth of Laboratory Training," *Business Horizons,* Vol. 14 (August 1971), pp. 87-95.

55.   The simulated business environment is from E. T. Hellenbrandt and John F. Stinson, *The General Business Management Simulation* (Athens, Ohio: Follett Book Co., 1955).

56.   Powell and Stinson, "The Worth of Laboratory Training," p. 91.

57.   For the measuring instrument, see Andrew W. Halpin, *Manual for the Leader Behavior Description Questionnaire* (Columbus, Ohio: Bureau of Business Research, Ohio State University, 1957).

58.   The cohesiveness subscale of the work group description questionnaire was used in the present case. See Ralph M. Stogdill, *Managers, Employees, and Organizations,* Monograph no. 125 (Columbus, Ohio: Bureau of Business Research, Ohio State University, 1965).

59.   Powell and Stinson, "The Worth of Laboratory Training," p. 93.

60.   Ralph M. Stogdill, "A Behavioral Model of Organizations." Paper presented at Annual Meeting, American Psychological Association, Washington, D.C., September 1969.

61.   Robert T. Golembiewski, "Small Groups and Large Organizations," in James G. March (ed.), *Handbook of Organizations* (Chigaco: Rand McNally, 1965), esp. pp. 88-94 and 101-106. See also A. Paul Hare, *Handbook of Small Group Research* (New York: The Free Press, 1976), esp. pp. 210-212 and 340-341.

62.   For example, assume that the laboratory experience in the family groups had satisfactorily dealt with inclusion or affection issues, but had either not begun or not completed work on power or influence concerns. Such an outcome seems possible, even probable, given knowledge of group phases of development and their likely sequencing; this outcome clearly would have impacted on the later performance of the family groups in simulation runs. For a summary view of stages of development of T-groups, consult Robert T. Golembiewski and Arthur Blumberg (eds.), *Sensitivity Training and the Laboratory Approach* (Itasca, Ill.: F.E. Peacock, 1977), esp. pp. 88-120.

63.   Powell and Stinson, "The Worth of Laboratory Training," p. 930.

64. Newton Margulies, "Organizational Culture and Psychological Growth," *Journal of Applied Behavioral Science,* Vol. 5 (October 1969), pp. 491-508; and John D. Aram, Cyril P. Morgan, and Edward S. Esbeck, "Relation of Collaborative Interpersonal Relationships to Individual Satisfaction and Organizational Performance," *Administrative Science Quarterly,* Vol. 16 (September 1971), pp. 289-296.

65. Attempts to develop operational definitions of "needs" and to relate them to personal and organizational outcomes have not progressed very far. For proof of the point, see Gerald R. Salancik and Jeffrey Pfeffer, "An Examination of Need-Satisfaction Models of Job Attitudes," *Administrative Science Quarterly,* Vol. 22 (September 1977), pp. 427-456. Hence, the formulation here basically rests on inferences rather than on some definitive research or experimentation.

66. John Neary, "Tilting at Windmills," *Saturday Review,* Vol. 76 (November 27, 1976), pp. 12 and 16.

67. Mildred L. Burns, "The Effects of Feedback and Commitment to Change on the Behavior of Elementary School Principals," *Journal of Applied Behavioral Science,* Vol. 13 (November 2, 1977), pp. 164-165.

68. Robert T. Golembiewski and Jack Rabin (eds.), *Public Budgeting and Finance* (Itasca, Ill.: F.E. Peacock, 1975), esp. pp. 236-286.

69. Bernard Lubin and William B. Eddy, "The Laboratory Training Model," *International Journal of Group Psychotherapy,* Vol. 20 (July 1970), pp. 316-317; and Edgar Schein and Warren G. Bennis (eds.), *Personal and Organizational Change through Group Methods* (New York: John Wiley and Sons, 1965), pp. 275-276, provide the basic model for this description.

70. Schein and Bennis, *Personal and Organizational Change,* p. 276.

71. Gene W. Dalton, "Influence and Organizational Change," in Anant R. Negandhi and Joseph P. Schwitter (eds.), *Organizational Behavioral Models* (Kent, Ohio: Comparative Administrative Research Institute, 1970), pp. 77-104.

72. Ibid., p. 84.

73. Robert H. Guest, *Organizational Change* (Homewood, Ill.: Dorsey, 1962), p. 62.

74. Dalton, "Influence and Organizational Change," p. 93.

75. The following discussion is based on Robert T. Golembiewski, "Organizational Properties and Managerial Learning," *Journal of the Academy of Management,* Vol. 13 (March 1970), esp. pp. 18-21.

76. John R. P. French, Jr., "A Formal Theory of Social Power," *Psychological Review,* Vol. 63 (1957), esp. pp. 181-194.

77. Leon Festinger, *A Theory of Cognitive Dissonance* (Evanston, Ill.: Row, Peterson, 1957), p. 18.

78. James O. Whittaker, "Resolution of the Communication Discrepancy Issue," in Muzafer Sherif and Carolyn Sherif (eds.), *Attitude, Ego-Involvement, and Change* (New York: John Wiley and Sons, 1967), pp. 168-169.

79. Fritz Heider, *The Psychology of Interpersonal Relations* (New York: John Wiley and Sons, 1958), p. 177.

80. Ibid., p. 211.

81. Robert T. Golembiewski and Robert Munzenrider, "Models of Change and OD Designs: Effects at the Individual Level." Unpublished ms.

82. Warren G. Bennis, *Organization Development* (Reading, Mass.: Addison-Wesley, 1969).

83. Roger Harrison, "Group Composition Models for Laboratory Design," *Journal of Applied Behavioral Science,* Vol. I (October 1965), pp. 409-432.

84. Likert, *The Human Organization.*

85. Douglas P. Crowne and David Marlowe, *The Approval Motive* (New York: John Wiley and Sons, 1964).

86. Robert T. Golembiewski and Robert Munzenrider, "Social Desirability as an Intervening Variable in Interpreting OD Effects," *Journal of Applied Behavioral Science,* Vol. II (July 1975), pp. 317-332.

87. Clayton P. Alderfer, "Organization Development: The Profession and the Practitioner," in Philip H. Mirvis and David N. Berg (eds.), *Failures in Organization Development and Change* (New York: John Wiley and Sons, 1977), pp. 101-104.

Section 2

SOME INTERVENTIONS FOR INDIVIDUALS

Chapter 4

DEALING WITH INDIVIDUALS WHERE THEY WORK
Applying Organization Development Values to Job and Career

The focus in the three concluding chapters of Part 1 begins to shift—from theoretical considerations to practical applications, from an emphasis on the human-processual approach to OD to a growing sense of its complex interrelationships with the technostructural approach, from an emphasis on the relationships between people to a growing concern about how "people" and "technology" come to simultaneously be reflected at work in human behavior or processes as well as in structures. Part 1 focuses first on individuals, then dyads, and finally on small groups. Part 2 of this second edition will follow through on this shift in focus, albeit in the context of large organizations.

To be more specific about the thrust of this chapter, it seeks especially to meet some long-standing criticisms against the laboratory approach to OD. And the catalog of those complaints is both detailed and formidable. To sample only: it is mawkish at precisely the time we need hard-nosed realism; it foolishly attempts to substitute group consensus for individual initiative; and it creates an illusion of emotional comfort in costly groups that perversely work to envelop themselves in an artificial and temporary environment when the life-and-death issues are everywhere around us with an immediacy that cannot be shut out. Malcolm McNair put this line of criticism as directly as anyone, although his target was broader than sensitivity training. He charges that too much "emphasis on human relations encourages people to feel sorry for themselves, makes it easier for them to slough off responsibility, to find excuses for failure, to act like children." The themes McNair would like to see more emphasized are: will power, self-control, personal responsibility, analysis, judgment, and decision-making. More and more, however, McNair sees a world "in danger of wallowing in self-pity and infantilism" rather than in thinking about the job and getting it done.[1]

Several features of McNair's broadside deserve highlighting. Thus, he is essentially correct, since most OD efforts emphasize the "pleasant side of the task," as in the emphasis on organizational growth as contrasted with economic recession, cut-backs, consolidation, and retrenchment.[2] Moreover, McNair's words imply an urgency, even an anger, that the tough challenges be dealt with better in the future than in the past.

Five themes in this chapter show how spin-offs from the laboratory approach can be all that McNair would like. This section describes designs based on the laboratory approach that face difficult issues for what they are, emphasize the role of individual initiative, and cope with critical issues that must be worked through to decision and implementation. The five sections below deal, in turn, with

- Demoted managers striving to make a decent adjustment to new jobs with less pay and status
- Individuals beginning to face the critical questions of what they would like to do, and can do, with the rest of their work lives
- The special case of individuals who face midcareer crises
- An early identification of those persons with managerial potential which has dual goals: to isolate individuals with desired qualities; and to reduce the probability that talent will variously get overlooked in large organizations
- A successful effort to reduce blue-collar absenteeism and turnover in industrial settings

Note also that OD designs relevant to individuals in organizations appear at several other points in this two-part revision, and especially in Chapter 5 of Part 2 which deals with separation as a major imperative in life. The focus here is more generally on integrating the individual in organizations.

Individual Adaptation to On-the-Job Trauma
The Case of the Thirteen Demotees

This section describes how one design consistent with the laboratory approach can be helpful for a new kind of OJT, on-the-job trauma. The traditional OJT, of course, refers to on-the-job training.

On-the-job trauma assumes a special significance in today's organizations, where rapid change attains a growing prominence as a commonplace part of work, trauma generated by reorganization, reassignments, demotions, upgrading some programs and downgrading others, the obsolescing of even newly acquired skills or knowledge, and so on. Not only will there be more such trauma than ever before, but adaptations to them must at once be more rapid and more effective than before.

The pace of change has accelerated so much that clock time can no longer be relied on as the universal healer. To begin, clock time was never all that effective. Moreover, in today's organizations, the game often will be over before the effects of clock time occur. Finally, it is often morally and practically awkward to wait.

There is only one way out of this dilemma. Ways must be found to accelerate healing effects in psychological time. This section suggests one such approach to engaging much psychological time in a few hours of clock time, to moderate the effects of demotions. The design is one way to apply in organizations the massive forces often observed in sensitivity training groups, one way to apply *in vivo* the values that commonly guide the development of the miniature societies that are T-groups. The action design, in sum, seems to accelerate effects in psychological time that would occur (if at all) only during far longer periods of clock time.

Integrating Disrupted Work Patterns*

This analysis fixates on the personal and organizational aspects of the demotion of thirteen field sales managers, many of whom were senior employees. The intervention sought to help ease the inevitable stresses on the demotees. These stresses inhered in diverse personal adaptations required of demotees as they changed jobs, schedules, and routines, and as they modified levels of aspiration and perhaps self-concepts. Stresses also inhered in the need to develop viable work relations between the demotee and his new manager, who formerly had been a peer. The demotions also meant major reductions in salary for most of the men.

For the organization, the design sought to preserve its valued human resources. Although they were demoted, the men's past efforts and their anticipated future contributions were perceived as significant enough to warrant risking

*This section draws heavily on Robert T. Golembiewski, Stokes B. Carrigan, Walter R. Mead, Robert Munzenrider, and Arthur Blumberg, "Toward Building New Work Relationships: An Action Design for a Critical Intervention," *Journal of Applied Behavioral Science,* Vol. 8 (March 1972), pp. 135-148. For other designs appropriate for individuals in organizations, see Chapter 5 in Part 2.

a difficult transition. Except for management's confidence in the laboratory approach, indeed, no doubt the men in question would have been released. Demotions are uncommon, because of the problems they imply.

The intent of the intervention also can be suggested by two crude equations.[3] Equation 1 sketches the grim consequences to be avoided.

$$\begin{matrix} \text{Imaginings} \\ \text{triggered} \\ \text{by demotion} \end{matrix} + \begin{matrix} \text{Relative} \\ \text{aloneness} \end{matrix} + \begin{matrix} \text{Relative} \\ \text{helplessness} \end{matrix} = \begin{matrix} \text{Initial} \\ \text{increases} \\ \text{in} \end{matrix} \begin{cases} \text{anxiety} \\ \text{depression} \\ \text{hostility} \end{cases} \quad (1)$$

It proposes that the imaginings or speculations induced by the demotions, given the aloneness of the field situation and the helplessness to do anything but resign, would generate immediate increases in anxiety, depression, and hostility. Such effects probably would not serve the individual, nor would they help in making necessary adjustments at work. In contrast, Equation 2 proposes to confront the imaginings induced by the demotions with the sharing of resources in a community setting that hopefully will increase a demotee's sense of mastery over the consequences of his demotion.

$$\begin{matrix} \text{Imaginings} \\ \text{triggered} \\ \text{by demotion} \end{matrix} + \text{Community} + \text{Mastery} = \begin{matrix} \text{Effective} \\ \text{coping, or} \\ \text{early reductions} \\ \text{in initial} \end{matrix} \begin{cases} \text{anxiety} \\ \text{depression} \\ \text{hostility} \end{cases} (2)$$

The Demoted Population

As part of a broader reduction in force, thirteen regional managers from the marketing department of a major firm faced two choices: accepting demotion to senior salesmen, or terminating. Most demotees would suffer a major reduction in salary, with the cuts ranging from less than $1,000 to approximately four times that amount for the demotees with most seniority. Several forces in tension influenced the decision of the thirteen men. In favor of choosing termination were such factors as the generous separation allowances available to those with seniority affected by reductions in force. To suggest the countervailing forces, the job market was tight, the company was considered a good employer, and market conditions required cutting as deeply as the thirteen managers, all of whom were satisfactory performers.

All but two of the managers accepted the demotion and, as Exhibit 1 shows, were given an early work assignment intended to facilitate their making the required adaptations as effectively and quickly as possible. The demotees knew that the "integrative experience" had been discussed with, and approved by, several managerial levels in the marketing department. In addition, almost all of the demotees and all of their superiors had long-standing relations of trust with

Exhibit 1   The Timing of the Action Design

Day 1	Day 2	Day 6	Day 7	Day 45
13 managers in-formed of choices:	Decision re-quired:	Three major ac-tivities:	Two major activi-ties:	Demotees and su-periors respond to MAACL:[a]
■ demotion to salesman ■ termination	■ 11 managers accept demotion	■ demotees and superiors re-spond to MAACL: pretest	■ demotees meet individually with their new superiors	■ test of per-sistence of changes
If demotion accepted, an early work as-signment would in-volve reporting to a midwestern city for an "integrative experience" along with their new su-periors		■ demotees spend bal-ance of day in discussion ■ superiors have briefing meet-ing	■ demotees and superiors re-spond to MAACL: post-test	

[a]Multiple Affect Adjective Check List.
Source: R. T. Golembiewski, *Renewing Organizations: The Laboratory Approach to Planned Change* (Itasca, Ill.: F. E. Peacock, 1972).

the four consultants who variously participated in the development and imple-mentation of this action design.

Four Broad Purposes

Five broad goals of the critical intervention may be distinguished. *First,* demo-tions challenged consultants to apply the norms of the laboratory approach in action-research that was personally and organizationally meaningful. Signifi-cantly, demotions involve difficult transitions, in emotions, in work routines, in relationships, and in salaries. The company had invested in a major way in a program of organization development, in which a voluntary offsite sensitivity training experience for organizational peers was a major early learning vehicle. Of the twenty-two participants, eighteen—the eleven demotees and their im-mediate supervisors—had such a learning experience earlier. The other four men had their sensitivity training postponed only by the major reduction in force at issue here. Moreover, nineteen of the men had been involved in various "team development" activities that attempted to extend the initial offsite training directly into organization activities.

Second, the special characteristics of the field situation encourage prompt action. For example, typically, the field salesman might spend perhaps 9 of 10 working days on his own, which creates special problems for supervisors as well as for the salesman who might want or need help.

Third, the design provided a specific action arena in which feelings could be expressed *and* worked through, if possible. The working symbolism was the cauterization of the wound, not pleasant but preferable to the possible or probable alternatives. The antigoals were obsessiveness and the postponement of a required facing-up to new work demands that would probably loom larger with the passage of time.

Fourth, the design provided diverse support to the demotees at a critical time. This support was to come from demoted peers, superiors, and the employing organization. The common theme was: "We want this to work for you as much as possible, and not against you."

The vicious cycle to be avoided can be sketched. Depression was an expected result of the demotions, for example, especially for the more senior men. Unless carefully managed, depression can work against the man. The consequences of believing "the organization is against me" can be both subtle and profound, especially for the field salesman. Incoming cues and messages might be misinterpreted, and outgoing projections of self might trigger unintended consequences. More broadly, Ari Kiev traces an unattractive catalog of the "manifestations of depressions," which include

> diminished incentive, interest, morale, and ability to concentrate, feelings of alienation, inability to assume responsibility or to follow a routine, diminished ability of self-expression, self-assertiveness and decreased pride, irritation with interference, feelings of being unappreciated or worthlessness. . . . [The] psychophysiological concomitants of early depression . . . include insomnia, loss of appetite, excessive worrying, indigestion, and decline in energy.[4]

Toward New Status and Relationships

A two-stage learning design was developed to meet these multiple goals. The first design component brought the demotees together for discussion of their concerns, problems, and needs. Approximately 4 hours were devoted to this exploration, with two resource persons available. The formal afternoon session was kept deliberately short, although it provided the model for several informal sessions in the evening. The announced design intent was to help prepare the demotees for the next day's sessions with their individual managers concerning work relations. This action thrust sought to harness emotional energies to organization purposes rather than to diffuse them through ventilation.

Resource persons sought to harness emotional energies rather than diffuse them, and their role was consequently complex and mixed. In capsule, the resource persons sought to direct attention to "content" as well as to "process." The model for interventions was the insight → action model, with the emphasis clearly on the action. Illustratively, assume that individual A was sending signals of fear and anger concerning some technical aspect of his new job. The resource persons sought to intervene at a process level as in a T-group, with the goals of making A aware of those signals and of putting him in touch with the inducing emotions, if possible. The seven old T-group hands among the demotees were very active in this regard, also. The capstone intervention here tended to be associated with the readiness of A to raise the concern and the associated feelings with his new manager, with whom he would meet the next day. The action thrust is patent. Moreover, the technical content at issue also would be explored. Sometimes the resolution was easy, as in clarifying a misunderstanding or a misinterpretation. When the resolution was difficult, interventions by the resource persons tended to be questions with an action thrust. What does individual A prefer? What are the other alternative strategies? What role can or should his new manager play in the matter, especially in the meeting between the two that was scheduled for the next day?

More specifically, the first phase of the design began with personal reactions to the demotions, and then trended toward a growing emphasis on the problems the demotees perceived as relevant in developing the required new work relationships. The following list provides some flavor of the main themes dealt with:

- Comparing experiences, especially about the diverse ways in which various relevant organization policies were applied to their individual cases
- Encouraging expression of anxiety or hostility about the demotions themselves or about the associated processes or their style, timing, and so on
- Surfacing and testing suspicion of management, as in the concern that another personnel purge was imminent
- Isolating and, as far as possible, working through demotees' concerns about authority and dependence, as in the complaint that the demotees did not see themselves being treated as adults, or that they were men enough to take the demotions without the integrative experience
- Dealing with a variety of issues on work relations—for example, explaining demotions to clients or other salesmen—to develop strategies and norms that would reduce the probability of either avoiding the matters or awkwardly handling them in the field
- Identifying relevant others with whom interaction had been stressful or with whom it might prove to be so, the emphasis being on strategies for handling such interaction

Surely success varied from case to case, but the intention of the resource persons was constant. That intention, in sum, was to: facilitate expression of feelings and reactions; help reveal the diversity of the demotees' experiences and coping strategies; and work toward a successful adaptation to the demands of the new job. More broadly, the resource persons were not advocates of management actions; nor were they neuters without emotional response to the sometimes tragicomic dynamics of the demotions. But they were committed to helping the demotees face their demotions as clearly and realistically as possible. Hence, demotees might decide to accept termination after the integrative experience. None of the men did so, but the option was announced to the men, after top-level management's agreement had been secured.

Two themes provide a useful substantive summary of the products of this first design component. Paramountly, almost all demotees emphasized the positive meaning of the integrative experience, whatever its specific outcomes. The design implied to them their value to the organization and reflected a continuing effort to provide resources which would help them do the job. The positive evaluation was variously shared by all the supervisors. One of the demotees took a different approach. He resented the integrative experience as "hand-holding" and "coddling."

The first component of the learning design emphasized some common elements among the demotees, as well as some differentiating factors. The training staff saw both the commonality and differentiation as being reality-based, and their conscious strategy was to avoid at all costs a strained display of ardent but feigned homogeneity or good fellowship among the demotees.

The elements of commonality that emerged in discussion among the demotees were expected ones. They include: the impact of the demotion on the self; experiences with important referents such as wives, colleagues, or salesmen from other firms; and concerns about taking on the salesman's job, about "picking up the bag again" to cover a sales territory, about participating in sales meetings, and so on.

The differentiating elements were harder for the men to openly identify, but they were no less clearly reality-based. For example, the demotees included both long-service employees and recent managerial appointees. Reasonably, on balance, the younger men felt more optimism about being repromoted at some future date. The prognosis for the longer-service men was far less bright, realistically, and they generally if sometimes grudgingly acknowledged the point. Relatedly, some men professed shock at being confronted with the choice of demotion or termination. Others maintained they had more-or-less expected some action, because of falling demand in the industry, or performance problems, or both. A few even expressed pleasure that the action was not as severe for them as it had been for those of their colleagues who were released outright.

The second component of the integrative experience took two approaches to extending demotee concerns into action, via the development of new working relations between the managers and their new subordinates. In the first approach, the managers met for some 2 hours to discuss the design for the next day and their role in it. The meeting's initial tone was a kind of gallows humor, which the training staff interpreted as understandable anxiety among the managers about their role. This initial tone quickly dissipated into the theme of making the transitions as easy as possible for all concerned. The basic thrust was to empathize with how the demotees were feeling and to channel those feelings toward making the most successful adaptation possible.

Each demotee spent approximately 3 hours of the second day of the design with his manager, one-on-one. The resource persons sat in on some of the dyads, as time permitted, and especially the dyads with senior demotees. The major concerns involving these dyads were

- The building of early supervisory relations, as in mutual pledges to work harmoniously together, which was easy enough in some cases because some of the demotees were able to choose their new managers as they exercised various options to relocate
- Technical problems such as going over sales territories, and so on
- Developing strategies by which the manager and man could be mutually helpful, as in discussing ways to moderate the formation of cliques that the demotions could encourage
- Isolating likely problems and cementing a contract to agree to meet any such problems mutually and early

Some dyads concentrated on one of these concerns, while others gave attention to several themes.

Measuring Intended Effects of the Design

The effects of the action design for helping integrate disrupted work patterns were judged by changes in the Multiple Affect Adjective Check List (MAACL), which conceives of affect not as a trait but as a state. That is, a time referent is specified for the respondent, who reacts as he feels "today" or "now" as opposed to how he feels "generally" or "occasionally." The researchers explain that MAACL

> was designed to fill the need for a self-administered test which would provide valid measures of three of the clinically relevant negative affects: anxiety, depression, and hostility. No attempt was made to measure positive affects but some of the evidence indicates that the scales are bipolar, and that low scores on the full scales will indicate states of positive affect.[5]

The instrument was not then yet recommended for routine applied use,[6] but a detailed bibliography suggests its validity.[7]

The expectations in this case were direct. The demotees would have high initial scores on anxiety, depression, and hostility, the three target variables, which a successful intervention would reduce significantly in a posttreatment administration of MAACL. Lower initial scores were expected for the managers, and the posttreatment administration was not expected to reveal any major shifts in scores, except perhaps on anxiety.

The design sought not only topical relief via temporary reductions in the target variables, however, but also to induce persisting reductions. Consequently, a third follow-up administration of MAACL was administered by mail approximately a month after the planned intervention. The purpose was to develop data about the persistence of any changes.

Sharp and Persisting Effects on All Target Variables

The design had the major intended effects, which can be characterized by six themes. *First,* as expected, the demotees initially generated high scores on all three MAACL scales, although they were not "unusually high."[8]

Second, the data meet all expectations concerning changes attributable to the training intervention. Specifically, demotees reported statistically significant decreases on all three scales on the second administration of the MAACL, and these sharp and sudden reductions were at least maintained through the third administration. Anxiety scores on administration 2 versus 3 also show a statistically significant reduction following the earlier major reductions.

Third, the scores of the managers showed a significant change only for anxiety. That reduction is most easily attributed to a successful intervention, a building down from a realistic prior concern about what the integrative experience would demand of the supervisor. Interestingly, scores on the hostility scale increased for the managers, although not significantly so. This may reflect a reasonable reaction against the action design, or against the training staff, whose clear bias was to help the demoted men rather than the managers. The moderate increase in hostility scores suggests a neglect of supervisory needs, in sum, which subsequent design variations should recognize.

Fourth, a variety of analytic approaches establishes that the design had quite uniform effects for all demotees, regardless of their other differences. To conserve space, these are not detailed here.

Fifth, the effects on individuals also establish the efficacy of the training design. For example, a comparison of the first and second MAACL administrations reveals that of the thirty-three comparisons—eleven demotees on three MAACL scales—twenty-six were reductions in scores and three were no-changes. In addition, no demotee had an increased score on more than one scale. Looked at from another point of view, the data show only a single demotee who had even one score that had significantly increased in the interval following the first administration.

Sixth, postexperience interview and questionnaire responses from the demotees and several levels of supervision underscore the value of the experience.

Many of the details cannot be revealed, since they tend to identify specific individuals. But, the respondents all but universally acknowledge the positive impact of the design. Similarly, the betting odds beforehand were that major problems could be expected with perhaps half of the demotees in the transition. Significantly, but not conclusively, all eleven demotees were still on the job some 6 months later, and the adaptations of ten of the men were rated by their managers as "in great shape" or "more than adequate" on a 20-point scale running through "adequate," "somewhat inadequate," and "critically inadequate." All the men were still doing satisfactory work 18 months later, and three had been repromoted to managers.

Real, if Restrained, Promise in the Results

The intervention, then, seems to have quickly reversed emotional states that could have generated consequences troublesome for the individual and the organization. Note also that it seems likely that the present learning design profited from earlier work in the host organization to develop norms, attitudes, and behaviors consistent with the laboratory approach. No concrete proof exists, but the training staff feels strongly that the observed effects derive in some substantial part from the earlier work in sensitivity training groups, as that training influenced individual behavior and as it helped develop appropriate attitudes and norms in the host organization. Consequently, this design may not be applicable in organizations as a first-generation effort.

Individual Assessment of One's Work
Career Planning as a Regular Concern

The analysis shifts from the ad hoc to the comprehensive—from a specific job action to the career. One of the many ongoing mini-revolutions in organizations involves "career planning." Such designs—often based on the laboratory approach—have attempted to extend its values and dynamics into a critical, practical setting. This seems a natural extension. To level with one's self about career, epigrammatically, certainly is consistent with leveling with others in interpersonal relations. Indeed, the extension appears to be widely perceived as an obvious given. That is, the substantial attention to career planning has not motivated the development of a supporting literature. As Super and Hall note: "In view of the great number of training activities in industry specifically devoted to career planning, it is disappointing that there is so little published research on their effectiveness."[9]

 In retrospect and in the broad perspective, in fact, this combination of great attention to the practice of career planning and paltry concern for research should not surprise. Much obviously needs doing, and the thrust of what needs doing seems equally obvious. A caricature might be useful. In days gone by, when one hired a "hand" the location of the rest of the person mattered little as long as that "hand" kept moving appropriately. Today, and for many operators as well as managers, it makes a great deal of difference where the total woman or man is—in complex physical, social, and emotional space. Many organization roles today demand so much of their incumbents that serious consequences increasingly occur if the individual is not "all there." For the individual, the costs may be a need-depriving job, of acting a role that has lost its attractiveness. For the organization, the costs might be decreased innovation or productivity, neglected opportunities, or a quality of life with the zest sucked from it.

Hence both practical and humanist reasons urge increasing organizational attention to career planning. For this design confronts the critical issue of whether a person's work is providing what he or she really wants and needs, and vice versa. If work is not need-satisfying enough, it is to the advantage of both the person and the organization that the fact be recognized early and that plans be made to do something to change the situation.

Costs and Benefits of Continuous Review

There are many possible kinds of career planning, and some elementary distinctions will be useful. Thus, approaches to career planning variously emphasize "can do" and "will do" issues.[10] The former deal with specific skills or knowledge, and the latter involve motivation. Relatedly, approaches to career planning differ in their concern with the psychometric measurement of skills or attitudes as a basis for career planning.[11] Various approaches also differ in their concern about validation of effects, although little research is available about the consequences of career-planning activities.[12]

The more general flavor of career-planning activities can be suggested by the introduction to an in-house seminar lasting 2 full days which is given in Exhibit 2. The participant gets these orienting cues at the very start.

Such a career-planning seminar has a dual purpose. It seeks to induce values and attitudes in participants that encourage more-or-less continuous review of career progress and individual needs. There are many possible focal questions. Is my career development so satisfying that I can really let myself get into my work? If so, fine. Or do I continuously hold back my efforts because I wonder: Is all this effort getting me what I really want? If not, the questions are legion. What needs are being frustrated in my present job? And why? And what skills do I need to develop in order to avoid the need-depriving consequences of my present job and career prospects? The antigoal is dying on the vine, which is both individually tragic and organizationally wasteful. The hope of career planning is that the tragedy and the waste can be avoided or at least reduced if

Exhibit 2   Introduction to Career-Planning Seminar

CAREER-PLANNING SEMINAR

The purpose of this seminar is to help you set personal career goals and plan how to attain them. This will be done by assessing and defining your present skills and strengths more precisely.

Many people in large organizations like this one have come into the company with a vague goal of "being successful." This meant moving "up" in the organization, making more money, having an office instead of a work space, supervising others, etc. The assumption was that good performance and appropriate behavior would be rewarded with increased status and money.

The trouble with this "success formula" is that it never asks the question, "What do *you* really want to *do?*" Instead of the job being rewarding in itself, many of us see it only as a *means* to get other rewards—newer, bigger cars, better furnished homes, more pleasant vacations, and a college education for our children.

People find work more meaningful and rewarding when they can relate it to their personal career goals. Unfortunately, many people have difficulty defining career goals.

In this two-day seminar you will
- Define who *you* are in terms of your aptitudes, skills, and strengths
- Define what *you* mean by success
- Define where *you* want to go
- Plan how *you* will get there

Source: Career-planning seminar designed and developed by Walter R. Mead, Corporate Personnel, Smith, Kline and French Laboratories, 1971.

the appropriate issues are confronted throughout a person's career, early as well as late.

Career planning can also have a special value at a variety of critical points in a work life.[13] Some of these critical points occur in every work life at more or less predictable times:

- You, like many persons in their forties, start to raise fundamental questions about how you wish to spend the second half of your life.

Other critical career points are difficult or impossible to program. Some examples include:

- You find an attractive job opportunity has become open, but it will require relocation of your family.
- You have a fairly senior technical position and are considering whether you should apply for a managerial position and whether you would accept one if it were offered.
- You have acquired a specialty which technological advance is making increasingly obsolescent. Do you hang on until the bitter end? Or do you seek to develop a new specialty as early as you can?
- You have come to doubt the value of what had been a life's calling, as in leaving business for the clergy or in leaving the celibate clergy to marry and raise a family.

Some Issues for Organizations

Whether viewed as continuous review or as applied to an immediate situation, career planning raises significant cost/benefit questions. Consider some typical costs from the organization's point of view. Thus, career planning is dangerous in organizations that will hold people in jobs that are need-depriving, or in jobs to which individuals are not committed. No value is placed on this organization strategy, for there are circumstances such as a just war which might justify it. The narrower point here, rather, is that a career-planning program that really works will encourage at least some people to try something new, either in the organization or outside of it. In a sense, the organization with a real career-planning program sanctions learning that will encourage some people to leave their present jobs, or even the organization. And these departures will not always be the persons for whom management would be pleased to host a going-away party, on short notice.

Career planning also would become a hollow effort if it is seen as an indirect way of getting rid of people, or of molding them to some master plan for their own destiny of which they are not yet enlightened enough to be aware. The real tests are who gets invited to participate in career-planning activities, and whether the organization can respond helpfully to even awkward products of career planning. If many clear organizational losers get invited, for example, the program may quickly develop a reputation as a kind of preparatory training for a separation anxiety. If only organizationally convenient career programs get acted on, similarly, invitees will no doubt become reticent about undertaking any real self-analysis.

Moreover, career planning can raise issues for individuals and the organization that might be better avoided unless a real commitment to following through exists. From the individual's point of view, disquieting questions may be raised that require time and patience to explore. Organizationally, career-planning programs may indicate that specific policies, procedures, or structures create impossible situations for people. Career development thus must be tied to the possibility of meaningful change in the organization. If the individual must adapt to a given organization—becoming the kind of peg the organization requires—a career-planning program is not likely to be productive. In fact, it may be bitterly resented. The individual probably will feel that he has sold his soul to the company store in this case; he is not likely to feel that he is directing and charting his own future in the ways that career planning intends.

In addition, organizations must face the issue of the advisability of worrying about whether one has the right job, as opposed to worrying about how to perform more effectively in the job one has. There is no single best response to such a concern. Different conditions will make different responses reasonable. In an economy of rapidly obsolescing skills, the priority often will be on whether a person is in the right job. For yesterday's training and experience will not necessarily suffice for today's job demands.

Finally, career plans are no better than their implementation. And here is a major rub. For an individual might plan, but implementation commonly requires the help of others, such as supervisors, and resources not controlled by the individual. Moreover, some career plans might require that the plans of others be modified, new strategies be developed, and so on. In sum, if career planning is viewed basically as a way of easing people out of the organization, it is a very involved and treacherous way of doing it because so many interlocking factors are involved.

Some Benefits for Individuals

The benefits for the individual can cover a broad range, although no real research literature exists that provides unchallengeable guidance. *First,* the individual may feel a new sense of control over her life as she struggles to determine whether her present course is the one she really desires. Even if no change results, the individual may feel a new commitment and dedication to a career pathway that she has analyzed and come to accept at a deeper level in her own way and time.

Second, and relatedly, the individual may come to feel a new sense of responsibility for where he is in his career. This is certainly the case if he decides to take some new direction as a result of career planning. An enhanced sense of personal responsibility is also likely even if the individual continues as before, after a hard look at career planning. As with the laboratory approach, the goals are to increase the degrees to which individuals can own their career choices, feel commitment to them, and have the sense and reality of having some control over what happens in their work lives.

The strategy of career planning is a transparent one, then, in these first two particulars. To choose is the ultimate human act, and to feel responsible for a choice is to announce ownership and commitment. Career planning attempts to create the conditions where greater opportunities exist for responsible choice, conditions that permit persons to affirm their existence in part of their life pace. In essence, then, career planning is oriented toward a new quality of life in organizations.

Third, conscious weighing of "musts" and "likes" with personal skills and abilities in career planning can put the individual in a more realistic attitude. Does he or she really need a certain source of satisfaction at work? Or is it more a matter of that source being an attractive but unessential feature? And does the person either have the skills to achieve her musts, or can she somehow reasonably expect to gain them? Or is she just engaged in wishful thinking? These are critical questions that a career-planning program seeks to have each participant confront.

A Sample Design[14]

Exhibit 3 sketches the outline of a career-planning seminar based on the laboratory approach, an opening experience that is intended to encourage organization
members to give continuing attention to their own development. Participation is
voluntary. Basically, the design can speak for itself, since it is quite transparent
in intent, as the column "Purpose of Design Element" in Exhibit 3 should establish. The internal logic of the design also should be clear enough. For example,
it begins with less-threatening elements and escalates to those that can be quite
threatening. Moreover, the design seeks a true collaboration between participants
that reinforces their sense of individual responsibility and initiative. Hence, the
design initially emphasizes feedback and inputs from others, as each participant
sharpens his own sense of career planning. Then, design elements 8 and 9 in
Exhibit 3 shift the emphasis to individual planning and action. That is, each
individual best serves herself as well as others by turning inward on her own
resources to take responsibility for actions or designs. The theme is paradoxical:
assertion of self through others. Finally, design element 10 returns to the group
locus for what can be done better there than by separate individuals: to share
ideas, stimulate further probing, and provide reinforcement as well as emotional
support for additional efforts toward career planning in the future.

Midlife Transition and Midcareer Crisis*
A Special Case for Individual Development

Accumulating knowledge and experience imply that high-resolution tuning is
both possible and necessary in career planning, as well as in what has come to be
known as "lifelong learning." That is, adult life is neither unpredictable nor of a
single piece. This section seeks to show why this is the case as well as to highlight some of the major organizational consequences of the fact that people
move through major stages or phases of life, more or less predictably.
      Three main points stake out the present concern. Thus, we are beginning to
distinguish phases in adult life, central among which is the midlife transition.
Moreover, it is increasingly meaningful to speak of midcareer crisis as a fact of
organizational life. Finally, the combined effect of midlife transition and midcareer crisis can be potent, as they were for the ex-city manager about age 40
who was experiencing both. He asked plaintively:

> Here I am coming into the peak of my career, and I am more down than I've
> ever been. And I've got my family well along, but somewhere they grew

*Paper presented at the Annual Meeting, American Society for Public Administration,
Washington, D.C., April 1976. Later reprinted with substantial modifications in *Public
Administration Review*, Vol. 38 (May 1978), pp. 215-222.

Exhibit 3   Design for a Career-Planning Seminar

Duration (minutes)	Description of Activity	Purpose of Design Element
?	1. Premeeting work. Each participant prepares a list of six "most satisfying achievements since leaving high school" and describes in writing specifically what he did. The list is to be brought to the first meeting of the Career-Planning Seminar.	1a. to start the individual thinking about what things he finds valuable and satisfying 1b. to start the individual thinking about his positive skills and abilities reflected in these achievements.
90	2. Groups of six individuals briefly introduce themselves, and then in turn: ■ Each individual describes and briefly discusses his first most satisfying achievement. ■ Other individuals jot down the skills and abilities seen as relevant in that achievement. ■ Each individual in turn describes the second most satisfying achievement, then the third, etc. ■ Notes about skills and abilities reflected in these other achievements are taken. ■ Each of the six persons in the Seminar ends up with five sets of notes about his skills and abilities, one set from each of the other five participants who heard each of his achievements described.	2a. to provide a positive start to self-analysis 2b. to provide each individual with lists of his positive skills and abilities as perceived by others 2c. to provide each individual with some gentle feedback concerning what others perceive as his strengths which he might later use to make his career plans as realistic as possible
35–40	3. Each individual prepares a list of how five specific individuals who know him well would describe him, with the instructions this time calling for both positive and negative features: ■ Participants prepare descriptions of "Me as Seen by Others." ■ Participants in turn share these descriptions by reading them aloud.	3a. to introduce gently the individual's negative features 3b. to provide some reality testing of these negative features by other participants, based on their probably limited acquaintance
5 5 15 5 15	4. The focus is on the various roles that participants assume in their work lives and at home. The subelements of the design variously expand on this theme: ■ In a deliberately brief period of time, participants prepare as long a list as they can of roles they play. ■ Participants in turn share their lists of roles. ■ Each participant adds to his own list as he hears roles shared by others that are reasonably applicable to himself. ■ Each participant then distinguishes two lists: a. roles that are most satisfying b. roles that are least satisfying ■ Taking only the list of least-satisfying roles, each participant deals with two critical questions: a. What do I dislike about the least-satisfying roles?	4a. to remind participants of the variety of roles they play, and of their diverse reactions to them 4b. to encourage participants to think of specific factors in roles that induce dislike or dissatisfaction 4c. to raise motivational issues with participants, to help determine whether there is any way of avoiding the performance of disliked/dissatisfying roles 4d. to heighten the sense of personal choice and individual responsibility by choosing to accept certain roles and to reject others

Exhibit 3   (Continued)

b. Why do I continue to fulfill these least-liked roles?

60–75

■ Participants share as much about answers to these two critical questions as they wish.

60–75

5. The focus is on "success patterns," dealing at greater depth with the six most satisfying achievements introduced in items 1 and 2 above:
   ■ Each achievement is rated in terms of 10 possible satisfactions, each of which is to be listed as a "major" or "minor" factor in each achievement.
   ■ A scoring system helps the individual to discern if there is an underlying consistency in which particular combinations of satisfactions define personal "achievement" or "success."
   ■ Based on these combinations, the individual develops "My Definition of Success" in writing.
   ■ The results are shared with the group of six, especially the definitions of success.

5a. to encourage the individual to think about what he needs to succeed or achieve, in terms of specific satisfactions relevant to Self

5b. to search for patterns in personally defined clusters of satisfactions

5c. to develop a written definition of "success" against which to measure current job roles, etc.

60–90

6. A "fantasy experience" concludes the design for the first day, with the focus on three things each participant would like to have done with his career:
   ■ Each participant draws three pictures representing these three unfulfilled desires.
   ■ The admonition is to draw a picture, not a projective image.
   ■ The pictures can be shared.

6a. to end the day with an ostensibly light exercise

6b. to induce some minor regression that may reveal insights controlled under other circumstances

30–45

7. Deliberately, the design begins to deal with more difficult issues:
   ■ Each participant describes Self in detail in writing, in the third person.
   ■ The third-person descriptions are read to the other participants, who react.

7a. to encourage the participant to be an observer of Self, to facilitate personal analysis by adapting an observational perspective of the Self

7b. to provide some measure of how realistic the person is in assessing his own qualities, in observing the Self

60–75

8. While preceding design elements were intended to sharpen insights, the focus here is directly on the present or future job, as well as on action steps to make it meet the individual's needs and values:
   ■ Each participant drafts an ideal future job description that would meet his needs
   ■ each participant must detail the specifics of what resources he has or requires in order to fill that ideal job description, e.g.:
     a. credentials
     b. information
     c. skills
     d. contacts
   These products are not shared.

8a. to encourage participants to develop their plans to fit their needs and values

8b. to encourage participants to match their resources, job preferences, and values with specific career plans

8c. to reinforce the critical notion that, beyond a certain point, career planning rests on individual decisions and initiatives

Exhibit 3   (Continued)

90–120	9. All participants are told that they cannot change their jobs, short of major and unexpected developments, and hence must improve their present jobs: ■ Each participant designs five initial steps for a job-improvement plan. ■ Each individual has one hour to begin or complete as many of the five initial steps as he can. ■ Six participants reassemble to share reactions to their efforts to implement their job-improvement plans.	9a. to encourage participants into an action mode, as a complement to the earlier analytical mode 9b. to provide an experience with the possibilities for improving a job environment 9c. to give the participant a sense of control over his environment and a feeling of individual responsibility for increasing the need-satisfying potential of his work
30–40	10. Each participant prepares a list of "Excuses for Inaction" and shares it by reading it to other participants, who discuss each list.	10a. to warn participants of the seductive quality of "excuses" or "reasons" for not acting after the Seminar 10b. to emphasize, from a negative perspective, that failure to act is often a self-imposed restriction and a lost opportunity to exercise initiative 10c. to reinforce any developing norms or values toward future action/planning re careers of participants
15	11. Wrap-Up and Evaluation.	

Source: R. T. Golembiewski, *Renewing Organizations: The Laboratory Approach to Planned Change* (Itasca, Ill.: F. E. Peacock, 1972).

away from me before I knew it was happening. Life's no longer sweet. My values seem to change just as I began to achieve what I long thought was important. Now I wonder about what I have. Why is that? It doesn't seem right!

These three realizations have come on full-force of late and—although far more questions exist than answers—useful experiences and research have begun to accumulate. Recent advances in knowledge at once reinforce the need for organizations and professional associations to provide facilitative experiences for midcareerists, and they also suggest some specifics about the "when" and the "what" of these experiences. Some useful attention has been given to "career planning," as the section above illustrates. What we are coming to know about adult life urges major qualitative and quantitative extensions of these newly won beachheads.

This discussion seeks to motivate greater attention to midcareer crisis, especially by professional associations and employing organizations, in a kind of new cooperative humanism to make the work site more responsive to individual needs. Generally, the argument is that such trauma are often the concomitants of a broader midlife transition through which we all must pass, whether lightly or with much wailing and gnashing of teeth. Specifically, the succeeding emphasis will be upon:

- Some general agreements about midlife transition
- The location of midlife transition in the broader flow of adulthood
- Some major issues in the midlife transition
- How the midlife transition has a special nowness, a contemporary significance in midcareer choices

General Agreements About Midlife Transition

At least six general agreements seem to have emerged from accumulating research and experience. *First,* there is a growing awareness of the subtle, developmental texture of the middle years. It was not always so; indeed, solid support of the awareness rests only on recent, even contemporary, research. In part, the growth of the awareness was squelched by long-standing dicta like that of Freud concerning "inelasticity of the ego" in people "near and above the fifties."[15] In part, also, awareness was muted by the lack until the late 1960s of longitudinal investigations of people as they moved through life, a lack which derived from the gargantuan difficulties of such research.[16]

Such common thoughtways had definite effects on research traditions. As late as 1974, for example, a distinguished group of behavioral scientists decried "the tremendous neglect of development and socialization in the main adult years, roughly 20-65, in psychology, psychiatry, sociology, and so on." They conclude: "We speak as though development goes on to age 6, or perhaps to age 18; then there is a long plateau in which random things occur; and then at around 60 or 65 'aging' begins."[17] Roger Gould colorfully paints the derivative and inadequate concept of these "main adult years." He observes:[18]

> Like a butterfly, an adult is supposed to emerge fully formed and on cue, after a succession of developmental stages in childhood. Equipped with all the accounterments, such as wisdom and rationality, the adult supposedly remains quiescent for another half century or so. While children change, adults only age.

Second, the period 35 to 43 is most favored[19] as dating the midlife transition. The time of onset, severity, and duration will vary from individual to individual however. Some persons are hardly affected during this transitional period; some experience a great torment; and most people feel some pangs in the transition.

Third, the transition seems to affect both men and women, coming at roughly the same ages but with some significant differences between the sexes as to mode of onset and coping.[20] Jacques effectively makes both points:[21]

> The transition is often obscured in women by the proximity of the onset changes connected with the menopause. In the case of men, the change has from time to time been referred to as the climacteric, because of the reduction in the intensity of sexual behaviour which often occurs at that time.

Fourth, depression is the common toxic reaction to midlife transition, and it seems to derive from a chronologically simple but psychologically momentous fact. "The individual has stopped growing up," Jacques observes, "and has begun to grow old." He concludes:[22]

> The first phase of adult life has been lived. Family and occupation have become established (or ought to have become established unless the individual's adjustment has gone seriously awry); parents have grown old, and children are at the threshold of adulthood. Youth and childhood are past and gone, and demand to be mourned. The achievement of mature and independent adulthood presents itself as the main psychological task. The paradox is that of entering the prime of life, the stage of fulfilment, but at the same time the prime and fulfilment are dated. Death lies beyond.

That is, the midlife transition fishes in deep and dark waters. Life may even proceed on two planes, as it were. In discussing eight major studies on aging, for example, Neugarten observes that they seem to fall in one of two clusters. Some studies indicate a range of individual differences largely independent of age; and other studies highlight differences in which chronological age seems a critical factor. Neugarten calls the first set of individual differences "socioadaptational," referring to those which focus "on more purposive processes in the personality, processes in which attempted control of the self and of the life situation are conspicuous elements." Revealingly, the individual differences ordered by chronological age Neugarten calls "intrapsychic" because they reflect processes "not readily available to awareness or to conscious control and which do not have direct expression in overt patterns of social behavior."[23] That is, the processes of aging go on at central levels of the personality, even if they may not be apparent at more superficial levels. Those processes seem to go on even if they are vigorously denied at conscious levels.

Fifth, evidence strongly implies the criticality of the midlife transition. Among persons of great accomplishment, for example, many observers have noted that the onset of the middle thirties often means that the prominent become "beset with misgivings, agonizing inquiries, and a loss of zest."[24] Jacques concludes that this common crisis can be resolved in three ways:[25]

- The career of accomplishment may come to an end, as in a drying up of creative work or even in death.
- A decisive change in the kind and quality of the accomplishment may occur.

- For a few, a successful midlife transition may express itself in major accomplishments.

The transition also seems important for Everyman as well.[26] A failure to come to grips with the midlife transition, Jacques notes, implies an "impoverishment of emotional life" and may even lead to "real character deterioration." Other observers chart an even sorrier catalog of the consequences of an ineffective transition. Commenting about professionals in their middle thirties, for example, Kaufman observes:

> During this period professionals perceive that what they have been doing is no longer fulfilling or important and that they have not attained the success in their careers that they expected. . . . It is during this period that careers, as well as marriages, go on the rocks and high rates of alcoholism, depression, suicide, and serious accidents occur. In fact, a peak in the death rate occurs between ages 35 and 40, and some have attributed it to the physical illness that is likely to accompany the emotional shock and severe depression that follow the individual's perception that he is on an irreversible downward path.

To be sure, many professionals continue to be effective throughout the transition, and some go on to even greater achievements. But the rates are not known.

Sixth, evidence suggests that midlife phenomena apply cross-culturally. One study, for example, finds basic similarities in the psychology of later life between lowland Mayans and urban Americans.[27]

Major Developmental Periods in Male Adulthood

It is useful to locate the midlife years in the context of full adulthood. Some interpretive restraint is necessary, however, because of the sometimes great variations in individual life experiences. Until recently, moreover, we paid little attention to the specific quality and texture of the long "middle years," that portion of life which roughly begins after school and ends just before retirement. Fortunately, some recent efforts have sought to fill that gap in knowledge, the specific interest being in "generating and working with hypotheses concerning relatively universal, genotypic, age-linked, adult developmental periods."[28]

Exhibit 4 sketches one view of male adulthood, in which the midlife transition is the entry to the last half of life through which all must pass. Successfully negotiated, the transition can lead to a long period of fulfilling life that is both stable and productive. An unsuccessful effort, alternatively, can lead to a frustrating life of turmoil and despair that seems endless.

The emphasis here is necessarily selective rather than exclusive, in at least two senses. Thus, the exhibit merely outlines the major developmental stages from an intensive study of only forty males, the major central tendencies in

Exhibit 4   Important Stages of Adult Male Development Centering on Midlife Transition

I. Early Adulthood (roughly, ages 20-40)

    A. Leaving the family

        A transition phase which begins at 16-18 and ends at perhaps 20-24, and sees the individual in the process of leaving the family of origin—a balance between "being in" and "moving out."

    B. Getting into the adult world

        Begins in the early twenties and typically extends to the early thirties, with the focus on building an adult life—"to explore the available possibilities of the adult world, to arrive at an initial definition of oneself as an adult, and *to fashion an initial life structure* that provides a viable link between the valued self and the wider adult world" (p. 247). A "dream" or vision of the future is a central feature of this period for many, often with an occupational focus. Early progress is checked against this dream or vision. Several patterns characterize this period of exploration and choice, including:

        1. For many males, a provisional commitment to an occupation and perhaps a marriage with, around 30, a transitional period focusing on whether to make a deeper commitment to the initial career and marriage choices

        2. For some males, a moderate or drastic change about 30 in initial occupation and life structure, which are seen as too constraining

        3. For some males, a transient and unsettled life in the twenties which leads around 30 to desperate attempts to "get more order and stability into . . . life" (p. 248)

    C. Settling down

        Begins in the early thirties for those who successfully make the transition. This typically occurs by the middle thirties, or not at all. Includes two central aspects:

        1. Order, stability, security, control

        2. "Making it"—planning, striving, moving onward and upward

        Overall, the individual "makes deeper commitments; invests more of himself in his work, family, and valued interests; and within the framework of this life structure, makes and pursues more long-range plans and goals" (p. 249).

    D. Becoming one's own man

        This is a time of peaking and of transition, often beginning in the middle or late thirties and lasting in cases until the forties. The prime feature is a sense of constraint and oppression in work, marriage, and other relationships. Whatever the accomplishments, that is, the indi-

Exhibit 4   (Continued)

vidual perceives self as insufficiently his own man. Central features of this striving for new autonomy typically include:

1.   A rejection or substantial modification of relationships with "mentors," older colleagues who have been supportive but parental ego-ideals, a process that usually has run its course by age 40

2.   The choice of some key event or achievement against which the individual will measure his affirmation or devaluation by society or relevant others—a promotion, new job, or some other achievement—which outcome may take 3 to 6 years to unfold

E.   Midlife transition

This is a pivotal time between two more stable periods, which usually peaks in the early forties. The transition can be smooth—or turbulent. The central issue is the disparity between what has been achieved and what is desired. Related issues involve:

1.   Bodily decline and the growing sense of mortality

2.   Aging

3.   The emergence and the integration of the "more feminine" aspects of the self

II.   Middle adulthood (roughly, ages 40-60)

A.   Restabilization. At around 45, the midlife transition is typically complete, and men come to a time of great threat or major developmental advance. For those who succeed, this can be a period of great vitality built on the new life structure evolved in the midlife transition.

III.   Late adulthood (roughly, ages 60+)

Source: Based on Daniel J. Levinson, Charlotte M. Darrow, Edward B. Klein, Maria H. Levinson, and Broxton McKee, "The Psychosocial Development of Men in Early Adulthood and the Mid-Life Transition," pp. 243-258, in David Ricks, Alexander Thomas, and Merril Roff (eds.), *Life History Research in Psychopathology,* Vol. 3 (Minneapolis, Minn.: University of Minnesota Press, 1974). Please also consult Daniel J. Levinson's *The Seasons of a Man's Life* (New York: Alfred A. Knopf, 1978).

complex data which were not obscured even by sometimes great variations in individual experiences. No judgment about the kind of developmental profile appropriate for females is made here. Patently, the common wisdom implies major differences between males and females, but that may more reflect the effects of role stereotypy than the dynamics of femininity. Some apparently major differences between males and females may moderate, for example, as a growing percentage of females assume work roles outside of the home and as a greater percentage strives for time-extended careers outside the home.

Major Issues in Midlife Transition

Exhibit 4 implies that there is reality to this common usage—the "fearsome forties." That is, the issues of the midlife transition are powerful ones, centering as they do on the disparity between what has been achieved and what is desired, a disparity to which urgency and poignancy are added by the growing consciousness of the inexorable march of time. Not only are those issues awesome, moreover, but they often are exacerbated by needs of adolescent children and/or a spouse, who may be contending with their own transitional concerns or traumas. In addition, the stakes are high. For success or failure in the transition probably will have a long time to influence all of us as we proceed toward our own rendezvous with death.

How to suggest the kinds of issues that may be encountered in midlife transition? Perhaps the most convenient approach is that of Roger Gould.[29] He studied 524 men and women, separated into seven age groups, one of which was 35 to 43. Each person was asked 124 questions, which referred to a broad sweep of life: relationships to parents, friends, children, and spouses; and feelings toward their own personality, job, time, and sexual behavior. Gould tracked the significance of each of these questions for each of the age groups, thereby getting a sense of the ebb and flow of specific issues for persons at various chronologic ages. Gould acknowledges the defects of his research design which, for example, was more convenient than—but not as elegant as—a longitudinal study of the same persons throughout their full life cycle.

Gould shows that persons in midlife transition differ markedly from other age groups on only a few of the 124 questions. These differences provide useful clues about the concerns that are central to the transition. In summary, the frequency and significance of these statements *decreases* markedly during the midlife years:[30]

- For me marriage has been a good thing.
- There's still plenty of time to do most of the things I want to do.
- I like a very active social life.

In summary, also, the salience of only eight statements *increases* during the same years. They are

- I don't make enough money to do what I want.
- I regret my mistakes in raising my children.

- It's too late to make any major changes in my career.
- My personality is pretty well set.
- I try to be satisfied with what I have and not think so much about the things I probably won't be able to get.
- Life doesn't change much from year to year.
- My greatest concern is my health.
- My parents are the cause of many of my problems.

It requires no great psychological insight to appreciate how momentous are the implied issues with which midlife transitionists seem to be grappling, or to see how even minor differences in the fine-tuning of adjustments might lead toward greater fulfillment or greater trouble. The feeling tone is one of chances lost, of pessimism, of an impending end before fulfillment in many critical areas of life. And, the chances of a kind of spiritual withdrawal seem high. Thus, parents can be used as scapegoats for any developmental failure; the pressure of time can encourage lassitude as well as its more efficient use; past mistakes can come to be seen as vexacious and irremediable; and pessimism about marriage and social life can deprive the individual of what he or she needs to cushion the transition as well as to extract value from it.

These dark possibilities seem to make a successful transition that much sweeter, however. This is implicit in Gould's description of what a successful adjustment seems to mean for those past 50, for whom there is a "mellowing of feelings and relationships" even as death becomes a newly real presence for them. Gould observes:[31]

> People of this age seemed to focus on what they have accomplished in half a century, and they were unrushed by the sense of urgency that accompanied the achieving 30s. At the same time, they were more eager to have "human" experiences, such as sharing joys, sorrows, confusions and triumphs of everyday life rather than searching for the glamor, the glitter, the power or the abstract. Precious moments of contact and deep feeling define the value of being in touch.

Some Perspectives on the Nowness of the Midlife Transition

Despite their somewhat speculative quality, ample reasons suggest that the midlife transition is an especially "now" phenomenon in multiple senses that heighten its contemporary impact. The transition is not merely with us—it is with us in significant senses for the first time. No argument can be definitive, but five interacting features imply that the impact of the transition is in crucial respects unprecedented. And this despite the fact that people patently have lived through their forties for many generations past.

First, midlife phenomena are being felt by increasing masses of people. The contrast with the past is something like that between scattered cases of a disease and an epidemic. As Longfellow observed,[32] we may really be seeing mass midlife transitions for the first time. The point does not apply only in the obvious sense that population burgeons. In addition, our lifespans have increased dramatically in just a few generations, and hence so have the proportions of live births that survive beyond their forties. Moreover, far fewer people than ever before are preoccupied with bare physical survival. The quality of life can get correspondingly greater attention, even as "killing time" becomes more of a necessary skill for many.

Second, the pace of social and technological change interacts with midlife transition. An appropriate image is numerous ships seeking to dock simultaneously in space. It is quite a trick in any case, and perhaps impossible to do without serious collisions or missed connections, since the ships are moving rapidly and in opposite directions. That is, midlife transition seems obviously easier when the changing individual can count on society and technology being relatively stable.

The unprecedented velocity of change in many of our institutions makes the midlife transition more dicey than ever in more than obvious ways. That is, the essence of the midlife transition is learning how to accept and deal with being out of control of some inexorable life forces. The pace of social and technological change grotesquely exagerrates this sense of being out of control over central life events, of being the acted-upon rather than the actor.

Third, to say somewhat the same thing, probably fewer people proportionately than ever before are role-bound or status-bound. This is consistent with high-velocity social change, of course, and it implies an increased freedom to choose among alternative life styles. Danger is the other side of this coin of opportunity, patently. Overabundance of choices can be as troublesome as a paucity of choices, and the latter at least has the superficial advantage of legitimating for many people the OK-ness of living lives of quiet desperation. Abundant choices can dramatically heighten the costs of failure to take adequate advantage of them, and it is at least the case that abundance can create major problems of choice as well as numerous opportunities to go wrong in seeking to select a life style attuned to one's inner rhythms.

Fourth, the point is easy to exagerrate, but probably greater proportions of people than ever before have substantially raised their expectations about what is acceptable, acceptable to them as persons and to the societies of which they are a part. The phenomenon may be world-wide; but it is at least pervasive in the Western world. T. George Harris incisively captures the new rhythms to which so many dance. "It's as if some idiot raised the ante on what it takes to be a person," he explains, "and the rest of us accepted it without noticing." The result? An "aspiration gap. What we are as individuals and groups fall short of what we now consider normal. We feel sent for and can't get there."[33]

The impact of raising this ante clearly complicates the midlife transition, not only because the task is more difficult but also because the objective is more attractive and the rewards for success are so much greater. For example, sex, race, class, and nation can lock people into roles that are unresponsive to individual qualities. Since they limit human potential, sexism, racism, and class consciousness must be neutralized in the person and in the society. This is a far taller order for quality personhood than was current not so very long ago. Harris also suggests the multiple binds inherent in raising the ante for effective personhood within the family, with increased and perhaps unreconciliable demands on its members. That is,[34]

> Family members assume that they ought to love each other, understand one another, or at least get their hostilities up front. [Few] mothers and almost no fathers used to seek such emotional luxuries. A wife who once considered sex a marital duty now expects to be an orgasmic playmate, intellectual companion, and growth partner, as well as an emotionally independent person, a cross between Mesdames Pompadour and Curie.

It also appears that the ante for personhood has been raised in organizations, and especially by many of those who have been more successful. Thus, one 1972 survey of managers indicated that over a 5-year interval nearly one-half were considering a complete change of career, or had actually switched.[35] And, popular management magazines have spotlighted the changes made by several key executives.[36] The reasonable presumption—this much smoke in such sources—indicates there is fire aplenty out in the world. Most of these midcareer changes seem to occur in the late thirties or early forties, the period of midlife transition.

Fifth, some observers argue that those entering the midlife transition in the mid-1970s may be especially vulnerable to the challenges of acknowledging and coping with that ultimate harshness: death. There are several ways to make the point, all more or less speculative but also intriguing. The overall sense of it is that those legions now coming into the midlife transition had unique early developmental experiences, whose major components include: a suddenly more benign environment, an affluence, a buoyant optimism about human perfectability, and an indulgence in place of the harshness of the Great Depression and its following war. The conclusion: the human products are somehow less able to deal with harshness by virtue of less consciousness about it and less practice with it.

This general argument can be given specific counterpoint. The early 1940s apparently saw the beginnings of pervasive changes in child-rearing practices, which presumably impacted on the postwar baby boom and—one guesses—would have been most accepted by the parents of the socioeconomic classes most likely to have raised today's midlife managers and professionals. These practices—a kind of generalized Dr. Spockism—were far more oriented toward encouraging personal growth and exploration than toward acknowledging specific and harsh limits on behavior and aspiration. Earlier, conventional practices emphasized parent-centered management of the child seen as a producer of problems and as a bundle of wants that often required curbing, harshly if necessary. The definite bias was that the child's maturation was to be scheduled in terms of adult preferences and convenience.

The magnitudes of this major shift in child-rearing practices can be illustrated briefly, relying on Martha Wolfenstein's analysis[37] of changes of emphasis in seven editions over the years 1914 to 1951 of the government publication *Infant Care.* The harshness recommended during the period 1914 to 1921 is patent, and implies the danger of not curbing the infant's impulses. Wolfenstein notes: "Thumb-sucking and masturbation, if not promptly and rigorously interfered with, would grow beyond control and permanently damage the child. While he was in bed, he was to be bound down hand and foot so that he could not suck his thumb, touch his genitals, or rub his thighs together."

Despite minor modifications, such views about infant care more or less prevailed until the 1942 and 1945 editions. Then, the volume's focus became drastically more child centered and gentle, on the baby as a "little person" whose wants had a sovereign status. Wolfenstein notes of this major change that the child becomes "remarkably harmless, in effect devoid of sexual or dominating impulses." The child's main aim is to explore the world, and the parents' job becomes one of gently facilitating this exploration that is a good per se. Wolfenstein concludes:

> While not engaged in his explanatory undertakings, the baby needs attention and care; and given these when he demands them, far from making him a tyrant, will make him less demanding later on. At this time, mildness is advocated in all areas: thumb-sucking and masturbation are not to be interfered with; weaning and toilet training are to be accomplished later and more gently.

The 1951 edition of *Infant Care* preserves this bias, essentially. Wolfenstein observes that "there is an attempt to continue this mildness, but not without some conflicts and misgivings." The revolution in child care backed up a little, but not much. For good or ill, so were many of today's midlife transitionists equipped to cope with what would come to those who survived.

Some Organizational Challenges/Opportunities

Adult life is neither unpredictable nor of a single piece, then, and therein lay several major challenges and opportunities for employing organizations and professional associations to join in a new cooperative humanism. For the next decade or two, increasingly large proportions of employables and members of professional associations will be experiencing a midlife transition. This will be one of the inevitable harvests of the postwar baby boom, as well as of the dramatic spurts in public employment that have occurred especially in state and local government. Employing organizations can provide useful learning experiences. But, given the kinds of issues raised in the transition, their delicacy, and their common rootedness in nonwork contexts, professional associations no doubt should take on the lion's share of this particular burden.

At least five challenges are involved in a constructive response to the midlife transition. *First,* a greater awareness of the organizationally relevant features of the phenomenon is required, for the full range of employees. The fearsome forties for males have received growing attention, of course, especially in the few dramatic cases of well-heeled successes who have chucked one blossoming career for a less exalted but more satisfying alternative.[38] Some other equally disenchanted but less financially cushioned souls have taken greater risks in attempting shifts in careers and life styles, perhaps most prominently in leaving the priesthood or orders of nuns. And, signs of midlife transition seem unmistakable in the "blue-collar blues,"[39] a social ferment suggesting that even the organizationally humble are no longer content to lead lives of more or less quiet desperation, variously locked into unsatisfying roles that they cannot or will not leave.

Second, organizations should develop a more acute ethical and especially economic sense of the costs/benefits of aiding their members through a midlife transition. The data do not exist. But there seem enormous costs, both psychic and economic, in awkward midlife transitions. Blue-collar workers seem especially prone to the blahs during this period, with both attitudes and productivity subject to substantial declines.[40] Similarly, organizational folklore has long recounted the ravages common in those who have been on the road 10 to 15 years. And, it seems no accident that midcareer crisis for professionals and managers—which "while hardly an epidemic, is no longer rare"[41] —tends to hit in the middle thirties. Transitions in personhood, that is, are reasonably linked to changes in career.

Looked at from another angle, enormous productive forces exist in the post-transition years. The point is sometimes too little appreciated. Recently available longitudinal studies indicate that, although physical decline often sets in and diminutions in energy will occur, even the December of life can be a period of psychological growth.[42] Moreover, the common notion of a massive deterioration in psychological functioning in those beyond, say, 70 years of age, gets no support from newly available studies.[43] In addition, many specific skills or attributes seem to have their own unique decay rates. Some steadily decline, beginning with the teens! Others hold steady or increase till the middle forties or later.[44]

Perhaps the most dramatic devaluing of the productive energies of the post-transition years lies in the prevalent myth that most outstanding creative work is done no later than the thirties, which many claim is a fact "as useless to bemoan . . . as to deny. . . ."[45]   Others point out that such widely accepted findings seem largely artefactual, resting as they do on calculations of "contributions which were made in each decade of life without regard to the number of contributors who were surviving in each decade." In the case of contributions by philosophers, for example, one student concludes that the apparent peak of productivity by philosophers at around age 30 is "primarily due to the fact" that many more philosophers lived in their thirties than in their seventies. In fact, philosophers who survived until their seventies made 22 percent of their total contributions in that decade![46]

The need for help from employing organizations or professional associations is no one-sided argument, of course, especially because midlife transition may mean radical midcareer change. It may seem perverse that an organization should apply its resources to create nonmembers, humanitarian motives aside. One can at least imagine, however, cases in which it is economically unsound to keep an individual in a job or profession that has lost its allure but which the individual cannot leave without help. Hence, some organizations have begun to subsidize midcareer changes for some of their employees, for multiple motives. Thus, early, insistent attention to matching individual needs with career development can signal the mutual concern about personal development which is the bedrock of solid personnel management. Moreover, such subsidization acknowledges past employee contributions, while it can slip between the horns of this central dilemma: of tolerating relatively senior officials for whom the go-go has largely gone but who nonetheless provide unfortunate role models for less-senior personnel; and of risking the spiritual and legal complications of purges via overt dismissals or "early retirement."

Third, relatedly, great emphasis should be placed on continuous checks of career progress against individual needs. The goal is to do something about growing mismatches, and especially when organizational convenience urges doing nothing. That is, perhaps the crucial ingredient in successfully making a midlife transition is active reflection—isolating what is important and attainable for the individual, assessing whether those important things are being worked toward, and doing something when things go otherwise. Such active reflection does not just occur when it is needed. It must be encouraged and nourished over the long-run, until it becomes part of an individual's attitudes about self and about seeing self.

The prevailing bias in most organizations is more go-go than look-see, of course, so this challenge is no easy piece. Hence, the value of the approach to career planning or life planning described above.

Fourth, the several rhythms of the life cycle must be acknowledged and responded to, both in individual behavior as well as in organization policies and procedures. "By recognizing the patterns," Gould notes, "we may gain some control over the forces by smoothing the transitions and muting the peaks and valleys of adult life phases." Without such mastery of the cycle, people are obliged to be its unknowing pawns. There is hope for making the inevitable somewhat more attractive. "While children mark the passing years by their changing bodies," Gould observes, "adults change their minds."[47]

Consider the schema in Exhibit 4, for example. It should be clear that the developmental profile there has significant implications for learning experiences designed for individuals at different life stages. For example, designs that emphasize the search for a "mentor" seem quite appropriate at stage 2 of early adulthood. By stage 4, in contrast, appropriate designs should emphasize humane and efficient ways for unbuckling from mentors, a delicate process that ideally should not meet developmental needs by a harsh rejection of the mentor's previous contributions and present needs. It is like parent and child → adult reaching a new and different relationship.

Fifth, employing organizations and professional organizations should better tailor their various systems and policies to human cycles and needs. The child-rearing years constitute one such cycle for most organization members. Similarly, Exhibit 4 reflects another common cycle. It implies that the midlife years enlarge the individual's focus from acquisition to integration, from a narrow emphasis on "making it," on acquiring or achieving one's key goals, to an emphasis on fulfillment of broader social and psychological needs.

The need for intellectual, emotional, and financial support for such transitions is as obvious as the fact that few employing organizations or professional associations do much by way of meeting that need. Some favorable straws in the wind are:

- Some organizations provide a "cafeteria" of possible fringe benefits, from which employees can tailor-make benefits packages (up to some common dollar value) responsive to their individual life situations.

- Some organizations hire husband-and-wife teams, each working half-time and sharing other duties at home.

- Some organizations are consciously negotiating contracts with "permanent part-timers" who are seeking some better balance between "making it" and satisfying broader needs or interests.

- Some organizations sponsor activities—ranging from full-fledged sabbaticals to episodic "life planning experiences"—that encourage individuals to get in more intimate touch with their own needs/aspirations/abilities, and to do something with such clarifications to improve their worklife and homelife.

Numerous other sections of this two-part volume also imply even more venturesome ways of being responsive to the stages of life in an OD mode. Career planning clearly helps respond to the changing texture of life, for example.

Other ways of encouraging or permitting responsiveness—as comprehensive as OD programs of total organizational change, or as simple as Flexi-Time—fill this volume.

Has an Organizational Rubicon Been Crossed?

The issues raised by this section are broad, then. One way of expressing them is to contrast two classes of motivators: one class is narrowly economic, as in the piece-rate or in fortunes to be made in days of low taxes; and the other class emphasizes broader human fulfillment.

It is just possible that we have crossed an organizational Rubicon where, for a variety of reasons, the relative salience of those two classes of motivators for numerous people has shifted in a significant way. Some of both classes of motivators have always been required but now, given tax laws, emphasis on seniority, the social ethos, or whatever, a sharp increase in human fulfillment has come to be seen by many as necessary to get the work of the world done.

If something like this thumbnail social history is appropriate, a new and subtle partnership will be required between employing organizations and professional associations. Organizations would have to adopt many systems and procedures to accommodate this significant change in emphasis toward human fulfillment.

There also seem real limits as to how far employing organizations can or should go in such matters, without raising specters of big brotherism or paternalism. This implies a very major role for outside contractors, and especially for the professional associations serving in such learning/helping roles. They would be vital in raising awareness about the need to adapt systems and policies to human developmental sequences and phases, in documenting the effects of such efforts, and in sponsoring learning experiences that it would be uneconomical or unwise for employing organizations to offer. That would really make professional associations—I hesitate to even write the word, given the multiple usages of the past few years—relevant to the needs of their members.

That related duo, midlife transition and midcareer crisis, seems like a high-priority target for a new cooperative humanism between employing organizations and professional associations.

Organizational Identification of Individual Potential
The Assessment Center Strategy

The laboratory approach also appears in various guises in other efforts to deal with individuals in organizations, as in the burgeoning tendency to use assessment centers to evaluate individual potential for new responsibilities. Briefly, the assessment center concept seeks to identify individuals with characteristics considered to be indicators of anticipated success in a specific position or level of management. The approach is especially favored for the early identification of potential for first-level supervision, that is, at the point the individual transitions from a functional or technical specialty to a job with integrative managerial responsibilities.

The assessment center concept has its immediate developmental roots in the multiple assessment procedures which can be traced to the period of World War II. The typical concern then was to determine which individuals had the potential to be effective spies, or military officers, or whatever, quickly and in large numbers.[48] Recognition of broader applications came quickly.[49] The basic approach is a simple one: Increases in predictive and explanatory power, relevant to estimating potential to perform effectively in some capacity, are sought via several independent assessment techniques. That is, multiple assessment would use such approaches to testing for potential for effective performance as:

- Personality testing, as in the use of projective tests
- Paper-and-pencil testing for specific abilities or skills, as for verbal facility
- Situational testing, as in exercises or simulations that are analogues of the situations that the assessed person will face in performing the task in question

Situational testing constituted the major breakthrough in multiple assessment, in at least three major senses. Paramountly, situational testing has the clearest obvious relevance for estimating performance on the target task. Relatedly, studies tend to show, at the least, that situational tests make "a substantial and unique contribution to the prediction of management success."[50] Moreover, many studies indicate that situational tests are not only useful but tend to be the most useful of the three types of assessment procedures. Paper-and-pencil tests of ability tend to be of intermediate value, and personality tests of least value, in assessing potential.[51]

Generic Features of the Strategy

Three central features characterize the assessment center strategy.[52] *First,* assessment centers deal with a number of individuals at the same time, say, twelve or so persons who are exposed to a design of variable length, depending usually on the level of management in relationship to which they are being assessed. Exhibit 5 outlines such a typical design, typical in that it includes individual, group, and interview situations keyed to a specific target position or level.[53]

Exhibit 5 Situational Exercises and Simulations in an Assessment Center Design

---

Day 1

- *Management Game.* Four-man teams seek to form different kinds of conglomerates by bartering companies. Each team sets its own acquisition objectives and policies and must organize to meet them.

- *Background Interview.* A 90-minute interview is conducted by an assessor.

- *Individual Fact-Finding and Decision-Making.* Each participant is told to imagine himself a division manager who has the immediate problem of reviewing a rejected request for funds to continue a research project. The research director appeals the decision of the previous manager to his successor. The participant gets a brief description of the situation and is given 15 minutes to ask questions that will provide additional data. He then must make a decision, deliver it orally, and be prepared to defend his decision under challenge from a member of the assessment panel.

Day 2

- *In-Basket Exercise.* The participant is told he has been suddenly promoted to a first-level supervisory position and is given a simulated in-basket left by his predecessor. The participant is to deal with the contents, as by scheduling and planning, delegating, making decisions, answering questions, and so on.

  An assessor reviews the results of the completed effort and conducts an hour interview with the man to gain insight into his strategies, thought processes, awareness of problems, and the like.

- *Assigned Role in Leaderless Group.* Each participant is instructed that he is a member of a compensation committee which will meet to allocate $8,000 in salary increases among six supervisors and managers from different departments.

  Each participant represents a different department and is instructed to do the best he can for the employee from his department.

  Participants and assessors rate the performance of members of the committee.

- *Individual Analysis and Presentation, Followed by Group Decision-Making.* Participants are each instructed to act as a consultant to an executive who faces two problems: a division that consistently loses money, and alternate plans for corporate expansion.

  Participants are given data about the company, from which they are to recommend courses of action.

  Each participant presents his recommendations in a 7-minute oral presentation.

  Following the presentations, participants form a group that is instructed to develop a single set of recommendations.

Days 3 and 4

- Assessment panel meets to share their observations, as well as to evaluate each participant as to: overall potential; each specific trait or attribute seen as relevant to the job; and training or development needs.

Source: William C. Byham, "The Assessment Center as an Aid in Management Development." Reproduced by special permission from the December 1971 *Training and Development Journal*, p. 19. Copyright 1971 by the American Society for Training and Development Inc.

Broadly, the design components are intended to induce behaviors and skills relevant to effective performance on the task. The task is formidable,[54] although its magnitude will only be suggested here. Clearly, for example, this intent implies a careful analysis of the task, of the demands it makes on the individual as well as the skills it requires. Clearly, also, this intent implies a range of knowledge about which specific exercises or simulations are appropriate to test for potential to perform specific tasks, how many such exercises provide the best assessment of potential, and so on.

Second, the assessors are a panel of people familiar with the demands of the position or organization level. Each panel includes perhaps four to six members, who are usually "line" personnel from one or two organization levels above that of the target against which individual skills and attitudes are being assessed. The assessors normally do not have a direct supervisory relationship with those being assessed. Individuals on such panels tend to serve only episodically. In such a large organization as AT&T, however, assessors serve a 6-month tour of duty.

The assessment panel typically operates at two evaluative levels. Assessors often make some overall rating of participants such as: Does Participant A have the potential to be promoted to middle management levels in the next 5 to 10 years? In addition, assessors typically rate each participant on a number of more or less discrete qualities. In one case, for example, assessors rated each participant on these twelve traits: (1) aggressiveness, (2) persuasive or selling ability, (3) oral communications, (4) planning and organization, (5) self-confidence, (6) resistance to stress, (7) written communications, (8) energy level, (9) decision-making, (10) interpersonal contact, (11) administrative ability, and (12) risk taking.[55]

This dual evaluation constitutes the heart of the assessment center. Assessment will be effective in uncovering potential for future growth as several conditions are simultaneously met. These conditions include: the specification of characteristics significant for performance on some task or at some organization level; defining those characteristics in behavioral terms; setting up exercises or simulations that highlight the strengths or weaknesses of specific individuals in behaving so as to meet the demands of the task; and training members of assessment panels to perceive and interpret that behavior correctly.

The assessing panel's major responsibility involves developing a report on each individual.[56] As Exhibit 5 indicates, the panel typically spends a day or so writing up reports concerning the performance of the participants on the interview as well as in the group and individual experiences or simulations. Typically, the reports are considered one part of each assessee's total record when he or she is later considered for promotion or a new job.

Third, assessment centers blend two sets of critical activities: assessment (or evaluation), and development (or training). For those assessed, the dual point should be patent. Thus, a typical goal of the assessment report is to suggest remedial or broadening experiences to meet inadequacies surfaced in the performance of individuals on any exercises or simulations. Relatedly, for those assessed, each design component can at once facilitate assessing an individual while it also suggests training opportunities. For example, the In-Basket[57] component of the illustrative design in Exhibit 5 has both potentials. Not incidentally, the assessed individuals are likely to be very interested in improving their performance during their stay at the assessment center and hence may be psychologically "unfrozen." In such a state, these individuals are unusually and perhaps uniquely open to training inputs.

Assessment centers also provide training and development opportunities for members of the assessing panel as they go about evaluating the skills and attitudes of others, a point which may not be so obvious. Assessors receive some prior and intensive training which, in combination with the actual experience of participating in specific runs of assessment designs, can be a powerful stimulus to their own development. For example, the development of assessors can be enhanced in senses such as:[58]

- Improved interviewing and listening skills
- Enhanced skills relevant to observing behavior
- Increased understanding of group dynamics and leadership styles
- New insights as to why specific individuals behave as they do
- Strengthening management skills via working with and observing various design components, such as In-Baskets, case studies, or simulations
- Broadening the range of their repertoire of responses to management problems
- Establishing and sharpening standards in terms of which to evaluate performance
- Developing a more precise vocabulary with which to describe behavior or group dynamics

Indeed, so compelling have such training advantages for assessors been to some wielders of power in organizations that they have deliberately increased the ratio of assessors to participants to expose more of the former to the training opportunities implicit in the assessment center approach.

Some Interfaces with Lab Approach

The assessment center strategy can variously rely upon and reflect facets of the laboratory approach. The clearest kinship is in their common experiential thrust. Thus, Robert Albrook explains that assessment centers basically deal with "observing how executive candidates perform in management games that often achieve startling realism." He explains:

> These techniques are powerful because they measure actual behavior in a standardized fashion. They do not depend upon a candidate's self-assessment as to whether, for example, he "likes people"—the approach often taken in ordinary interviewing or psychological testing. Nor do they

depend upon the sometimes suspect "reference" from a friend, teacher, or former employer. . . . The games provide a live demonstration of such factors in a realistic setting.[59]

Three points establish other specific points of articulation between assessment centers and the laboratory approach. *First,* a process orientation is at the heart of the assessment center concept. This is patently true for the assessors, who focus on behavior, leadership, and group dynamics that are seen as relevant for performance in the specific position or level of organization which is the standard for assessment. Simulations or exercises provide the context for such a process orientation. And, they also provide a measure of how the participants can bring to bear a variety of skills, such as financial management, planning, and so on. Since process and content issues are ineluctably mixed in assessment centers, a premium is placed on the skill of the assessment panel in being aware of both. Various learning designs based on the laboratory approach, including T-groups, can help sharpen assessor competence in identifying and managing process issues.

Assessment centers also commonly induce a strong process orientation in participants, whether by intent or merely in the nature of the design. Thus, William Byham notes that "a 'T-group' atmosphere is often created to increase self-learning." Interestingly, also, the job-boundedness of assessment center designs may provide a safeguard against the negative effects of sensitivity training. Byham explains that "Conditions . . . are sufficiently well-controlled . . . that none of the negative effects which have occasionally characterized the T-Group session have been noted. . . ."[60] In any case, participants are understandably concerned about how and why things happen as they do in the simulations and exercises, as well as about how they can improve their interpersonal and technical competence in achieving what they intend to accomplish. Many assessment centers accentuate this natural tendency, in a variety of ways. Typically, participants rate themselves and others on total performance as well as on such process-related dimensions as leadership, ideas contributed, and so on. Such data gathering encourages a process orientation, of course. More elaborately, participants as part of the design also often[61]

- Analyze and discuss their performance in exercises or interviews as they watch videotape replays
- Engage in critiques of their performance in discussion groups led by outside resource persons
- Meet in small groups of participants to share their responses and strategies in specific exercises or simulations, to have their reasoning tested by others, and to enlarge their repertoire of possible administrative responses by listening to others explain their approaches

Second, feedback to participants is emphasized in assessment centers. Because the focus is on feedback related to performance of the tasks or exercises, it consequently has technical as well as interpersonal emphases. The quantity and character of the feedback processes vary broadly in different assessment programs. The amount of feedback will vary in proportion to the level of the assessment target, for example, as will the formality of the feedback processes. Thus, the approaches to process orientation above will create many opportunities for feedback, and some assessment centers go much further, especially for higher-level positions. A written commitment to action, by individual and/or organization, often follows.[62]

Third, the values guiding any assessment center seem to be critical. If the values emphasize a helping relationship and the primacy of the needs of the participants, that is one thing, even given the potential for difficulty in the effort. Other values could trend in radically different directions, as toward the creation of organizational look-alikes patterned after some monolithic grand design. Such values would induce more repression than psychological owning of any learning.[63]

Some Attractions and Qualifiers

Although a creation of the past few years only, the assessment center strategy has spread widely. Many thousands of businesses now employ the approach, and a number of government agencies have also begun to experiment with the strategy.[64] The subsection will sketch the broad attractions of assessment centers that seem to explain their burgeoning popularity. Five factors below suggest the fuller rationale.

First, the growing scale of the assessment problem has forced experimentation with new approaches. In AT&T alone, for example, 70,000 candidates for first-level supervisory positions have been assessed in recent years. The assessment load has roots in industrial and population growth, clearly enough. In addition, the dramatic 1960s decline in the size of the critical 35 to 45 age group[65] places a special premium on the early identification of those with managerial potential, so that they may get suitable developmental experiences. The decline reflects the lack of Depression babies and the low birth rates of 1930 to 1940. Finally, affirmative action programs place a very heavy burden on early and accurate assessment of potential for promotion, especially of those unlikely to have educational or other credentials.

Second, traditional methods of assessment apparently have left much to be desired, at least as far as many organizations are concerned. The intent of assessment centers is to help do better what must and will be done, in one fashion or another. The goal is to provide an additional, and hopefully a well-informed, source of information to help guide evaluation and promotion decisions. Perhaps the archetypal block to evaluation or promotion is the lower-level functionary who defensively devotes himself to assuring a hard time for any young employee who is better trained, or whatever, than he.

Hence, perhaps the key potential weakness of some assessment center plans is that they rely on nomination of participants by their immediate supervisors. As Byham delicately observes: "Some high potential employees may never be nominated because qualities of aggressiveness, curiosity and intelligence that might make a person successful at higher levels of management are not always appreciated by lower-level supervision."[66] This may be especially probable today, given the relative flood of unprecedentedly trained youngsters in many fields with skills beyond those of persons only a few years senior to them. Consequently, a number of organizations have resorted to self-nomination as a bypass around obstructive supervisors. And, the voluntarism of self-nomination probably also would help intensify the training and development aspects of assessment centers.

Third, several validation studies support the effectiveness of assessment centers for identifying both organizational winners and losers.[67] Significantly, also, these studies usually indicate the superiority of the center concept over such approaches as supervisory appraisals or paper-and-pencil tests.[68] One study is especially convincing, showing as it does that assessment panel correctly identified 95 percent of those who did not attain promotion to middle management.[69]

A mixed conclusion seems appropriate. The assessment center concept is still in a developmental stage, and a specific assessment effort is no better than the clarity with which job-relevant behaviors and skills are defined, induced by the design, and perceived accurately by assessors. Research does suggest just those things tend to happen, more rather than less, but the magic is clearly not in the concept but in its implementation, and especially in the careful tailoring of assessment designs to specific jobs in specific organizations.

Fourth, the usefulness of the assessment center's emphasis on performance is perhaps greatest in the case of assessing minority and female employees.[70] Many paper-and-pencil tests, that is to say, discriminate against the culturally deprived. Moreover, the relevance of such tests to performance at work often has been obscure or indirect. Court decisions, such as *Griggs et al. v. Duke Power,* encourage special care that selection and appraisal standards and procedures be job-relevant.[71]

Fifth, the use of assessor panels has variously aided acceptance of the assessment center concept, especially via greater understanding of its strengths and weaknesses. Use of line managers as assessors, for example, has eased acceptance of the concept by other managers and by the participants as well. Greater involvement in the assessment program goes hand in hand with greater understanding, which Byham considers an "extremely important result." He cites the contrasting illustration of psychological testing, on whose results managers typically overrely or underrely. Byham explains that managers "have difficulty determining the correct emphasis because they are not familiar with the tests, tester or intent of the program." Assessment center reports can be misused for similar reasons, of course, but the probability seems lower because of the participation of line managers in developing specific assessment designs as well as in assessing itself. "When a manager who has been an assessor gets the assessment report," Byham concludes, "he knows the basis for the observations and judgments and can more accurately weigh them against data on job performance and other available information."[72]

Decreasing Turnover and Absenteeism by Making the Work Site More Rewarding
Dealing with Blue-Collar Blues

We turn from potential to pain, specifically to the "blue-collar blues," especially as that "mysterious but obvious malaise"[73] is reflected in high employee turnover and absenteeism. It is not clear when the term "blue-collar blues" was first used, but the underlying syndrome seems to have taken on massive proportions only of late.[74] The term itself seems to have been coined in 1970,[75] in response to growing evidence that more and more of "them simply do not seem to want to work anymore." Settled opinion has it that these "blues" have two basic causes: American blue-collar workers are more educated than ever before,[76] which by implication makes it more difficult to accept discipline or conditions at work that seemed natural to their parents and grandparents; and rampant simplification of tasks reduces the degree to which employees can control their work,[77] with the hypothetical results being a heightened sense of powerlessness and a burgeoning alienation.

An Organic OD Design in a Growing Firm*

A small but rapidly growing construction firm was experiencing the blue-collar blues. Specifically, one important job category had a yearly turnover rate of some 300 percent. And, management was losing the struggle to stay even, as the problems of managing a young and transient work force pyramided. The

---

*This section is based on Jacob E. Hautaluoma and James F. Gavin, "Effects of Organizational Diagnosis and Intervention on Blue-Collar 'Blues,' " *Journal of Applied Behavioral Science,* Vol. 11 (October 1975), pp. 475-496. For an earlier effort to reduce absenteeism by increasing participation, see Edward F. Lawler and J. R. Hackman, "Impact of Employee Participation in the Development of Pay Incentive Plans: A Field Experiment," *Journal of Applied Psychology,* Vol. 53, no. 6 (1969), pp. 467-471.

prevailing view among management was that the new breed of employee was poorly motivated, and that they simply moved on when the work posed any real challenge.

An "organic design" programmed a systemic solution to the blue-collar blues, essentially a two-phase approach to planned change involving diagnosis and then intervention. The consultants offered this "rather terse definition" of OD: "the alteration of a system's 'culture' via planned interventions, and stresses diagnosis as *sine qua non,* but provides little clarification of the [specific intervention] to be employed. In fact," the consultants conclude, "the process of changing an organization rarely follows a set pattern."

The basic feature of the OD effort was that both diagnosis and interventions were conceived as part of a step-by-step process, with explicit contracting by both client and consultants at each step, with renegotiation where necessary at subsequent steps. "This allowed the client to determine the depth of the intervention effort," the consultants emphasize, "while recognizing our inability as consultants to specify a predetermined program at the outset."[78] Moreover, the effort involved the entire system, and was designed around participation by all members and all its relevant subgroups. Finally, consultants played an active role, but worked hard to assure that responsibility for making any diagnosis or changes remained where it belonged, within the firm. As the consultants observe:[79]

> The consultants' role included being helpful and supportive, and they worked hard to surface problems. They took responsibility for gathering data, presenting them in an understandable form, and insisting on attention to them. They did not offer easy, expeditious solutions but instead attempted to have the organization members themselves decide what should be done. After decisions were reached, the consultants designed interventions, which were then submitted for approval by the organization. During each intervention, the consultants acted as facilitators, supporters, probers, and task leaders—not masters—of problem solution.

Design for Diagnosis

The troubled firm employed about seventy employees, about fifty of whom were blue-collar workers, so it was possible to involve all employees in various ways at the several stages of the OD effort. Basically, employees were involved as individuals and also as members of three aggregates: management, clerical, and blue-collar. Thus, interviews with all employees were held, and they all responded to a standard questionnaire. In addition, various meetings were scheduled for the whole work force as well as for a variety of subgroups.

The data gathering was basically compressed into a single day, using eleven intervenors, and a set of feedback meetings were held 2 weeks later to share the data and consultants' interpretations. The feedback sessions were extensions of the diagnosis, in part, and their central emphases can be summarized briefly. Previously, that is, the firm's problem was seen as a poorly motivated work force, and especially among its younger employees. After the feedback sessions, in contrast, *the* problem came to be perceived as more complex and differentiated. To summarize:

- Major issues inhered in the fact that, while still small, the firm had experienced rapid growth recently, with a range of attendant stresses and tensions.
- The "management team" was variously split concerning its major goals and approaches, which differences were variously magnified and elaborated by the daily give-and-take in the firm.
- The firm's management had basically come up through the ranks, and supervisors lacked perspective on the managerial job and were generally unaware of alternative supervisory styles and strategies.
- Blue-collar workers, especially younger ones, were strongly dissatisfied with the Theory X approach to supervision that was dominant in the firm.
- Most blue-collar tasks were simplified and short-cycle combinations of a few stereotyped activities.

Designing Interventions

Three kinds of interventions were developed in response to this broader concept of the firm's problem, and their effects were to variously make the work site more rewarding (or less punishing) for the blue-collar employees. The interventions include:

- A team-building experience for management, which was split and working at cross-purposes
- A skills workshop for all first-line supervisors, participation in which included some blue-collar employees
- An expanded role for the firm's advisory committee, a joint labor/ management forum

Such interventions helped make the work site more rewarding for blue-collar employees in several senses. Initially, blue-collar feedback established the need for such interventions. Being truly heard and responded to, of course, can be very rewarding. Beyond that, blue-collar inputs were important during the three interventions. In the case of the supervisory skills workshop, for example, blue-collar employees provided data about the style of supervision they preferred and the kind they actually received from first-line supervisors. These data provided powerful contrast with supervisor reports about the kind of supervision the blue-collar workers required, which was an extreme form of Theory X supervision. Blue-collar employees acknowledged that this was the supervisory style they experienced but to which they took strong exception. This was especially true of the younger employees. This contrast supported a variety of role plays based on realistic work situations, a kind of "how we do it now" and then a "how we might do it in the future." As the consultants explain:[80]

> role plays concerning critical incidents at the plant . . . lasted 10 to 15 minutes and [were] observed by the non-role-playing participants; they were also videotaped and immediately reviewed and discussed by the whole group. This method was especially effective in facilitating the supervisors' "ownership" of their supervisory styles and in evoking a commitment to personal development and improved skills. The workers observed the supervisors honestly struggling to improve their methods, and they showed considerable empathy for them. At the end of the day the supervisors felt they had learned some important skills, and the workers were impressed with a change effort that used their responses to the questionnaire administered during the diagnostic stage.

Finally, the work site would become more rewarding for blue-collar employees to the degree that the interventions triggered changes in day-to-day management.

Sketching Some Consequences

Major changes observed in the postintervention period are consistent with a more rewarding work environment for blue-collar workers. Three emphases do the job here; and the interested reader can refer to the original report for details.[81] *First,* absenteeism fell sharply after the interventions. Specifically, it averaged 8.65 percent before the interventions, and 5.88 percent afterward.

Second, turnover also decreased, and especially so for longer-service employees. For the latter, turnover dropped from nearly 10 percent to less than 4 percent.

Third, employee attitudes reflected credible patterns in before versus after comparisons. Thus, perceptions about the work itself did not change, which is expected because no changes in jobs were made. Work was initially seen as dull and tedious, and remained that way. Employee attitudes about the quality of supervision did improve dramatically, in contrast, and that also is expected from such interventions as the supervisory skills workshop. Similarly, satisfaction with pay also increased sharply. This is reasonable, since management did raise rates of pay after the intervention.

Such effects suggest two levels of change. Thus, the broad participation in the processes of diagnosis and intervention by employees credibly made the work site more rewarding and aided employees in giving themselves more fully to their work. Moreover, in a related but distinct way, the diagnosis and interventions also seem to have improved the quality of the work site, as in the changes in supervisory style in directions desired by employees.[82] In cases, increases in productivity may result from changes in attitudes about roles or styles. But convincing evidence implies that improvements in the emotional quality of work can occur without necessarily increasing productivity.[83] So designs seeking to improve both morale *and* productivity should include technical as well as attitudinal enhancers.

Note also that other OD efforts report similar success with the same kinds of tough problems.[84] Based on a problem census, these other cases made use of a survey/feedback design to motivate skill-training capable of inducing the appropriate changes at the work site. In a number of experimental districts, to illustrate, turnover was reduced by approximately one-half.[85]

Notes

1. Malcolm P. McNair, "What Price Human Relations?" *Harvard Business Review,* Vol. 35 (March 1957), pp. 15-22.

2. Jay H. Heizer, "Transfer and Termination as Staffing Options," *Journal of the Academy of Management,* Vol. 19 (March 1976), p. 115; and R. D. Brynildsen, "Some Thoughts on Broadening Career Development Thrusts," *OD Practitioner,* Vol. 9 (January 1977), pp. 13-15.

3. Richard M. Jones, *Fantasy and Feeling in Education* (New York: New York University Press, 1968), p. 77.

4. Ari Kiev, "Crisis Intervention in Industry," p. 2. Paper delivered at Annual Meeting, New York State Society of Industrial Medicine, Occupational Psychiatry Group, December 10, 1969.

5. Marvin Zuckerman and Bernard Lubin, *Manual for the Multiple Affect Adjective Check List* (San Diego, Calif.: Educational and Industrial Testing Service, 1965), p. 3. Reproduced with permission.

6. Ibid., pp. 6-16.

7. Marvin Zuckerman and Bernard Lubin, *Bibliography for the Multiple Affect Adjective Check List* (San Diego, Calif.: Educational and Industrial Testing Service, 1970), 8 pp.

8. Bernard Lubin and Marvin Zuckerman, "Levels of Emotional Arousal in Laboratory Training," *Journal of Applied Behavioral Science,* Vol. 5 (October 1969), p. 488.

9. Donald E. Super and Douglas T. Hall, "Career Development: Exploration and Planning," in Mark R. Rosenzweig and Lyman W. Porter (eds.), *Annual Review of Psychology,* Vol. 29 (1978), p. 360. Herbert A. Shepard has been the central figure in developing such designs. See Herbert A. Shepard and John A. Hawley, *Life Planning: Personal and Organizational* (Washington, D.C.: National Training and Development Service, 1974); Herbert A.

Shepard, "Life Planning," in Kenneth D. Benne, Leland Bradford, Jack R. Gibb, and Ronald O. Lippitt (eds.), *The Laboratory Method of Changing and Learning: Theory and Application* (Palo Alto, Calif.: Science and Behavior Books, 1975), pp. 240-251; and John Van Maanen and Edgar H. Schein, "Improving the Quality of Working Life: Career Development," in J. Richard Hackman and J. Lloyd Suttle (eds.), *Improving Life at Work* (Los Angeles: Goodyear, 1976), pp. 30-96.

The approach also has some sex-specific variants. For example, see Janice Kay, "Career Development for Women: An Affirmative Action First," *Training and Development Journal,* Vol. 30 (May 1976), pp. 22-24. For a comprehensive bibliography, consult Marlys Hanson and Lynn Allen, *Career Planning for Adults: An Annotated Bibliography* (Lawrence Livermore Laboratory, University of California, Livermore, Calif. UCRL 77109).

10. The distinction is made by Bernard Haldane and is reflected in his "Managerial Excellence Kit" (Washington, D.C.: Bernard Haldane Associates, 1968).

11. For a career-planning program that uses attitudinal measure heavily, see Behavioral Science Center, Sterling Institute, *Achievement Motivation: A Seminar for Managers* (July 1970).

12. For one evidence of the impact of a Haldane program, see *U.S. Employment Service Review* (December 1965), p. 15.

13. See Jack K. Fordyce and Raymond Weil, *Managing with People* (Reading, Mass.: Addison-Wesley, 1971), pp. 132-133.

14. The seminar was developed by Walter R. Mead, Corporate Personnel, Smith, Kline and French Laboratories, 1971. For another variant of career-planning programs, see Marlys Hanson and Lynn Allen, "Career Planning for Adults at Lawrence Livermore Laboratory," *Training and Development Journal,* Vol. 30 (March 1976), pp. 12-14.

15. Cited in Harold Geist, *The Psychological Aspects of the Aging Process with Sociological Implications* (St. Louis, Mo.: Warren H. Green, 1968), pp. 17-18.

16. Joseph H. Britton and Jean O. Britton, *Personality Changes in Aging* (New York: Springer, 1972), pp. ix, 1.

17. Daniel J. Levinson, Charlotte M. Darrow, Edward B. Klein, Maria H. Levinson, and Braxton McKee, "The Psychosocial Development of Men in Early Adulthood and Mid-Life Transition," in David Ricks, Alexander Thomas, and Merrill Roff (eds.), *Life History Research in Psychopathology,* Vol. 3 (Minneapolis, Minn.: University of Minnesota Press, 1974), p. 244.

18. Roger Gould, "Adult Life Stages: Growth Toward Self-Tolerance," *Psychology Today,* Vol. 9 (February 1975), p. 78. See also his "The Phases of Adult Life: A Study in Developmental Psychology," *American Journal of Psychiatry,* Vol. 129 (November 1972), pp. 33-43.

19. Ibid., pp. 74, 76; and Elliott Jacques, "Death and the Mid-Life Crisis," *International Journal of Psychoanalysis*, Vol. 46 (October 1965), p. 502.

20. Henry S. Maas and Joseph A. Kuypers, *From Thirty to Seventy* (San Francisco: Jossey-Bass, 1974), p. 2; and Jack Block, *Lives Through Time* (Berkeley, Calif.: University of California Press, 1973), pp. 137-168 and 189-246.

21. Jacques, "Death and the Mid-Life Crisis," p. 502.

22. Ibid., p. 506.

23. Bernice L. Neugarten, *Personality in Middle and Late Life* (New York: Atherton, 1964), p. 192.

24. Richard Church, *The Voyage Home* (London: Heinemann, 1964), p. 127.

25. Jacques, "Death and the Mid-Life Crisis," p. 502.

26. Ibid., p. 511; and H. G. Kaufman, *Obsolescence and Professional Career Development* (New York: AMACOM, 1974), p. 47.

27. David Gutmann, "Aging Among the Highland Maya: A Comparative Study," *Journal of Personality and Social Psychology*, Vol. 7, no. 1 (1967), pp. 28-35.

28. Levinson, Darrow, Klein, Levinson, and McKee, "The Psychosocial Development of Men," p. 244.

29. Gould, "Adult Life Stages."

30. Ibid., pp. 76-77.

31. Ibid., p. 74.

32. Layne A. Longfellow, "Toward Understanding Societal Influences," unpublished. Copyright ® 1975, Layne A. Longfellow, Ph.D., The Menninger Foundation. For another attempt to motivate study of mid-career phenomena, see L. Eugene Thomas, "Why Study Mid-Life Career Change," *Vocational Guidance Quarterly*, Vol. 24 (1974), pp. 37-40.

33. T. George Harris, "Some Idiot Raised the Ante," *Psychology Today*, Vol. 5 (February 1972), p. 40.

34. Ibid.

35. Dean C. Dauw, *Up Your Career* (Prospect Heights, Ill.: Waveland, 1975), p. 125. Of all mid-career changes, available but inconclusive data suggest that involuntary changes outnumber the voluntary by nearly two-to-one. See Thomas M. Driskill and Dean C. Dauw, "Executive Mid-Career Job Change," *Personnel Journal*, Vol. 54 (November 1975), pp. 562-567.

36. "Don't Call It 'Early Retirement,' " *Harvard Business Review*, Vol. 53 (September 1975), pp. 103-118.

37. Martha Wolfenstein, "Trends in Infant Care," *American Journal of Orthopsychiatry*, Vol. 23 (1953), p. 121; see also esp. pp. 128-130.

38. *Harvard Business Review*, "Don't Call It 'Early Retirement.' " For the beginnings of rigorous research about such cases, see L. Eugene Thomas,

Richard L. Mela, Paula I. Robbins, and David W. Harvey, "Corporate Drop-outs: A Preliminary Typology," *Vocational Guidance Quarterly,* Vol. 25 (March 1976), pp. 220-228.

39. The malady was especially highlighted by the HEW report *Work in America.* For a more chilling description, see H. L. Sheppard and N. Q. Herrick, *Where Have All the Robots Gone?: Worker Dissatisfaction in the 70's* (New York: Free Press, 1973).

40. The rigorous evidence is sparse and not consistent, but such blue-collar flame-out seems growing if perhaps not yet epidemic. For early hints, see Patricia Cain Smith, "The Prediction of Individual Differences in Suscepti-bility to Industrial Monotony," *Journal of Applied Psychology,* Vol. 39 (October 1955), pp. 322-330.

41. Allan J. Cox, "How to Love Your Job—and Yourself, Too," *Advertising Age,* Vol. 46 (June 23, 1975), p. 39. See also Kaufman, *Obsolescence,* esp. pp. 46-48.

42. Britton and Britton, *Personality Changes in Aging,* pp. 169-170.

43. Maas and Kuypers, *From Thirty to Seventy,* pp. 200-201.

44. Geist, *Psychological Aspects of the Aging Process,* pp. 36-37.

45. The central study by Harvey C. Lehman is conveniently reprinted in Bernice Levin Neugarten (ed.), *Middle Age and Aging* (Chicago: University of Chicago Press, 1968); see esp. pp. 104-105.

46. Ibid., see the study by Wayne David, esp. pp. 113.

47. Gould, "Adult Life Stages," p. 78.

48. OSS Assessment Staff, *Assessment of Men* (New York: Rinehart, 1948), gives credit for the emphasis to German psychologists seeking those with potential as military officers.

49. The advantages of multiple-assessment procedures are detailed by John C. Flanagan, "Some Considerations in the Development of Situational Tests." *Personnel Psychology,* Vol. 7 (Winter 1964), pp. 461-464. That efforts to capitalize on such advantages came thick and fast is patent in the fact that there have been hundreds of articles and reports published in the past 10 years about the assessment center strategy, many of which have penetrated the general management literature. See "Where They Make Believe They're the Boss," *Business Week,* August 28, 1971, pp. 34-35; Robert C. Albrook, "How to Spot Executives Early," *Fortune,* Vol. 78 (July 1968), pp. 106-111; William C. Byham, "Assessment Centers for Spotting Future Mana-gers," *Harvard Business Review,* Vol. 48 (July 1970), pp. 150-160; and John J. McConnell and Treadway C. Parker, "An Assessment Center Pro-gram for Multi-Organizational Use," *Training and Development Journal,* Vol. 26 (March 1972), pp. 6-15.

50. Herbert B. Wollowich and W. J. McNamara, "Relationship of the Compo-nents of an Assessment Center to Management Success," *Journal of Applied Psychology,* Vol. 53 (October 1969), p. 352.

51. Douglas W. Bray and Donald L. Grant, "The Assessment Center in the Measurement of Potential for Business Management," *Psychological Monographs,* Vol. 80, no. 17, whole no. 625 (1966), p. 24. See also J. R. Hinrichs, "Comparisons of 'Real Life' Assessments of Management Potential with Situational Exercises, Paper-and-Pencil Ability Tests, and Personality Inventories," *Journal of Applied Psychology,* Vol. 53 (October 1969), pp. 425-432.

52. For a critical overview, see Ann Howard, "An Assessment of Assessment Centers," *Journal of the Academy of Management,* Vol. 17 (March 1974), pp. 115-134.

53. For other designs, see Bray and Grant, "The Assessment Center," and J. M. Greenwood and W. J. McNamara, "Interrater Reliability in Situational Tests," *Journal of Applied Psychology,* Vol. 51 (June 1967), pp. 226-232.

54. For a comprehensive treatment, see Donald E. Super and John O. Crites, *Appraising Vocational Fitness* (New York: Harper and Row, 1962), esp. pp. 29-55.

55. Hinrichs, "Comparisons of 'Real-Life' Assessments," p. 427. The qualities to be rated vary from position to position, and from one assessment center to another for the same position. For another list of qualities to be rated, see John H. McConnell, "The Assessment Center: A Flexible Program for Supervisors," *Personnel,* Vol. 48 (September 1971), pp. 36-37.

56. For a sample, see William C. Byham, "The Assessment Center as an Aid in Management Development," *Training Directors Journal,* Vol. 25 (December 1971), pp. 20-21.

57. The In-Basket is a training technique which uses 10-20 letters, memos, transcripts of phone calls, etc., to test an individual's ability to organize work, handle complexity and uncertainty, and so on. The trainee is instructed to act as the holder of a job, the features of which are usually specified, who has to deal with the pending business in his in-basket.

58. Byham, "The Assessment Center as An Aid in Management Development," p. 12.

59. Albrook, "How to Spot Executives Early," p. 106.

60. Byham, "Assessment Centers for Spotting Future Managers," p. 152.

61. Byham, "The Assessment Center as An Aid in Management Development," p. 12.

62. Ibid.

63. William C. Byham and Regina Pentecost, "The Assessment Center: Identifying Tomorrow's Managers," *Personnel,* Vol. 47 (September 1970), p. 23.

64. Tennessee Valley Authority, *TVA's Experiment in the Assessment of Managerial Potential* (Knoxville, Tenn., not dated).

65. David Nadler, *The NOW Employee* (Houston, Tex.: Gulf Publishing, 1971), pp. 4-5.

66. Byham, "The Assessment Center as an Aid in Management Development," p. 16.

67. Steven D. Norton, "The Empirical and Content Validity of Assessment Centers vs. Traditional Methods for Predicting Managerial Success," *Academy of Management Review*, Vol. 2 (July 1977), pp. 442-453. See also William C. Byham, "How to Improve the Validity of an Assessment Center," *Training and Development Journal*, Vol. 32 (November 1978), pp. 4-6.

68. Hinrichs, "Comparisons of 'Real-Life' Assessments."

69. Bray and Grant, "The Assessment Center," esp. p. 18.

70. Allen I. Krant, "New Frontiers for Assessment Centers," *Personnel*, Vol. 53 (July 1976), pp. 30-38.

71. William C. Byham and Morton E. Spitzer, "Personnel Testing: The Law and Its Implications," *Personnel*, Vol. 48 (September 1971), pp. 8-19.

72. Byham, "The Assessment Center as an Aid in Management Development," p. 13.

73. Jacob E. Hautaluoma and James F. Gavin, "Effects of Organizational Diagnosis and Intervention on Blue-Collar 'Blues,' " *Journal of Applied Behavioral Science*, Vol. 11 (October 1975), p. 476.

74. Sheppard and Herrick, *Where Have All the Robots Gone?*

75. Judson Gooding, "Blue-Collar Blues on the Assembly Line," *Fortune*, Vol. 80 (1970), pp. 69-71, 112-113, and 116-117.

76. Hautaluoma and Gavin, "Effects of Organizational Diagnosis," p. 476.

77. Special Task Force to the Secretary of Health, Education and Welfare, *Work in America* (Cambridge, Mass.: MIT Press, 1973).

78. Hautaluoma and Gavin, "Effects of Organizational Diagnosis," p. 477.

79. Ibid., p. 486.

80. Ibid., pp. 484-485.

81. Ibid., pp. 486-492.

82. Ibid.

83. William A. Pasmore and Donald C. King, "Understanding Organizational Change," *Journal of Applied Behavioral Science*, Vol. 14 (December 1978), esp. pp. 462-466.

84. Marvin R. Weisbord, Mark A. Frohman, and J. Johnston, "Action-Research on Turnover as an OD Entry Strategy." Paper presented at Fall 1971 Meeting of OD Network, Minneapolis, Minn.; and Mark A. Frohman, Marvin R. Weisbord, and J. Johnston, "Turnover Study and Action Program." Unpublished MS, Organization Research and Development Co., Merion Station, Pa.

85. Mark A. Frohman, Marshall Sashkin, and Michael J. Kavanagh, "Action-Research as Applied to Organization Development," in S. Lee Spray (ed.), *Organizational Effectiveness: Theory, Research, and Utilization* (Kent, Ohio: Kent State University Press, 1976), pp. 150-151.

Chapter 5

DEALING WITH DYADS, WHEREVER
Applying Laboratory Values to Work, Home, and Social Settings

Relations between pairs are both ubiquitous and significant. Husband and wife, superior and subordinate, parent and child, clinician and patient, and so on: the catalog of possible dyads goes on and on. Their potential for good or mischief needs no underscoring here. Some observers even see pair relations as *the* most central in nature. That conclusion comes close enough to being correct that there is no real point in arguing about it. For those readers who need more convincing, convenient summaries of the empirical literature should make the point with plenty to spare.[1]

So, this chapter hunts big analytic game, albeit with full recognition that the available OD research must be rated more sparse and suggestive than exhaustive and definitive. The limited approach here, specifically, illustrates dyadic-level designs in five contexts:

- In complex issues between multiple pairs influencing a work unit's performance, as those issues are released for inquiry by process analysis

- In the conflict between pairs, especially at work, as a third party seeks to help them out of their mutual impasse

- In the clash of domestic and business priorities, as husband-wife pairs seek to manage the impact on home life of the spouse's travel on-the-job

- In bargaining between organizational superior and subordinate about the content of roles, with special emphasis on roles in organizations

- In the interaction of significant social dyads, especially in black-white relationships

Patently, much of the juice of life, both sweet and acidic, runs through these five emphases.

Note that the designs here have a mixed orientation. Several of them straightforwardly focus on interaction. But notice how technostructural features—reflected in work policies, procedures, and structures—ineluctably influence the personal and organizational processes in several cases. This interaction seems clearest in two cases: husband-wife strife deriving from business travel, and role negotiation.

Pairs Coping with On-the-Job Problems, I
Process Analysis and the Manager
Who Loved in Nonobvious Ways

Process analysis often can help come to grips with problems between pairs at work. So much unfinished business has accumulated as to clog the communication pipeline between pairs, as it were. Process analysis can isolate and perhaps remove that interpersonal garbage.

Consider the case of the manager who loved so that you could know it only with difficulty. The basic pair relationship in this case was in fact with someone who was even not a member of his work unit. But that unfinished business influenced, perhaps even determined, the manager's relationships with several of his employees. If perhaps dramatic, however, the use of process analysis in this case is no different from cases where the issues are more direct.

The case's background is relatively simple. A new manager was appointed to head a field marketing group, after a short but astounding record as a salesman. Almost from the start, by his own admission and from the complaints of his men, it was clear that his managerial problems were mounting. Some difficulties in adjustment had been expected, especially since the new manager was promoted over several other salesmen with greater seniority and fine records. But, the difficulties lasted longer than the new manager or his superiors either expected or felt comfortable with. A "process conference" was called to see if relief were possible. The manager and his men were to arrive in time for Sunday dinner, and the conference would conclude at Wednesday noon.

From the earliest stages of the process conference, the new manager reflected behaviors and attitudes that created cross-pressures for his men. Four points deserve special emphasis. *First,* the new manager reflected a strong desire to win every point even when the relevance of the issue was obscure and the manager's position was a tenuous one; and he assiduously kept selling his role and himself even when they did not seem at issue. *Second,* the new manager was "helpful," in his view, or "needlessly dominant," as his subordinates saw it. His concern included keeping the water pitchers full and iced. "You guys want cold water. Right?" And perhaps his favorite expression was: "I know you all like to do things in ways you are accustomed to, but you ought to do it this way." "This way" was, of course, his way. *Third,* he expressed dislike of, and even contempt for, most blacks. The company had an affirmative action program, but the new manager would have none of it. He would not voluntarily attempt to seek out potential black salesmen, he announced, although he might be a "good soldier" if a "lot of pressure" were put on him. If blacks were so lazy and unmotivated that they did not answer his help-wanted ads for salesmen, he explained, too bad. His generalizations did not extend to all blacks. Fred, one of his salesmen, was an exception to the new manager. Fred was black, but he had "worked his way up by his own efforts, and not by looking for handouts." *Fourth,* with it all, the new manager expressed a strong need for acceptance by his men, even for their love.

The potential dilemmas in these behaviors and attitudes of the new manager were triggered constantly in the first day of the conference, one might even say deliberately. For example, the manager might push very hard to get his men to accept some position. They often would resist, sometimes out of annoyance at being badgered, and often for what they considered sufficient technical or market reasons. The new manager would read rejection in their behavior and he would then emphasize how difficult it was to work under conditions where he was not accepted as a person.

Considerable attention was focused on the quality of the processes generated by the new manager, attention that carried into the early morning hours over cards and drinks. The subordinates confirmed that their reactions at the conference were like those at work, and for the same reasons. And, the new manager gave increasing signs of awareness of the impact of his behaviors and attitudes. "I'll be damned," he commented several times in effect, "there I go damning you if you do and cursing you if you don't."

During a long session on Tuesday night and early Wednesday morning, the new manager organized much of the data into a new level of insight. No verbatim report is available, but during Wednesday's regular session the new manager spelled out his understanding. This summary contains the sense of his new understanding of himself and of his work relations:

> None of this stuff is entirely new, but it fits together now. I put it all together last night.
>
> I like all of you, and I probably even would like your love, but I have been pushing that need too much in this group. I have been jumping all over to be helpful, and I know I alienate people by doing what they don't want to do, or want to do in their own way. I've got to let some things be. And I know

I have tried to win every point, even the very doubtful ones. I really don't need to be a big man that way.

I have been bad-mouthing all blacks, too, and saying that if others before them could work their way up, they could too. I know only a small percentage are the welfare chiselers and revolutionaries. And I know that it is tougher to work your way up today if you don't have skills, or the cultural background.

How does all this go together? I love my father, I realize, and need his love. He has always held back from me, and that made me feel unworthy. I have tried to make it all up with you guys, and my subordinates, and probably my family too. It's that simple, and that complex.

But I really don't need all from you that I have been asking. I like you guys, and respect you. But I have been asking too much from you. I want you to accept me, but I have been forcing myself on you. I want you to consider me a competent guy, but I have been trying to do it all.

Hell, Fred, I don't even hate blacks.

I just love my father, who worked his way up from the bottom. My business is basically with him, not you.

I'm ready to get to work. I feel like a big weight has been lifted. I'll try not to impose it on you guys again.

The evidence indicates that both the manager and his men did in fact subsequently get to work in mutually satisfying ways. They cite the value of the process conference in "getting over the hump." But, only a continuous attention to their own processes will conquer similar humps, as the sense and sentiment of that one meeting fade in memory and possibly get violated in practice.

This illustrates a major breakthrough via a process orientation and goes as far in the laboratory approach as it is advisable to go. In some cases, follow-up with individual therapy might be indicated. In this case, the new manager seemed thoroughly in command of the learning situation. Indeed, only he had the relevant data, which he had assembled and organized. Revealingly, the manager notes that it was easier for him to recognize and reorganize that data because he was "so tired" from all the late talking and card-playing that his "conscious controls were weakened." Since late-night activities were not usual ones for the manager, one might also say that he also controlled, or even created, that aspect of his own learning environment.

Pairs Coping with On-the-Job Problems, II
Character and Consequences of Third-Party Consultation

Two opposed forces are at the heart of organizational life: conflicts that separate many people; and interdependencies that for good or ill require that many of the very same people integrate their efforts as smoothly as possible. This section deals with the central dilemma inherent in these forces in opposition, via emphasis on the character and consequences of third-party consultation, one of the growing family of spin-off technologies of the laboratory approach.

Interpersonal Conflict as Real and Relevant

If there were an organizational Book of Genesis, it no doubt would start with these words: "From the beginning, there was interpersonal conflict; and technological development begat increasingly more interpersonal conflict." In fact, formal organizations are in an important sense vehicles for coping with diverse and often opposed interests and desires, which puts them in the interpersonal conflict business in a big way. The extent of this involvement is suggested in Richard E. Walton's definition of the term: "Interpersonal conflict is defined broadly to include both (a) personal disagreements over substantive issues, such as differences over organizational structures, policies, and practices, and (b) interpersonal antagonisms, that is, the more personal and emotional differences which arise between interdependent human beings."[2] Moreover, the two general bases of interpersonal conflict—substantive and emotional—can develop in diverse interacting ways.[3]

Powerful forces imply that such interpersonal conflicts will be a constant feature of life in organizations. *First,* today's organizations are characterized by escalating interdependencies—between units of the same organization;[4] between units of different organizations linked as major contractors and subcontractors; and between organizations and government as coparticipant, or buyer, regulator, or even competitor,[5] and more besides.

Second, interpersonal conflict also has a variety of advantageous features, so that there would be important reasons to preserve it even if it could be eliminated. Given that it is easy to overdo any useful thing, a certain amount of interpersonal conflict can encourage a sharpening of job descriptions or definitions of work roles. Such clarification in turn could make it easier to establish responsibility for performance. Again, "a certain amount" of interpersonal conflict might serve to bring out the best in people at work.

Third, however, interpersonal conflict in all organizations often goes beyond the "certain amount" which can be a good thing. To begin with a conclusion, multiple forces act to discourage the early raising of interpersonal conflicts, with the consequence that any organization is likely to have a substantial backlog of unfinished business to which additions are continually made. If nothing else, this backlog can serve to create a state of readiness that can be escalated into interpersonal conflict by apparently minor episodes.

Consider only a few forces that impede the resolution of unfinished business deriving from interpersonal conflict in organizations. Inhibitions about raising interpersonal issues, especially of the emotional kind, exist in all organizations.

Conservation of energy also dictates avoiding some interpersonal conflicts. This may be a short-run saving that turns out to have major long-run costs. But the plain fact remains that many interpersonal issues are set aside in any organization in the rush of other immediate business. Finally, there are risks in surfacing interpersonal conflict in all organizations. If nothing else, that requires that at least two parties be willing to disclose or reveal themselves, and there can be a risk in such disclosure. As a general rule, in addition, the risk is greatest where interpersonal conflict is most pronounced. Consequently, the explicit raising of interpersonal conflict is least likely precisely where it is most necessary.

A Learning Design for Aiding Conflictful Pairs

A wide variety of interventions have been developed to either resolve or manage interpersonal conflict, however it gets triggered. Three more-or-less traditional models can be distinguished. Thus, the work can be restructured or reorganized to make variously sure that the parties in conflict do not interact with one another, or the jobs of the individuals might be changed to reduce or eliminate the previous interdependency.[6] Alternatively, a legal-judicial model might be followed. Here the resolution or control of the conflict depends on determining what are the applicable rules and precedents and somehow adjudicating the difference between the contending parties.[7] Or, one might follow a bargaining model, where the resolution will be influenced by issues of equity but only as they are significantly mediated by the relative power potential of the parties in dispute.[8] Of course, combinations of these three basic strategies also are possible.[9]

A more-or-less distinct strategy has recently begun to emerge for resolving or controlling interpersonal conflict, what Walton calls "social science analysis and intervention."[10] This strategy, in partial contrast to the three models above, "would take into account many additional facets of the social system and would attempt to find a resolution to the dispute consistent with the objective of preserving or changing the social system, or certain of its characteristics."

Third-party consultation is one kind of social science intervention applicable in organizations which recently has been spun off from the laboratory approach, largely through the efforts of Richard Walton.[11] Basically, the approach calls for a confrontation between two parties in interpersonal conflict, in the presence of a qualified facilitator who seeks to help the parties move toward resolution or control of their differences. Often, the confrontation *à trois* takes place after the consultant has interviewed both parties. Third-party consultations have diverse intended effects, which may be illustrated by the results of the technique's application to the three examples of interpersonal conflict introduced earlier. The results cover the range from resolution of the issues in conflict, to managing or controlling some of the consequences of issues that remained unresolved:[12]

- A recurrent conflict between two managers was based on a misunderstanding of motives, with one manager suspicious that the other sought the former's job. Third-party consultation convinced the parties that there was a discrepancy between perceived intention and actual intention, and they developed a new understanding which eliminated that discrepancy.

- Two organization members got into a mutually destructive conflict, due to contrasting personal styles and contradictory definitions of their work roles. Third-party consultation permitted the individuals to explore these differences. No changes were made in personal styles, but the emotional conflict was reduced and the definitions of work roles were modified to reduce the contradictions.

- Two managers who were directly competing for the same job pursued their mutually exclusive goals with such abandon as to support the cause of Self by undercutting Other. The third-party consultation helped the antagonists reach an agreement that outlawed certain destructive tactics, in the sense of an interpersonal treaty of nonaggression in certain areas.

The more specific character of third-party consultation can be circumscribed in terms of four elements. *First,* the technique is a confronting one for exploring and clarifying issues in conflict, assessing the nature and magnitude of the needs or forces involved, and highlighting the feelings generated in the two parties. As Walton observes:[13]

> If well managed, the confrontation is a method: for achieving greater understanding of the nature of the basic issues and the strength of the principals' respective interests in these issues; for achieving common diagnostic understanding of the triggering events, tactics and consequences of their conflict and how they tend to proliferate symptomatic issues; for discovering or inventing control possibilities and/or possible resolutions.

Second, the third party serves two basic functions in the role of helping the pair to confront their conflict in constructive ways. Thus, he or she serves as a process consultant in observing the interacting pair; attempts to reflect a process orientation in his/her own interventions, and also seeks to encourage the pair to increasingly respect the same values in their interactions in the learning situation as a prelude to later self-maintenance of their interaction at work. In sum, this means (to use Edgar Schein's definition again) that the consultant attempts to generate "a set of activities . . . which help the client to perceive, understand, and act upon process events which occur in the client's environment."[14] In this role, the consultant may:[15]

- Regulate interaction between pairs, as by terminating a discussion that is repetitive or counterproductive
- Suggest items for discussion between the pair

- Constantly summarize what he understands has been said or projected nonverbally by the principals, to clarify and perhaps even redefine issues, with the goal of increasing the consensus about what all three participants understand as the sense of ongoing communication and, hence, of increasing the credibility and reliability attributed to the communicative signs being exchanged
- Encourage feedback between the principals, and between the principals and himself
- Make observations about the processes that exist between the pair in conflict, and perhaps himself and them
- Diagnose the sources of conflict
- Prescribe techniques that may facilitate discussion
- Suggest ways to resolve or manage the conflict

Perhaps the most crucial role of the consultant is encouraging adherence to the values and goals of the laboratory approach. These values relate especially to openness, willingness to risk interpersonally and to experiment, owning the conflict as well as the emotions associated with it, and acceptance of the responsibility for the consequences of the confrontation. This is not usually as difficult as it appears, because the principals often have had a T-group experience before they begin a third-party consultation and the two parties identify their consultant with the laboratory approach. In any case, the effects are central to the success of third-party consultation. As one source explains: ". . . because of the nature of the third party's professional identity and the clients' prior experience with persons in the profession, his presence by itself tended to provide emotional support and reinvoke some of the behavioral norms which were instrumental to the conflict confrontation and resolution process."[16]

Third, since interpersonal conflicts tend to be cyclical, a major task of the third-party consultation is to isolate those factors which trigger the conflict as well as those which dampen it. Such information can serve one of two purposes. An elemental strategy for managing conflict would straightforwardly seek to minimize the occurrence of trigger events and to maximize the dampeners. Beyond that, knowledge of the specific triggers and dampeners may spotlight the causal issues which must be dealt with by any real resolution of the conflict.

Fourth, a variety of conditions seems to be necessary for a productive third-party consultation. These conditions may be sampled here briefly, since a fuller treatment with illustrations is conveniently available.[17] The conditions often can be influenced markedly by the consultant. They include:

- Mutual and synchronized positive motivation by both principals seems a prerequisite, apparently in that it is a measure of willingness to invest in the confrontation and to own its consequences, both of which no doubt are powerful factors predisposing toward a successful experience.

• Some balance in the power of principals in the learning situation seems important, which the consultant can help supply by interventions that help both parties get air time or that draw attention to the domination by one of the pair. For example, the subordinate in a manager-employee pair might feel that he "will lose every time" in the learning situation as well as outside of it, in the absence of efforts by the consultant to achieve some relative balance of power or influence.

• Of critical importance is the appropriate pacing of the two basic phases characteristic of third-party consultation, differentiation and integration. These may occur several times, especially when a complex string of issues is involved.

Differentiation often is time consuming, as each party develops his own sense of the conflict, elaborates other differences between the two parties, and ventilates feelings and reactions toward the other. The level of tension is likely to be high.

Integration often can occur in brief if important episodes, as in stressing the commonalities between the pair, expressing a new respect or even a mutual warmth, and moving toward commonly accepted solutions that manage or resolve the interpersonal conflict.

• An intermediate tension level seems useful for learning in third-party confrontations. Low levels of tension imply low motivation, and very high levels of tension apparently bind principals in ways that confound and complicate the learning situation.

Inadequate Research Literature

No ample research literature establishes the unqualified value of third-party consultation, or even the conditions under which success is probable. But the presumptive case is strong, supported as it is by some systematic research and by developing practice in a variety of organizational, institutional, and family settings, as well as by the logic of the laboratory approach developed above. Indeed, even when the goals of a specific third-party consultation are not achieved, real progress may have been made. As Walton concludes:

> The very fact of having vested personal energy in a relationship usually increases respective commitments to improve the relationship, provided there is some small basis for encouragement. Even when there is no emotional reconciliation, if the parties are able to explicitly or implicitly arrive at better coping techniques, they tend to feel more control over their interpersonal environment and less controlled by it.[18]

Whatever the case, Walton points to a number of researchable propositions with which the next developmental stage in third-party consultation must deal.

Perspectives on a Failure*

Despite the lack of explicit research, much experience implies the validity of
Walton's prescriptions for effective third-party consultation. An application in a
five-member work group which obviously failed, for example, provides patent
support for Walton's approach. For many purposes, please note, the case below
basically involves two overlapping pair relationships:

- A mollifying subordinate and the manager
- An emotional subordinate and the manager

The intervenor, in effect, is the third party in both cases.

A Troubled Mini-History

As part of a larger organization, the work unit was recently established to analyze
policy for potential legislation. The unit's four staff members held degrees, some
advanced, in the areas of political science and public administration; all had practical work experience. The unit's supervisor held a law degree and had spent 2
years with a law firm. The unit promised to be a compatible one that would
produce quality reports.

Within 3 months, however, the unit was crippled by interpersonal conflict.
Initially, the disagreements centered around different concepts of a satisfactory
management style. The unit director took an authoritarian approach to running
the division, expecting formal, written progress reports; staff members had anticipated a looser approach to structure: more brainstorming and free discussion.
Problems also arose regarding each member's autonomy over projects assigned to
his or her supervision. The unit director made it plain he felt he had ultimate
say-so over a project, but all staff members felt their suggestions should be given
equal weight in the final project.

The Third-Party Intervention

The director of the parent organization made the decision to employ a third-
party consultant, at the 5-month point in the unit's life. The intervenor was a
member of the parent organization, although unknown to any of the staff
involved.

Since the unit clearly had polarized into four (the staff) "versus" one (the
supervisor), the intervenor held separate introductory meetings to determine
what each "side" saw as the greatest problems facing the group. In both

*Written expressly for this volume by Frances Rauschenberg, a graduate student at the
University of Georgia.

meetings, the intervenor acted as a sounding board, sometimes clarifying or re-stating an idea, but primarily playing the listener.

The first meeting was with the staff. Discussion emphasized problems of miscommunication, as well as lack of communication; each member's thwarted expectations of duties and responsibilities; and perceptions of real (compared to ideal) unit organization. The four also discussed some of the degrading and criti-cal personal remarks that were being exchanged between the director and some staff members. Silences, sometimes of several days, resulted. The problems were especially critical for one staff member, Flo. The other three had other projects which provided them respite and shelter. Flo was on unit work fulltime, and her complaints were strongest. The other three staff sympathized with her vulner-able position, and encouraged her to confront the supervisor while noting they had less need to do so themselves. The four staff members worked well together, shared similar goals for the unit, and all felt isolated from the supervisor.

There is no record of the meeting of the intervenor and the supervisor but later recollections indicate that discussion centered on the supervisor's frustration at being isolated and screened from *his* superiors.

The third meeting, held a few days later, was the first opportunity for the unit to meet in toto. The atmosphere was strained. One of the staff members—more experienced, and with greatest informal status—opened the meeting with a rambling discourse about the job the unit was trying to accomplish, and how well it was being done. He referred to recurring problems, but avoided their person-ality aspects. This member later revealed his intent was to relieve obvious tension; other staff members believed it only aggravated the situation. About 45 minutes were taken up in this way, with only minor interventions by either participants or the third party.

Eventually, the supervisor says to the intervenor: "I am interested in know-ing how Flo feels about all this." Everyone turns and looks at her.

Flo shifts uneasily in her chair. Her headache suddenly becomes a full-blown migraine, it seems. Her thoughts are racing as she weighs alternatives: Should she say it or not? She looks to the intervenor for encouragement, but he is studying his cigarette with fascination.

"I must say *something*," she thinks, "or I'll regret it the rest of my life." When she opens her mouth, she is appalled to hear a squeaky little voice emerge. She thinks: "Can it be mine? I sound like I am going to cry! *I* know I'm not, but everyone else looks nervous."

The words pour out. "I'll be honest: I've felt cheated in this job. You promised some pretty great things—you said you needed someone who could do more research than secretarial work, but I haven't seen much research yet. Some days the only thing I come in for is to clip articles out of three newspapers and maybe file a little. I know the menial things have to be done, too, but it seems like that's all there is."

"I've tried to be honest about what I thought fell within the demands of my job. Like not getting coffee for you in the morning—I think you know a lot more about how you like your coffee than I do. And also about screening your phone calls—no one else in the entire department has it done. I know you were used to some of this where you worked before but things here aren't so formal. I think you should try to fit in more with what's accepted here."

Flo is pretty elated that she's said some of these things. But by now she's hyperventilating, so she tries a new tack. She starts to feel a little sorry for the supervisor. "He hasn't said a word in self-defense. I'll take a little of the blame, too. It seems only fair!" she thinks.

"I know I'm stubborn and hard to get along with. I've refused to do things I probably should have done," she continues. "I'm feeling like a real rat."

This prompts a flurry of activity by the other staff members, the first real participation in perhaps 15 minutes. They note Flo is too hard on herself; that she has done a good job.

But the conversation soon becomes desultory. The heated invitation to confrontation seems embarrassing to all, including the intervenor. The supervisor pays virtually no attention to the emotional outburst which centered around specific personal problems that Flo has with her supervisor. Did he ask the question only for appearance? The "discussion" soon returns to its earlier orientation, centering mostly on what kinds of information were not being shared between the supervisor and the rest of the staff. The supervisor did not reveal to the staff the problems which he encountered with significant people outside the immediate unit, about which he had complained to the third party.

The session ends after about 2 hours, with all members feeling there had been some initial sharing within the group. But the basic problems, vast differences in personal style and work expectations, had been ignored.

The intervenor thanks the members for their participation and indicates his availability to the group in the future, but makes no suggestion of a next meeting date. There are no additional meetings.

A Retrospective Look

This intervention seems a failure, however viewed. According to the unit's members, the "we" and "him" polarized even further after the intervention. One staff member said: "We simply gave up." The director made no further efforts at rapproachment; and the intervenor scheduled no follow-up meetings. The work unit was abolished 6 months later.

Why the outcome? What follows is a personal explanation of the failure based upon failure to respect four basic elements identified by Walton as necessary for an effective third-party consultation.

The Technique Is Confrontation not Exhortation.[19]   The intervenor was perceived as more boundary setting, or even as more hierarchy serving, than Walton recommends. The meeting's dominant mode from the start was to do better, period. Specifically, the intervenor "helped" the supervisor more than the other four staff members by:

- Restating the supervisor's views and feelings, but not those of the staff
- Indicating the supervisor's interest in certain issues rather than others, yet failing to bring up the issues that had been mentioned by the four staff members in their group session
- Not encouraging or even legitimating the open discussion of the emotions and feelings that were involved
- Not dealing with behavior, such as the various mechanisms that triggered conflict

Staff members sensed that confrontation would only be "allowed" to take place on certain levels. The single time a member attempted to move toward more personal issues, the effort was not reinforced. Thereafter, discussion centered on safe topics, such as ways to revise the unit's structure and improving patterns of communication.

Intervenor Should Adopt a Process Orientation.   Walton prescribes that the third parties adopt the same values in their personal style of confrontation that they seek to engender in the conflictful pair. Eiseman focuses attention on a critical related point in the third party's role. "Although being neutral implies being impartial," he observes, "it does not imply being value-free." In fact, Eiseman advises, "the third-party must be prepared to champion the values underlying collaboration."[20]   The intervenor's behavior in this case did not foster a process orientation, nor a confronting mode. Specifically, the intervenor

- Did not regulate the group's interaction. He should have actively involved all members of the group instead of allowing two members of the group to dominate discussion, one of them for a 45-minute stretch.
- Did not suggest topics and issues for discussion based on the fact-finding of the two introductory meetings, even though it was obvious that two very different perspectives of the unit's problems existed.
- Did not attempt to deal with the conflict source, as perceived and described by staff members.
- Did not "process" the "emotional outburst."
- Did not reveal, or get the supervisor to reveal, that part of the supervisor's authoritarian behavior inhering in the controls exercised over the supervisor by his hierarchical superiors.

This catalog implies both missed opportunities and awkward modeling by the third party. The consultant should have reflected openness, willingness to risk and experiment, and should have encouraged owning behavior and emotions. He played an inactive, listening role. Some of the staff members showed a desire and readiness to share on a personal level, at some anticipated personal risk, but they were rebuffed by the lack of acceptance by the third party and the supervisor.

Isolate Factors Which Trigger or Dampen Conflict.[21] Walton suggests that interpersonal conflict be viewed as a cyclical process. Triggering events may not actually escalate the conflict, but may cause conflictful recycling. Minimizing the events which trigger, and maximizing the issues which have a dampening effect on conflict, can break the cycle.

The intervenor made little effort to deal forthrightly with the basic causes of conflict or to discover the actions which would lead to conflict reduction. More attention was paid to preaching that the unit had to run more smoothly than to seeking elimination of problems which hindered that smoothness.

Create Conditions for Productive Confrontation.   Walton also prescribes that at least four elements characterize an effective third-party intervention. They are:

- Equal motivation[22]
- A balance of power[23]
- Pacing that provides due attention to both differentiation and integration of the parties in conflict, basically in that order[24]
- An appropriate level of tension[25]

The third-party consultant did not respect such elements, on balance.

First, there was no real test of participant motivation, because no choice was given. Two members probably would not have participated if an option had been available. Some members felt they had too much to lose, especially if they were honest. There were also differences in staff status which accounted for some apprehension.

Second, "balance of power" does not refer to equal status or influence among members, but to the situational balance of participation in the confrontation. The intervenor failed to insure or even encourage each member's opportunity to participate. Therefore, most members hung back, waiting to be addressed directly. The result was domination by the director and one staff member, whose approach was to defuse the conflict from the first moments of the combined meeting. The other three participants grew more defensive and withdrawn as the meeting wore on, and they received no help in situationally counter-balancing the director's formal power.

Third, pacing of the confrontation requires a delicate shifting between differentiation and integration phases. Differentiation emphasizes the differences in the group. Integration should then follow, emphasizing the common goals and similarities. Often, there will be several cycles of differentiation ↔ integration in a third-party consultation.

Basically, the combined meeting never got very far into the sources of differentiation, probably because of the very long attempt by one staff member to emphasize integration from the start. The "emotional outburst" about the 45-minute mark probably was heightened by the delay in getting on with it. Moreover, and perhaps because of the unexpected intensity of the outburst, the consultant did not seem to know quite what to do with the emotional aspects of differentiation. In fact, he seemed to ignore and avoid attempts to deal with them. He did not seem at ease dealing with the emotional aspects of differentiation, even seemed to ignore and avoid attempts to deal with them. He did not seem at ease dealing with the personal problems and frustrations that four members had voiced to him privately as the main causes for concern. The four staff members did attempt to balance their "attacks" with integrative interchange. These latter efforts were virtually ignored by the supervisor. The intervenor did not draw attention to the lack of response from the supervisor, nor did he encourage feedback.

Fourth, the tension level in the combined meeting escalated to a point at which it was difficult for any learning to occur. One member recalled getting a migraine headache during the meeting. Yet the intervenor seemed unaware of any unusual tension, and made no efforts to discuss it.

The intervenor in this case was interviewed, and his views and feelings are interesting. At his request, he was given only nominal briefing from the parent organization regarding the unit's problems. He stated his preference to observe and listen to each faction as impartially as possible. He then determined the underlying issues and formulated a strategy. He indicated that his confrontation strategy varied with each situation, the primary goal being to remain totally unbiased. He viewed the role of intervenor as a sounding board, and he comments only when he seeks clarification or sees a need to sum up what has been said. He studiously avoids the role of moderator, preferring to be inactive in structuring the discussion.

Consistent with this preferred role, the third party did not actively encourage the transfer of confrontation values back to the worksite. Also, future dialog was made more difficult because no follow-up meeting was set. The third party merely mentioned his future availability.

This posture about follow-up meetings seems counterproductive. One meeting on a problem of this scope scarcely scratches the surface. In this case, it only heightened the tension that the members were experiencing. Three staff members felt the single meeting actually had destructive effects. One member initially thought it was constructive, but altered that opinion after learning there would be no follow-up.

Husband and Wife Deal with Problems of Business Travel
Interfaces Between Work and Home

Work is often like an octopus, its tentacles penetrating into many areas of life. And where work extends, there also must the laboratory approach to OD establish its applicability. That is the spirit of this section.

The focus here is both generic and specific. Broadly, this section focuses on how problems at work can influence marriages, even tear them apart.[26] The specific focus is on an OD design which attempts to ease the problems of heavy travel schedules of husbands and wives as they impact on spouses and marriages, certainly a common and probably a growing concern.

The present design seeks to develop a more satisfying interface between two systems that impinge on one another only in part, and should be kept that way. The basic value prescribes involvement of all parties in matters that influence them, while largely separate spheres for work and family also ought to be maintained. Perhaps the difficulty of drawing the line tends to inhibit efforts at working on the interfaces between work and family. In any case, organizational issues seldom get defined in ways that emphasize the relevance of family involvement.[27] This section deals with one of the exceptions.

Boundaries to Preserve Privacy

The interface between work and family systems in this case was bounded in two ways, by restrictive policies as well as by a learning design with a strong privatizing bias. A number of policies defined the restricted interface between the demands of work and of family. An acceptable design would

- Restrict attention to the stresses of travel, not the entire marriage; other family businesses would remain private
- Involve organization members only by their own choice, based on full information about the design
- Not force or pressure participants into discussing subjects they did not wish to discuss
- Emphasize the strengthening of current problem-solving capabilities associated with the stresses of travel, as opposed to criticizing deficiencies

A Design for Problem-Solving

The present narrow if significant interface of family/work systems were explored by a design with a strong privatizing bias, as Exhibit 1 details. Basically, each husband-wife pair worked on the several design elements in a separate motel room, with a change agent available if desired. The several pairs did meet together to get instructions about design elements, and for some minor sharing of reactions. But the design overwhelmingly involved only the private husband-wife pairs. The brevity of the design—two gently paced days—also no doubt contributed to limiting the experience to the individual married pairs.

A variety of considerations urge caution in responding to this prototypical design, but it does seem promising. The main cautions relate to representativeness: the small size (six couples) of the trained population, which limits the confidence that can be placed in the results; and a special condition, such as the "fairly conservative morality" of the couples, which may account for important effects.

Given such cautions, however, the design seems to have induced the desired outcomes for five of the six couples. Culbert and Renshaw note that an independent research program provides tentative support for the basic hypotheses guiding the design:

- The problem-solving resources of husbands and wives seem to have been augmented, as reflected in self-reports about changes in attitudes, changes in perceptions of norms relating to problem-solving in their marriage, and anecdotes about increased effectiveness in problem-solving.
- The abilities of couples to cope with the stresses of travel seem to have increased, as aided both by greater personal planning and by organizational changes inspired by the learning design.
- Changes seemed to occur which applied to other areas of work, and the easing of family pressures made available more potential energy for dealing with issues at work.

The sixth couple responded neutrally to the OD intervention, although they were pleased to have some time together away from the children.

Whatever replications of this design may show, it illustrates the broad family of limited exchange contract OD efforts which are sensitive to the guidelines sketched above. These guidelines seek at once to preserve the sense of the historic development of the laboratory approach and to suggest directions for the future drawn from the experience of the past.

Exhibit 1   "Limited Exchange Contract" OD Design for Functional Interfacing of Work/Family Systems

Approximate Time (minutes)	Purpose of Design Exercise	Design Steps
15	1. to introduce design	
45	2. to establish individual differences	2a. Each person draws on a sheet of paper his "life-line" from birth to death and indicates his present location on that line. 2b. Separate pairs of spouses share and discuss their life-lines. 2c. All couples share their reactions, in part to legitimate the range of differences.
120	3. to develop awareness of, and empathy for, the different ways in which spouses view themselves as a prelude to later formulating specific strategies for coping with the stresses of travel	3a. Each person takes 10 minutes to reflect on his distinguishing characteristics—a role, idiosyncrasy, or whatever. 3b. Each person writes one of these characteristics on each of 10 slips of paper. 3c. Each person rank orders his own slips of paper from most-essential to least-essential. 3d. Each pair of spouses returns to own motel room to share self-descriptions. 3e. Each spouse takes a turn, with the listening spouse being instructed to ask questions to increase understanding of the self-descriptions but not to try to change them. 3f. Couples reassemble to share reactions.
60–90	4. lunch	4a. Same-sex groups, so as to: 1. provide some relief from design 2. gain perspective from others with a similar role
120	5. to recognize forces acting upon the marriage	5a. A general session of "force-field analysis,"[a] a method for analyzing complex situations. 5b. Couples return to own room, where each person independently develops a large graphic of those forces driving toward a more satisfying relationship with his wife or husband and those forces restraining such a relationship. 5c. Couples share and discuss with each other their individual force fields.
at least 60	6. to reflect on and integrate the events of the day	6a. "alone time"
	7. dinner and evening	7a. married couples
90	8. to use feelings as data	8a. A fantasy exercise is used to provide an indirect way to express feelings that might be difficult in normal situations, the fantasy being that the husband had just left on a long business trip. 8b. Couples reflect on the emotional experience induced by the fantasy and write each other a letter describing that experience.

Exhibit 1   (Continued)

		8c. Couples return to separate rooms and read aloud the letters they have just written to each other.
90	9. to demonstrate empathy for their spouses	9a. Consultant describes and demonstrates "brainstorming."
		9b. Each person uses this technique to list all the stresses expected during an upcoming period of peak travel.
		9c. Each person rates intensity of each stress on 1–10 scale.
		9d. Spouses exchange lists, with their focus for analysis being the specific behaviors in terms of which the other partner responds to each specific stress.
		9e. Couples return to separate rooms to discuss the accuracy of their perceptions of the other, as well as their feelings about being understood.
	10. lunch	
90–120	11. to build support, to legitimate the giving and receiving of support by each partner	11a. Using lists of stresses due to travel, each partner develops a list of actions he or she would *like* to take themselves and of the kinds of support they would prefer to receive.
		11b. Discussion by couples of the supporting actions they prefer to give and receive.
30–45	12. closing	12a. reactions to learning design
		12b. recommended organizational changes that would aid coping with stress of travel

[a]Robert T. Golembiewski and Arthur Blumberg (eds.), *Sensitivity Training and the Laboratory Approach* (Itasca, Ill.: F. E. Peacock Publishers, Inc., 1970), pp. 293-294.
[b]Sidney J. Parnes and Harold F. Harding (eds.), *A Source Book for Creative Thinking* (New York: Charles Schribner's Sons, 1962), pp. 251-304.
Source: Based upon Samuel A. Culbert and Jean Renshaw, "Coping with the Stresses of Travel as an Opportunity for Improving the Quality of Work and Family Life," *Family Processes,* Vol. 11 (September 1972), pp. 321-337.

Organization Members Deal with Influence and Job Boundaries*
An Exercise in Role Negotiation

Power, competitiveness, and coercion may be viewed from many perspectives. At one extreme, this trying trinity may derive from inadequate skill, lack of knowledge of the issues or the persons involved, from unfortunate mistakes or

*The leading article on such matters is Roger Harrison's "Role Negotiation: A Tough Minded Approach to Team Development." Reproduced by special permission from W. Warner Burke and H. Hornstein (eds.) *The Social Technology of Organization Development* (Washington, D.C.: NTL Learning Resources, 1972), pp. 84-96.

regrettable departures from a basically collaborative human spirit, or from repressive social institutions that warp an otherwise generous human spirit. At another extreme, power, competitiveness, and coercion may be seen as organizational analogues of death and taxes. That is, the trio may be seen as basic and ubiquitous in all human relationships. And efforts to curb the trio would be seen as quixotic and doomed to failure, even if such efforts are not positively dangerous.

This section illustrates one approach to slipping between the horns of such extreme positions. The goal is to do something about power, competitiveness, and coercion, but a relatively modest something.

Distinguishing Interventions of Two Depths

Let us briefly begin to build toward the basic sense of the "relatively modest something" at issue here. Where one sits philosophically can have profound effects on OD designs of choice. As Harrison observes,[28] it matters significantly how one conceives *the* basic problem of organizational change:

- As one of *releasing* human potential for collaboration and cooperation
- As one of *controlling* or *checking* the human appetite for seeking advantage and being competitive in win-or-lose terms

These two ways of conceiving the problem of organization change imply interventions of two different depths, or levels. Consider a bitter struggle between two colleagues in an organization, which boils down to the question of who will be dominant. The *releasing* concept encourages a broad and deep search for repressed or partially recognized contributors to the white-knuckle experience. The key questions are deeply probing, that is. How do superior and subordinate feel about each other, since their conflict may be explained by mutual personal dislike? And what factors underlay such feelings? Once expressed, goes the implied rationale, this repressed material can be worked through, releasing much energy for task performance.

The *controlling* concept has more modest ambitions. Hence its key question is: What do we have to do to operate effectively, without necessarily understanding all the bases of the conflict between us? The goal here is to manage adequately, as opposed to resolve finally.

The choice of an appropriate depth for an intervention is not always simple, in principle or in practice. To be sure, in some cases, what it takes to release and control may be exactly the same. For example, efforts to control may be stymied unless release occurs, with the effort to control being like squeezing a balloon filled with water. In many cases, however, what it takes to control usually is very much more limited than what it takes to release.

Role Negotiation as a Controlling Strategy

Roger Harrison developed "role negotiation" as an intervention more oriented toward controlling than releasing. Briefly, these descriptive snippets from Harrison serve to circumscribe the intervention. That is, role negotiation[29]

- "includes not only the formal job description but also all the informal understandings, agreements, expectations, and arrangements with others which determine the way one person's or group's work affects or fits in with another's"
- "intervenes directly in the relationships of power, authority, and influence within the group. . . . It avoids probing into the likes and dislikes of members for one another and their personal feelings about one another"
- "[it is] more consonant with the task-oriented norms of business than are most other behavioral approaches."

Five more detailed features also characterize role negotiation as an OD intervention.[30] *First,* the design is applicable to a range of role-bound social units, including executive teams, project teams or task forces, as well as husband-wife combinations or other dyads. Despite the design's applicability to groupings of many sizes, it is dealt with here in the chapter on dyadic interventions as an organizing convenience, and also because the design is applicable to dyads as well as to larger collections.

Second, although the design is appropriate for groups of a wide range of sizes, Harrison advises that multiple learning groups be formed when the number of those involved gets as large as eight or ten. Representatives from each of these several learning groups might then perform a second-order role negotiation exercise on any issues broader than the individual learning groups.

Third, role negotiation makes only one basic assumption, that most individuals will almost always opt for some acceptable bargain rather than for continuing tension. As Harrison notes:[31] "most people prefer a fair negotiated settlement to a state of unresolved conflict and they are willing to invest some time and make some concessions in order to achieve a solution." In short, many people would rather switch than fight.

Fourth, role negotiation requires that participants be willing and able to specify, with substantial accuracy and detail, what they want and what they are willing to bargain away for what they want. That is, change here rests basically on negotiated bargains, giving up this to get that. Relatedly, all participants must be open to some degree of exchange, to know what they are willing to give up themselves in return for what they want from others.

Fifth, the role negotiation makes real but limited demands for mutual trust between participants, including consultants or intervenors.

The Basic Contract in Role Negotiation

The modicum of trust just mentioned essentially appears in the form of a mutual willingness of participants and consultant to agree to, or contract for, a relatively specific intervention. Harrison advises a written contract, which has six prime features. These contractual features, as it were, define the norms of the temporary social system in which the role negotiation will take place. Hence the centrality of contracting, for it will pervasively affect all that occurs subsequently.

Harrison's own development of the six contractual features will be relied upon here. Please consult Exhibit 2.

Role Negotiation as Bargaining Made Overt

Basically, then, role negotiation seeks to make as explicit as possible processes that are always ongoing, although usually subtly and in ways of which participants may be unconscious. The participants' motivation for overtness is direct. Except for the manipulator who seeks to gain leverage from incomplete information and from subsurface or even unconscious negotiation,[32] most participants understand that such processes on balance are often more mischievous than useful. If nothing else, such secret processes probably increase the potential for awkward decisions, based on partial or misleading information, unclear perceptions of what participants need, what they want, and what they may settle for. Relatedly, role negotiation increases the average influence that group members can have on one another, although some participants may find that their influence as individuals is reduced. This is a powerful motivator for participating in such a design except, obviously, for the skilled and resourceful manipulator.

The details of role negotiation clearly reflect the senses in which the design makes overt the usually secret game of bargaining. Perhaps the central feature is an Issue Diagnosis Form, which each group member completes for self as well as all other members. The form solicits responses to three key questions, for each participant:

- What should (   ) do more of, or do better?
- What should (   ) do less of, or stop?
- What should (   ) keep doing?

Exhibit 2   Main Elements in a Role-Negotiation Contract

It is not legitimate for the consultant to press or probe anyone's *feelings*. We are concerned about work: who does what, how, and with whom. How people *feel* about their work or about others in the group is their own business, to be introduced or not according to their own judgment and desire. The expression of non-expression of feelings is not part of the contract.

Openness and honesty about behavior are expected and essential for achieving results. The consultant will insist that people be specific and concrete in expressing their expectations and demands for the behavior of others. Each team member is expected to be open and specific about what he wants others to do *more* or *do better* or *do less* or *maintain unchanged*.

No expectation or demand is adequately communicated until it has been *written down* and is clearly understood by both sender and receiver, nor will any change process be engaged in until this has been done.

The full sharing of expectations and demands does not constitute a completed change process. It is only the precondition for change to agree through negotiation. It is unreasonable for anyone in the group, manager or subordinate, to expect that any change will take place merely as a result of communicating a demand or expectation. Unless a team member is willing to change her own behavior in order to get what she wants from the other(s), she is likely to waste her and the group's time talking about the issue. When a member makes a request or demand for changed behavior on the part of another, the consultant will ask what he is willing to give in order to get what he wants. This goes for the manager as well as for the subordinates. If the former can get what he wants simply by issuing orders or clarifying expectations from his position of authority, he probably does not need a consultant or a change process.

The change process is essentially one of bargaining and negotiation in which two or more members each agree to change behavior in exchange for some desired change on the part of the other. This process is not complete until the agreement can be *written down* in terms which include the agreed changes in behavior and make clear what each party is expected to give in return.

Threats and pressures are neither illegitimate nor excluded from the negotiation process. However, group members should realize that overreliance on threats and punishment usually results in defensiveness, concealment, decreased communication and retaliation, and may lead to breakdown of the negotiation. The consultant will do her best to help members accomplish their aims with positive incentives whereever possible.

Source: The leading article on such matters is Roger Harrison's "Role Negotiation: A Tough Minded Approach to Team Development." Reproduced by special permission from W. Warner Burke and H. Hornstein (eds.), *The Social Technology of Organization Development* (Washington, D.C.: NTL Learning Resources, 1972), pp. 84-96.

After completion, each group member gets all[20] the lists on which her name appears in the parentheses, that is, those lists relating to her own behavior.

The Issue Diagnosis Form essentially provides each group member with a comprehensive survey of what may be expected of him, and of what he has going for him that he may use in exchange for what he would like from others.

The exchange of Issue Diagnosis Forms is critical, and the design is here most vulnerable to failure. As Harrison explains:[33]

> If sufficient anger and defensiveness are generated by the problem sharing, the consultant will not be able to hold the negative processes in check long enough for the development of the positive problem-solving spiral on which the process depends for its effectiveness. It is true that such an uncontrollable breakthrough of hostility has not yet occurred in my experience with the method. Nevertheless, concern over the negative possibilities is in part responsible for my slow, deliberate and rather formal development of the confrontation of issues within the group.

Hence Harrison firmly monitors the sharing of the forms. Only clarification is to take place, initially: items on the lists, beyond understanding their referent, are all only more or less suitable for the exchange process that will follow. The goal is to absolutely restrict any rebuttal or defensiveness to the lists which each individual collects, to avoid dissipating the group's total energy for the mutual influencing and problem-solving which is to come.

Beyond this point, the process of role negotiation is direct:

- Issues for negotiation are chosen by group discussion, with the reality constraint being that unless all parties are at least willing to consider behavioral change there is no particular point even in discussion.
- The overriding tone that the behavioral change usually requires exchange, some quid pro quo, although changes may sometimes occur because the parties are persons of goodwill, or because they are indifferent between several alternative behaviors.
- Each individual indicates those issues on which he or she
  Most wants to exercise influence
  Is most willing to accept influence
- Consultant leads the development of a sample negotiation, with any agreements being written down and formalized with open discussion of sanctions for failure to respect the agreement.
- Other group members then engage in other role negotiations, sometimes several simultaneously, in various combinations as the specific issues require, but with any results being made available to all group members.

Simply, then, the design takes an elemental form: "If I do X, which you really want me to do, will you do Z, in which I have a strong interest? Also remember that I cannot do P, so don't ask me now. It's off-bounds. Maybe later." Participants keep at it until they believe they have struck tolerable bargains, some reasonably probable and valuable return for what is given.

Typically, also, some follow-on meetings are scheduled to check on adherence to the role negotiations. Sometimes, failure merely means a reversion to the status quo. At other times, specific incentives or disincentives may be marshalled to reinforce the agreements.

Role Negotiation in Retrospect

The design, then, cannot do it all. There is no guarantee that a specific intervention will lead to agreements that stick, or even to any agreements at all. And no available research permits comparisons of the consequences of role negotiation with (for example) team development or sensitivity training designs.

However, the case for the design is presumptively strong, and it clearly is the case that these attractions may be sketched briefly.[34]

> First, role negotiation focuses on work relationships: what people do, and how they facilitate and inhibit one another in the performance of their jobs. It encourages participants to work with problems using words and concepts they are used to using in business. It avoids probing to the deeper levels of their feelings about one another unless this comes out naturally in the process.
>
> Second, it deals directly with problems of power and influence which may be neglected by other behavioral approaches. It does not attempt to dethrone the authority in the group, but other members are helped to explore realistically the sources of power and influence available to them.
>
> Also, unlike some other behavioral approaches to team development, role negotiation is highly action oriented. Its aim is not just the exposing and understanding of issues as such, but achieving changed ways of working through mutually negotiated agreements. Changes brought about through role negotiation thus tend to be more stable and lasting than where such negotiated commitments are lacking.
>
> In addition, all the procedures of role negotiation are clear and simple, if a bit mechanical, and can be described to participants in advance so they know what they are getting into. There is nothing mysterious about the technique, and this reduces participants' feelings of dependency upon the special skill of the consultant.

In addition to these attractive features, role negotiation makes fewer demands on the skills and insight of the intervenor than some designs such as sensitivity training or even team-building. Harrison emphasizes that internal consultants need have no special training in the behavioral sciences to use the intervention, which implies that role negotiation is not a high-cost venture.

Perspectives on a Potentially Explosive Social Dyad
Facilitating Black-White Relationships
in Large-Scale Enterprises

Now comes an up-front problem in large-scale enterprise, which sometimes waxes and then wanes, but is always there as a potentiality for disruption and violence. The daily news provides evidence enough of the eruptions of this potentiality: the Navy experiences racial problems on some of its ships so serious that major damage to life and property results;[35] the American armed forces in Europe have been at the racial flash-point many times over the past few years;[36] racial disturbances have become an unfortunate way of life in many schools and communities, though fortunately many exceptions exist;[37] and all organizations have had to learn to recognize the various rhythms of black-white relationships, which sometimes run smoothly and then erupt into personal or collective tragedies.[38]

Range and Character of OD Interventions

OD applications have been somewhat responsive to the need for improving black-white relationships in large organizations, but those applications have had certain self-limiting characteristics. Both points get illustrative attention here.

It is possible only to suggest the range of OD interventions directed at black-white relationships in complex systems. For example,

- The U.S. Navy exposed approximately 200,000 officers and enlisted men to a form of sensitivity training—what might be called "racial encounters"—as a first-stage effort to deal openly with profoundly disruptive issues.[39]
- Many school systems used various laboratory designs to ease the transfer of teachers and students to approach goals of racial balance.[40]
- Laboratory designs were used to train small groups of the "hard-core" unemployed.[41]
- Some OD designs have focused on relationships between, for example, police and urban dwellers[42] or those from different economic classes, using organizational/community-action specialists in efforts to identify and help resolve conflict.[43]

This catalog could be extended substantially, but the examples provide sufficient support for several generalizations about such OD efforts. *First,* many of these designs came long after the fat was already in the fire. That is, the racial disturbances of the mid-1960s motivated a spate of ameliorative OD designs. Like many kinds of interventions, however, OD no doubt is more useful as a preventative measure rather than as a Band-Aid applied after the fact. Too often, OD interventions were utilized after all else failed. That seems awkward.

Second, and in part because of the emergency character of many of the interventions, too few of them seek to track design consequences in any rigorous way. Exceptions to this generalization exist,[44] but golden opportunities were missed to document two significant classes of outcomes of specific OD designs:

- Such *processes* as those leading to an improved self-concept of participants which would facilitate direct and immediate feedback
- Such *outcomes* as heightened racial harmony, collaboration, and so on

In addition to lack of planning time, such research may have been inhibited by attitudes that derogate research as just more elitist, honky claptrap, as an activity that can only sap any emotional arousal and thus inhibit action. No doubt, of course, "research" can get used for just such purposes.

Third, such OD designs require very careful fine-tuning. Specifically, they may be too oriented toward providing whites only with an experience of the "distinctiveness of blackness," or blacks only with a reaffirmation of white "caring and concern." The danger in either case is that the design will remain unidirectional, that it will not facilitate reciprocal linkages. If blacks only harangue whites, or if whites are only eager to establish their real understanding, such designs probably will be counterproductive. Needless to say, reciprocity is difficult to achieve in such designs.

Fourth, many observers have emphasized that participants having different cultural and socialization experiences will respond differently to the same OD design. Consider socioeconomic class as a rough differentiator, given the necessary imprecision about how we classify and label various conditioning experiences as middle class or non-middle class. For example, Mill notes that:[45]

> Middle-class participants, black *or* white, tend to accept with much greater docility a training activity that requires them to react, to exhibit behaviors, and to think and respond to one another in ways different from everyday life. They can allow themselves to do this for a short period in order to learn from the behavior that has been produced.

Non-middle-class participants have a different bias. To rely on Mill again, "their thoughts and behavior are directed toward obtaining immediate satisfaction, reducing the amount of talk, and increasing the amount of action.[46] Having come out on the short-end so consistently, perhaps, they want to get to the bottom-line as quickly as possible, to save energy if it appears to be the same old runaround.

Fifth, evidence strongly suggests that OD designs dealing with racial issues can be especially destructive if they do not go beyond the limited (if often accurate) notion that "talking about problems will be helpful." Such a notion is limiting for middle-class participants as well, but it seems especially counter-productive for non-middle-class participants. Hence, any management authorizing such a design must be very specific about its goals. If management will provide support for change as a result of such designs and the information they generate, Mill concludes, "such training sessions can be justified." But Mill also posts some clear warning signs. He draws attention to some common management objectives, asks some central questions, and then comes to a firm conclusion:[47]

> Is the training only a means to examine white racism? Is the training only to provide a soundingboard for blacks? Is it only for limited political or economic ends, such as to improve the liberal image of the company? *All these ends are dysfunctional in the long run.*

The U.S. Navy captures the essence of the present point in one of its objectives for an executive seminar for junior officers, which utilized a sensitivity training variant "to confront the issues of racial attitudes, presumptions and prejudice, both institutional and individual, within the National and Naval Societies."[48] Objective 8 warns and prescribes:

> We cannot be satisfied with evangelism. Conducting an emotional three-day experience that culminates in something called "awareness" does not get at the core of institutional racism. All executive level seminars must have the development of Equal Opportunity Action Plans as their primary objective.

The dual objective, in short, was to generate awareness, and then to directly transfer that awareness into a specific plan of action.

Sixth, such OD interventions clearly can impact on the authority structure of an organization, especially when, as is often done, learning aggregates contain people of different hierarchical ranks. If an organization intends to move away from directive or autocratic managerial styles, such an impact can be most welcome, even ardently desired. On the other hand, if the autocratic quality of the authority structure is to be maintained, the only available strategy is to seek to compartmentalize radically what happens in the OD training from what occurs in the real-time organization. This is not easy to do: most OD consultants probably would resist a contraceptive experience, and in any case mixing ranks only runs a foolish risk, given the determination to retain a directive or auto-cratic style of supervision. These concerns are reflected by one observer's reaction to the Navy's "race relations training classes" which used "group encounter techniques and mixing ranks." The observer goes on[49]

> there is no censored subject. Everything is free and frank and out in the open, admittedly in a classroom environment. Everybody is free to say what he wants to say regardless of his rank or position. I wondered what place this type of training has in a military organization and whether or not such training is a beneficial or a negative effect on the chain of command?

To fill in some of the implied argument, lower-level Navy managers no doubt felt threatened in two ways. Thus, the race relations program was imposed and monitored by headquarters, which by definition curbed local autonomy and flexibility.[50] Moreover, increased awareness of racial issues motivated bypasses of the normal chain of command to air problems quickly in the spirit of new consciousness, and perhaps even encouraged violence to draw attention to local abuses.[51] In short, local managers were uncomfortably whipsawed, and perhaps provided with a convenient rationale to let headquarters "take its medicine" when things got rough.

Not surprisingly, then, the Navy's Phase II sought to reemphasize local initiative, and also provided local commanders with OD resources to isolate and remedy local issues and problems.[52] It does not appear that Phase II had been an overt part of the original game plan. Clearly, however, knowledge of Phase II by the Navy's managers might have been helpful as they struggled with Phase I. In a nutshell, as it were, Phase I took some things away from local managers, and Phase II bestowed some others on them.

Flow and Consequences of a Design for Changes Between Blacks and Whites

Given the broad range of possible objectives, OD designs relevant to black-white relationships can differ profoundly. Some such designs are *interactive* in the sense that they intend simultaneous changes *between* members of the two races. Exhibit 3 illustrates one interactive design. The design involves a staff of two, with some forty participants, approximately one-third of whom are black.

The rationale underlying the design seems clear enough, given the basic objective of easing an upcoming introduction of a substantial number of blacks and Puerto Ricans into the work force of an industrial plant. At least these five stages are reflected in the design.

- Introductory sessions seek to permit and thus legitimate the release of tensions and frustrations; that is, the airing of "old business" was to serve as an intended facilitator of design segments to follow.

Exhibit 3   Schema of a Design for Black-White Issues in an Industrial Plant

First half-day	1. Introduction of staff
	2. Explanation of the goals of the program: to help prepare for the impending introduction of a large number of blacks and Puerto Ricans into an industrial plant
	3. Rap session between blacks and whites, culminating in an affirmative answer to the question: "Do you really feel there is a racist problem in this company?"
Second half-day	1. Rap session continues, with general mood of hostility
	2. Collaborative exercise to test more specific readiness to confront a peer, subordinate, or boss; design used quartets, with each participant in turn being a confronter, a confrontee, and an observer
	3. T-groups are formed to provide opportunities for direct and immediate feedback
Third half-day	1. In as many cross-racial pairs as possible, similarities and differences between racial groups are listed and shared
	2. A listening exercise in triads of one black and two whites, focusing on a list of discussion topics relevant in the plant; basically, each speaker had to reflect the meaning of the previous speaker before developing own position
	3. T-group time
Fourth half-day	1. Experiment with being dependent, via use of blindfolds
	2. Lecturette on Jo-Hari window, followed by quartets with two charges
	a. to share something that would not ordinarily be shared with a new acquaintance
	b. to provide feedback to each about first impressions
	3. T-groups
	4. Cross T-group pairs met in quartets to learn what was happening in the other T-group
Fifth half-day	1. Theory session which emphasized three kinds of situations:
	a. lose-lose, as by rioting and violence

Exhibit 3   (Continued)

	b. win-lose, as by fighting or power
	c. win-win, as by collaboration
	2. An intergroup competition/collaboration exercise
	a. each T-group to come up with ten ideas to reduce racism in plant
	b. each T-group selects three representatives to negotiate a final list of ten items
Sixth half-day	1. Negotiations re ten items on final list
	2. Fishbowl arrangement
	a. blacks observe whites discussing: "How do you feel now about your own white racism?"
	b. blacks detail any cop-out statements by whites
	c. whites give blacks feedback on the theme: "This is why I see blacks as hard people to work with"
	3. Free exchange as a concluding design element.

Source: Based on Cyril R. Mill, "Training the Hard-Core Unemployed," esp. pp. 36-39, in Howard L. Fromkin and John J. Sherwood (eds.), *Intergroup and Minority Relations: An Experiential Handbook* (La Jolla, Calif.: University Associates, Inc., 1976).

- To provide variously specific and immediate opportunities for feedback and disclosure from a variety of sources—in pairs, quartets, T-groups, cross-T-group pairs, and so on—as if to provide concrete counterpoint to the global and powerful frustrations and tensions more likely to be triggered by the design's initial elements.

- To describe and illustrate the application of conceptual models for dealing with conflict, at both interpersonal and organizational levels, that can induce the development of new attitudes/behaviors already in the repertoires of participants.

- To encourage and ease transfer, that is, to facilitate the application of any off-site learning to organization problems.

- To reinforce any learning and to suture any wounds induced or exacerbated by the design.

No specific evaluation of the design was attempted, but two general outcomes seem certain and deserve emphasis. *First,* the design seemed to be most impactful for the whites, which is the way it should be, given the focus on sensitizing people to white racism so as to reduce its impact when the new employees are added. Mill thus concludes that "the whites undoubtedly learned a great deal about black feelings and attitudes and about their own prejudices, whereas the blacks appeared to learn much less along these lines."[53]

Second, characteristic of such designs, the initial release of tensions and frustrations remained incomplete. Black participants, especially, kept recycling back to the global and powerful issues of social injustice whose release began early in the design. This is not surprising, since a need frustrated over time can be a powerful motivator of behavior even in situations where the behavior is not appropriate. In part, also, this recycling may reflect the reasonable doubt that this time is any different from those many other past times. That is, a testing process might be involved. The recycling also may characterize attitudes/ behaviors that are so set that continued emphasis on them may be counterproductive, at least for a time.

The basic need is to be able to fine-tune the dynamics to such a degree as to distinguish reasonable testing (which profits from continued emphasis) from unredemptive suspicion and hostility (where continued emphasis might be self-defeating, as in convincing whites that relationships with blacks are far worse than they previously imagined). Patently, this is no simple matter.

Flow and Consequences of a Design for Changes Within Whites

Alternatively, another set of designs seek a kind of one-way amelioration of black-white relationships. Their focus remains *within* a race rather than between races.

"Within" designs imply some good news, but probably also some bad news. Thus, such designs may seek to make whites more sensitive to the various forms of organizational and personal racism, without the risky fine-tuning referred to above. Such designs are intentionally less complex than interactive designs— which involve blacks and whites simultaneously—and they may be safer. But, it is not yet clear whether they sacrifice impact for safety and simplicity.

Bass and his associates recently developed an intriguing and careful design of this second kind.[54] The design's acronym is PROSPER—a self-guided training activity which includes a method for stimulating an awareness of racism, as well as provides before and after measurements of that awareness. PROSPER differs in significant ways from usual designs for attitudinal change. Basically, Bass adopted an "engineering strategy," a relatively structured approach to heightening awareness of and sensitivity to quite specific discriminatory behaviors based on race. The interactive design introduced immediately above, in contrast, is relatively unstructured. Its outcomes are thus heavily dependent on the trainer's attitudes and skills, as well as on the mix of participants and their expectations about outcomes.

Specifically, PROSPER is "relatively structured" in these four major senses. *First,* the basic target goals were developed empirically, by factor analysis of survey data that sought a definite working definition of "racial awareness." Conventional factor analytic methods isolated five clear awareness components which can be identified briefly as follows.

- The system is biased.
- Affirmative action policies are implemented in limited ways only.
- Black employees need real inclusion.
- Black employees are competent.
- Black employees need to build self-esteem.

Second, these five factors were built into PROSPER's learning design in numerous and reinforcing ways. For example, that design includes a role play in which each of five players takes the role of a person with heightened racial awareness who is to spontaneously argue for one of the factors above. A sixth role player, a manager, seeks to stimulate inventive responses from the five others by asking pointed questions. In this way, participants get multiple experiences: they must improvise on one of the awareness factors, whatever their own actual racial awareness; and they also hear others do likewise on the other four factors. The underlying theory is that the role players will shift their own opinions to correspond more closely to what they say as "managers," and what they hear others say when in the "manager" role.[55] A discrepancy model clearly is implied by this aspect of the design, but the discrepancy basically unfolds in a private or personal setting, to reduce defensiveness by learners, one supposes.

Third, the five factors permit independent measures of change. This yields double value. Thus, one need not only rely on global evaluations or self-reports as to whether the design "worked," thereby avoiding ticklish judgments about the faking of participant reactions. Moreover, the use of orthogonal measures raises one's confidence that five phenomenal domains are being measured, as contrasted with measuring one domain five times.

Fourth, PROSPER is designed to be self-administering,[56] being packaged in a single booklet for each participant. The underlying assumption is crucial. As Bass and his associates observe:[57] ". . . the program was designed to help white managers become aware of racial stereotypes in American institutions, including industry. It was assumed that as managers became more aware of key factors which generate racial bias, they would be better able to understand their own feelings and to improve their effectiveness in dealing with minorities—especially blacks."

This brief description does not do justice to PROSPER, but an analysis of data from 2293 managers and professionals exposed to the design implies its potency. A posttest revealed that significant changes occurred on all five PROSPER dimensions. Less satisfactory data suggest that much of the change on all five dimensions was retained 5 months after the posttest.[58] Note, however, that PROSPER was only the major component of a somewhat broader learning experience entitled Management Awareness Training and Education Seminar (MATES).[59] So, the effects sketched above in some part reflect the impact of all developments during the observational period, as well as the impact of MATES.

The Fundamental Dyad as It Appears in Collective Enterprise
Male-Female Relationships in Organizations

Under the recent stimulus of affirmative action and equal employment opportunity initiatives, the centrality of accommodating both female and male perspectives in organizations has increased sharply. As a result, both self-development for women and male-female interaction has received some OD attention, although the research literature still remains slim.

What follows is a brief introduction to OD work in three arenas relevant to female-male relationships in organizations, written by a person who specializes in such work, Sharon L. Connelly. She looks at three self-development arenas: individual, interpersonal, and organizational. The *individual arena* involves issues related to a woman developing herself for herself. The *interpersonal arena* covers ideas related to developing women for their relationships, both work and personal. And the *organizational arena* focuses on developing women for their organization.

The Individual Arena of Development*

This first arena of self-development includes many options for personal awareness, growth, contemplation, and activity. Convenient sources amply illustrate the diversity and range of designs for individual growth by women, from consciousness raising to assertiveness training, from cultural to sexual emphases, from broad cultural roles to quite specific but still complex organizational roles.[60] Often these designs are for women only, a basic design choice that cuts several ways.[61]

Available designs could support extensive discussion and analysis, but here I want to emphasize only one theme in individual development, if a critical one: roles and role conflicts of professional women. One important kind of role conflict felt by professional women has been studied extensively by Douglas T. Hall. Hall points out the significant differences between the sequential role conscious-

---

*This section was written for this volume by Sharon L. Connelly, organization consultant, Arlington, Va.

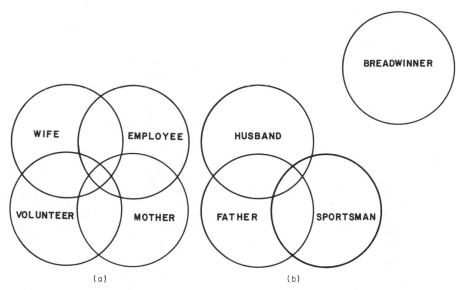

Figure 1   Two kinds of role-consciousness illustrated. (a) Traditional female role constellation: continuous consciousness. (b) Traditional male role constellation: sequential consciousness. [Based on Douglas T. Hall, "A Model of Coping with Role Conflict: The Role Behavior of College Educated Women," *Administrative Science Quarterly,* Vol. 17 (December 1972), esp. pp. 472-74.]

ness of men and women's continuous role consciousness. Traditionally, male professionals have been permitted to submerge their consciousness of other roles while emphasizing their role as breadwinner. See the diagrams in Figure 1. Women, on the other hand, are expected to retain consciousness of their roles of wife and mother even while employed, and often are judged negatively if they seem to put career ahead of these responsibilities.

What is so dreadful about this problem is that women have an average work life of 35 years after their children go to school, and we still have trouble getting permission from others *and ourselves* to succeed to our greatest capacity. Working through such role-related issues implies substantial OD challenges that relate to individuals, organizations, and institutions.

The Interpersonal Arena of Development

Developing interpersonal skills, and particularly those between men and women in work situations, requires time, patience, and a sense of humor. People experience varying degrees of uncertainty, anger, and anxiety as values and norms change in this delicate area. Certainly, male-female relationships are as emotionally laden as any I can think of.

The present contributions to illustrating the interpersonal arena of development concern the changing of male-female relationships, and also the restructuring of boss-subordinate roles. The first emphasis suggests a way of looking at the different sorts of relationships that result from changing values and attitudes about women and work. The second emphasis briefly lists several considerations one should keep in mind in trying to create better boss-subordinate relationships through role restructuring.

Changing Male-Female Relationships: A Conceptual Model

People's attitudes, values, awareness, and behaviors in male-female relationships vary so greatly as to preclude generalization. One hears a lot about equal employment opportunity, or about suggested legal and organizational remedies to reduce discrimination. At the same time, however, one hears very little about coping with the distinctive differences that derive from different combinations of values and attitudes brought to action arenas by specific women and men.

As a preliminary way of illustrating what I mean, let us simplify and hypothecate that men's attitudes, feelings and behaviors regarding women (all measured highly subjectively) will fall on a continuum somewhere between "traditional dominating male" and "liberated egalitarian male." Likewise, one can hypothecate that women's attitudes, feelings, and behaviors regarding the role of women and their relationships with men (again measured subjectively) will fall on a similar continuum between "traditional deferring female" and "liberated egalitarian female."

By combining these two continua, we get a matrix which describes four prototypical male-female relationships. Figure 2 isolates and names those four types of relationships.

Figure 2 implies a range of OD challenges in male-female relationships, challenges ranging from those implying ready growth for both sexes to those challenges requiring substantial changes to get beyond ground-zero. Quadrant I, the open and equal arena, is most benign. It may best be understood in terms of Nena and George O'Neill's "open marriage" concept. In such a relationship both individuals share in their attempts to facilitate the personal and professional growth of the other. Roles are not stereotyped, equal treatment of the sexes is valued, and open communication takes place though not without conflict.

Quadrant II—the "combat zone" arena—refers to *female actualization at the expense of the relationship* with males. It reflects the prototypical situation in which the ambitious woman experiences considerable frustration seeking her own professional development in a relationship with a husband or colleagues who

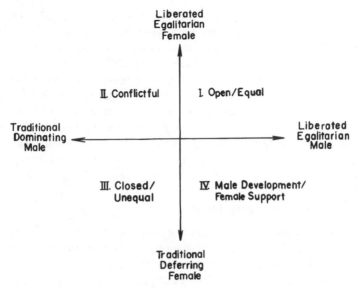

Figure 2   Four prototypical male-female relationships.

customarily frown upon female assertiveness and ambition as "unladylike." In extreme situations, such a women may rebel and "leave the nest" entirely through divorce or resigning her job. Alternately, in such a relationship at work she may experience continual conflict, and she may be terminated by an unsympathetic boss. Value conflicts and misunderstanding abound; one might think of this quadrant as the "combat zone."

Quadrant III, the closed and unequal arena, can be thought of as the "closed marriage" prototype inasmuch as a pair tends to follow rather traditional patterns of relating in terms of male and female roles, male dominance, and female deference. Such features minimize both the opportunity and the likelihood that the female will be highly motivated toward a professional career. Such a female, if widowed or divorced, will have great difficulty with that kind of independence, and will quickly seek a partnership with another traditional male.

Quadrant IV refers to *male actualization* which develops because of, or apart from, the development of the female. For example, a male might feel he gets a great deal of support and devoted helpfulness from a secretary, assistant, or spouse. In a marriage, similarly, he might feel he has outgrown his partner leading him to seek the support and companionship of other women who can relate to him in ways other than his wife/partner is able. Both people in such a relationship might be happy, but his growth ends up being more important than hers in each case. Moreover, if he "outgrows" her they might lead rather compartmentalized lives, as when he encourages her to grow but she cannot or will not.

Figure 2 has a most interesting use in teaching, counseling, and in OD designs emphasizing male-female relationships. One can utilize it to demonstrate the different kinds of relationships that can exist, depending on one's values and attitudes toward women in careers. Likewise, in counseling male-female pairs, one can ask each pair to locate themselves. In this way, each has a visual description of how the other sees the relationship, and differences in perceptions and subjective realities can readily be identified. Better ways of understanding value conflicts and resolving problems in relationships may be discovered through such discussions.

Boss-Subordinate Role Restructuring

Apart from the feelings and attitudes that may exist between a woman and her boss about women in careers, a second interpersonal concern relates to a woman's actual job content and responsibilities. Related issues are especially subtle, given the possibility of adding new responsibilities and restructuring old ones. By participating in boss-subordinate role restructuring, one can take steps to expand work potential in a very concrete fashion.

One should focus on the boss-subordinate relationship as the main locus of potential change, and indicate to the boss that "I could do my job better if you . . ." While doing this, one should keep in mind the principles of *exchange theory*. This theory demonstrates that a person is more likely to get a desired something if some other is also getting a desired something. In other words, the subordinate who wants more responsibilities can appeal to the boss's self-interest by showing him or her that their load would be positively affected by a redistribution of responsibilities.

Another way of restructuring the boss-subordinate relationship is for the subordinate to introduce, slowly, new and probably more assertive behaviors into the relationship. An employee who may always have waited for her boss to suggest a training or development activity might instead ask her boss to talk about her future with the company, as well as about ways she might prepare for her next promotion.

Whether the relationship with a boss is improvable, moreover, a woman should be cultivating relationships with others in the organization who may be of help to her. She should find a mentor and role models from whom advice might be gotten about important work issues, and she should be sure that those around her know what she has to offer and what her ambitions are. As a last resort, she should keep her eyes and ears open to possibilities outside her organization, and consider them as serious options if she feels underutilized in her current job and is not particularly hopeful of changing it significantly for the better.

The Organizational Arena of Development

The more I work in the area of women's career development and equal employment opportunity (EEO), specifically, the more aware I am of the *deep* difficulties that there are in accomplishing individual and organization change in these areas. Not only do the equal employment opportunity laws require certain changes regarding men and women, but they, as a logical conclusion of the written law, require more complex organizational, attitude, and value changes which do not necessarily fall into the sex discrimination category. Major OD challenges inhere in such changes.

What follows is a quick list of some of these issues and dilemmas which act as obstacles to the successful implementation of EEO in organizations:

- New levels of personnel efficiency are being required by EEO legislation . . . a greater level of sophistication than may ever have been reached before in the organization.
- Organizations are being asked to "grow up" regarding fairness towards others, open communication, and trust.
- Men are now faced more often with their "soft" parts—their emotions, dependencies, insecurities, especially when working for a woman.
- Women are now required to exhibit more assertive, persuasive, "hard" characteristics as they take on more responsibilities. At the same time, many women fear losing their femininity by doing so.
- Open dealing with conflict becomes necessary but very difficult when dealing with EEO issues.
- There is a trend toward an integration of task and emotion which is uncharacteristic of many businesses.
- Dealing with sexuality with peers is unavoidable; men in the office no longer have the power advantage they have been accustomed to with secretaries and with other females in the office not on their level.
- Dealing with insecurities about competence, competition, and the next promotion are more likely; a mediocre male may no longer be sheltered from challenge from women, or be promoted simply because "all supervisors are male."
- Financial costs of recruiting and hiring women, providing facilities, and equalizing salaries are high. How would men feel, on the other hand, if their salaries were *reduced* to equal those received by women?
- New ways of doing work are necessary to adapt to women's various role demands, for example, scheduling, job redesign, benefits, role negotiations, job sharing, day care, and so on.
- Men are most familiar with women as servants, secretaries, mothers, and sex objects, and have difficulty adapting to new female roles as competent and contributing peers.

- Most organizations have antagonism toward the government for telling them what to do.
- A redistribution of power is necessary for organizations to be in compliance with EEO laws; laws say that homogeneous organizations are no longer legal, that they should be heterogeneous reflecting the population.

Patently, major changes are implicit in this selective catalog. The challenges for OD efforts seem substantial.

Three Action Strategies

I have suggested some survival skills for women who manage, and looked at some issues and ideas related to three self-development arenas. By now you must be suffering from information overload! Yet, before I close I want to share with you three very important things—possibly the three most important things I've learned as a manager and consultant:

- Career and life-planning
- Role negotiation between partners
- Time and stress management

Career and Life-Planning

Briefly, career and life planning is a systematized approach to considering personal values and goals, skills and weaknesses, career objectives, and life styles. The goal is to discover and develop action strategies to meet goals and objectives. It is often done in a small-group workshop, or via a workbook that may be done alone or in groups. It is most effective if done regularly and viewed as a positive road map from which opportunities spring, rather than as a deterministic strait-jacket. It is thoughtful hard work, but also enjoyable and rewarding.

Chapter 4 illustrates one example of a career-planning design. For further information and career-planning exercises refer to:

Richard N. Bolles, *What Color Is Your Parachute? A Manual for Job Hunters and Career Changers* (Berkeley, Calif.: Ten Speed Press, 1972).

John C. Crystal and Richard N. Bolles, *Where Do I Go from Here with My Life?* (New York: Seabury, 1974).

George A. Ford and Gordon L. Lippitt, *Planning Your Future* (La Jolla, Calif.: University Associates, 1972).

Sam Keen and Anne Valley Fox, *Telling Your Story* (Garden City, N.Y.: Doubleday, 1972).

Role Negotiation Between Partners

As more and more women seek professional careers, the life styles of such women and the couples of which they are a part will rapidly change. The decision-making process regarding career choice and mobility becomes more and more complex, and defies easy answers. Role negotiation, not unlike boss-subordinate role restructuring in its approach (though hopefully different in terms of power and authority dynamics), offers a means of dealing with some complex interpersonal issues.

One application of role negotiation in an organization has already been illustrated. For further information, including several approaches to role negotiation, refer to the following:

Clark Carney and S. Lynne McMahon, "The Interpersonal Contract," in *The 1974 Annual Handbook for Group Facilitators,* Pfeiffer and Jones (eds.), (La Jolla, Calif.: University Associates, 1974), pp. 135-138.

Nena O'Neill and George O'Neill, *Open Marriage: A New Life Styles for Couples* (New York: Evans, 1972).

Rhona Rapoport and Robert Rapoport, *Dual Career Families* (London: Penguin, 1972).

John J. Sherwood and John C. Glidewell, "Planned Renegotiation—A Norm-Setting OD Intervention," in *The 1973 Annual Handbook for Group Facilitators,* Jones and Pfeiffer (eds.), (La Jolla, Calif.: University Associates, 1973), pp. 195-202.

Time and Stress Management

Managing time poses a major dilemma, and skills for doing so give any manager a great deal more leverage for success and productivity. Moreover, as work tasks and interpersonal interactions become more complex, the hurried professional is increasingly prone to emotional and physical stress. Time and stress management, therefore, constitute two skills that will become increasingly important. In a society marked by a shrinking globe and future shock, success will demand tools and techniques for selecting the most important tasks, and unwinding after periods of hard work.

The three best references on time and stress management that I have seen are the following:

Cary L. Cooper and Judi Marshall, *Understanding Executive Stress* (New York: Petrocelli, 1977).

Alan Lakein, *How to Get Control of Your Time and Your Life* (New York: Wyden, 1973). (There is also a superb film of the same name.)

Walter McQuarde and Ann Aikeman, *Stress* (New York: Bantam, 1974).

Such activities, undertaken alone or with the help of a trainer or consultant, immeasurably increase the focus and problem-solving skills a woman brings to bear on any career or personal situation affecting her. With her goals firmly in mind, her family behind her, and her time and stress factors skillfully managed, the career of her choice should be attainable. For women who manage, who chart paths for successful futures, a satisfying work life is a well-deserved reward.

Costs and Benefits of Interventions for Individuals
Some Generalizations

This chapter and the preceding one illustrate the range of OD designs that focus on individual learning, in singles or in pairs, and they permit eleven generalizations. Note that several other chapters (for example, especially most of Chapter 5 in Part 2) also bear on present concerns.

Generalization 1.   Despite the paucity of specific research, a number of impactful and relevant designs or interventions exist. The T-group is not the only vehicle for individual learning. Clearly, there are a variety of ways of applying OD values to the work site for singles and pairs. Moreover, much has been learned about practical ways to reflect such values. The point applies broadly to the "process analysis" reflected at several points in Chapters 1 and 3, as well as to the guidelines for third-party consultation dealt with in this chapter. The latter source also illustrates what may happen when those guidelines are not respected.

This accumulating knowledge and experience has concerned some observers, of course. One Luddite view sees OD as a kind of ultimate vehicle for enslavement to the "organization imperative."[62] The more effective the design, in short, the more insidious. What you know can hurt you, to be sure, but that is hardly an argument against knowledge.

Generalization 2.   Much of the available literature is bounded—by white, North American, male, and "nonradical" perspectives and orientations, for example. These biases may sharply limit the applicability of the available literature. For example, the business-travel design seems useful for bringing married couples closer together, and for encouraging organizational changes that reduce the issues between partners. But we have no good designs for effectively rupturing such a relationship, even if that were ethically and practically a very good thing, or even the best thing. Much the same point applies to the demotion design which neglects those few individuals who chose to leave the firm rather than accept downgrading. Chapter 5 of Part 2 directs additional attention to this critical bias in the existing OD literature.

Generalization 3.   Note that the designs above typically seek some delicate balance. Both interaction-centered and more structual interventions seem useful, for example, sometimes in combination. Moreover, group contexts are often used to facilitate individual choice and change. Or the designs seek to test the boundaries between home and work.

Generalization 4.   The OD technology is not the only approach to change by individuals or pairs, even though it clearly constitutes the major approach that emphasizes choice. For example, much recent attention in the managerial literature has been devoted to "behavior modification."[63] In fact, some recent experimentation[64] with behavior modification reports effects much like those in the section on decreasing turnover and absenteeism in Chapter 4.

This is no place for an exhaustive comparison of BM versus OD, but several points seem clear enough. *First,* both BM and OD—at least at a certain level— have the common goal of building more rewards into the work site. Some have even argued that BM and OD are therefore similar, if not identical. Gamboa,[65] for example, proposes that BM is simply a more specific way of understanding and especially operationalizing what is meant by "participation."

Second, however, BM and OD differ in the basic directionality of the reward:

- If you will do X, implies BM, then you will get reward Z.
- If you wish to satisfy certain individual needs, implies OD, here are a number of values and designs that can be useful.

In some particulars, the approaches are identical. In numerous other essentials, the differences can be profound. Thus, BM is likely to

- Be more elitist in orientation than OD, as in the choice of the rewards, the need to monitor performance closely so as to detect deviations, and so on
- See the individual more as a changer rather than a choice-maker, as acted-upon rather than actor
- Raise more ticklish ethical issues than OD, as in the matter of informed consent
- Be based on a simple individualistic stimulus $\rightarrow$ response psychology

Third, BM seems more unilateral than OD. Consider certain possible difficulties. What happens in BM, for example, when A is trying to get B to perform Z while B is simultaneously trying to get A to get B to do non-Z? The problem is not a basic one in OD, where the values of the approach can be negated only by their opposites—closedness versus openness, for example—rather than by themselves. OD is designed for multiples to play, basically; BM stresses separate actors and responders.

Such difficulties with BM suggest that it is basically unilateral or even elitist. Certainly, most of its more successful applications have been in "closed systems" such as mental hospitals. OD, in contrast, is intendedly and even determinedly multilateral, granted that there have been and will be attempts to use the technology in more narrowly manipulative ways.

Fourth, BM has not established its effectiveness in cases of relatively complex behavior, for example, the kind of change in interpersonal and intergroup climate discussed in Chapter 6. BM proponents would argue that it is all a matter of "shaping," of appropriate "reinforcements," of effective "schedules." That may be. Critics would no doubt note that BM has usually been applied in cases of quite specific, perhaps even simple, behavior. But proponents might retort: Is a reduction in absenteeism a "simple" behavior? The BM technology has proved able to induce changes in it.[66]

Fifth, decay rates for neither OD or BM learning have been established. The questions are momentous. For example, does BM imply low ownership of change and commitment to it? Similarly, will given reinforcers lose their potency over time, requiring more rewarding reinforcers for decreasing increments of behavioral change? These questions cannot now be reliably answered. However, they do illustrate the kinds of comparative analyses of learning technologies that have great theoretical and practical importance, and which desperately need major and timely attention.

Sixth, BM is not as value-conscious as OD. The emphasis is too much on shaping, reinforcers, and schedules—to hazard a simplification—and too little on what behaviors should be shaped, reinforced, and scheduled.

Seventh, BM does not seem to take specific advantage of group contexts as reinforcers of behavior.

Generalization 5. Several of the designs above suggest the usefulness of a focus on roles, as opposed to individuals or even behavior. This is patently the case with role negotiation, for example. Such designs may be of especial usefulness where low legitimacy exists, or should exist, for dealing with interpersonal relationships. Localizing the focus of an intervention to a role also may be useful, and less defense-inducing than alternative designs.

Generalization 6. The extension of OD designs to situations of racial or cultural conflict is especially useful. Results are quite encouraging, even as documentation remains still scarce. Far more data are required as to the persistence of any changes, under which conditions, given specific learning designs. The usefulness of "noninteractive" or "within" training—for one sex only, or one race only, and so on—seems worthy of special attention. Some experience and conjecture suggest significant problems with "interactive" or "between" designs. In the case of individuals who differ in power, for example, the two most likely outcomes seem to discourage the latter type of design. First, the more powerful will undervalue and perhaps exploit others, while the less powerful may swing toward obeisance and apathy.[67] Interactive designs in this case may be counterproductive, for obvious reasons. Second, when the less powerful become more assertive, their emphasis is more likely to be on constraint than inducement or persuasion, as Brown notes, on power building to develop "a resource base from which they can persuade the powerful." Since power building is likely to generate a self-heightening cycle of counterconstraints and counter-counterconstraints, Brown argues convincingly, this second case does not offer much early "hope for moving from conflict to cooperation. . . ."[68]

Generalization 7. Pretty clearly, choice or change by individuals or pairs often will imply change in the institutions in which the individuals are enmeshed. This raises a critical design consideration. Some evidence suggests, in fact, that change/choice at the individual level generates some special risks if corresponding change does not occur at institutional levels.[69] In this sense, the situation sketched by Culbert and Renshaw in connection with family life and work travel approaches the ideal, with reciprocal changes occurring in both husband-wife pairs and in the employing organization.

Generalization 8. Chapters 4 and 5 both reveal potential aplenty for a mutual satisfaction of numerous individual needs and organization demands. Much exchange is clearly possible, an exchange which can help OD walk that line between being either a servant of those in power or a fraudulently humanistic front for a destruction of real and imagined establishments.

Generalization 9. Much OD literature places a distinct premium on process skills, but several of the interventions in Chapters 4 and 5 require other skills. Consider this general flow of part of an "awareness workshop" for either or both sexes:[70]

1. Surface assumptions and stereotypes about women at work, either by buzz-groups or by reliance on instruments that direct thought.[71]

2. Share assumptions and stereotypes and the supposed underlying "evidence."

3. Present research findings and social science materials relevant to testing assumptions and stereotypes.

4. Discuss persistence of "facts" in light of the facts.

5. Deal with the socialization of women and generalizations about their related social training and role pressures.

At stages 1 and 4, particularly, process skills by the intervenor or convenor patently will be useful. But, at other stages of the design, as Kanter notes, the resource person must "also make available 'expert' knowledge on women in organizations. This is a departure from the usual view of the OD specialist as an expert on 'process' independent of 'content'; in this case content knowledge is critically important."[72] For example, the conventional wisdom usually provides that women will be absent more often than men, for the usual "female reasons." However, Kanter notes that the social science data do not present a homogeneous picture. "Among clerical and government workers," she notes, "women's rates of absenteeism overall are the same as men's."[73]

The significance of "content" skills also will be manifest at numerous points in the second volume. Working in an OD mode basically involves dealing with the balance between freedom and repression. "Process" skills often will help increase an individual's freedom, especially in face-to-face situations. But "content" skills very often will be necessary to do so when the aggregates are large, or when (as in organizing work) knowledge about both technical features and behavioral consequences will be necessary to shift the balance of freedom and repression.

Generalization 10. Designs that are fully instrumented (as in PROSPER) or in which the intervenor is available only on-call (as in the business travel design) often have significant advantages, and may even be critical to success.[74] Intervenorless designs can facilitate such OD values as learner and ownership control over the learning.

Generalization 11. Overall, this chapter and the preceding one reflect a sense of beginnings. Witness that career-planning designs have just fairly got started, and only exceptional designs focus on retirement in its socioemotional as well as economic fullness.[74] Certainly this neglect does not inhere in the logic of the laboratory approach, which prescribes that one begin with people *where they are*, and that one go on from their present developmental stage.

Notes

1. Ted L. Huston and George Levinger, "Interpersonal Attraction and Relationships," pp. 115-56, in Mark R. Rosenzweig and Lyman W. Porter (eds.), *Annual Review of Psychology*, Vol. 29 (1978), pp. 115-156.

2. Richard E. Walton, *Interpersonal Peacemaking: Confrontations and Third Party Consultation* (Reading, Mass.: Addison-Wesley, 1969), p. 2.

3. Ibid., p. 6.

4. Leonard R. Sayles, *Managerial Behavior* (New York: McGraw-Hill, 1964), pp. 58-82.

5. Don K. Price, *The Scientific Estate* (Cambridge, Mass.: Harvard University Press, 1967).

6. The classic catalog of such strategies to affect the flow of interaction is provided by William F. Whyte, "The Social Structure of the Restaurant," *American Journal of Sociology*, Vol. 54 (January 1949), pp. 302-310.

7. The labor mediator often stresses this strategy, especially in the adjudication of grievances and disputes. See Ann Douglas, *Industrial Peacemaking* (New York: Columbia University Press, 1962).

8. This model tends to be characteristic of international relations, but note that the relative power potential of a country can vary with many conditions other than its wealth or armed might. See Oran Young, *The Intermediaries:*

Third Parties in International Crisis (Princeton, N.J.: Princeton University Press, 1967).

9. Usefully, consult Alan C. Filley, *Interpersonal Conflict Resolution* (Glenview, Ill.: Scott, Foresman, 1975).

10. Walton, *Interpersonal Peacemaking,* pp. 12-13.

11. Richard E. Walton, "Third Party Roles in Interdepartmental Conflict," *Industrial Relations,* Vol. 7 (October 1967), pp. 29-43; "International Confrontation and Basic Third Party Functions: A Case Study," *Journal of Applied Behavioral Science,* Vol. 4 (July 1968), pp. 327-344; and *Interpersonal Peacemaking.* For other behavioral applications of the third-party notion, see Virginia Satir, *Conjoint Family Therapy* (Palo Alto, Calif.: Behavioral Books, 1964); and L. Dave Brown, John D. Aram, and David J. Bachner, "Interorganizational Information Sharing," *Journal of Applied Behavioral Science,* Vol. 10 (December 1974), esp. pp. 551-554.

12. Walton, *Interpersonal Peacemaking,* pp. 6, 15-70.

13. *Interpersonal Peacemaking: Confrontations and Third Party Consultation* (Reading, Mass.: Addison-Wesley, 1969), p. 95. Quoted by permission.

14. Edgar H. Schein, *Process Consultation* (Reading, Mass.: Addison-Wesley, 1969), p. 9.

15. Walton, *Interpersonal Peacemaking,* pp. 122-129.

16. Walton, "Interpersonal Confrontation and Basic Third Party Functions," p. 327.

17. Walton, *Interpersonal Peacemaking,* pp. 94-115.

18. Ibid., p. 95.

19. Ibid., pp. 94-105.

20. Ibid., esp. pp. 107-111, for the general point. The quotation comes from Jeffrey W. Eiseman, "A Third-Party Consultation Model for Resolving Recurring Conflicts Collaboratively," *Journal of Applied Behavioral Science,* Vol. 13 (October 1977), p. 303.

21. Walton, *Interpersonal Peacemaking,* esp. pp. 73-79.

22. Ibid., pp. 96-98.

23. Ibid., pp. 98-101.

24. Ibid., esp. pp. 105-107.

25. Ibid., pp. 111-114.

26. " 'Til Business Do Us Part,' " *Harvard Business Review,* Vol. 54 (January 1976), pp. 9-101.

27. Samuel A. Culbert and Jean Renshaw, "Coping with Stresses of Travel as an Opportunity for Improving the Quality of Work and Family Life," *Family Process,* Vol. 11 (September 1972), pp. 321-337.

28. Roger Harrison, "When Power Conflicts Trigger Team Spirit," *European Business,* Vol. 9 (Spring 1972), p. 57. See also Harrison, "Role Negotiation:

A Tough-Minded Approach to Team Development," in W. Warner Burke and Harvey A. Hornstein (eds.), *The Social Technology of Organization Development* (Washington, D.C.: NTL Learning Resources Corp., 1972), pp. 84-96.

29. Ibid., p. 58.

30. Ibid., pp. 58-59.

31. Ibid., p. 58.

32. Robert J. Ringer, *Winning Through Intimidation* (Los Angeles, Calif.: Los Angeles Book Publishers, 1974).

33. Harrison, "When Power Conflicts Trigger Team Spirit," p. 61.

34. Ibid., p. 65.

35. U.S. Congress, House Committee on Armed Services, *Report,* Special Subcommittee on Disciplinary Problems in the U.S. Navy, 92nd Congress, 2nd session, 1973, esp. pp. 17674-17679.

36. Charles Moskow, "The American Dilemma in Uniform: Race in the Armed Forces," *Annals,* no. 406 (March 1973), pp. 94-106.

37. At the present writing, the prime publicized difficulties appear to be in South Boston, Lexington, Kentucky, and Pensacola, Florida.

38. Little comprehensive evidence is available about either racial cooperation or conflict in organizations, but the latter gets the most attention.

39. For a useful review of the Navy program, consult William B. Hildreth, "Sensitivity Training and Race Relations in the Organization." Unpublished MS (December 1975). Hildreth's work is relied upon at a number of points in this subsection. More specifically, see U.S. Congress, House Committee on Armed Services, *Hearings before the Special Subcommittee on Disciplinary Problems in the U.S. Navy,* 92nd Cong., 2d sess., 1973, esp. pp. 1069-1121.

    The estimated number of participants is from OPNAVINST 53006A, Part II, p. 2, a memo from the Office of the Chief of Naval Operations. Such encounters were used basically in Phase I of the Naval Human Goals Program inaugurated by Admiral Elmo Zumwalt, Jr., then Chief of Naval Operations. Phase I focused on activities of the confrontive mode, and began in early 1971. See U.S. Department of the Navy, Office of the Chief of Naval Operations, *Navy Human Goals Plan* (Washington, D.C.: U.S. Navy, 1973). Phase II began in fall 1974, with a specific OD orientation to build on the heightened racial awareness generated by Phase I. Phase II's major expression was a flexible program that could be used by local commanders to institutionalize equal opportunity and to counter racism. Consult U.S. Department of the Navy, Bureau of Naval Personnel, *Phase II Equal Opportunity Race Relations Program: Consultant Guide* (Washington, D.C.: U.S. Navy, not dated).

40. Such designs were used in Atlanta, Georgia, for example, as well as in a substantial number of other local school systems.

41. Thomas H. Patten, Jr., and Lester E. Dorey, "An Equal Employment Opportunity Sensitivity Workshop," *Training and Development Journal,* Vol. 26 (January 1972), pp. 42, 44, 46-53.

42. Robert T. Golembiewski and David Sink, "OD Interventions in Urban Settings, II: Public-Sector Success with Planned Change," *International Journal of Public Administration,* Vol. 1, no. 2 (1979). In press.

43. Arthur M. Freedman, "Hang-up in Black and White: A Training Laboratory for Conflict Identification and Resolution," in Howard L. Fromkin and John J. Sherwood (eds.), *Intergroup and Minority Relations: An Experiential Handbook* (La Jolla, Calif.: University Associates, Inc., 1976), pp. 45-49.

44. Philip G. Hanson and Ruth G. King, " 'I Am Somebody:' Black Students' Self-Concept," in Fromkin and Sherwood, *Intergroup and Minority Relations,* pp. 22-28.

45. Cyril R. Mill, "Training the Hard-Core Unemployed," in Fromkin and Sherwood, *Intergroup and Minority Relations,* p. 40.

46. Ibid.

47. Ibid., p. 41.

48. Quotations come from official Navy materials prepared for resource persons and participants in executive seminars.

49. U.S. Congress, House Committee on Armed Services, *Hearings,* pp. 1120-1121.

50. Based on several interviews with race relations instructors in the Navy.

51. The official report of major racial flare-ups on two aircraft carriers in 1972 suggests or implies such a complex linkage: weakening of the local commanders by headquarters' actions; overemphasis on racial issues compared to the fuller naval mission-and-role; perceptions by lower-level managers that they should "lessen the discipline"; and perhaps a growing feeling that headquarters would understand, perhaps even welcome, dramatic evidences of racial injustice. See U.S. Congress, House Committee on Armed Services, *Report,* pp. 17674-17679.

52. U.S. Department of the Navy, Bureau of Naval Personnel, *Phase* II, Vol. I; and Charles F. Fauch, "Navy Human Goals Plan," *Commanders' Digest* (February 1974), esp. p. 4.

53. Mill, "Training the Hard-Core Unemployed," p. 41.

54. Bernard M. Bass, Wayne F. Cascio, J. Westbrook McPherson, and Harold J. Tragash, "PROSPER: Training and Research for Increasing Awareness of Affirmative Action in Race Relations," *Journal of the Academy of Management,* Vol. 19 (September 1976), pp. 353-369.

55. Harold C. Kelman, "Attitude Change as a Function of Response Restriction," *Human Relations,* Vol. 6 (1953), pp. 185-214.

56.   Bernard M. Bass, Wayne F. Cascio, and J. Westbrook McPherson, *PROS-PER: A Program about Problems of Race in the Working Environment* (Scottsville, N.Y.: Transnational Program Corporation, 1972).

57.   Bass, Cascio, McPherson, and Tragash, "PROSPER: Training and Research," p. 354.

58.   Ibid., pp. 365-366. Data are scarce, but it appears that most studies reveal only short-term if statistically significant changes. Illustratively, see David A. Tansik and John D. Driskill, "Temporal Persistence of Attitudes Through Required Training," *Group and Organization Studies*, Vol. 2 (September 1977), pp. 310-323.

59.   Bass, Cascio, McPherson, and Tragash, "PROSPER: Training and Research," p. 365.

60.   Fortunately, available resources are growing in number and sophistication. Selectively, see: Louise Yolton Eberhardt, *A Woman's Journey: Experiences for Women with Women*, Vol. I (Columbia, Md.: New Community Press, 1976); Rosabeth Moss Kanter, *Men and Women of the Corporation* (New York: Basic Books, 1977); and Alice G. Sargent (ed.), *Beyond Sex Roles* (New York: West Publishing, 1977). For an empirical test of the effects of personal growth and assertiveness training, see Susan A. Wheelan, "The Effect of Personal Growth and Assertive Training Classes on Female Sex-Role Self-Concept," *Group and Organization Studies*, Vol. 3 (June 1978), esp. p. 239.

61.   Alma S. Baron, "Special Training Course for Women: Desirable or Not?" *Training and Development Journal*, Vol. 30 (December 1976), pp. 30-33.

62.   David K. Hart and William G. Scott, "The Organizational Imperative," *Administration and Society*, Vol. 7 (November 1975), pp. 259-850.

63.   Conveniently, see Victor V. Gamboa, *Beyond Skinner with Dignity: An Investigation of the Application of Behavior Modification in Industrial Settings.* Unpublished doctoral dissertation, University of Michigan, 1974. For a rousing critique, consult Edwin A. Locke, "The Myths of Behavior Mod in Organizations," *Academy of Management Review*, Vol. 2 (October 1977), pp. 543-553. Jerry L. Gray provides a rejoinder in "The Myths of the Myths About Behavior Mod in Organizations," *Academy of Management Review*, Vol. 4 (January 1979), pp. 121-129.

64.   Ed Pedalino and Victor U. Gamboa, "Behavior Modification and Absenteeism: Intervention in One Industrial Setting," *Journal of Applied Psychology*, Vol. 59, no. 6 (1974), pp. 694-698.

65.   Gamboa, *Beyond Skinner with Dignity*, pp. 35-36. See also Lyman W. Porter, "Turning Work into Non-Work: The Rewarding Environment," Marvin D. Dunnette (ed.), *Work and Non-Work in the Year 2001* (Monterey, Calif.: Brooks/Cole, 1973), pp. 113-132. Significantly, also, behavior modification gets significant attention in a major overview of OD.

See Edgar E. Huse, *Organization Development and Change* (St. Paul, Minn.: West Publishing, 1975), pp. 278-830.

66. Gamboa, *Beyond Skinner with Dignity*, esp. pp. 42-56.

67. Walter R. Nord (ed.), *Concepts and Controversy in Organizational Behavior* (Pacific Palisades, Calif.: Goodyear, 1976), esp. pp. 437-450.

68. L. Dave Brown, "Can 'Haves' and 'Have-Nots' Cooperate?: Two Efforts to Bridge A Social Gap," *Journal of Applied Behavioral Science,* Vol. 13 (June 1977), pp. 212-213.

69. The difficulties are especially severe in the case of individuals exposed to supportive interpersonal relationships in small groups, while their broad reference groups are locked in conflict. Consider Arab and Jew, Irish Protestant and Irish Catholic, and so on. For some evidence, see Leonard W. Doob and William J. Foltz, "Voices From a Belfast Workshop: Conflict/Consensus," *Social Change,* Vol. 5, no. 3 (1975), pp. 1-2, 6-7.

70. Rosabeth Moss Kanter, "Women in Organizations: Change Agent Skills," in W. Warner Burke (ed.), *Current Issues and Strategies in Organization Development* (New York: Human Science Press, 1977), p. 123.

71. For one such useful instrument, consult Bernard M. Bass, *Profair—A Program About Working with Women.* (Scottsville, New York: Transnational Programs Corporation, 1971).

72. Kanter, "Women in Organizations," p. 122.

73. Ibid., p. 123.

74. For example, the developers of the Grid argue that participant learning did not differ in trainer-led versus trainerless groups that were guided by pre-formed instructions and instruments. But back-home applications of learning were enhanced for those experiencing trainerless, instrumented designs. See *Group and Organization Studies,* Vol. 3 (December 1978), pp. 403-404. Also consult Jane S. Mouton and Robert R. Blake, *Instrumented Team Learning: A Behavioral Approach to Student-Centered Learning* (Austin, Texas: Scientific Methods, 1975).

75. For emphases on preretirement and postretirement in an OD framework, to illustrate the slim literature, see: John B. Kenny, "Pre-Retirement Planning Seminars: A Canadian Experience," *Training and Development Journal,* Vol. 32 (August 1978), pp. 68-74; Leland P. Bradford, "Retirement and Organization Development," in W. Warner Burke (ed.), *Organization Development, 1978* (La Jolla, Calif.: University Associates, 1979); and Leland P. Bradford and Martha J. Bradford, *Coping With Emotional Upheavals at Retirement* (Chicago: Nelson-Hall, 1978).

Section 3

SOME GROUP INTERVENTIONS

Chapter 6

BOUNDED AND EXTENDED
INTERVENTIONS IN SMALL GROUPS
Some Developmental Trends and Two Case Studies

This chapter provides breadth and depth. Broadly, it provides a review of trends in the small group's role in the process of change. It also details case studies of two small management teams at critical points in their history. Specifically:

- An introductory section sketches three stages in the history of small group studies, whose latest tendency is to use small groups as the agents of change, and especially in "family" settings.
- "Team development" is described as the most common way of using small groups as agents of change in "family" settings.
- Two case studies of team development are presented, one being time-bounded and narrow in scope, and the other being time-extensive and comprehensive.

This chapter's intent may be approached in another way. Basically, it illustrates two OD designs which begin with a human-processual approach, which are interaction-centered, and—in a direct sense—which seek to induce members of the two small organizations to get their things together by an emphasis on the real and incompletely recognized problems inherent in how they deal with one another. The first case is an easier piece: the work group is smaller and just getting started, the work relationships are less formalized, and fewer policies and procedures inhibit change. The second case study takes the illustration one crucial step forward, in showing how an interaction-centered approach can provide a kind of launching pad for changes in the technostructural realm. In essence, the work group in the second case sought to change broader organizational processes and structures to make them more congruent with the prior changes that occurred in their interaction as people.

Group Change via Laboratory Methods
Some Overall Tendencies

The laboratory approach should have gone to school on the experience of other behavioral science approaches to groups, to use the golfer's idiom, but it did not. Some of the consequences thereof are severe and negative, as substantial detail will make clear.

Three Stages in Studying Groups

Three chronological stages adequately trace the developmental history of behavioral science approaches to the small group. To begin, early observers dating back to Aristotle and at least through LeBon were impressed by a common observation: that the behavior, attitudes, and beliefs of individuals are rooted basically in interpersonal and intergroup relations. Observers did not agree whether what they saw was for good or ill, to be sure. Aristotle in his *Politics* saw nobility in man's social nature, and LeBon saw man's groupiness as the source of much mischief,[1] if not all of it.

In this elemental sense, the group is a *medium of control.* Groups provide the major context in which people develop their concepts of who they are, or—to say almost the same thing—of how they relate to others.

The basic observation that groups influence behavior generated two major conceptual extensions.[2] One developmental notion was a product of the 1930s and 1940s, basically. If groups can influence or control behavior, attitudes, and beliefs, goes this core insight, then why not think of the group as a *target of change?* A variety of theoretical and applied work leaped at the challenge of gaining the leverage inherent in a group's influence over its members to change either individual or group behavior. Group contexts were used to induce mothers to feed orange juice regularly to their babies, to encourage industrial workers to raise output, and to get housewives to use unpopular cuts of meat to ease wartime shortages. Several principles of group dynamics[3] resulting from this interest have had wide impact in teaching, healing, and work contexts:

- The greater the attractiveness of a group for its members, the greater the influence it can exert over its members, and the more widely shared are a group's norms by its members

- The greater the attractiveness of a group for its members, the greater the resistance to changes in behavior, attitudes, or beliefs which deviate from group norms
- The greater the prestige of an individual among group members, the greater the influence he can exert

One particular weak link bedevils attempts to apply such principles of group dynamics, especially in industrial or administrative situations. There is no guarantee that groups will "do the right thing" as far as formal authorities are concerned. For example, if workers view their group as attractive on social grounds, that group will not necessarily be a useful medium for changing attitudes about output levels in the way that management desires. A more attractive group might only better mobilize its sources to resist management, in fact,[4] as by lowering output.

Consequently, it became increasingly clear that other principles of group dynamics were necessary to predict whether, and especially in what direction, a group's influence would be applied in specific cases. Some significant other principles illustrate the broader field:

- The greater the sense of belonging to a common group that is shared by those people who are exerting influence for a change and those who are to be changed, the more probable is acceptance of the influence.
- The more relevant are specific behaviors, attitudes, or values to the bases for attraction of members to a group, the greater the influence a group can exert over these behaviors, attitudes, or values.

Such principles imply a profound conceptual development of the primal observation that groups influence behavior. Directly, much of the resistance inherent in the use of the group as a target of change could be avoided by using the group as the *agent of change*.

The radical implications of the concept of a group as the agent of change are reflected nowhere so clearly as in the T-group. Within very wide limits, members of a T-group can determine their own destiny as a temporary social system,[5] and this enhances the probability of undiluted group influence. Crudely, the T-group needs to apply fewer of its resources to resisting outside authority and thus can devote more of them to learning or influence. The experience with T-groups consequently reflects the effect of several other major principles of group dynamics:

- The greater the shared perception by group members of the need for a change, the more the pressure for change that will originate within the group, and the greater the influence that will be exerted over members.

- The more widely information about plans for change and about their consequences is shared among group members, the greater is member commitment to the change and to its implementation.

Group Power Utilized in "Stranger" Settings

The concept of the group as the agent of change encouraged two basic uses. The first historic use involved small populations of participants in stranger T-groups, an especially convenient context for quickly generating fundamental group processes, research concerning which could add to basic knowledge in important ways.[6] Moreover, the T-group was linked with in-depth understanding of group processes by participants, as well as with practice and mastery of specific "basic skills,"[7] in about equal measure. Consistently, participants in these early T-groups tended to be members of the various "helping" professions or occupations: teachers, industrial trainers and personnel officials, pastors and clerics, youth workers, staff from service and charitable organizations, counselors and clinicians, and so on. These early populations clearly had strong needs to understand their experience, to develop instrumental skills consistent with it, and to evaluate that experience in terms of the institutions or professions or occupations which they tended to represent.

The power of the T-group as an agent of change also generated a second usage.[8] That is, the T-group was used for large numbers of participants in stranger experiences for the broad purpose of confronting the self-in-relation. Overall, the T-group experience was intense and impactful. Simply, learning designs focused on affect and emotion, and far less on understanding or specific skill-practice. Significantly, also, participants increasingly sought to alleviate feelings of alienation or loneliness, for example, and many anticipated or even demanded the experience of an "emotional high."

These two uses of the T-group as an agent of change rest on several commonalities, while they differ profoundly. The critical commonality is that openness will occur best where participants feel psychologically safe. The stranger T-group encourages this sense of safety in several critical senses:

- It meets for an extended period on a "cultural island."
- Its members will probably never meet again, which reduces or eliminates one major source of threat.
- Its culture is intentionally different from the back-home world, more supportive and less evaluative.
- It is a temporary system, and hence encourages members to express themselves and experiment in ways they probably would not risk in more permanent systems.

Tying Group Power to Change in Family Settings

The emphasis on the stranger T-group as the agent of change implied a definite trade-off: Emotional impact of the T-group experience was emphasized more than transfer of learning. Recognition of the basic point came slow and hard, in many circles.

The evidence underlying this crucial conclusion may be sketched in terms of three propositions. *First,* the early research literature generated mixed results concerning the persistence of changes induced in stranger T-groups, as well as about their contribution to increased effectiveness in various back-home situations.[9] Such findings demonstrated that transfer of learning into real-time contexts was subtle. Learning in one context did not get more-or-less directly transferred to other areas of a person's life.

Second, concern grew that stranger experiences with no planned back-home design loops might actually create problems for learners. Indeed, mischief might result, in rough proportion to the initial impact on the individual, mischief far more serious than simple fade-out, or decay, of learning. As Warren G. Bennis, Kenneth D. Benne, and Robert Chin cautioned as early as 1962: "Isolating the individual from his organizational context, his normative structure which rewards him and represents a significant reference group makes no sense. In fact, if it sets up countervailing norms and expectations, it may be deleterious to both the organization and to the individual."[10]

Hence, *third,* the growing need "to be concerned with altering both the forces within an individual and the forces in the organizational situation surrounding the individual."[11] The shift in focus is critical. Increasingly, the initial experience with laboratory values came in the family group, at work or wherever, and that constituted a great leap forward. "It was learning to *reject* T-group stranger labs," Robert Blake noted, "that permitted OD to come into focus."[12] The trade-off? Blake proposes that any losses in impact of the initial learning experience will be compensated for by the more direct application in relevant contexts of whatever learning does occur.

The Growing Emphasis on Team Development
A Prime Way of Applying the Laboratory Approach to Groups

"Team development" is the most common organizational expression of the laboratory approach in small, family groups. Basically, it seeks to build analogues of T-group processes and dynamics into ongoing groups. Sometimes this is accomplished by the direct use of T-groups. Most often, however, "process analysis" constitutes the prime learning mode.

The Anatomy of Team Development

Specifics about team development[13] can be detailed under three separate headings. They refer, in turn, to the unit considered a "team"; the way in which the team experience gets analyzed; and the differentiated range of activities which an effective team will balance. These three themes constitute a prelude to some heavy work. A following section will distinguish types of team-building, a significant set of distinctions to be followed by two case studies.

Focal Units

At its foundation, team development assumes that small task groups of five to twenty members—such as the manager and the first level or two of his or her subordinates—are basic.[14] The organization is seen as a complex clustering of such teams. Consequently, when changes in the behavior, attitudes, or values of individuals are necessary, the norms and culture of several variously inclusive teams at several levels of organization might also have to be changed.

Analysis of Experience

Team development designs variously analyze existing team activities and relationships to lead to a plan of action for influencing future outcomes. Three general steps consequently are involved in all team-development designs, which otherwise can vary widely in their details. The general steps are

- Collection of information about team activities or relationships
- Feedback of this information to the team
- Action-planning by the team, based on the feedback and reactions to it

Beckhard calls this team-development approach an action-research model of intervention.[15]

A wide variety of designs have been utilized to help move a team-development experience through the three steps above:

- A sophisticated and open team might periodically meet to work toward action-planning based on answers to these questions: How are we doing? And why? How can we do better?
- An outside resource person could interview members of the team, for the purpose of reporting back his or her aggregate impressions of their responses to such questions: How can we improve the efficiency and effectiveness of this team?
- A team might collect information and get feedback by arranging a "mirror design," as when a service group asks a marketing unit how it is

perceived by this important customer, with the intent of using the feedback for action planning by the service group.

- A team can choose a T-group experience to generate data and provide feedback about internal interpersonal relationships, with the goal of using that data to improve communication and decision-making.

Normally, these designs are scheduled for perhaps 2 to 5 days at a neutral site. Not uncommonly, work teams will schedule a team-development activity at intervals of 6 to 12 months.

Differentiated Focus of Activities

Each team must develop a viable and dynamic balance between at least five sets of simultaneous demands. Neglect of any of these demands will have a long-run impact on the others and, consequently, on team effectiveness. Hence the need for periodic fine-tuning, if not gross adjustment, of the allocations of resources made by a team to the several demands.

Two such demands are "external":

- Organization expectations about team performance, which may be expressed in terms of production standards, acceptable levels of quality, broad policies and procedures, and so on
- *Relations with other groups,* which can be critical in at least three general cases:

    Where two or more teams work simultaneously on subsystems of some project or product which must be integrated

    When two or more teams perform sequential steps on some project or product, so that the work pace and quality of one team is either dependent upon and/or directly influences another team or teams

    Where two or more teams are related as seller/buyer or producer/consumer of some service, as in typical line-staff relationships

The challenges in integrating these two levels of demands are multiple and should be more-or-less obvious. For example, organization expectations about productivity might force two interdependent teams into win or lose competitive situations, as when each blames the other for lower-than-expected production. In the vernacular, successfully "throwing dead cats" by one team into the backyards of other teams might help the first team meet organization expectations about productivity, but only at the cost of polluting relationships between the teams.

Each team must also give attention to three "internal" demands. They are

- The *group task*, whose short-run demands may be so compelling as to be overwhelming

- *Group maintenance,* which refers to the management of what team members do "*to* and *with* each other" as they work on the common task, for a team "needs to have a growing awareness of itself . . . , of its constantly changing network of interactions and relationships, and of the need to maintain within itself relationships appropriate to the task"[16]
- *Individual needs* of team members, which variously influence and relate to how a team does its work, and whose relative satisfaction crucially determines the individual's involvement and commitment to the team

From a second and related perspective, the thrusts of team-development activities can be suggested in terms of what "teamwork" requires. Team development often centers around balancing such components of teamwork, to rely basically on Gordon L. Lippitt, as:[17]

- An understanding of, and commitment to, common goals
- The integration of resources of as wide as possible a range of team members, to use their contributions and also to increase their owning of and commitment to a team's goals or products
- The ability and willingness to analyze and review team processes, to prevent the accumulation of unfinished business and to improve team effectiveness
- Trust and openness in communication and relationships
- A strong sense of belonging by its members

Team-development activities commonly seek to realize these individual "shoulds," while managing potential and painful conflicts between them. Thus, a strong sense of belonging to a team can become dysfunctional, as when the team's mission changes or is curtailed while team members seek to protect their comfortable relationships.

Five Characteristic Team-Development Situations

Despite such commonalities, however, team-building designs can vary in important ways. Such designs must be particularly sensitive to the initial condition of the target group, for example. This should come as no surprise, in general, but that recognition does not preoccupy OD intervenors.

How will this analysis seek to encourage recognition of differences to which team-building designs should be sensitive? Dyer's useful analysis distinguishes and illustrates five different kinds of team-building situations,[18] and those situations provide the basic structure for the consciousness-raising that immediately follows.

Facilitating Start-Up

As Beckhard notes,[19] start-up situations tend to have common features that encourage team-building or development activities.[20] Basically, start-up typically involves one or a few groups operating under stress and time pressure, with major costs associated with any integrative problems,[21] whose success or failure can set profound precedents for later steady-state operations.[22] Moreover, start-up typically involves:

- Substantial confusion about roles and relationships
- Fairly clear understanding of immediate goals but lack of clarity about provisions to be made for longer-run operations
- Fixation on the immediate task, which often means that group maintenance activities will receive inadequate attention and individual needs will be neglected[23]
- A challenge to team members, which will induce superior technical effort, but which may also have serious consequences for personal or family life[24]

Start-up usually generates significant opportunities for team development and generates substantial leverage for the OD intervenor. For example, Case Study I below illustrates how a one-shot design was capable of providing sufficient impetus for an executive group at start-up. That design has features which should not be overlooked, reflecting substantial experience that start-up designs should:[25]

- Emphasize "structuring" versus "unfreezing" interventions, as in setting up project teams rather than surfacing interpersonal conflicts
- Give precedence to task-oriented versus process-oriented interventions, as in role negotiation or instrumental process analysis
- Contribute to managing a burgeoning anxiety rather than to inducing a "creative tension" as via T-group or confrontation designs
- Provide relief from the demands of the project—as in prescribing "away time" or decoupling activities—in contrast to "getting us all together all the time"
- Create protection from some pressures and inputs, which contrasts with the objective of many OD interventions to generate a sensitivity to the broadest possible range of data and data-sources
- Focus on conflict-resolving and boundary-setting activities, in more or less direct opposition to confronting or experimental activities

Managing Chaos and Conflict

A host group with a long history of conflict and contention presents quite a different challenge for a team-building intervention, and the prognosis typically will be more dicey than for start-up efforts. Case Study II below details a beautiful example of what must be and can be done—in terms of a useful initial design as well as follow-up activities—so we need not dwell here on that which gets such vivid statement there.

Note here only two features of using team-building designs to manage chaos and conflict that complicate the task of intervening successfully. First, the OD intervenor must design and maintain a context for dealing with substantial emotionality. Smothering probably will not work, and there may be no place for the timid to hide. In Case Study II, for example, some participants got their dukes up and were ready to go at it, right then. Second, typically, extensive and extended reinforcement of learning will be necessary to help avoid regression and recidivism. Case Study II reflects special strength and concern in this regard: extending the initial team-building design into policy and structural changes, and tracking the consequences of such changes with standard indicators over a long period of time.

Case Study II provides apt illustration of how to use team-development designs to manage conflict and chaos, but it hardly stands alone. The literature provides valuable counterpoint and supplement to the report below.[26]

Overcoming Unhealthy Agreement

Although too seldom diagnosed, it seems useful or even critical to distinguish a "crisis of conflict or difference" from a "crisis of agreement."[27] Typically, OD intervenors assume that only one type of crisis exists, and design appropriately. That seems an error. For reality seems to come in at least two major varieties which defy blending.

The issue is so significant that major parts of Chapter 4 of Part 2, a chapter which deals with various integrative linkages between roles or positions in large organizations, distinguish the two kinds of crises in detail. So, only brief notice will be provided here. Later treatment in Part 2, as well as other convenient sources,[28] provide illustrations and also reveal how two classes of designs should be tailored to the two distinct kinds of crises.

But the reader will not be left completely waiting for Chapter 4 of Part 2. By way of whetting the analytical appetite, note here only that the two kinds of crises relate to different primary risks. In the crisis of disagreement, the individual's basic risk involves "unsatisfactory inclusion," and the central question gets framed in these terms: How do I keep from being incorporated with that different/strange/conflictful "them"? So, the basic intervention strategy seeks variously to reveal that the "we" and "they" share significant common ground, as when efforts are made to reduce the "social distance" between two parties, when putting Self in the Other's position seeks to induce a greater empathy and understanding of some "Them," and so on. In a crisis of agreement, in contrast, fear of separation seems the dominant motive. The key question thus becomes some variant of: How do I avoid risking a dilution of my membership in some "us"? Key interventions in this second case will center around nonthreats to membership that still permit progress—as by seeking to defuse risk by demonstrations that "the worst" that could happen as a result of a specific threat to membership has less than catastrophic consequences.

A single comparison will have to be relied upon, for now, to support the basic distinction between the two types of crises and to urge reliance on different kinds of designs for each of them. Case Study II below makes use of the three-dimensional image in a confrontation design, for example. When individuals reveal differences on such images that are acknowledged and recognized, given a crisis of conflict, that implies success because the evaluators thereby show they are in touch with the other's reality. In a crisis of disagreement, awareness of that difference thus reveals a common ground on which a more secure relationship might be built. Oppositely, the same images in a crisis of agreement imply failure. When individuals report a "difference," that is, that threatens the maintenance of membership in an "us." Hence, a correct perception of the other in such cases will tend to be less attractive than an incorrect perception that does not threaten membership. In this sense, a crisis of agreement might be heightened by designs quite serviceable in a crisis of disagreement.

Revitalizing a Complacent Team

"Pumping-up" a team once the air has escaped from its balloon, as it were, constitutes a major challenge for the OD intervenor. Causes of such deflation cover a broad range, and designs must be sensitive to such differences.[29] For present purposes, consider only three situations to which different designs no doubt will be appropriate.

- A small R&D firm has "hit it big," escalating prices of its stock have made several partners instantly rich, and the "get up and go" has suddenly gone.

- A large public agency has made a 30-year transition from innovative to hide-bound reactionary status, essentially with the same managerial group—which got on board around start-up, got promoted rapidly, and all but universally stayed on until most top managers now approach retirement together.

- A "new-venture" search group has had a strong track record, but over the last year supervising executives have grown increasingly concerned that the group's hubris has set it to "chasing wild hares," although they do not act because the new-venture group's track record rests firmly on having "done it their own way" in the past.

Similar design elements might be used to confront the differently rooted complacencies in these three cases, but design variety would more likely be the order of the day. Thus, forceful notice might suffice to encourage the new-venture group to confront its complacency, but the complacent agency faces a far more complicated task: training, recruiting, opening up new and substantial areas of delegation to juniors, planning to relinquish control rather than waiting for retirement, and so on.

Dealing with Interteam Conflict

Moving from an intrateam to an interteam level poses some challenges of its own, especially in that issues of power and pecking order typically will be involved. Moreover, the complex and ad hoc character of cases in point all but precludes brief illustration.

Useful models exist for such efforts, however. Chapter 4 in Part 2 details an appropriate design and its consequences; Chapter 5 deals with several related topics; and other convenient sources provide illustrations of both diagnosis and prescription relevant to cases involving interteam conflict.[30]

Two Illustrations

OD applications in small groups could take many directions, then, even if the focus narrows only to team development. Two examples get explicit attention here, one time-bounded and the other time-extended as well as broad-ranging in encompassing the substance of policies and structures in addition to interpersonal and group processes.

One-Shot Intervention with an Executive Group
Case Study I

Let us begin with an OD application at start-up of a small executive team. The design was explicitly limited as a kind of pump-priming venture, and thus is bounded in terms of time, planned reinforcers, and coverage. The case deals with one of the still small but growing number of applications in university and college administration.[31]

Mirror Design for an Executive Group

The classic OD design[32] for an analysis of a small group's processes—the inter-view/feedback design which relies heavily on a consultant or change agent—was the choice in this case. In effect, the intervenor serves as a mirror, reflecting back the image projected to him or her by some group. The design is economical in some important ways, as in the sense that only the change agent requires initial skills and values consistent with the laboratory approach. Group members thus can have a quick and easy experience of what things would be like if they took the time themselves to enhance such skills and values, and if they behaved congruently with them.

The interview/feedback design is now standard for OD openers, and can be a gentle one for a group intent only on surveying or auditing its own processes. "How are we functioning?" is the guiding question. Or, it can be an opener for extended programs of change in a group's processes, with the interview/feedback serving to highlight the need to develop attitudes and skills consistent with the laboratory approach. "How can we change our processes to get more of what we want?" is the basic question underlying this second use of the interview/feedback design.

A Typical Interview/Feedback Design[33]

There are diverse varieties of this classic design, and it is far easier to illustrate one than it is to describe them all. Consider the top executive group of a major state university: the university president and his six immediate subordinates.

Preliminary diagnosis indicated that an appropriate learning design would need only to indicate quickly and forcefully to all executives how bad the current situation was—a kind of shock treatment to accelerate getting on with it. Five major contributors to this diagnosis can be sketched. *First,* the president was new in his job, which was a major step upward from his previous responsibilities. The president exercised his prerogatives with a very gentle hand, and his initial role was sharply limited.

Second, several new members had been recently joined the president's executive team. The normal processes of adaptation were no doubt still working themselves out at the time of the OD intervention.

Third, major jurisdictional issues stressed relationships in the executive group. These disputes may have been caused by personal conflicts among the president's subordinates, as some maintain. In any case, the consequences of the jurisdictional issues strained the relationships between several members of the executive group.

Fourth, these jurisdictional and personal issues had a special edge because they occurred during a period of consolidation, following an unprecedented decade of budget increase upon increase upon increase. Priorities became a very real issue. Various interest groups among students, faculty, and legislators encouraged their particular champions in the executive group to get the best of suddenly scarcer resources. The stakes were major ones. Different interests and priorities would be served by the several diverse policy positions that leading members of the executive group were known to support.

Fifth, diverse images of the executive group held by various relevant publics were made known to the author. The president saw his executive group as deliberately getting its ducks in a row, under very difficult conditions. The common stereotype among administrators one or two levels removed from the top provided a stark contrast. They saw the executive group as a hard-working one which spent enormous amounts of time in wheel spinning, in dealing with minutiae, and in laboriously redoing their own work and that of their subordinates. And all this fiddling was going on while, figuratively speaking, the university Rome was at least threatened by fire, if it was not already burning merrily away.

Influentials who were concerned about this public and private contrast in images paved the way for the author. The influentials persuaded the president to raise the question of a "socioemotional audit" with his executive group, following a simple design. The author would privately interview each executive and report back to the group his findings in ways that would preserve the anonymity of his sources. Some reading material was provided, should the president or his executives like an idea of the kinds of issues that could be raised by the design.

The executive group quickly agreed to the design. The explicit contract was for a one-time effort, with most members of the executive team maintaining that this provided some guarantee that the consultant would not withhold any "tough talk" in the interest of generating more business. The consultant did emphasize that it often was better not to start such process analysis unless a real possibility of following through existed, and he also stressed that the design would be a poor delaying tactic to relieve some of the heat that the executive group might be feeling. Beyond these common preliminaries, interviews of at least 90 minutes were scheduled, with the added hope that executives could clear their calendars for a longer period if that were possible. Follow-up interviews thus could be avoided. The average interview ran somewhat under 2.5 hours.

The interviews were broadly standardized, and also sought to explore specific targets of opportunity. Each interview opened in the same way. The consultant briefly made the following six points.

- Any management group can improve its operations.
- Effectiveness of such groups is important, if only as preparation for stress situations such as student disturbances.
- Review of interpersonal and intergroup processes is one way to improve operations.
- The interviews were an initial approach to surveying group processes.
- Summary data from the interviews would be fed back to the total group, as far as it was possible to do so and protect anonymity.
- The executive group might decide to look at their processes in more depth later, based on their positive reaction to the consultant's feedback session.

The interviews themselves all touched some common bases, as they were guided by the same general outline. At a minimum, and in this order, respondents were asked to do the following.

- Sketch the major challenges that they felt top management would have to face in the immediate future.

- Rate the quality of their functioning as an executive team (especially in their weekly meetings, which typically lasted several hours and might last all working day), from three perspectives:

   Respondent's rating,

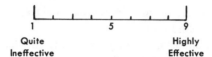

   Quite   Highly
   Ineffective   Effective

   Respondent's estimate of the average rating of other executives,

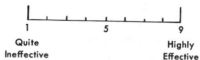

   Quite   Highly
   Ineffective   Effective

   Respondent's list of specific executives with highest and lowest ratings.

- Discuss the special strengths of the executive group in their meetings.

- Discuss the special weaknesses of the executive group in their meetings. If the points were not spontaneously raised, the respondent was asked to comment on at least these three characteristics of their group processes:

   The openness of executives with one another, in public sessions and in private,

   Problem-solving effectiveness in group meetings, as in dealing with the real problems, coming to timely decisions, and so on,

   The ways in which conflicts were resolved.

- Discuss the clarity of role definitions and lines of authority in the internal relationships of the executive group.

- Discuss the president's managerial style, as it influenced group meetings and the relationships between executives.

Why Bother, Especially with a Consultant?

What features of interview/feedback encourage groups to devote time to the design? Reasons for rejecting such a design come easily. The pressures of time, and incredulity that an outsider can gain much perspective in a brief series of interviews, illustrate the broad range of negative motivators.

What is there on the positive side? Each situation has its own idiosyncratic motivators, but some general motivators also usually encourage having a go at such a design. *First,* concern about interpersonal and intergroup processes is common, even (perhaps, especially) in effectively functioning groups, and especially at higher levels of organization, where interpersonal and intergroup relationships tend to dominate.

Second, concern about socioemotional processes can be especially intense under two conditions. Typically, much data will be in the hidden area of the Johari window of several or all members of a group. Members may be unwilling to raise such issues because of the perceived risk, or they may simply lack the time, the skills, or the persistence necessary to work through the issues they clearly perceive. Similarly, but more potentially ticklish, one or two group members may have a major blind spot.

Third, the consultant-as-mirror might variously enrich a group's appreciation of its own processes. At a minimum, the consultant might only confirm what every member already knows. This may seem a small blessing, but some things cannot be confirmed too often lest people come to doubt their reality. A little more ambitiously, the change agent's intervention might contribute to greater self-maintenance of regenerative communication systems, even if the specific feedback by the consultant is not particularly helpful or enlightening. More expansively, the consultant may induce the release of hidden data or perceive the significance of factors which group members undervalue. In some cases, the change agent also may be able to put the proverbial two and two together, and here the change agent can really earn his or her salt.

Fourth, the interview/feedback design is a safe one for the participants. Potentially delicate issues can be brushed aside, for example, with varying degrees of delicacy. Hence, "It is unfair to expect that consultant could have really tuned-in to how we do things here, given the short time he could devote to us. You know, sometimes we really ought to set aside the time necessary to do the job well." Legion are the other devices by which a group can avoid hearing what is being communicated by the consultant in feedback sessions, if that becomes necessary.

Specifics of an Executive Group Being Mirrored

Two hours had been set aside for the feedback session to the executive group described above, and the meeting began pleasantly enough with the high hopes for learning expressed by the president. The consultant introduced his feedback in terms of the notion of a degenerative communication system introduced earlier, which was greeted with knowing nods as accurately describing the state of affairs among other groups of university executives. The consultant also noted that the feedback session could be quite short. In sum, despite the variations on a theme that could be detailed, a dominant pattern emerged from all interviews. And this pattern could be conveyed via a simple illustration. Several more complex ways of making the same point had been prepared, the consultant added, and the executive group could later decide whether it wished to go into them. But it would in no sense be necessary to do so.

As the simple illustration was developed, the pleasant tone of the feedback session changed appreciably. Apparently, the executives interpreted the presentation as implying that their interaction system had major degenerative properties. Whatever the case, the presentation developed two aspects of a single theme:

- On almost all issues, the executive group contained two or more subgroups with significantly different perceptions, expectations, and evaluations concerning their interpersonal and intergroup relations.

- More significantly, on almost all issues, the executives were either unclear or mistaken about the perceptions, expectations, and evaluations of their fellow executives.

The two points were illustrated by detailing how the executives responded to rating their effectiveness as a group in meetings, on a low/high scale running from 1 through 9. Some highlights may be sketched, with uncommunicated but interesting data being presented in parentheses:

- There were two clusters of scores about group effectiveness, especially at meetings: 2-4 and 7-8.

- Almost without exception, each executive's rating for self was 2-4, while his estimate of the average ratings of his fellow executives was 7-8. (The one exception was the president, whose self-rating was 7 and who was unwilling to guess the ratings of the others "because I just don't know." This datum was not communicated.)

- The executives guessed poorly as to which of their fellows rated the executive group highest/lowest on effectiveness: in fact, over half of the executives made at least one maximum error, for example, guessing that executive A was the lowest rater of the group's effectiveness whereas in fact he reported the highest rating in the consultant's in the interviews. (There is much food for thought in this one. Were executives merely unaware? Or had they conveyed a false impression to their colleagues, while being straight with the consultant? Or, had they been putting-on the consultant, while they were four-square with their colleagues? These questions were not raised explicitly. More food for thought: The president correctly picked the executive who scored his group the lowest on effectiveness, but his guess about the highest scorer was far off. The assumed highest scorer was in fact next to lowest.)

- One executive refused to give a single rating, but he did provide three ratings for effectiveness of the executives as a group, and especially in their meetings:

To learn what's going on: 7
To get at basic problems: 2-3
To create a sense of cooperation or team identity: 4

Presenting this illustration took only a few minutes of clock time, almost as long as the silence that followed the consultant's request for reactions! The logjam was broken by a brief statement from the elder statesman of the group. "Damn," he said, "you heard everything I told you, and most of the stuff I was thinking." ("That saved you," I was told later by one of the executives in a private review of "the" meeting. "Two or three of us, including me, were ready to sandbag you at the first opportunity." I agreed.)

The exchanges flew thick and fast for awhile, and then the request: "Well, what else do you have for us?" That established the pattern for a meeting that ran 3 hours beyond the originally scheduled time. We went back to similar wells six times in all, each time being a replica of the other. The consultant would summarize data on one point; the usual silence would follow, as if the group were catching its breath; someone would confirm that there seemed substantial-enough reality reflected in the summary; and discussion would follow. These major topics were considered, in this order:

- Major challenges facing the executive group
- Various formal role definitions that influenced the group's interpersonal and intergroup relations
- Contrasting personal and analytical styles of the several executives
- The ways of dealing with conflict in the executive group
- The role of the president and its impact on interpersonal and intergroup relations

Several recommendations were made for follow-on, but these were not implemented in the form presented. The executive group did take a 3-day "retreat" to work on their relationships, but they decided against using a process observer when I proved to be unavailable.

The retreat was held, and the president and most of the other executives have gone out of their way to emphasize its value and especially that of the feedback session. "It got us down to elementals with one another," reads one letter. Another letter tickles me: "We have started to waffle with one another 3 or 4 times in meetings since you were last here. And then someone would say: 'If we keep this up, Big Bob will come get us again.' That always breaks us up, and gets us leveling again."

Time-Extended Intervention with a Law Enforcement Team
Case Study II

The research literature also contains models for more time-extended and deliberate efforts to build laboratory values into small groups.[34] Frank Friedlander's training/research effort clearly introduces what such efforts intend to accomplish, and how.[35] He uses family groups exposed to what he calls "organizational training laboratories" to overcome the perceived shortcomings of an initial resort to stranger experiences. As Friedlander explains:

> these training sessions deal with the intact work group as an integrated system into which is introduced procedural and interpersonal change, rather than with a collection of strangers representing different organizations—or unrelated components of the same organization.

> The organizational training laboratory is directed at helping the individual bridge the hazardous, yet critical transition from his trainee role to the "real life" role of his back-home environment, and at preventing dissipation of the training effects. Since much of the discussion centers upon the relevant work problems which the group actually faces, and since the members of the training group are also the members of the organizational work group, ideally there is a perfect consolidation of the training and organizational membership roles.

Friedlander concludes succinctly on his use of family groups: "The back-home and the here-and-now are one and the same."

Some Background

The focus here is on a family setting to induce relatively specific changes among a small group of police officials,* changes which in turn triggered longer-run changes in Metro County law enforcement. The county is a study in contrasts. Its population of 170,000 is sharply divided between the university and professional communities and the county's agricultural and business communities. The problems facing the Sheriff's Department extend from issues affecting the farmlands and rapidly growing communities on the plains, to problems most often associated with mountain communities. This enforcement range includes urban drug problems and plane crashes on isolated peaks.

---

*The case study here is essentially the report of R. Wayne Boss, "Organization Development in a Metropolitan Law Enforcement Agency (mimeographed, 1975). See also Boss, "The Not-So-Peaceful Incident at Peaceful Valley: A Confrontation Design in A Criminal Justice Agency," in Arthur G. Bedeian, Archilles A. Armenakis, William H. Holley, Jr., and Hubert S. Field, Jr. (eds.), *Proceedings* (Annual Meeting) Academy of Management, August 1975, pp. 357-359.

In November 1970, a 29-year-old police officer was elected Sheriff of Metro County. After taking office in January 1971, he began staffing his department with young, educated, and dedicated law enforcement officers whom he perceived as willing to "work hard and get the job done." He also began implementing the kinds of law enforcement programs viewed as futuristic in most parts of the country.

Problems began to surface within the fast-changing, progressive department. Interpersonal differences, competition, and hostility among subordinates emerged; and discontent with the Sheriff's administrative style ran deep. A spring 1972 antiwar demonstration added fuel to the fire, and existing discontent was further aggravated in 1973 by a major change in the Sheriff's administrative approach. Prior to that time, he had an open-door policy. However, in the summer of 1973 the Sheriff directed that all employees, including his top administrative staff, should channel all business through the Undersheriff. If the matter could not be settled there, only then would the Sheriff be notified. The top administrative staff responded to the surprise change with noteworthy vehemence, especially because they suspected that the Sheriff was only beginning his run for reelection at their expense.

Shortly thereafter, a move was begun at the lower levels of the department to unionize. The movement rapidly gained support, and by late summer nonadministrative personnel seemed almost certain to unionize.

In early October, the Sheriff called in two organizational consultants. Consultants first attended the weekly administrative staff meetings as observers. In addition, extensive interviews were held with each member of the staff: the Sheriff, the Undersheriff, and the five Division Heads.

Subsequently, the consultants and staff agreed that an off-site team-building session should be held for the purpose of increasing collaboration among team members and providing an opportunity for solving interpersonal and departmental problems. In preparation for the off-site meeting, each of the seven managerial personnel participated in a private, semistructured interview and responded to such open-ended questions as the following.

- What are the most critical issues currently facing the Sheriff's Department?
- What are the most critical issues between divisions in the Sheriff's Department?
- What do other staff members do that make it difficult for you to fulfill your responsibilities?
- Do some people get preferential treatment? If so, please explain.
- What does the Sheriff do well?
- What should the Sheriff do more of?

- What should the Sheriff do less of?
- If you could make any five changes in the department, what would they be?

Each participant was told that all answers to each question would be posted anonymously on large sheets of newsprint and shared during the team-building session. Each person could own up to his comments if he so desired, but no one would be required to do so.

Such interview sessions serve a number of valuable functions. For example, they provide consultants and department members an opportunity to develop a relationship. Most important, the interviews provide the participants with a safe vehicle for ventilating their feelings and raising issues that would otherwise remain "unfinished business" or "interpersonal garbage"—problems that are not openly confronted, resulting in decreased interpersonal effectiveness and the loss of psychological energy because the private and hidden areas of the Johari window are so large relative to the public area.

During the interview sessions, seven especially significant problems surfaced. Most obvious, *first,* was the overwhelming disapproval of the personality, attitudes, and managerial style of the Undersheriff. An example: "It is not so much what he does that bothers me. It is the way he does it. Everyone agrees that he is an outstanding cop—but I think he is a lousy manager. If I had the authority, I would fire him."

Much of the frustration and anger, *second,* was triggered by the lack of access to the Sheriff. This resulted not only in a lack of effective upward and downward communication, but also in a significant loss of access to the top official in an organization.

Third, the department was plagued by an extremely high turnover rate. For the 3 years prior to the organizational effort, the turnover rate had fluctuated between 40 and 60 percent.

Fourth, the frequent absence of the Sheriff from the department was troublesome. Because the position of Sheriff is an elected office, he opted to attend numerous meetings and activities not directly related to departmental operations. The staff did not like it. As one staff member put it: "I think the Sheriff ought to forget about politics and get back to work as the Sheriff. If we do a good job, it will speak for itself. That is the most important thing."

Fifth, a formal atmosphere existed in the department, defenses were high, and communication suffered. Even though many of them had known each other for a number of years, for example, they continually referred to each other by their title: Sheriff, Undersheriff, Captain, or Lieutenant.

Sixth, how departmental policy was made and implemented caused serious problems. Decisions were made arbitrarily by the Sheriff and Undersheriff, and then transmitted either by a memo or an announcement in staff meetings. These "bolts from the blue" infuriated the staff members, and the problem was magnified even further when subordinates would learn of critical decisions through the grapevine before the staff members found out about them.

Finally, and most important, the staff members' trust for the Sheriff and Undersheriff had degenerated to the point where almost everything they attempted to do was looked upon with suspicion.

These seven features weighed heavily on the officials. By early November, four of the five Division Heads were seriously considering resigning and three had already written letters of resignation.

Confrontation/Team-Building Design

It was in this context that the Sheriff and his six top aides, along with the consultants, began a 6-day confrontation/team-building meeting in a rural area that will be called Peaceful Valley. The Peaceful Valley retreat sought to convert a fragmented and hostile group of managers into an effectively functioning team, to provide participants with the opportunity for working through the unresolved socioemotional "garbage" that was so manifest in the interviews. The week's activities, however, proved to be anything but peaceful.

A Cathartic and Serendipitous Incident

An early critical point in the process occurred Monday evening, the first full day of the team-building. Following an exercise in consensual decision-making, a discussion ensued concerning the degree to which the chaotic decision-making process manifested in the exercise was like staff meetings at the office. The Captain of the jail division said the exercise was identical to the staff meetings. The Sheriff angrily denied any resemblance. The rest of the staff immediately took sides, and all the hidden agendas and unfinished business that had been cluttering up the interpersonal relationships for the past 3 years began surfacing. Accusations were made, tempers flared, and an explosive confrontation took place. The Captain of the patrol division described the situation this way. "For a few minutes I was convinced that there would be six homicides—and I'll guarantee that one of them wasn't going to be me. I can't remember when I have been so angry. I have known all of those guys for years, but I have never seen them explode like that. It all seemed to come out at once." The Captain was central in these dynamics, especially in his physical confrontation with the Sheriff. Each stood facing the other, fists clinched, arguing: the Sheriff at 5 feet 6 inches, and the Captain at 6 feet 4 inches.

The consultant interrupted and suggested that the group take a short break to cool off. All were sitting in a semicircle facing the consultant 10 minutes later. He began explaining what he had observed, traced the details of the previous 20 minutes, and suggested some possible reasons for the explosion, based upon what he had observed in the staff meetings and learned during the interviews. He also reminded the group of the preconference interviews, and their responses to the following questions:

- To what degree are you willing to accept the fact that many of the problems you are experiencing in this organization may be caused by your own behavior?
- To what extent are you willing to work to change that behavior in order to solve those problems and make the organization function more effectively?

Each staff member had previously admitted that he was at least partly at fault and had made a commitment to work on correcting any dysfunctional behavior over which he had control. The consultant then explained the possible implications of the conflict and explored with the group the alternative solutions to the current situation. During the next hour, the group temporarily worked through the immediate problems and settled the issues to the point where each was willing to continue to work on the causes of the interpersonal difficulties, rather than the symptoms.

Confronting as a Planned Activity

Such critical incidents cannot be planned, of course, but they are consistent with the spirit of the present design, which emphasized confronting attitudes and behaviors. Confronting refers to dealing openly with the various issues and problems that threaten interpersonal and organizational effectiveness. Generally, this means that team members must learn to do the following:[36]

- Become more aware of their own reactions and feelings, as well as those of the other members
- Accept and maintain a norm that encourages the expression of the full range of necessary information, reactions, and feelings
- Become more aware of the impact of their own actions on those working with them
- Develop skills to share their concerns in ways that encourage others in similar expression

In the Peaceful Valley design, confronting behavior was manifest in two forms: The sharing of three-dimensional (3-D) images,[37] and the sharing of responses to the preconference interview questions.

For the 3-D images, the staff was divided into two groups: the "administration," composed of the Sheriff and the Undersheriff, and the "staff" cluster of

the other five participants. Each group worked separately, preparing three lists
of descriptions in response to the following questions:

- How do you see yourselves in relation to the staff?
- How do you see the staff?
- How do you think the staff sees you?

The two sets of descriptions were written on large sheets of newsprint, taped to
the wall in the central meeting room, and read by all participants. Exhibit 1
shows the two sets of responses. The basic ground rule for sharing images was
direct: communication would consist of giving and requesting examples and clarification of the meaning and intent of the various items listed on the newsprint.
Defensive and argumentative behavior was to be avoided. As can be imagined, a
lively discussion followed the sharing of the 3-D images. Although the two
groups found that their perceptions were congruent in some areas and incongruent in others, the technique provided a positive base upon which to continue the
team-building activities, primarily for the following reasons.

- Participants' need such information, discomforting or even initially
  hurtful though it may be.
- Participants typically understand that the best—indeed, perhaps the
  only—way to raise the probability of receiving such needed information
  in the future is to be accepting of the 3-D images in the present. Acceptance, however, does not necessarily mean agreement.
- Confronting with 3-D images is a shared experience that can build
  mutual identification and understanding, which is what many participants are seeking.
- Most individuals are uncomfortable if their verbal or nonverbal behavior
  is at substantial variance with what they really know or believe. The
  sharing of information usually reduces this discomfort when one sees
  that others are willing to be open and own up to their feelings, attitudes,
  and perceptions.
- Substantial agreement typically exists between pairs of 3-D images. This
  agreement almost always increases the participants' sense of mutual
  competence and acceptance, by confirming that one person or group
  shares perceptions with another, as well as by signaling that the actual
  process of exchange has begun.[38]

The second confronting aspect of the design took place the following day
when the responses to interview questions were shared with the entire group.
The answers to the questions were assembled so that all responses provided by the
individual staff members to each question appeared on a sheet of newsprint. The

Exhibit 1   Results from the 3-D Image Design

How staff sees the administration:	How the administration sees staff:
1. Fiercely dedicated	1. Good cops
2. Somewhat lonely	2. Hard working
3. Unyielding	3. Together—clique
4. Hard working	4. Backbiting
5. Aloof	5. Hard to work with
6. Attitude of superiority	6. Stubborn—closed minds
7. Politically motivated (in negative way)	7. Unconcerned about political pressure
8. Impossible to please	
9. Insensitive	
10. Unwilling to give credit where due	
11. Lack of administrative skills	
12. Caught up by their power	
13. Overreaction oriented	
14. Good cops	
15. "Rooting"	

How the staff sees themselves in relation to the administration:	How the administration sees themselves in relation to the staff:
1. Professional	1. Intelligent
2. Diligent	2. Dedicated
3. Worthy of respect and consideration	3. Experienced
4. Competent	4. Fast to react
5. Untiring	5. Opinionated
6. Unyielding	6. Stubborn
7. "Super cops"	7. Put in long hours
8. Dedicated	8. "Rooting"
9. Intelligent	
10. Humorous	

How the staff believes the administration sees them:	How the administration believes the staff sees them:
1. Hard working	1. Talented
2. Wave makers	2. Picky, picky, picky
3. Rebels	3. Overzealous

Exhibit 1   (Continued)

4. Unprofessional	4. Authoritarian
5. Self-serving	5. Hard working
6. Not concerned with departmental effectiveness	6. Pushy
7. Overly concerned with personal factors	7. Dedicated
8. Irresponsible about budget	
9. Insensitive	
10. Underpaid	

numerous sheets papered a large room, all being taped side-by-side to the wall. The following are a few examples of the eighty-four pages of responses:

- *What are the most critical issues facing the Sheriff's Department?*

  We are putting out fires rather than directing our efforts toward long-range goals.

  I feel as if my authority and ability are constantly under question.

  The county commissioners are not paying personnel what they are worth.

  The election next year. Who will run against the Sheriff? Where do we stand in the election process? What image do we have with our County citizens? Do they support our programs?

  Lack of training because of lack of time. Either a man has to give up his day off, come in on his own time, or you are taking him away from his duties on the job.

  Morale because of pay, lack of job security, and the administration changes after every election.

  I can't think of any time when the department has done something good that they've been praised for it, but if we do something wrong, watch out!

  Turnover.

- *What are the most critical issues between divisions in the Sheriff's Department?*

  A general feeling of empire building.

  People are working as separate organizations rather than as a team.

  Instead of the captains working out their problems between themselves, they run them through the staff meetings and the administration. If it affects the entire department it is an administrative matter; if it is just affecting two divisions it should be dealt with at that level, between the two captains.

Inability of a man in one division to understand the problems of another division.

Nobody cares whether I quit or not; the attitude is that there are plenty of others around who can replace me or anyone else who expresses dissatisfaction.

An effective chain of command. People are afraid to make decisions because they are afraid their decisions will not be backed.

The administration does not accept our opinions and ideas.

Space and geographical problems.

The continual competition for adequate manpower.

Note a basic complementarity of these two components of the design. The 3-D images basically sought to surface relational issues between the administration and the staff, while the interview responses were more intended to surface specific substantive issues between and among individual team members. In this sense, in turn, the design focused attention on "process" and "content." Again, the same ground rules prevailed: Communication was restricted to clarifying and giving examples of various items in a nonjudgmental manner. Each person was encouraged to ask questions dealing with material pertaining to himself, with emphasis on specific examples for clarification and/or illustration. Considerable time was spent reviewing the various responses, and the degree to which each team member acknowledged his own answers to the interview questions was surprising to all. As one staff member put it: "I never thought I could say, 'I was the one who said that.' But at the time it seemed to be not only the appropriate thing to do, but it was also easy, and in some ways refreshing, to attack the problem rather than running from it as I had done earlier."

Contracting as Planned Follow-On

These discussions served to generate a list of priorities for the problem-solving aspect of the session, which came in the form of interpersonal *contracting*. The basic purpose of contracting is to insure that action will be taken on the issues raised during the confrontation stage. The participants realized that change on the part of any member would be impossible without the full cooperation and assistance of other members of the group. Therefore, as each person solicited feedback, lists were prepared in response to the following questions:

- What I will do to help the organization function more effectively?
- What will the rest of the group do to help me?

This technique provided for both a commitment on the part of the individual requesting the feedback, as well as a corresponding commitment on the part of the remaining six staff members. The commitment from the group also implied support which would be necessary in times of difficulty.

As mentioned earlier, the Undersheriff was a focal point for much of the preconference hostility. Exhibit 2 shows the changes he was willing to make and the commitment each staff officer made to assist him in fulfilling his contract to function more effectively. It also suggests the degree to which each staff member was willing not only to examine his own behavior, but also to make a determined effort to work more effectively as a member of the management team. Each person, in turn, received individual feedback from the rest of the group and participated in the interpersonal contracting procedures. These contracts were then reproduced, and all participants received copies of all of them.

Once the interpersonal contracting was completed, the focus changed to the solution of organizational problems. The remainder of the session was spent resolving problems associated with organizational and interdepartmental communication, decision-making methods, and use of control processes.

Some Attitudinal Results of the Peaceful Valley Experience

Three instruments were used to measure the effectiveness of the confrontation-team-building design: a single-item trust scale, Likert's Profile of Organization and Performance Characteristics, and Friedlander's Group Behavior Inventory (GBI).

Impact on Trust

The trust scale was composed of the following single item:

Please indicate the degree to which you trust the other members of this management team.

           1   2   3   4   5   6   7   8   9   10

Not at all   Completely

This question was valuable as a sensing device for roughly determining the progress of the group, since evidence suggests that trust is central to group effectiveness.[39] On Sunday evening the average score was 1.5. By Wednesday, the trust level had risen to 6.8. By the end of the session, the average score was 9.56.

Impact on Organization Climate

The Likert Profile is composed of forty-eight items designed to measure organization climate. Each of the items is represented by a 20-point scale and describes four separate systems of organization. All respondents are asked to mark the

Exhibit 2   Interpersonal Contracting Between the Undersheriff and the Rest of the Staff

---

What the Undersheriff will do to help the organization function more effectively

 1. Feel commitment to better interpersonal relationships
 2. Control my temper
 3. Speak in positives
 4. Open communications with departmental personnel
 5. Never make snap decisions when avoidable
 6. Provide an open path for feedback
 7. Place myself in the other man's chair
 8. Remove my authoritarian attitude
 9. Develop a trust relationship
10. Make a forum for fair and equal decisions
11. Follow the chain of command
12. Guarantee input
13. Provide assistance to staff members in their problems
14. Provide feedback to staff
15. Deal on a first-name basis
16. Recognize staff officers' positions
17. Improve the image of my fellow officers
18. Forget the past
19. Avoid coloring of information
20. Try to remain happy with good attitude
21. Not send direct letters to any officers
22. Won't take disciplinary action on any officer outside my direct control
23. Will deal with people on a one-to-one basis on problems with people when I have to
24. Recognize attributes (good things people do)
25. Avoid dwelling on the negative
26. Stop rooting
27. Recognize and work with "them" on a colleague basis

What staff will do to help the Undersheriff

 1. Rectify the "Bad Undersheriff" image
 2. Open communication with the Undersheriff—not turn him off—and deal from a high-trust basis
 3. Recognize and support his position as Undersheriff

---

position on the continuum which best describes their organization at the present time. In all cases the responses are uniformly coded so that scores run as below.

Score	Management System
1-5	Exploitative-coercive
6-10	Benevolent-authoritative
11-15	Consultative
16-20	Participative-group

The average responses by Metro County top staff on the seven clusters of variables measured by the Likert Profile are shown in Table 1. Virtually no change occurred during the 5 weeks prior to the training session. Organization climate markedly improved following the team-building, and the changes were maintained over the following 2 years. These effects are expected, marked, and persisting, obviously.

Impact on Basic Group Dimensions

The Group Behavior Inventory (GBI) is designed to measure the quality of group performance and interaction in an organizational setting. The first five comprehensive dimensions are measured on a 5-point scale, with possible answers ranging from "strongly agree" to "strongly disagree." Worth of meetings, on the other hand, is measured along a 7-point scale. The six dimensions are defined as follows:[40]

1. *Group effectiveness* in solving problems and in formulating policy through a creative, realistic team effort. Groups high on this dimension arrive at creative team solutions, sharing responsibilities and problems openly.

2. *Leader approachability* describes groups in which members feel that the leader is approachable and that they can establish a comfortable relationship with him or her. Groups low on this dimension withdraw from the leader, do not push their ideas, do not behave according to their feelings, and seem intent on catering to the leader at the possible sacrifice of group output.

3. *Mutual influence* describes groups in which members mutually influence one another and the leader and assume responsibility for setting group goals.

Table 1   Average Responses for the Metropolitan County Top Staff on Likert's Profile[a]

| | Average Responses on Likert Profile | | | | | |
Processes	5 Weeks Before	Before Peaceful Valley	After Peaceful Valley	6 Weeks After	1 Year After	2 Years After
Leadership	9.04	9.02	14.82[b]	15.53[b]	15.70[b]	16.80[b]
Motivation	9.62	9.40	14.77[b]	15.66[b]	15.52[b]	16.33[b]
Communication	9.59	10.02	15.39[b]	15.23[b]	16.25[b]	15.85[b]
Interaction	10.87	10.88	15.92[b]	15.04[b]	15.45[b]	16.03[b]
Decision-making	8.35	8.91	15.08[b]	15.31[b]	15.81[b]	16.23[b]
Goal-setting	10.09	9.83	15.55[b]	15.61[b]	16.12[b]	16.85[b]
Control	8.53	7.52	14.28[b]	14.92[b]	15.83[b]	15.95[b]

[a]Five administrations of the Profile during a 2-year period.
[b]A difference statistically significant at the 0.05 level or beyond, using "Before Peaceful Valley" score as the base for comparisons.

4. *Personal involvement and participation* is descriptive of groups in which members want, expect, and achieve active participation in group meetings. The combination of high expectations and actual participation implies a fulfillment that is reflected in the desire to continue group meetings.

5. *Intragroup trust (versus intragroup competitiveness)* depicts a group in which the members hold trust and confidence in one another. Groups low on this dimension can be characterized more as a collection of individuals who are reluctant to alter their individual personal opinions and ideas for the sake of working consensus. Competition among members then tends to be destructive and submerged.

6. *Worth of meetings* is a generalized measure of the feelings about the meetings of group—as either good, valuable, strong, and pleasant, or as bad, worthless, weak, and unpleasant.

The before and after results from the GBI are shown in Table 2. The Metro County Sheriff's Department improved in five of the six categories, while comparison group scores remained essentially the same. The results are expected, based on several replications of the same design in both public organizations (like the Metropolitan Atlanta Rapid Transit Authority) and business firms (the Long Times Division of AT&T, several loci in Smith, Kline and French, Inc., and locations in Procter and Gamble).[41]

Some Organizational Restructing Triggered by Peaceful Valley

Those at Peaceful Valley often voiced dissatisfaction with many of their specific duties and responsibilities. Therefore, the first major effort to which the team addressed itself upon returning to Metro County involved reorganization of departmental responsibilities. The reorganization was undertaken in five separate steps, to which attention will be given below. In order, discussion will turn to:

- Changes in the organizational structure
- Number of personnel assigned to each division
- Specific personnel to be assigned to each division
- Reallocation of space
- The method to be used in notifying the total departmental personnel of the proposed changes

Table 2   Average Responses for Metro County and a Comparison Group on Friedlander's GBI

Category	Metro County (N = 7)		Comparison Group (N = 5)	
	Before Peaceful Valley	After Peaceful Valley	Before Peaceful Valley	After Peaceful Valley
Group effectiveness	2.38	3.83[a]	3.20	3.22
Leader approachability	3.61	3.88	2.80	2.73
Mutual influence	3.57	3.97[a]	3.45	3.44
Personal involvement and participation	2.71	3.17[a]	3.24	2.57
Intragroup trust	3.00	3.66[a]	3.64	2.92
Worth of meetings	4.20	5.16[a]	3.62	3.61

[a]A difference statistically significant at the 0.05 level or beyond, comparing before versus after scores.

Reorganizing the Agency

Since most of the top staff had expressed dissatisfaction with their current responsibilities, each was asked to submit to the Sheriff and Undersheriff a list of
specific responsibilities he would like and areas in which he preferred to work.
The Sheriff and Undersheriff then examined the requests and made their recommendations, adhering as closely as possible to the individual requests while also
aggregating functions as much as possible.

The new organization chart was drawn, posted on large sheets of newsprint,
and shared at a special staff meeting. It was made clear that the new organizational structure was tentative, subject to the input and approval of the staff. The
Undersheriff explained the organizational structure, the reasons for specific responsibilities assigned to a particular person, and the reasons why some requests
had not been honored. With only two minor exceptions, each staff member
agreed completely with the proposed changes. The two exceptions related to two
staff members who had special programs in which they had strong interests; they
quickly traded responsibilities, and unanimous agreement was reached. Figure 1
shows the pre-Peaceful Valley organization structure. Figure 2 reflects the basic
department changes that were made during the course of the systemic phase of
the OD intervention.

Personnel Reassignments

The ongoing struggle over personnel generated much dispute in staff meetings
prior to the Peaceful Valley retreat. Each division commander protected his own
complement and did all in his power to obtain additional personnel. Since the
total number of departmental personnel was limited by budget and legal constraints, difficult decisions often had to be made; and win or lose situations
developed frequently.

Once the changes in organizational structure were finalized, each staff member submitted the number and rank of personnel needed to fill the responsibilities in each of the areas under his jurisdiction. The Sheriff and Undersheriff then
examined the lists, made tentative decisions about the number of personnel in
each division, and presented the proposal at a special staff meeting. The staff
then spent 2 hours discussing the needs of each division and the proposed manpower allocation. The prevailing cooperative spirit is illustrated by one staff
member who previously had been extremely possessive of personnel. He said,
"I don't see how you can function with that many people. It just can't be done.
Why don't you take two of my people? I really don't need that many, anyway."

Another important concern related to the specific people assigned to work in
each division. The staff agreed to abolish the existing Corporal positions and use
the remaining money to appoint three new Sergeants. Again, each staff member
submitted a list of his preferences; this time the list contained the specific people

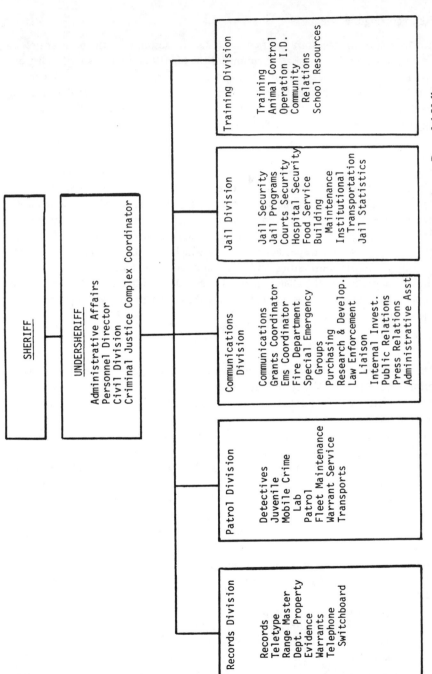

Figure 1 Metropolitan County Sheriff's Department organization chart prior to Peaceful Valley.

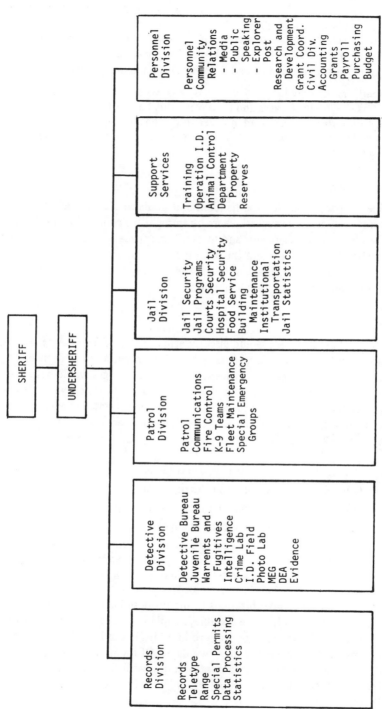

Figure 2 Metro County Sheriff's Department after reorganization.

with whom each would like to work. The lists were examined, and the proposed changes were presented to the staff. The following statement illustrates the cooperative spirit that again pervaded the decision-making process:

> I need Frank badly in my division. He has worked there for two years and knows the job backwards and forwards. But I also think he deserves to be promoted to Sergeant. And in order to do that, he will have to work in your division. I'll tell you what, I will give you Frank if I can have Lloyd to take his place.

Space Allocation

The issue of space allocation was handled in a similar manner. Each division commander was asked to suggest where he thought his office should be located, given the changes in assignments and the available space. Tentative decisions were reached by the Sheriff and Undersheriff, and the proposed changes were presented to the staff for final approval. The meeting took less than 30 minutes, and the resulting decisions were unanimous.

Announcing Changes

Since the proposed changes would directly affect 85 percent of the personnel, a critical step in the organizational change involved presentation of decisions to the entire department. Prior to Peaceful Valley, the changes would have been announced by a "bolt from the blue." New times called for new ways. The staff adopted the following strategy for implementing the proposed changes. The employee, his new division commander, and either the Sheriff or the Undersheriff met together in a 10-minute meeting. During the meetings, the employees were:

- Shown the new organization structure chart
- Told where they would fit in the organization
- Informed as to who would be their superiors, peers, and subordinates
- Asked how they felt about the changes
- Told that if they had any objections to the proposed changes, they should so state them and feel free to discuss the changes privately with either the Sheriff or Undersheriff the following day

Each was also told that any objections to the proposed changes would receive serious consideration and, where possible, people would be reassigned. If that was not then possible, the person was promised his desired position as soon as it became vacant. This procedure took two days. Of the ninety-one people interviewed, only one person expressed dissatisfaction with the change. The entire organizational change had taken place within 3 weeks after the staff returned from Peaceful Valley.

Reinforcement Sessions

During the following 10 months the OD process continued, and the staff also participated in two additional off-site retreats. Although the formats for the two meetings varied, the general purpose of each was to follow-up on previous commitments and departmental problems. Each retreat was preceded by data collection and diagnosis by the consultant. Training in effective managerial skills was also an integral part of each session.

Some Broader Ripples of Effects

Assessing the value of organizational interventions ultimately rests upon the efficiency and effectiveness with which the organization uses its resources in achieving its goals and objectives. For the Metro County Sheriff's Department, the long-range goals are to decrease crime and to increase the rehabilitation of the offender, and one can expect that a single law enforcement agency would have a significant impact on either only over a long period of time, if ever. However, in the short run, a number of significant developments related to performance have taken place since Peaceful Valley.

Changes in Organizational Climate in the Entire Agency

The organizational climate for the entire department, as measured by the Likert Profile, moved from a benevolent authoritarian to a consultative system, despite the fact that only the top staff participated in the OD design. This implies a powerful rippling effect, a second-order change. Table 3 shows the before and after scores for the entire department and for a comparison group. The comparison group is a law enforcement agency located in a political, cultural, and geographical environment similar to the Metro County Sheriff's Department. The major differences between the two organizations are their size, the fact that Metro County prison houses all inmates and suspects, and the substantially higher salaries in the comparison group. Metro County scores show marked increases on all seven variables measured by the Likert Profile, while the comparison group show no significant changes over the 2-year period between measures.

Turnover Rate Falls

The turnover rate in the Sheriff's Department also decreased significantly. Table 4 shows information pertaining to employee termination, department population, and turnover rates for the Metro County and the comparison group during the period 1971 to 1975. Note that the Metro County turnover rate decreased from almost 60 percent in 1971 to about 20 percent in 1974 and 1975. Employees explain the low turnover rate by the fact that the organization has become a more enjoyable and comfortable place in which to work. This is partic-

Table 3   Average Responses for Metro County Sheriff's Department Total Personnel and a Comparison Group on Likert's Profile[a]

	Metro County			Comparison Group		
Processes	Before Peaceful Valley (N = 89)	1 Year After (N = 100)	2 Years After (N = 133)	Before Peaceful Valley (N = 38)	1 Year After (N = 38)	2 Years After (N = 55)
Leadership	11.40	12.95	13.51[b]	10.93	10.27	8.78
Motivation	10.66	12.52[b]	13.61[b]	10.27	9.64	9.16
Communication	10.46	13.36[b]	14.14[b]	11.34	10.86	9.37
Interaction	10.56	13.27[b]	13.97[b]	10.76	10.35	9.28
Decision-making	9.90	12.40[b]	13.50[b]	9.48	8.65	9.10
Goal-setting	10.90	13.16[b]	13.44[b]	10.71	9.72	9.00
Control	10.69	13.18[b]	14.26[b]	11.22	10.05	9.38

[a]Responses are over a 2-year interval.
[b]A difference statistically significant at the 0.05 level or beyond, comparing before versus after scores.

Table 4   Termination, Department Population, and Turnover Rates for Metro County Sheriff's Department and a Comparison Group, 1971-1975

Year	Metro County			Comparison Group		
	Number Terminated	Department Population	Turnover Rate (%)	Number Terminated	Department Population	Turnover Rate (%)
1971	40	67	59.7	25	56	44.6
1972	30	75	40.0	23	56	41.0
1973	48	93	51.6	30	66	45.4
1974	20	104	19.2	27	68	39.7
1975	32	135	23.7	7	63	11.1

ularly significant, since Metro County personnel are paid only about 70 percent as much as their counterparts in the Metro area.

Other Probable Effects

Three other classes of probable effects of the OD effort also deserve notice. Thus, the strong movement toward unionization was soundly defeated in a secret ballot during spring 1974.

Moreover, the Sheriff overwhelmingly defeated his three opponents in the 1974 general election, receiving over two-thirds of the total votes. This success is attributed in the largest part to the increased effectiveness and quality of law enforcement service rendered by department personnel. The victory holds a special significance, since prior to Peaceful Valley the Sheriff had considered it only a remote possibility that he would seek reelection.

Finally, the interpersonal behavior of the Undersheriff has drastically changed. In an off-site meeting 5 months after the beginning of the OD project, the top staff unanimously agreed that the Undersheriff had lived up to every commitment he had made at Peaceful Valley. Furthermore, he has subsequently developed process and intervention skills to the point where he is functioning effectively as an internal change agent within his own organization, as well as an external change agent in other criminal justice agencies.

Concluding Notes

The Metro County experience demonstrates that OD technology can be used effectively in bringing about positive changes in a law enforcement agency, given a commitment from the organization's leadership in general, and from the chief executive officer in particular.[42] It will take more data and time to determine whether the OD effort will succeed in helping the organization achieve its long-range goals and objectives. The accomplishments during the first years are clearly substantial, however.

A Generic Issue in Group Designs
Fitting OD Interventions to the Properties of Different Groups

Note a prime danger in the two cases above. They do reflect general purpose designs that seem broadly applicable and adaptable to varying group conditions. But those cases should not encourage neglect of a basic probability: that different group conditions may be variously responsive to different OD interventions. Moreover, some group conditions might even contraindicate a specific OD design.

Despite the intuitive attractions of fitting interventions to group conditions, little available research deals with that topic. But, three conclusions seem appropriate. First, despite the substantial attention to isolating individual group characteristics,[43] no generally accepted typology of groups yet exists. Patently, this crucial basic research lacuna substantially explains the failure of the OD literature to test the relative appropriateness of specific OD interventions to different group properties.

Second, some short-cuts to isolating a typology of groups do exist, however, as via the use of statistical procedures such as hierarchical grouping. Basically, such procedures simultaneously assess differences and similarities between research units—individuals, groups, or organizations—and estimate the number of separate types necessary to account for the variation. Michigan researchers applied such a technique to a number of work groups, in fact, and sought to determine whether the types corresponded to distinct diagnosed conditions to which five OD interventions would be differentially responsive. The interventions include:

- Survey/feedback
- Data hand-back only
- Interpersonal process consultation
- Task process consultation
- Laboratory training or T-grouping

They isolated seventeen distinct types of groups, and also established tendencies for the five alternative OD interventions to impact differentially on different types. "Interventions must be carefully chosen to match the characteristics and practices of the group being studied," Bowers and his coworker conclude. "Even in its present crude form, [our approach] provides a guide for intervention choice."[44]

Third, despite the reasonableness of the notion that different diagnosed conditions in groups would be more responsive to different OD designs, establishing the more precise nature of the fit will require very large research programs. For example, procedures like hierarchical grouping can provide appropriate types only for the characteristics being measured. Measure meaningless characteristics, in short, and you get accurate but useless typologies. The issue of which group characteristics require measurement is still an open one. Relatedly, a research design with 17 group types × 5 OD interventions—like that of the Michigan study—provides 85 separate cells for data. Providing a minimum of ten cases per cell would no doubt require several thousand groups, which is clearly in the high-roller league. Even if each cell of such a design had exactly the same probability of cases falling into it, 850 groups would be required to provide ten cases per cell. Such equidistribution is highly unlikely, of course. Some kind of Manhattan Project for OD seems required.

Exhibit 3 Predicted Effects and Results of Standard Team-Building Design

Group Behavior Inventory Dimensions	Predicted Effects of Team-Building Experience	Actual Results of Team-Building at AT&T		
I. Group effectiveness; high scorers see creative and realistic team effort in problem-solving	Most members will report *higher* scorers	7 score significantly higher (1, 2, 3, 4, 5, 6, 7)	1 scores same (8)	0 score lower
II. Approach vs. withdrawal; high scorers see manager as approachable, as one with whom an unconstrained and comfortable relationship can exist	Many members will report *higher* scores, but manager is a probable exception as are those who tried "approach" but saw it as not working or were punished for their try	4 score significantly higher (1, 3, 5, 7)	3 score same (2, 4, 6)	1 scores lower (8)
III. Mutual influence; high scorers see themselves and others as having influence with others and work-unit manager	Will *increase* for most members, with probable exception of manager and the "exception(s)" described under II	5 score significantly higher (1, 2, 5, 6, 7)	1 scores same (3)	2 score lower (4, 8)

IV. Personal involvement and participation; high scorers are those who want, expect, and achieve active participation	Will *increase* for most or all members, with possible exception of manager	7 score significantly higher (1, 2, 3, 4, 5, 6, 7, 8)	0 score same	1 scores lower (4)
V. Trust vs. competitiveness; high scorers see a group whose members have trust and confidence in one another	Will *increase* for most or all members, with possible exception of manager	6 score significantly higher (1, 2, 4, 5, 6, 7)	2 score same (3, 8)	0 score lower
VI. General evaluation; high scorers see group as good, valuable, or pleasant vs. bad, worthless, unpleasant	Will *increase* for most or all members, with possible exception of those scoring lower on II, III, or IV	5 score significantly higher (2, 4, 5, 6, 7)	1 scores same (1)	2 score lower (3, 8)

Costs and Benefits of Group-Level Interactions
Some Generalizations

Generalization 1. Data like those above suggest that potent group-level interventions based on the laboratory approach can be designed. This may understate the case substantially, in fact, as can be established by a brief review of a "standard" design.

Common Effects of a Standard Group-Level Design

The point can be supported by my own experience with a standard team-building design—whose basic components are illustrated in the two case studies detailed above—which I have run perhaps twenty-five or thirty times over the years. After a set of diagnostic interviews designed to acquaint myself with work-unit members and issues as well as to test whether major team problems sufficiently reside in matters over which the team has reasonable control, the standard design has generated quite uniform results in a wide variety of contexts.[45]

The general flow of the design may be sketched briefly, and the all but invariable outcomes can be illustrated by one application. A group of middle-level managers in AT&T requested the team-building and, using the first two columns in Exhibit 3, the intervenor noted that: "If you would like the effects predicted on the six Group Behavior Inventory dimensions, my experience is that a standard team-building design will do the job. No lead-pipe cinches exist. But the probability is very high that the intervention will yield the predicted effects."

Exhibit 3 promises no rose garden, especially for the unit's formal head. Thus, *decreases* due to intervention may be expected for the work-unit head on the influence dimension, for example, and decreases are possible on that person's involvement and trust. The reasons should be patent. Team-building often sees expressions of concern directed at the formal supervisor; the design also results in new patterns of involvement and influence, with the manager losing some traditional perquisites of rank, such as monopolizing the conversation; and for many formal heads, team-building implies their own failure. Overall, however, the predicted effects are sanguine.

In my experience, the AT&T results reported in the last three columns of Exhibit 3 represent the usual range of outcomes. The work-unit had eight members (1, 2, 3, . . .), with 8 being the manager. The posttest came about 3 days after the team-building experience, which lasted about 2 long work days. The pretest or benchmark data were gathered about 1 week before the training experience began.

Note several points about the results. *First,* over 70 percent of the work-unit members report statistically significant increases on the GBI dimensions, with increases usually interpreted as attractive or positive.

Second, as predicted, the unit manager accounts for half of the negative changes.

Third, additional administrations—even as far as 6 months after the intervention, or more—typically show two sets of effects. Thus, the prevailing positive character of changes is maintained even in the absence of other reinforcing interventions. And the manager's scores, when they have dropped as in Exhibit 3, tend to increase and become like those of other work-unit members.

Fourth, perhaps once in every three or four replications of the design, at least one member will develop and maintain a pattern of low scores. For that person, the intervention fails. Most often, in my experience, this failure case has one or both of two characteristics. That person had previously been in somewhat successful competition with the formal head, and abreacts from what he correctly perceives as an improvement in the work situation which reduces the leverage that he previously enjoyed. Often, in addition, the criticism of the formal head characteristic of early phases of team-building may encourage the competitor to boldly take-on the formal head. Typically, the now overt antagonist loses group support in the process. "The formal head is not all that bad," most group members seem to say. "This team-building seems to be working. Let's give the boss a chance." If the antagonist does not hear these new attitudes, trouble for him can be predicted. In the rare case, the antagonist may succeed in unhorsing the formal supervisor during the team-building. But, powerful forces support the supervisor, especially if he shows any hopeful signs of learning from the team-building. A supervisor in very deep trouble with his work unit before team-building should very carefully consider adopting that intervention. In most cases, however, the team-building experience is seen as an act of good faith and reinforces the superior's position. Manipulative supervisors have learned that lesson, but may be making trouble for themselves by authorizing periodic but contraceptive team-building experiences which only let off steam, period.

Alternatively or complementarily, the "failure case" represents a person for whom the new climate or style is seriously unattractive. "I just can't take the confessional aspects of this new thing," one such person reported. "I just want to do my job, period. Let others do theirs. And we all should take care of ourselves."

In short, a strong case can be made for the potency of available group-level OD designs.

Generalization 2. Six significant limits on this attribution of substantial power to group OD designs seem appropriate. *First,* not every individual or every grouping of individuals will respond similarly to such training interventions. In one of the two cases above, enough individuals and groups responded as expected to generate statistically significant differences. No specific data were gathered in the other case, but impressionistic reports are all positive, indeed glowing. But aggregate analysis is only a start. Too little is known about deviant cases—the individuals or groups for whom the experience does not "take" or for whom even hurtful consequences occur. And Exhibit 3 clearly shows deviant cases, although often they are expected.

Second, what it means to "respond similarly" to similar OD designs may differ profoundly, depending upon whether the judgment is made by informed observers or whether it is based on participant responses to questionnaires. Scientific progress will often be served by the use of standard questionnaires, applied in many replications of the same or similar designs. But such instruments are not always available or appropriate.

Third, even where instruments are appropriate and are utilized, any conclusions about the efficacy of a training design assume the usefulness of the measuring instrument. Only many replications of the training-research design will establish that usefulness. Since some questions can be entertained about the validity and reliability of any measuring instrument, a tentativeness is appropriate when interpreting results such as those above. An awkward measuring instrument can, in any single study, either mask relations that are really there or isolate regularities that are only apparent.

Fourth, studies of group-level interventions would profit from tests other than those provided by self-reports. Unobtrusive measures are ideal, such as measures of change in interaction pattern following training that can be rated from tape recordings in terms of detailed classification schemes.[46] If nothing else, this makes compliant self-reporting more unlikely. Some have charged that self-reports can tell more about how much respondents like the experimenter than about what the stimulus situation really was.

The use of unobtrusive measures avoids two dangerous positions that are easy enough to fall into. One position essentially argues that changes such as those in the GBI cited above are morally desirable ends in themselves, no matter what their other consequences. The other extreme position urges that changes in interpersonal and intergroup competence such as those apparently measured by GBI will directly lead to improved performance, as conventionally defined in terms of higher productivity or lower turnover. The first position is mindless of several factors, one of which is that science is nothing if it is not an expanding network of multiple cross-checks. Without a passion for such multiple cross-checks, an approach runs the risk of rigidifying into an ideology to be protected rather than evolving into a growing network of relations. The second position is too simplistic, because complex intervening variables no doubt must be specified in linkages of interpersonal competence and such outcome variables as productivity.[47]

From this point of view, Boss' intervention in a law enforcement agency is especially attractive. He includes both measures of changes in processes, as well as in outcomes such as decreased employee turnover.

Fifth, formulations like Boss' do not distinguish phases in which the several GBI variables may become critical. Figure 3 suggests the significance of the omission by a model which differentiates two sets of effects over time. Without some pump-priming level of trust, the model implies, the processes of approaching the values of the laboratory approach do not begin.[48] That level either exists when training begins, or it must be induced. Some ongoing groups have achieved that level; and it appears that some ad hoc groups quickly decide that high trust is appropriate. Model I in Figure 3 covers these two cases. Other ongoing groups have not achieved that requisite level, and it appears that some ad hoc groups quickly decide that low trust is appropriate. These cases are detailed by Model II in Figure 3. Here, the initial strategy is a delicate building of shared influence and personal involvement to help generate a requisite level of trust. The going is difficult. In Model II, until the cycle is somehow broken, every issue eventually ends up in a demonstration that the trust level is not adequate to support work toward changes consistent with the laboratory approach.

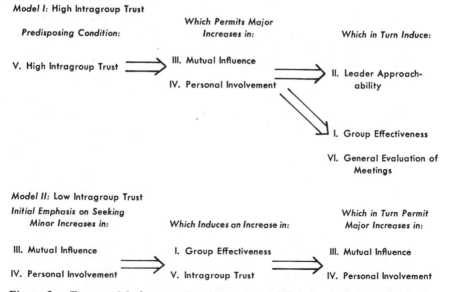

Figure 3 Two models for engaging dimensions of Friedlander's Group Behavior Inventory. [From R. T. Golembiewski, *Renewing Organizations: The Laboratory Approach to Planned Change* (Itasca, Ill.: F. E. Peacock, 1972).]

It requires only a little imagination to explain results like Boss', or anyone else's, by assuming various combinations of high-trust and low-trust groups as they enter training. Suffice it here to note that different developmental phases for groups can be conceived, and that groups can truly enlarge their competence even if they achieve only relatively low plateaus of learning. The same point applies to both cases. Any attempt to measure several groups by the same standard of progress, or change, involves an oversimplification. Unfortunately, not enough is yet known to avoid this convenient oversimplification.[49]

Sixth, working with individual groups, whether as singles or as multiples in a parallel design, can induce significant problems. Changing a group's internal processes can cause relational problems with other groups which have not experienced a similar learning experience, for example. Two conditions minimize such an effect: when the group is at or toward the top of its particular hierarchy, and/or when the group is substantially autonomous. Boss' study seems to take advantage of both conditions. The case study of the university executive team may reflect less insularity, as in reasonable member concern about the reactions of state legislators to any signs of "weakness" or "inefficiency."

Notes

1. Gustave Le Bon, *The Crowd,* 16th impression (London: T.F. Unwin, 1926).

2. The following argument was suggested by Dorwin Cartwright, "Achieving Change in People: Some Applications of Group Dynamics Theory," *Human Relations,* Vol. 4 (October 1951), pp. 381-392.

3. Robert T. Golembiewski, *The Small Group* (Chicago: University of Chicago Press, 1962), esp. pp. 8-33; and A. Paul Hare, *Handbook of Small Group Research* (New York: The Free Press, 1976), esp. pp. 384-395.

4. Full realization of this fact came slow and hard. Arnold Tannenbaum and Stanley Seashore, *Some Changing Conceptions and Approaches to the Study of Persons in Organizations* (Ann Arbor, Mich.: Institute for Social Research, University of Michigan, not dated).

5. Leonard Horwitz, "Transference in Training Groups and Therapy Groups," *International Journal of Group Psychotherapy,* Vol. 14 (November 1964), p. 208.

6. Dorothy Stock and Herbert Thelen, *Emotional Dynamics and Group Culture* (Washington, D.C.: National Training Laboratories, 1958).

7. The T-group was originally called a "basic skill-training" group, in fact. See the revealing history in Kenneth D. Benne, "History of the T-Group in the Laboratory Setting," in Leland P. Bradford, Jack R. Gibb, and Kenneth D. Benne (eds.), *T-Group Theory and Laboratory Method* (New York: John Wiley and Sons, 1964), pp. 87-113. See also Leland P. Bradford, *National*

Training Laboratories: Its History, 1947-70 (private publication, 1974), esp. pp. 31-57; and Kenneth D. Benne, Leland P. Bradford, Jack R. Gibb, and Ronald O. Lippitt (eds.), *The Laboratory Method of Changing and Learning* (Palo Alto, Calif.: Science and Behavior Books, 1975).

8. Martin Lakin, "Some Ethical Issues in Sensitivity Training," *American Psychologist,* Vol. 24 (October 1969), pp. 923-928; and Arthur Blumberg and Robert T. Golembiewski, *Learning and Change in Groups* (London: Penguin, 1976), Chapters I and II. Far more critical is Kurt Back, *Beyond Words* (New York: Russell Sage Foundation, 1972).

9. Floyd C. Mann, "Studying and Creating Change," in Warren G. Bennis, Kenneth D. Benne, and Robert Chin (eds.), *The Planning of Change* (New York: Holt, Rinehart, Winston, 1962), pp. 605-615.

10. Ibid., p. 620.

11. Ibid., p. 612.

12. Quoted in Wendell French, "A Definition and History of Organization Development." Paper presented at NTL Conference on New Technology in Organization Development, New York, October 8-9, 1971, p. 11.

13. For systematic overviews, consult Frank Friedlander and L. Dave Brown, "Organization Development," *Annual Review of Psychology,* Vol. 25 (1974), pp. 328-329; Glenn Varney, "Building an Effective Management Team," *The Business Quarterly,* Vol. 41 (Spring 1976), pp. 38-45; and Michael Beer, "The Technology of Organization Development," pp. 955-961, in Marvin D. Dunnette (ed.), *Handbook of Industrial and Organizational Psychology* (Chicago: Rand McNally, 1976).

    For other efforts to describe the characteristics of team development, see such sources as Gordon L. Lippitt, "Team Building for Matrix Organizations," in Gordon L. Lippitt, Leslie E. This, and Robert G. Bidwell, Jr., *Optimizing Human Resources* (Reading, Mass.: Addison-Wesley, 1971), pp. 158-170. A case study of a team-development experience is provided by Iain L. Mangham, J. Hayes, and Cary L. Cooper, "Developing Executive Relationships," *Interpersonal Development,* Vol. 1 (1970), pp. 110-127.

14. Richard Beckhard, *Strategies of Organization Development* (Reading, Mass.: Addison-Wesley, 1969), p. 16.

15. Ibid., pp. 16, 27-28.

16. Gordon L. Lippitt, *Organization Renewal* (New York: Appleton-Century-Crofts, 1969), p. 102.

17. Ibid., pp. 107-113.

18. William G. Dyer, *Team-Building: Issues and Alternatives* (Reading, Mass.: Addison-Wesley, 1977), pp. 73-124.

19. Beckhard, *Strategies of Organization Development,* pp. 28-29.

20. Roger Harrison, "Effective Organization for Start-up." Development Research Associates, Inc., Boston, Mass., July 8, 1970. Mimeographed.

21.   See, for example, Pat M. Keith, "Individual and Organizational Correlates of a Temporary System," *Journal of Applied Behavioral Science,* Vol. 14 (April 1978), esp. p. 195.

22.   For perspective on how this early experience can be generalized into profound patterns, consult Laird W. Mealiea, "Learned Behavior: The Key to Understanding and Preventing Employee Resistance to Change," *Group and Organization Studies,* Vol. 3 (June 1978), pp. 211-223.

23.   The point is strikingly suggested by changes in supervisory styles in power plants after start-up observed by Floyd C. Mann and L. Richard Hoffman, *Automation and the Worker: Social Change in Power Plants* (New York: Holt, Rinehart, Winston, 1960). See also Mann, "Toward an Understanding of the Leadership Role in Formal Organization," in Robert F. M. Dubin (ed.), *Leadership and Productivity* (San Francisco: Chandler, 1965), pp. 68-103.

24.   The phenomenon is especially marked in aerospace project teams, which no doubt illustrate an increasingly significant organizational form. For a broad perspective, see Philip Slater and Warren G. Bennis, *The Temporary Society* (New York: Harper and Row, 1968).

25.   For summary perspective, consult Roger Harrison, "Prescriptions for Organization Startup." Situation Management Systems, Inc., Berkeley, Calif., 1978. Mimeographed.

26.   Conveniently, see Robert T. Golembiewski and William Eddy (ed.), *Organization Development in Public Administration,* Part 2 (New York: Marcel Dekker, 1978), pp. 36-48, 160-177, 297-312; and Dyer, *Team-Building,* pp. 84-92.

27.   Consult Jerry B. Harvey, "Consulting During Crises of Agreement," esp. pp. 165-168, in W. Warner Burke (ed.), *Current Issues and Strategies in Organization Development* (New York: Human Science Press, 1977).

28.   Ibid., esp. pp. 169-171; and Dyer, *Team-Building,* pp. 93-104.

29.   Dyer, *Team-Building,* pp. 115-116.

30.   Ibid., pp. 117-122.

31.   Ronald Boyer, "New Applications in OD: The University." Paper presented at Annual Meeting, Academy of Management, August 1974, Seattle, Wash. He provides overview concerning one OD program in an institution of higher learning.

32.   Chris Argyris, *Interpersonal Competence and Organizational Effectiveness* (Homewood, Ill.: Dorsey, 1962), pp. 57-132.

33.   This author has used this design five times with several groups of university administrators. The case study reported here is typical. Some details have been altered to preserve anonymity.

34.   Support for this position can be found in such sources as Clayton P. Alderfer and Ray Ferris, "Understanding the Impact of Survey Feedback." Unpublished MS, Yale University, New Haven, 1971; and David A. Nadler,

"Use of Feedback for Organizational Change: Promises and Pitfalls," *Group and Organization Studies,* Vol. 1 (June 1976), pp. 177-186.

Particularly significant here is a recent attempt to test the adequacy of a survey feedback design, compared to a control condition. The results suggest higher satisfaction of needs in the former condition, but with no significant differences in performance. Herbert H. Hand, Bernard D. Estafen, and Henry P. Sims, Jr., "How Effective Is Data Survey and Feed-Back as a Technique in Organization Development?" *Journal of Applied Behavioral Science,* Vol. 11 (September 1975), esp. pp. 342-343.

35. Frank Friedlander, "The Impact of Organizational Training Laboratories upon the Effectiveness and Interaction of Ongoing Work Groups," *Personnel Psychology,* Vol. 20 (Autumn 1970), pp. 289-307.

36. Robert T. Golembiewski and Alan Kiepper, "MARTA: Toward an Effective, Open Giant," *Public Administration Review,* Vol. 36 (January 1976), pp. 46-60.

37. Ibid., p. 6.

38. Ibid., pp. 6-7.

39. For example, see Dale E. Zand, "Trust and Managerial Problem Solving," *Administrative Science Quarterly,* Vol. 17 (June 1972), pp. 229-239; Frank Friedlander, "The Primacy of Trust as a Facilitator of Further Group Accomplishment," *Journal of Applied Behavioral Science,* Vol. 6 (1970), pp. 387-400; and Robert T. Golembiewski and Mark L. McConkie, "The Centrality of Interpersonal Trust in Group Processes," in Cary Cooper (ed.), *Theories of Group Processes* (New York, John Wiley and Sons, 1975), pp. 131-185.

40. Frank Friedlander, "A Comparative Study of Consulting Processes and Group Development," *Journal of Applied Behavioral Science,* Vol. 4 (October 1968), pp. 377-400.

41. For example, see Golembiewski and Kiepper, "MARTA."

42. For a recent summary treatment, consult A. Paul Hare, *Handbook of Small Group Research* (Riverside, N.J.: Free Press, 1978). For evidence of the leader's centrality, see R. Wayne Boss, "The Effects of Leader Absence on a Confrontation Team-Building Design," *Journal of Applied Behavioral Science,* Vol. 14 (December 1978), esp. pp. 469-471.

43. David G. Bowers and Doris L. Hausser, "Work Group Types and Intervention Effects in Organizational Development," *Administrative Science Quarterly,* Vol. 22, no. 1 (March 1977), pp. 76-94.

44. Chris Argyris, "The CEO's Behavior: Key to Organizational Development," *Harvard Business Review,* Vol. 73 (March-April 1973), pp. 55-64.

45. Two major caveats are in order here. First, despite the confidence I have in this design, no comprehensive assessment of it has been made by me using a large batch of comparable cases. In fact, the team-building literature also lacks such comparative research. For a model of what badly needs doing,

consult Reuben T. Harris and Jerry L. Porras, "The Consequences of Large
System Change in Practice: An Empirical Assessment," in Jeffrey C.
Susbauer (ed.), *Proceedings '78* (Annual Meeting) Academy of Manage-
ment, August 1978, pp. 298-302. See also Porras and Harris, *An Empirical
Assessment of the Process and Outcome of an Organizational Change
Project Aimed at Improving the Quality of Work Life.* Final Report to the
U.S. Department of Labor, Grant No. 21-06-77-09, Stanford University,
Stanford, Calif., March 1978. Second, the experience summarized here re-
lates only to teams I diagnosed as having a "crisis of disagreement," as
distinguished from a "crisis of agreement." The distinction was sketched
earlier in this chapter. Details can be found in Chapter 4 of Part 2.

46. Chris Argyris specifically designed one classification system for this pur-
     pose. See his "Explorations in Interpersonal Competence," *Journal of
     Applied Behavioral Science,* Vol. 1 (July 1965), pp. 255-269.

47. This was the outcome of the efforts to link satisfaction and productivity,
     and there is no reason to expect linkages of competence and productivity
     to be different. For example, an interpersonally competent individual
     should be able to develop better relations with others, which could permit
     higher productivity. But he/she might also be better able to keep output
     low while preserving a superior's good graces.

48. The primacy of preexisting trust is suggested by several studies. See, for
     example, Friedlander, "The Primacy of Trust as a Facilitator of Further
     Group Accomplishment." Indeed, Gibb concludes that ". . . trust level
     is the key leverage variable in world change." Jack R. Gibb, *Trust: A New
     View of Personal and Organizational Development* (Los Angeles, Calif.:
     The Guild of Tutors Press, 1978).

49. Note that Michael L. Moore suggests one useful approach to diagnosis of a
     group's need for team-building in his "Assessing Organizational Planning
     and Teamwork: An Action Research Methodology," *Journal of Applied
     Behavioral Science,* Vol. 14 (December 1978), esp. pp. 479-484.

Author Index

Subject Index

Absenteeism
   design for, 233-236
   as distinct from productivity, 237
   trends in, 233
Action research
   examples of, 194-203, 233-237,
      246-261, 276-288
   spurious contrast with Organiza-
      tion Development, 18
Affect, human (*see also* Disclosure;
      Feedback; Trust)
   eight relevant levels of, 106-109
   and laboratory approach, 109
   as measured, 202-203
   in OD designs, 11-13, 20-21, 30-
      73, 89-95, 105-109, 116-
      121, 156-162, 199-203
Aha! phenomena, 33-34
American Telephone and Telegraph,
      123, 228, 231, 338-341
Anxiety, measurement of, 202-203
Assessment center designs
   costs/benefits of, 231-233
   development of, 225-226
   and Equal Employment Opportun-
      ity, 232
   features of, 226-229
   and laboratory approach, 229-231
   process orientation in, 230-231
Attitude, defined, 108

Authenticity, 69-70, 90
Awareness workshop, 287

Balance model, Heider's, 176-177
Behavior Modification
   contrast with OD, 119-121
   determinism in, 118
   and OD designs for individuals,
      285-286, 292
   values in, 116-121
Belief, defined, 108
Black/white designs
   features of, 271-274
   interactive vs. noninteractive, 286-
      287
   and PROSPER, 274-276
   range of, 268-269
   some consequences of, 274-276
Blues, blue-collar, 233
Business travel
   design for, 259-261
   some consequences of, 259
   as stressing family relationships,
      258

"Cafeteria" benefits, 224
Career planning designs (*see also*
      Assessment center designs)

355